Politics and Policies
in Divided Korea

Also of Interest

†*The Politics of North Korea,* edited by Jae Kyu Park and Jung Gun Kim

†*The Security of Korea: U.S. and Japanese Perspectives on the 1980s,* edited by Franklin B. Weinstein and Fuji Kamiya

††*Korea and Indonesia: Toward Inter-regional Cooperation,* edited by Jae Kyu Park

U.S.-Korean Relations, 1882–1982, edited by Tae-Hwan Kwak, John Chay, Soon Sung Cho, and Shannon McCune

U.S. Policy Toward Korea: Analysis, Alternatives, and Recommendations, Nathan N. White

South Korea, David I. Steinberg

Irrigation and Agricultural Politics in South Korea, Robert Wade

††*Nuclear Proliferation in Developing Countries,* edited by Jae Kyu Park

U.S. Foreign Policy and Asian-Pacific Security: A Transregional Approach, edited by William T. Tow and William R. Feeney

Critical Energy Issues in Asia and the Pacific: The Next Twenty Years, Fereidun Fesharaki et al.

†*The Women of Rural Asia,* Robert Orr Whyte and Pauline Whyte

Communist Nations' Military Assistance, edited by John F. Copper and Daniel S. Papp

†Available in hardcover and paperback.
††Available only in paperback.

Westview Special Studies on East Asia

*Politics and Policies in Divided Korea:
Regimes in Contest*
Young Whan Kihl

This comparative study of North and South Korea is unique in its analysis of Korean politics as a manifestation of the politics of a divided nation. Professor Kihl discusses the details of developments in the two Koreas in the context of the political dynamics and processes in each state, explained from the perspective of Korea's political tradition, its culture, and its links with the external environment. After surveying changes occurring between 1945 and 1980, he focuses largely on the politics of transition in the era of the 1980s, interrelating domestic and foreign politics with specific domestic policies, foreign policy behavior, and unification policy pursued by the Korean regimes. He concludes with hypotheses that aim at explaining Korea's recent past and speculates about the future of Korean politics.

The most up-to-date book available on Korean politics, this textbook will be useful to scholars and students of East Asia, as well as to those interested in political change in the Third World.

Young Whan Kihl is professor of political science at Iowa State University, where he teaches international politics and comparative Asian politics. He is the author or coauthor of *Conflict Issues and International Civil Aviation Decisions: Three Cases* (1971), *Party Politics and Elections in Korea* (1976), and *World Trade Issues: Regime, Structure, and Policy* (forthcoming).

To the memory
of those who fought for freedom
in Korea

Politics and Policies in Divided Korea: Regimes in Contest

Young Whan Kihl

Westview Press / Boulder and London

Westview Special Studies on East Asia

All rights reserved. No part of this publication may be reproduced or transmitted in any form or by any means, electronic or mechanical, including photocopy, recording, or any information storage and retrieval system, without permission in writing from the publisher.

Copyright © 1984 by Westview Press, Inc.

Published in 1984 in the United States of America by Westview Press, Inc., 5500 Central Avenue, Boulder, Colorado 80301; Frederick A. Praeger, Publisher

Library of Congress Cataloging in Publication Data
Kihl, Young W., 1932–
  Politics and policies in divided Korea.
  Bibliography: p.
  Includes index.
  1. Korea—Politics and government—1945–1948.
2. Korea (South)—Politics and government. 3. Korea (North)—Politics and government. I. Title.
DS917.35.K5 1984   320.9519   83-19711
ISBN 0-86531-700-3
ISBN 0-86531-701-1 (pbk.)

Printed and bound in the United States of America

10   9   8   7   6   5   4   3   2   1

Contents

List of Illustrations ix
Preface xi
Acknowledgments xv

1 Comparative Korean Politics: An Overview 5

    Political Systems in Contrast 6
    Analytical Framework: Approaches and Methods 9
    Dominant Features of Korean Politics 16
    An Organizational Overview 22

Part 1
Historical Dimensions

2 Divided Korea and Its Political Development, 1945–1970 27

    The Partition of Korea (1945) 28
    National Liberation and Civil War (1945–1953) 32
    Estrangement and Consolidation (1954–1970) 42
    Concluding Remarks: Divided Nation Politics 52

3 Authoritarian Adaptation, 1971–1980 55

    Korean Response to Major-Power Rapprochement 55
    Park Chung Hee's Yushin Korea 59
    The Land of Kim Il Sung 65
    Concluding Remarks: Korea's Authoritarian Politics 72

4 Regimes and Stability in the 1980s 74

    The Fifth Republic Emerges: The South 75
    The Son Also Rises: The North 90
    Concluding Remarks: Regimes in Contrast 101

Part 2
Policy Patterns and Processes

5   Political Culture and Leadership............................ 107
    Korea's Political Culture................................... 107
    Leadership Style and Traits 114
    Supreme Leadership... 119
    Concluding Remarks: The Politics of Contestation 127

6   Political Economy and Performance......................... 130
    Economic Systems in Contrast 130
    Policy Choices and Consequences 136
    Comparative Data: Endowment and Performance.............. 140
    Concluding Remarks: The Dynamics of Competition.......... 157

7   Domestic and Foreign Policy Behavior 160
    Consolidation and Development: South Korea............... 160
    External Links and Security: South Korea 172
    Mobilization and Revolution: North Korea 179
    Manipulating Foreign Relations: North Korea 189
    Concluding Remarks: Linkage Politics 199

Part 3
Future Prospects

8   Unification Policy Issues................................... 205
    The Basic Premises of Unification Policies................... 206
    Unification Policies in the 1980s 212
    Comparative Assessment: Continuity and Change............ 223
    Concluding Remarks: Power and Motivation 228

9   Conclusion: Regimes in Contest............................ 231
    Systems and Regimes in Perspective 231
    Explaining System Transformation.......................... 234
    Problems and Prospects 242

*Appendix: Countries Maintaining Diplomatic Relations with
    South Korea and North Korea as of June 1982* 247
Notes 249
List of Abbreviations... 281
Bibliography 283
Index 297

Illustrations

Maps

Divided Korea in Its Asian Setting.............................. 1

North Korea, Administrative Units............................. 2

South Korea, Administrative Units............................. 3

Tables

1.1 Contrasting Models of South and North Korean Polities..... 10

2.1 Casualties of the Korean War, 1950–1953 42

5.1 Political Participation of South Korea's Adult Population.... 111

5.2 World Views Shared by South Korea's Elites and
    Mass Public, 1973 113

5.3 Level of Trust Among South Korea's Elites and
    Mass Public, 1973 114

6.1 North Korea's Economic Performance, 1947–1978, by
    Major Sectors: Aggregate Indicators and Growth Rates...... 134

6.2 South Korea's Economic Performance, 1962–1986, Growth
    Rates by Major Sectors: Achievements Versus Targets 135

6.3 Strategic Choices for Development: Policy Emphasis as
    Indicated by Allocation Decisions, 1953 and 1971.......... 137

6.4 North and South Korea's Policy Performance in
    Three Key Sectors, 1960 and 1980....................... 139

6.5 Socioeconomic Profile of North and
    South Korea: A Comparison............................. 142

x   Illustrations

6.6 Military Expenditures: North and South Korea 146

6.7 Comparison of Military Postures: North and
South Korea, 1982 148

6.8 Number of Countries Maintaining Diplomatic Relations
with North and South Korea 151

6.9 North and South Korea's International Trade, 1970–1980 ... 154

6.10 North and South Korea's Direction of International
Trade, by Principal Countries, 1971–1980 155

Figures

6.1 The Political Economy Model Applicable to
North and South Korea 132

8.1 South Korea's Unification Formula Based on a
Step-by-Step Approach 226

9.1 Explaining System Transformation in Divided Korea 235

Preface

Korea, known historically as "the Land of the Morning Calm," has become in the 1980s a nation divided into opposing armed camps. Two hostile states confront each other across the heavily fortified Demilitarized Zone (DmZ). The Korean Peninsula is thus a highly inflammable region, a powder keg that a spark could ignite at any moment as a result of accident, miscalculation, or erroneous decisions made by the respective political leaders of divided Korea. Why has this anomalous situation been allowed to develop? Why do the two Korean states and societies, a socialist north and a capitalist south, confront each other as separate regimes in contest, rather than agree to reconcile and tolerate each other as twins in destiny?

The roots of the Korean problem are geopolitical and historical, and its development reflects the dynamics of the policy patterns and processes of Korea as a divided nation. Geopolitically, the Korean Peninsula is the strategic fulcrum of East Asia, where the interests of four major world powers (the United States, the Soviet Union, the People's Republic of China, and Japan) converge. It is not surprising, therefore, that in the preceding one hundred years three major international wars have been waged over the control of the Korean Peninsula: the Sino-Japanese War of 1894–1895, the Russo-Japanese War of 1904–1905, and the Korean War of 1950–1953, which involved the United States and China, among others, as major belligerents. Divided Korea, the product of U.S.-Soviet ideological and military rivalry in the Cold War, continues to reflect the respective Korean states' inability to attain mutual reconciliation and accommodation.

The era of divided nationhood for Korea from 1945 to 1983, the focus of this book, is unique in many ways, although it also shares certain characteristics with earlier eras of Korea's modern history. During the period since 1945, for instance, as during the era of the Hermit Kingdom of Korea at the end of the nineteenth century, the interplay of forces internal and external to Korea has led to political crisis and the tragedy of external wars. What makes the present era of Korea basically different from the earlier situation, however, is that the intense rivalry between the two political regimes across the DmZ makes the balance of power surrounding the Korean Peninsula that much more precarious and unstable.

The politics and policies of divided Korea, in short, are more complex and difficult to analyze than those of previous historical epochs; this is also true of the study of the two regimes and societies of divided Korea. An added complexity and difficulty in attempting an impartial analysis of North and South Korean politics is that the hostility that prevails between the two halves of divided Korea pollutes the scholarly environment. The rhetoric of self-justifying claims by both regimes makes an objective interpretation of the political and socioeconomic processes going on in the respective halves of divided Korea most difficult.

For instance, *Juche* is touted by North Korea as the doctrine of self-reliance and independence. Yet North Korea is a tightly controlled and regimented society in which the "Great Leader" Kim Il Sung and his son are extolled and in which individual freedom and human rights are more apparent than real. Western reporters who recently visited North Korea described the country as "Marxism's First Monarchy" (*Reader's Digest,* February 1982) and as a "Hermit Kingdom" that practices the Kim Il Sung cult and preaches the Juche Idea (*Time,* May 30, 1983). The obvious contradiction of North Korea is that the virtue of "self-reliance" that Juche stands for is recognized only at the collective national level, while the individual initiative and self-reliance also required to make democracy possible are ignored.

South Korea's economic miracle of the 1962–1979 years, which propelled the country to newly industrializing country (NIC) status in the 1980s, was accomplished through a degree of authoritarianism that undermined the democratic aspirations of the population and the human rights of the individual. Although South Korea has attained greater economic welfare, the distribution of benefits is not equitable, and the practice of authoritarianism has undermined its economic accomplishments.

A scholarly study of Korea as a divided nation is a challenge because the two Korean "regimes in contest" epitomize the global contest between capitalism and socialism. As East Asia, since 1945, has been the center of the world struggle between capitalism and socialism, so divided Korea in the 1980s continues to be a sensitive indicator of shifts in the global balance between these two socioeconomic ideologies. East Asia has witnessed communist and socialist revolutions in China, North Korea, and Vietnam and has also seen some of the most impressive capitalist achievements in the postwar era, in Japan, South Korea, Taiwan, Hong Kong, and Singapore.

The engine for rapid economic growth in the capitalist East Asian countries, as in South Korea, has largely been the outward economic policy of positive interaction with the global economy and an export-led strategy of industrialization. Socialist East Asian states have also switched their orientation toward the global economy by assuming a more positive and aggressive foreign economic policy. North Korea since the early 1970s, like China in the post-Mao era, has expanded its trade relations with Japan, Western European countries, and some members of the non-aligned nations movement, going beyond its traditional trade interactions with the Soviet bloc countries.

The present book clarifies the politics and policies in divided Korea by examining three topics: (1) the historical dimension of political developments in Korea since 1945, which provides the context for understanding the political dynamics of the 1980s, (2) the policy patterns and political processes of the respective Korean regimes, and (3) the future prospects for the Korean Peninsula, seen in the light of the regimes' pursuit of the policy goal of Korean unification.

Divided nations, like divided families, are difficult to reconcile. Once partition takes place, it is difficult to rectify the mistakes and restore the status quo ante. Rapprochement, attempts to normalize the relationship following a period of estrangement, will improve the situation but not erase wounds already inflicted. The reunification of a divided country is an ideal that, like a rainbow, inspires the people to act but is difficult to attain. Although the Korean people continue to "dream the impossible dream" of reunification, the reality of inter-Korean competition and great power rivalry surrounding the Korean Peninsula frustrates hopes for an early attainment of this goal.

Dividing Korea was a tragic mistake, imposed upon the Korean people by outside forces in 1945. Subsequent events and the processes of political dynamics led to the emergence and entrenchment of the two rival systems and hostile regimes. It is my hope that by examining the factors and forces that led to the institutionalization of the political movements in the two Korean states, the prospects for normalizing inter-Korean relations and eventually achieving reunification may be assessed. It was in the spirit of promoting understanding of the Korean problem and its possible solutions that this project was undertaken.

I have been studying Korean politics for more than a decade. My first meaningful scholarly encounter with Korea, apart from the fact that I am a native-born Korean and now a naturalized U.S. citizen, was in 1973, during a visit to the Asiatic Research Center of Korea University on a Fulbright Senior Research Fellowship. My field research in 1972 and 1973, supported by a grant of the Joint Committee on Korean Studies of the ACLS-SSRC (American Council of Learned Societies and the Social Science Research Council), gave me an opportunity to rediscover my native land. This time I was ostensibly an outsider looking inside a country with which I thought I had been very familiar. The origin of this particular project, the comparative study of North and South Korean politics, may be traced to the invitation to prepare a conference paper for the Workshop on the Comparative Study of North and South Korea, sponsored by the Joint Committee on Korean Studies of the ACLS-SSRC, in San Juan, Puerto Rico, January 16–17, 1976.

Although I have been working on this particular book on and off for about seven years, I did not feel comfortable writing about North Korea until the summer of 1981, when I visited North Korea for fifteen days. That trip gave me an invaluable firsthand opportunity to observe and experience the situation of North Korea. I have had the occasion to visit South Korea more regularly—every other year for the past ten years. Such field experience has been indispensable, but I have also made a special effort in this book to try to approach the subject of Korean politics from the perspective of a student in comparative politics. The present book therefore is an attempt to study Korean politics comparatively, focusing not only on the two halves of divided Korea but also contrasting divided Korea on the one hand with other political systems in the world on the other, including those of both democratic and authoritarian developing countries.

As a general rule all Korean names are given in the text according to the McCune-Reischauer system of transliteration, with some stylistic modifications. Exceptions include individual names that are widely recognized and accepted in their idiosyncratic renderings, such as Syngman Rhee, Kim Il Sung, Park Chung Hee, Chun Doo Hwan, and Kim Jong Il. Other exceptions are certain place names, such as Seoul, and official terms like Juche. Otherwise, family names precede given names, and the given names are hyphenated (Kim Dae-jung or Cho Man-sik). As for the ordering of individual authors' names in the reference material, I have tried to follow individual preferences (e.g., Chong Lim Kim or B. C. Koh) or style (Chong-Sik Lee or Dae-Sook Suh) if they are known to me.

Young Whan Kihl
Ames, Iowa

Acknowledgments

The central themes of this book are original and are presented here for the first time in printed form. Some portions of the material in individual chapters, however, have appeared elsewhere as journal articles or as conference proceedings. These previously published materials are listed below with the corresponding chapters noted in parentheses.

"Comparative Study of the Political Systems of South and North Korea: A Research Note," *Korea and World Affairs* 5, 3 (Fall 1981): 383–402. An earlier version, "Comparing Political Systems of South and North Korea: A Preliminary Note on Research Strategies," appeared in *Proceedings,* Fourth Joint Conference of the Korean Political Science Association and the Association of Korean Political Scientists in North America, August 10–13, 1981 (Seoul: Korean Political Science Association, 1981), pp. 53–64 (portions of Chapters 1 and 6).

"Korea's Fifth Republic: Domestic Political Trends," *Journal of Northeast Asian Studies* 1, 2 (June 1982): 37–56; "North Korea: A Reevaluation," *Current History* 81, 474 (April 1982): 155–159, 180–182; and "Korean Politics in the 1980s," *Problems of Communism* 30 (September-October 1981): 66–70 (portions of Chapters 4 and 7).

"North Korea in 1983: Transforming 'the Hermit Kingdom'?" *Asian Survey* 24, 1 (January 1984): 100–111 (portions of Chapter 7).

"South Korea's Unification Policy in the 1980s: An Assessment," *Korea and World Affairs* 7, 1 (Spring 1982): 73–95; "North Korea's Unification Policy in the 1980s," *Korea and World Affairs* 7, 4 (Winter 1982): 602–614; and "The Issue of Korean Unification," in C. I. Eugene Kim and B. C. Koh, eds., *Journey to North Korea: Personal Perceptions* (Berkeley: University of California Institute of East Asian Studies, 1983—reprinted here by permission), pp. 99–117 (portions of Chapter 8).

The author wishes to acknowledge, with appreciation, the permission given to use portions of the preceding materials.

A number of institutions assisted me directly or indirectly in completing the current project. In addition to the Fulbright program and the ACLS-SSRC grants already mentioned, I am grateful to the ACLS-SSRC for a second grant in 1978, to Iowa State University for a university research grant in 1976, a faculty improvement leave grant in 1978-1979, a World Food Institute research grant in 1980–1984, and to the George Washington University Institute for Sino-Soviet Studies for my residence there as a visiting scholar in the fall 1978 semester.

In completing this project I have talked with and learned from various individuals, all of whose names cannot necessarily be included or revealed. I owe special thanks to many individuals whom I interviewed during my field trips. I hope that their confidence in me as a scholar has not been diminished as a result of my writing and the interpretations included in this book. Among many colleagues and friends, I would like to single out the following for special thanks: Dong Suh Bark, Roger Benjamin, William Boyer, C. I. Eugene Kim, Chong Lim Kim, Ilpyong J. Kim, Samuel C. Kim, Young C. Kim, B. C. Koh, Chae-jin Lee, Chong-Sik Lee, James McCormick, Larry Niksch, Victor Olorunsola, Han-Shik Park, Jorgen Rasmussen, Ross Talbot, John Turner, Edward Wright, and Sung Chul Yang. For research assistance and for typing the manuscript, thanks go to S. S. Yoon and Virginia Lee respectively. I was fortunate in working with a group of dedicated professionals at Westview Press that includes Lynne Rienner, Deborah Lynes, Holly Arrow, and Vicki Gundrum, whose assistance I cherished greatly. Finally, I would like to acknowledge the special contribution that my wife, Mary, made toward this project. Without the affection and criticism she gave me in-between her busy schedule, this book would not have been completed in its present form.

Y.W.K.

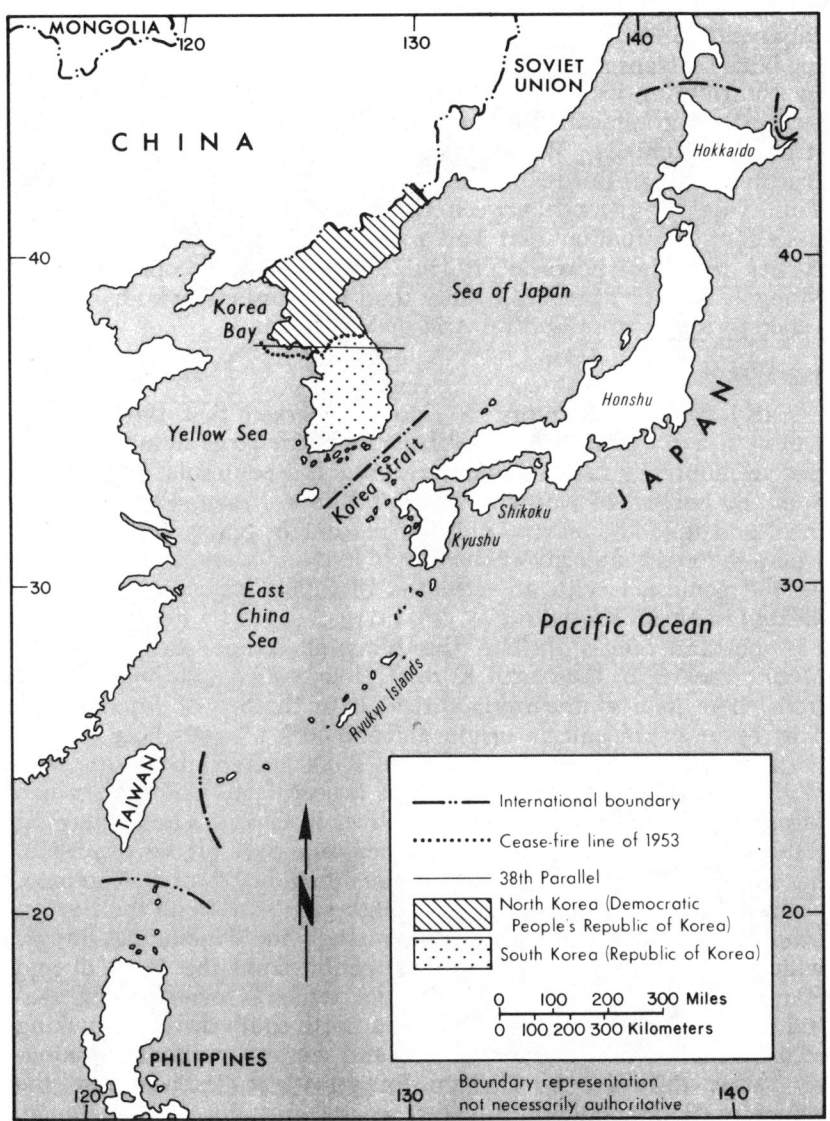

Divided Korea in Its Asian Setting

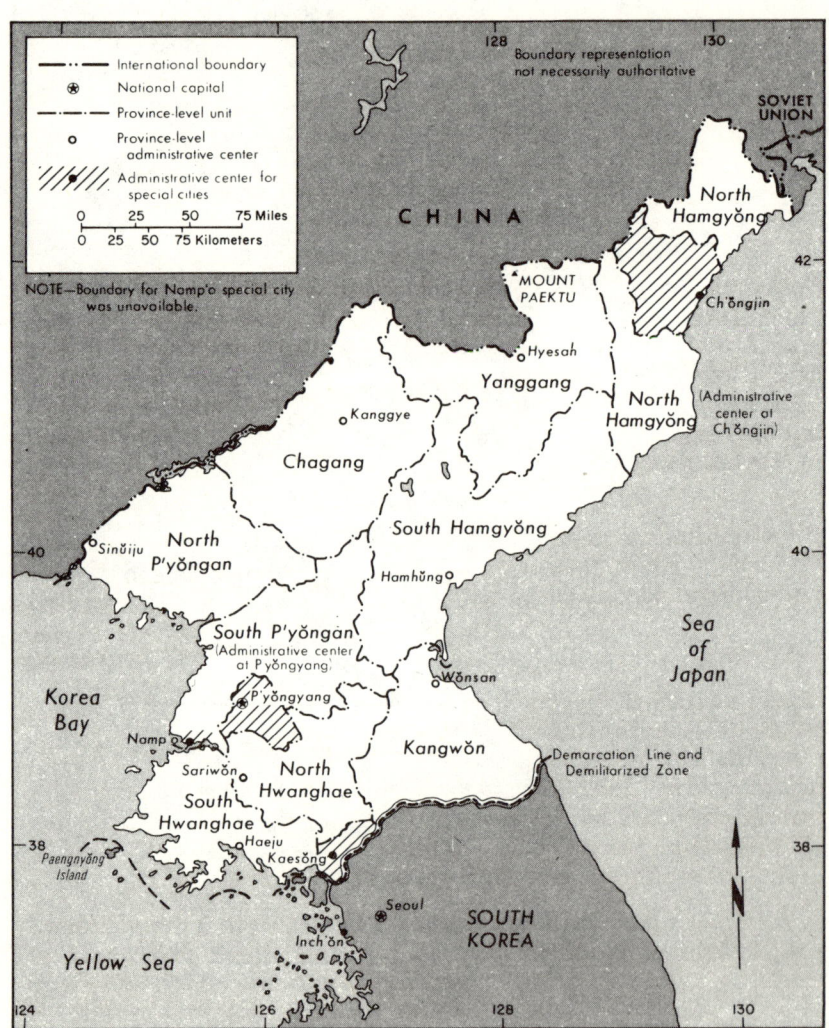

North Korea, Administrative Units

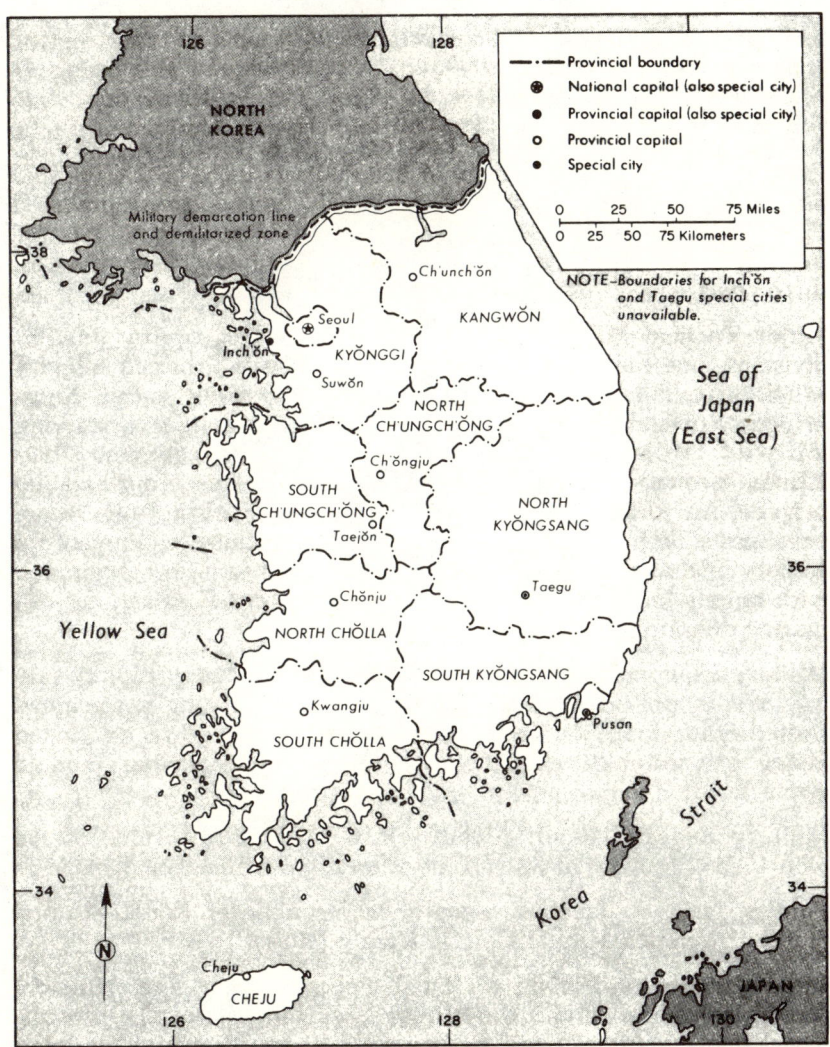

South Korea, Administrative Units

1
Comparative Korean Politics: An Overview

The two political systems that emerged in divided Korea are in sharp contrast. They are radically different in political ideology and organization as well as in value orientation and leadership style. This contrast is even more striking in view of the high degree of uniformity that characterizes the traditional culture and society of Korea. The Koreans are known for their homogeneous ethnic, linguistic, and cultural characteristics, but since 1945 divergent political systems and separate states have emerged in Korea that are mutually antagonistic. They are engaged in the politics of competing legitimacy. The political regimes in the respective Koreas typically hold the view that the policies and programs pursued by the opposing camp are not compatible with the broad national interests of the Korean people, especially on the question of national reunification. This self-righteous posture toward the opposing regime breeds inter-Korean rivalry and accentuates the level of political conflict.[1]

The degree of hostility between the North and South Korean regimes is so intense that the two Korean states are engaged in a high-risk zero-sum game of politics. The anomalous situation of Korea as a divided nation led Gregory Henderson to claim that "it is hard to think of a more homogenous national or cultural entity anywhere [in the world] than the Korean peninsula; no other has been divided with a more mindless artificiality by purely external powers; in none are communications so utterly ruptured or conflict positions more implacable."[2] Glenn Paige was impressed by "Korea's remarkable potential as a 'natural social science laboratory.' "[3] He refers to the possibility and promise of undertaking a comparative study of politics in North and South Korea, especially on the role of political leadership in the development of two divergent political systems in what was a highly homogeneous nation until partition in 1945.

As Han-Kyo Kim recently noted, "different patterns of development in two regions of Korea in the postwar years may be attributed to political factors (political leadership according to Paige) inasmuch as the social and cultural factors could safely be assumed to be fundamentally identical throughout Korea at the onset of national division."[4] The impact of political factors on the pattern of societal development may therefore be analyzed, according to Paige, under conditions "roughly approximating those of a controlled laboratory experiment."[5]

In comparative research, the similarity and the difference between two sets of phenomena are a matter of degree and perspective. For this reason both similar-nation and different-nation designs may be employed in comparative social research, as Przeworski and Teune point out.[6] In view of the anomalous and unique situation of Korea as a divided nation, this study will highlight the contrast between North and South Korea as two divergent political systems. More particularly, this chapter will explicate three matters of theoretical concern for the study of comparative Korean politics: a profile of the political systems of divided Korea, the analytical framework employed for the present study, and a specification of the dominant features and characteristics of Korea's political culture.

Political Systems in Contrast

Neither the political system of North Korea nor that of South Korea can truly be called democratic, despite constitutional provisions and claims to the contrary. Instead, both political systems of divided Korea are modifications of forms initially intended to be democratic that have been transformed into more or less "Koreanized" political systems. While the political system in the south embodies a type of authoritarianism, resembling what some students of Latin American politics call a "bureaucratic authoritarian state," the political system of North Korea epitomizes an extreme form of modern totalitarianism revolving around the life of the founding leader. North Korea's monolithic and unitary state is reminiscent of the Orwellian 1984 superstate, except that it is smaller in scale and thoroughly familistic in leadership composition. Under Kim Il Sung, North Korea has become a Confucian communist state. Within the confines of authoritarian and totalitarian structure, North and South Korea have developed divergent political systems and styles of leadership.

As a communist state, North Korea has an official ideology that guides its political life, and a ruling political party that applies this ideology in developing workable policies and programs. The ruling party leaders and cadres are entrenched in key positions of power in the north. They are instrumental in formulating the party line and translating it into government policies. Like other communist systems, the ruling party in North Korea controls the government through a system of lateral controls such as the overlapping of key positions in the party and government agencies at the center and the periphery. The political ideology of North Korean communism, known as *Juche* (Chuch'e) or *Juche Sasang* (Chuch'e idea), is claimed to be an application of the theory of Marxism-Leninism to the Korean experience. The ideology is also known as Kimilsungism (*Kim Il Sung Chuûi*), after the supreme leader of North Korea, Kim Il Sung, who personally provided a leadership role in developing it. In the socialist economic system of the north, the means of production and distribution are collectively owned and controlled by the people, and the state administers the people's property.[7]

South Korea, in contrast, is a praetorian state tempered by a constitutional form of government. Like many developing countries in the Third World, South Korea lacks a firm tradition of democratic rule, and it has been influenced by extraconstitutional measures throughout its political history. The constitution enacted in November 1980 stipulated that South Korea was a "democratic state" in the sense that the government was set up to carry out policies and programs formulated and approved by a duly elected body, the National Assembly. However, since the military has intervened in politics in 1961 and 1980, the tradition of civilian control of the military—essential for democratic rule—has been undermined in South Korean politics. In recent years, as South Korean society has become more complex with the progress of industrialization, the military has come to exert influence in South Korean politics more as an institution than through individual leaders or personalities, as was the case in earlier years. In its rule the military attempts to mobilize the support of civilian bureaucrats, technocrats, and some intellectuals and entrepreneurs. Under the capitalist economic system of South Korea, the means of production and distribution are privately owned and operated, at least in theory. South Korea does not practice pure capitalism, however, as some key enterprises—such as utilities, rail transportation, and steel mills—are government owned and operated. Its economic system is often said therefore to be semicapitalism or state capitalism. Yet South Korea does recognize the principles of entrepreneurship, incentive, and profit that are basic to a capitalist system.[8]

The political systems of North and South Korea converge, in spite of divergent ideological perspectives and orientation, in their heavy reliance on coercive instruments of political rule and in their use of state agencies in carrying out programs of planned socioeconomic change. The state administration has captured the attention of various socioeconomic groups in Korean society north and south—groups such as the military, the bureaucracy, party elites, entrepreneurs, students, workers, and so on. Whereas in the north the KWP (Korean Workers' Party), as the ruling communist party, supervises the administration of the state through the interlocking and overlapping membership of party and government bureaucracies, in the south the military faction that has emerged by usurping power supervises the administration of the government through the civilian bureaucracy and technocracy. In both cases the state has become the motive force for attaining socioeconomic modernization and managing the national economy.[9]

States, in Max Weber's conception, are "compulsory associations claiming control over territories and the people within them."[10] Although this definition of statehood remains valid in the Korean context, the states of divided Korea, once established, became more than the contested *objects* of varying social groups and individuals that they were at the outset. Rather, they became *subjects* or autonomous actors, sponsoring and initiating public policies and programs of socioeconomic change and modernization. The state, in North and South Korea, is the originator of comprehensive programs of reform directed from above. In the north the state is the exclusive agency for planned socioeconomic change and modernization; in the south the state provides the policy direction, sharing with other social agencies and the business community the responsibility for executing the programs and policies of socioeconomic transformation.[11]

The state also readily intervenes in the "market" in the south; in the north it controls and operates the economy and directs the cultural life of the population as well. In terms of the basis of political participation however, the political systems of North and South Korea are somewhat varied.

The 1961 and 1980 coups in South Korea were "conspiratorial" coups carried out by career military professionals.[12] The prime movers of these coups were career military officers who, by going through officer training schools and service experiences, acquired not only conventional and traditional military skills but also uniform perspectives and values on matters such as national economic planning, security and welfare, and anticommunist ideology. These military officers installed a "corporatist" regime in 1980 in response to perceived crises of political order and to perceived needs for continuing economic development following the collapse of the Yushin system in 1979. Unlike the 1961 coup, the 1980 coup established a corporatist state, with the military using state power not only "to stave off or deflect threats to national order from subordinate classes and groups"—such as workers, students, and activist Christians—but also "used state power to implement socioeconomic reforms or plans for further economic growth."[13] It also promoted close ties between the state on the one hand and big business, as well as officially sanctioned political parties, labor unions, and noncompetitive interest groups, on the other.

In North Korea, the 1980 Sixth KWP Congress was the epitome of carefully planned and executed social engineering imposed from above. Important policies, including political succession and economic development, were carefully laid out by the top leadership and party bureaucracy prior to the congress. The party congress acted merely as a "ratifying" instrument, rather than as a substantive decisionmaking body.[14] The use of the state by party elites in the north in 1980 was thus deliberate in both speed and design. The "due process" facade was maintained throughout to legitimize the act of political succession that had already been decided upon prior to the official announcement in 1980.[15] Like the 1980 coup in South Korea, the 1980 KWP congress had far-reaching consequences; yet it was more or less a routine and regularized process, in contrast to the extraordinary and extraconstitutional process of political change represented by the coup in South Korea.

Analytical Framework: Approaches and Methods

A meaningful and systematic inquiry into the politics of North and South Korea is long overdue. The prevailing mode of scholarly inquiry into Korean politics is largely monosystemic rather than comparative or cross-systemic. The majority of studies in the literature tends to focus on one of the two rival political systems of Korea.[16] Studies that use a method of comparative research based on a common analytic framework are rare.[17]

To advance a knowledge of Korean politics that is cumulative and not dated, however, systematic inquiry into the politics of Korea as a divided nation is needed. A comparative approach to the politics of North and South Korea that incorporates a common analytical framework may be more enduring and useful than separate studies of each half, transcending the current situation of divided Korea and viewing the phenomenon of national separation since 1945 from a broader historical perspective.

The research strategy of comparative studies of North and South Korean politics may adopt any one or several of the various approaches used in the discipline of political science today. These approaches include analyses of political culture and tradition, political leadership and performance, the formation and implementation of developmental policies and programs, and the dynamics of factionalism.[18] In view of the timely and topical nature of these and other approaches, it is important that the relevance to our study of any of these conceptual approaches be first demonstrated. This chapter introduces a framework for analyzing the comparative dynamics of the North and South Korean political systems. The four specific approaches or perspectives to be employed are: (1) typological analysis, (2) political culture and leadership analysis, (3) political economy analysis, and (4) policy analysis and linkage politics. Taken together, these perspectives will provide the basis for generating some intersystem questions and hypotheses regarding Korean politics.

Typology of Political Systems

The literature on Korean politics abounds with monosystemic accounts of North and South Korean political development.[19] In describing the political characteristics of each half of divided Korea, these studies have generally adopted—either implicitly or explicitly—typologies derived from the experience of other countries that are also useful as shorthand descriptions of the political process and reality evident in a particular society. For instance, some observers characterize North Korea under Kim Il Sung as a "Stalinist regime" (Chong-Sik Lee); others depict it as a "mobilizational regime" (Ilpyong J. Kim), a "personalist" system (C. I. Eugene Kim), or a monocracy (R. Scalapino and Chong-Sik Lee). Recently, Kim Il Sung's position of power in the north has been described as "hereditary or dynastic rule" (Dong-bok Lee). Some students of South

TABLE 1.1
Contrasting Models of South and North Korean Polities

South Korea	North Korea

Authoritarianism
  Praetorian State
  Repressive Regime
	Totalitarianism
	  Stalinist State
	  Unitary System

State Capitalism
  Market Economy
  Government-managed
	State Socialism
	  Command Economy
	  Centrally Planned

Dependent Development
  Managed Interdependence
	Independent Development
	  Autonomy & Self-reliance

Korean politics have also characterized South Korea under Syngman Rhee and Park Chung Hee as an "authoritarian regime" (James Palais) or a "repressive dictatorship" (Bruce Cumings).[20]

When these conceptions of the Korean political systems are taken into account, at least three themes, associated with the role of the state in society and economy in the two Koreas, stand out as noteworthy in the literature. These conceptual schemes generally use either dichotomies or polarities in describing the political systems of South and North Korea.[21] The contrasting models are shown in Table 1.1.

Although all three models in Table 1.1 reflect macrosystemic views of politics, each is based on a set of specific assumptions regarding the nature of political rule and the role of the central government in the political process. For instance, the political systems of South and North Korea may be depicted as "authoritarian" and "totalitarian." This reflects the view of a political analyst who is concerned with defining the proper relationship between the ruler and the ruled. An implicit assumption is that (in both North and South Korea) when a conflict arises between the ruler's interest and the general interest, the former often prevails, even though the ruler's interest is always defended as promoting the welfare of the governed. Under this scheme, no competing systems or elites are tolerated, and politics becomes a matter of life or death that reflects a high-risk system.[22]

The nature of economic activities and the role of the central government in the market are the bases for the second characterization of the political systems of North and South Korea listed in Table 1.1. While North Korea follows the ideology of socialism and employs the centralized planning of a command economy, South Korea subscribes to the principle of capitalism based on the dynamics of the market, although the government frequently intervenes to direct market forces in a particular policy direction.[23]

The third dichotomy in Table 1.1 contrasts styles and approaches to economic development. Whereas the developmental strategy of North Korea is allegedly based on the principle of Juche (autonomy and self-reliance) in mobilizing domestic and indigenous resources, that of South Korea is more flexible, taking greater risks with external forces by exposing its economy to outside sources of capital inflow and technology input.[24] In theory, North Korea practices autarky, although out of necessity it has been increasingly participating in the world economy through expanded foreign trade and purchases of technology from other countries, including advanced Western nations. South Korea, on the other hand, is actively involved in the world economy through expanded international trade and the inflow of foreign capital and investment activities. In short, South Korea is committed to a policy of coping with and managing complex interdependence within the international system, while North Korea advocates the idea of Juche, which makes a virtue of autonomy, independence, and self-reliance.[25]

From the world systems perspective South Korea is a peripheral state in the world capitalist system, engaged in performing a specific role in the world economy's international division of labor. By pursuing its economic policy of industrialization through an export-led strategy of economic development, South Korea has emerged as a semi-industrial or newly industrializing country (NIC) in the world system. Its heavy dependence on the markets of Japan and the United States for both import and export, however, makes South Korea's economy vulnerable and dependent. North Korea, in contrast, is a socialist peripheral state that is relatively isolated and immune from the world capitalist system.[26] North Korea's economy is smaller in scale than South Korea's, and is well-integrated as an autonomous system. It is also relatively free from external pressures and disturbances. Whereas South Korea has an outward-oriented economy, North Korea has an inward-oriented economy. South Korea is a capitalist dependent nation, and North Korea is a socialist independent country.[27]

Political Culture Perspective

Although the political systems of North and South Korea differ, some argue that the two Korean states have similar political cultures and propensities for political activity. In spite of apparent institutional variations—in terms of contrasts between communist and noncommunist ideology as well as between socialist and capitalist economic systems—the political systems of North and South Korea are seen to exhibit several "latent" characteristics deeply ingrained and rooted in Korea's political culture and tradition. This conceptualization of Korean politics in terms of common political culture has some practical significance, although one must be careful about the explicit meaning of political culture employed as a concept in analysis.

For the sake of convenience, two usages and meanings of political culture analysis may be differentiated. The first considers political culture as stemming from the traditional beliefs and historical experience of a people; the second treats political culture as largely based on the contemporary political experience of the elite and the citizenry, including their socialization. The present study applies both concepts of political culture to the phenomenon of Korean politics.

To explain Korea's political culture in terms of "traditional beliefs" is intuitive and interpretative; to do so in terms of "contemporary beliefs, attitudes, and behavior" is empirical and positivistic. Proponents of the first approach to Korea's political culture would argue that since North and South Korea share a common culture and tradition, with a continuous record as a unified and homogeneous nation since the seventh century A.D., the present generation of Koreans must consider the territorial division of the country since the end of World War II as a transitory phase in the longer historical perspective of the Korean people's existence. According to this view, sources of inspiration and interpretation for the analysis of the present political developments in divided Korea must be sought in the cultural heritage and past experience of the Korean people. More specific examples that interpret Korea's political culture in terms of traditional sources—and the resultant controversy and rival hypotheses regarding Korea's political culture—will be presented in Chapter 5.

The second approach starts with an examination of the changing pattern of attitudes and behavior of present-day Koreans. Political behavior and activities may be treated as dependent variables explainable in terms of sociological and psychological theories of human behavior. What, then, is the behavioral concept of political culture, and how is it relevant to the study of Korean politics?

The interdisciplinary analysis of political attitudes and behavior popularized by Gabriel Almond, Lucian Pye, and Sidney Verba can be applied to the study of the comparative political culture of North and South Korea.[28] After all, Korean political culture consists of "the system of empirical belief, expressive symbols, and values which defines the situation in which political action takes place," to borrow from Verba. The "link between the events of politics and the behavior of individuals in reaction to those events" must be clarified first and foremost because, as the same author put it,

> although the political behavior of individuals and groups is of course affected by acts of government officials, wars, election campaigns, and the like, it is even more affected by the *meanings* that are assigned those events by observers. This is to say no more than that people respond to what they *perceive* of politics and how they interpret what they see. From the cultural point of view, for instance, we would look at political history

not so much as a series of objective events but as a series of events that may be interpreted quite differently by different people and whose effects on future events depend upon this interpretation.[29]

The consciousness of the Koreans is affected, in short, not only by the historical experience they went through but also by the *subjective* meanings they attached to these historical events. The older generation is affected by such experiences as Korea's national liberation in 1945 and the tragic internecine war in 1950–1953. The legacy of the anti-Japanese guerrilla fighting and resistance movement prior to 1945 has definitely colored not only the world view and perception of North Korea's political elite under Kim Il Sung but also that of North Korea's new generation of leadership and youth through the deliberate inculcation of these values and myths. The anticommunist orientation of South Korea's ruling circle, moreover, is influenced by a large number of refugees from the north who fled communist rule prior to the end of war in 1953. Likewise, the 1960 Student Revolution and the 1961 military coup are given varying meanings and interpretations by the generations that experienced these tumultuous events. The 1980 Kwangju insurrection and its suppression will no doubt also receive different interpretations by Koreans supporting or criticizing the measures taken by the Chun Doo Hwan government in response to the Kwangju riots.

Political Economy Perspective

The capacity of the political regimes in North and South Korea to implement their public policies varies. It is true that state officials are inclined to formulate policies that seem to them to be most plausible and feasible. It is also true, however, that states often pursue goals that are beyond their capacity and their means to achieve. What the Korean regimes profess as policy is not to be equated with what they are capable of implementing and attaining. For this reason, we need to examine the carrying capacity of each Korean state and the performance of each regime in socioeconomic development. Political economy and policy analysis, our third and fourth analytical perspectives, may prove to be highly useful for the comparative study of North and South Korea.

The typological approach to the study of North and South Korean politics is, as noted, predominantly sociological in orientation, while political cultural analysis is largely historical-sociological and psychological in emphasis. Both sociological and psychological approaches, however, must be used skillfully and supplemented by what may be called political economy and policy analysis.

Political economy has become fashionable as a mode of scholarly inquiry in comparative politics. One reason is that this approach makes it possible to undertake an analysis of public policymaking and implementation by a particular regime.[30] Although it is not always clear what political economy as a concept entails, we may safely assume that in the Korean context political economy has something to do with the interaction of government in the allocation of power and wealth. Whatever the Korean governments do in the production, manipulation, and distribution of power and wealth may therefore be considered to fall into the proper domain and scope of political economy.[31] The importance of political economy as an approach in political science was highlighted recently by Joe Oppenheimer:

> Political economy has developed as a fugue, with at least two closely related themes: how politics determines aspects of the economy, and how economic institutions determine political process. . . . Inherent in these themes are the great ideological questions of politics: what can and should be the structure of political and economic institutions? Who should get what? What should be the role of liberty and property?[32]

The task of utilizing the concept of political economy for a study of comparative Korean politics is to discover links between the political regime and the business or entrepreneurial sector of the society that maximize the conditions and climate for the productive activities of the national economy. The Harvard Business School, in its case studies of political economy based on the experience of Japan from 1854 to 1977, also described political economy as "the study of economic policymaking as it takes place in its political and institutional context."[33] "Typically," it went on to state, "it is the study of economic policymaking at the highest levels of government of the nation. The problems considered have to do with choice of goals, formulation of supporting policies, development of institutions, and mobilization of resources. Government, and particularly the executive branch of government, is charged with influencing or 'managing' an economy."[34] The establishment of a proper relationship between the government as the regulator and the market as the arena of economic activities is thus what political economy is expected to accomplish in a society.

The political economy approach, thus conceived, has a potential for generating important hypotheses and questions regarding the comparative study of Korea as a divided nation. The political dynamics of divided nationhood have kept the two Korean regimes isolated from each other for nearly four decades, and during this period different sets of economic policies and measures have been put into effect. This means that divided Korea, with its two competing political regimes, provides a unique laboratory for the political economy studies of other countries of the world as well. Another reason the political economy perspective is useful for comparing the North and South Korean regimes is that the socio-economic reality of the two Korean societies has changed radically due to rapid industrialization and its effect on society at large. The Koreas of the 1970s and 1980s are obviously not the same as the Koreas of the 1950s or the 1960s.

A comparative study of North and South Korean regimes using political economy perspectives is difficult primarily because of the unavailability of systematic data across the systems. For this reason our study will be limited to an analysis of several key factors for which data are available. As will be shown in Chapter 6, the political economy approach to comparative Korean politics clarifies three interrelated issues: (1) the role of the government in the market, i.e., the production, distribution, and exchange of goods and services in the two Koreas, (2) the performance of the national economy during a given period of time as affected by government policies, and (3) the nature of external links established by the economy with the world economy, i.e., the dependent or independent orientation of the national economy. The North and South Korean approaches to each of these aspects of political economy are radically different.

Policy Analysis and Linkage Politics

The fourth perspective adopted in our comparative study of North and South Korean politics will be policy analysis and linkage politics. To grasp the essence of modern government, whether socialist or capitalist, it is important to know how public choices and decisions are formulated under different political regimes. To anticipate the direction of change and to estimate the consequences of adopting a particular course of action or policy, the orientation of policy analysis must be predominantly ex ante, rather than ex post facto like the typological or political culture approaches already discussed. In view of the scarcity assumption that the economist generally adopts, the policy analyst will also need to predict behavior rather than viewing behavior as either random or unique—the predominant orientation of many political scientists.

The linkage between domestic and foreign policy considerations will need to be clarified in the policy analysis. The policies and programs implemented by the Korean regimes undoubtedly reflect the strategic considerations of the political elites in promoting a set of policy goals and values. Examining the regimes' policy behavior in domestic and foreign policy arenas is the best way to detect and isolate the policy goals and values that underlie specific policies and programs of the regimes. Because domestic and foreign policy behavior is often linked in the Korean context, an analysis of their linkage patterns will give us some clues in determining the nature and character of the political regimes operating in divided Korea.[35]

A further task of policy analysis will be the consideration of policy patterns and processes in terms of specific sectors of the economy and the regime. Sectarian policies dealing with agriculture, industry, and foreign trade are necessary, and the political consequences of choosing specific policy goals and implementation strategies are important to an understanding of North and South Korean politics. Analyzing regime policies that cope with demand and support by certain sectors in society, such as functional groups and regional constituencies, is likewise important in determining the success or failure of the political systems and performance of the two Korean regimes.

The heart of policy analysis is thus to study the available choices open to the political leadership and their probable consequences. The strategic choices available to the Korean regimes vary. They range, for instance, from basic economic development policy decisions, such as production and market decisions, to sectoral support policy decisions, such as a price support policy for agricultural goods or subsidies for food prices for the urban and industrial sectors. Illustrations of policy behavior and linkage politics will be presented in Chapters 6 and 7.

Dominant Features of Korean Politics

The characteristic traits of Korean political culture may be seen from the twin perspectives of sociological and psychological approaches. Korean politics is noted for a set of five distinguishing cultural characteristics, manifest in the pattern of contemporary political beliefs, attitudes, and behavior in North and South Korea. These five traits of Korean politics are: (1) the politics of hierarchy and deference, (2) the politics of voter mobilization, (3) increasing participatory orientation, (4) widening elite-mass cleavage, and (5) the politics of defiance during acute crises. These cultural traits may serve as a checklist of Korea's contemporary politics against which the discussion of Korea's historical political development may be presented.

The Politics of Hierarchy and Deference

Both in the north and the south dominant characteristics of Korean political culture are hierarchy and deference in authority relations.[36] Those in leadership positions perceive their role to be one of active command; those on the receiving end accept their role as one of blind submission. Vertical and unequal relations prevail in Korean society at both the interpersonal level and between ruler and ruled, elite and masses—a manifestation perhaps of the hierarchical principle of Confucianism. The ruler tends to take a paternalistic attitude toward the masses—perhaps also in line with the Confucian culture mores—and the ruled in Korea generally exhibit total submission and compliance toward authority.[37]

This hierarchical structuring of authority relations in Korea has brought about a system of political stratification based on power and influence. At the apex of the power pyramid is the supreme leader, Kim Il Sung and Chun Doo Hwan in North and South Korea respectively. The supreme leader, called *suryong* in the north and *taet'ongryong* in the south, is supported by a group of loyal followers who are party cadres in North Korea or military generals and higher civil servants in South Korea. This group constitutes the ruling elite in whose hands the day-to-day responsibility for decisionmaking is vested. The supreme leader and the ruling elite in each Korean society attempt to reach the base of the power pyramid to increase the level of political support among the masses. Political participation by the masses, however, is tightly controlled and manipulated by the supreme leader, who uses the rhetoric of participatory democracy—the mass-line principle in the north and the Saemaul movement in the south.[38] It is clear, however, that the supreme leader in each Korean state employs gimmicks of political mobilization to suit the interests of the ruling elite.

Political participation in divided Korea is largely confined to the elites and, in the case of South Korea, the counterelites (opposition party leaders), who play the game of influence and power in an effort to reach the supreme leader for support. The supreme leader, realizing the importance of political participation by key groups, tends to exploit the tendency toward centralized bureaucratic control to consolidate his personal power.[39] Since the ruler is concerned about maintaining political authority, he manipulates opportunities for political participation by the elites and masses to enhance the power and legitimacy of his position. The supreme leader in each Korean state is constantly reminded of the "logic of the ruler's imperative," which states that the political leader must consolidate his power by whatever means are available to him and that maintaining political authority is the ultimate goal.[40]

The Politics of Voter Mobilization

Political participation by the masses in Korean society is largely the result of directives from above with which the citizenry is expected to comply. For this reason political participation in Korea might be termed "mobilized participation" or "political mobilization"; it is intended mainly to serve the interests of the ruling elites. Political participation Korean style is not the autonomous and voluntary kind of participation generally found in Western democracies. The citizenry in Korea is compelled to play an essentially passive role in politics, as "subject" rather than as "participant." As a result, the prevailing political behavior of the masses is habitual compliance with the order and command of authority, not willing and voluntary support of authority. Although a political culture of centralized control and hierarchy is partly to blame, the paternalistic and manipulative orientation of the political leadership is equally responsible for suppressing voluntary and autonomous citizen political participation in Korea.[41]

This pattern in Korean politics is deeply ingrained in the political consciousness of the Korean people, especially in the day-to-day political attitudes and behavior of the elites and masses.

Voting behavior in both North and South Korea may be used to illustrate the phenomenon of "mobilized participation" in Korean politics. Elections in Korea are often carried out as a matter of routine, as a formalistic act of ratifying decisions already made by the central authority, rather than as a matter of genuine choice among the alternative candidates or policies by the voting public.[42] This is especially true in North Korea, where elections are more or less a ceremonial matter, a ritualistic exercise of state sovereignty. A typical claim by the North Korean authorities, in electing members of the Supreme People's Assembly (a nominal legislature) or members of the local assemblies is that 100 percent of the eligible voters turned out to vote and cast their 100 percent supportive votes for representatives who are nominees of the Korean Workers' Party. This is an unbelievable and impossible assertion from the standpoint of electoral statistics familiar in the West.

In South Korea, the situation is less extreme, but the ruling elites in South Korea also use the referendum as a means of obtaining a popular mandate and sanction on important policy matters such as constitutional amendments or political reform. This practice of conducting "politics by plebiscite" is often misleading, and it is subject to manipulation of voter sentiment by those in power. Although referendum voting in South Korea in recent years has never produced a 100 percent affirmative vote, as might have happened in the more regulated society of North Korea, the fact remains that no referendum advanced by the governing elites has ever been defeated in South Korea.

The phenomenon of "mobilized voters" in South Korea's national elections is another manifestation of the top-down approach to Korean politics. Mobilized participation distinguishes South Korean election behavior from that of voters in western democracies. One study estimates, for instance, that at least 9 percent of the voters in South Korea in 1973 belonged to the category of mobilized voters.[43] Mobilized voters in South Korea are identified in this study by three primary characteristics: (1) their voting decisions depend heavily on the advice or pressure of another person; (2) they do not know the names of the two representatives from their district; and (3) they feel totally ineffective regarding their role in politics.[44] Mobilized voters, as compared with the remaining voting public, are generally less informed and knowledgeable about democracy and "express antipathy to key democratic values."[45] Mobilized voting explains, at least partially, why South Korean politics is noted for high voter turnout in elections, especially in the rural areas. Rural voters in South Korea are more susceptible to government pressure for political mobilization.[46] In fact, the electoral results of South Korea's national elections show that the countryside tends to favor the progovernment candidates and the cities—especially the metropolitan regions—tend to elect the antigovernment or opposition party candidates.

Increasing Participatory Orientation

Expansion of the scope of political participation is the third trait of contemporary Korean politics. Increasing participation in South Korea, however, has been largely the result of progress in socioeconomic development and the impact of modernization, not of deliberate efforts by the ruling elites to promote democracy or to institutionalize democratic procedures. As noted by a perceptive student of Korean political participation, Chong Lim Kim, "seldom has the extended participation in postwar Korea been a direct result of conscious choice by the ruling elites. With the possible exception of a brief but chaotic period of Chang Myon's liberal regime" in 1960-1961, according to Kim, "popular participation has expanded, if at all, as a result of deliberate and selective mobilization efforts of the government or as an unintended effect of socioeconomic growth in the country."[47] Therefore, the two routes to political participation, which Huntington and Nelson have described as "participation as a means" and "participation as a by-product," have been the dominant processes in South Korea.[48]

Autonomous or voluntary participation in North and South Korean politics—as contrasted with induced or mobilized participation—may therefore be interpreted to be "participation as a by-product," associated with the impact of socioeconomic development and modernization of society. In spite of the centralized and hierarchical tendencies in Korea's political culture, which are deeply ingrained in Korea's leader-follower relationship, Korean societies are not immune to the impact of the rapid socioeconomic change that has characterized both Korean states in recent decades. This process of Korea's development and its effect on politics is noted by Kim:

> As the society becomes more modern, so do individuals, acquiring a higher level of individual modernity. This would erode the social basis of mobilized voting, depriving the regime in power of its once-secure electoral advantages . . . the march of modernization seems almost indubitable. In Korea today, urbanization is occurring at a rapid rate; illiteracy is already a thing of the past; mass media are spreading at a phenomenal rate, penetrating into the remotest villages and hamlets; and industrialization . . . is here to stay. All of these social and economic changes are bound to have a profound impact upon the belief systems and attitudes of the citizen, especially those who until now remained highly susceptible to the pressure of mobilized voting.[49]

The political attitudes and beliefs of Koreans may be ascertained by analyzing some of the opinion surveys conducted in South Korea. Although no survey data are available on North Korea's elite and masses, one can conjecture that North Korea is no better off than South Korea insofar as the democratic orientation and attitude of the mass public is concerned. In fact, because of the highly elitist nature of North Korea's political system, close attention to the leadership style and traits will yield many invaluable data necessary to the interpretation of North Korea's communist politics. The results of content analysis of the leadership principle in North Korea's communist system and the survey findings in South Korea will be presented in Chapter 5.

Widening Elite-Mass Cleavage

The ever-widening gap between the elite and the masses in their perception of political issues is the fourth characteristic of contemporary

Korean politics. Although this problem is not unique to Korea, the elite-mass gap will continue to widen in the future with the progress in industrialization and with the rapid socioeconomic change that are noticeable in Korean society.[50] An analysis of the world view and trust level shared by the elite strata and mass public in South Korea may be used to illustrate the point.

The level of political trust and the world views shared by the public in South Korea have implications for the society's future politics. They definitely have an impact upon the ways in which political activities are carried out in contemporary Korean society. If a gap exists between elite beliefs and mass opinions, the potential for disruption is immense in a country like Korea, whose political culture is noted for a high degree of hierarchy and centralization in authority relations. The smaller the elite-mass gap in perception and preference on conflict issues, the greater the possibility of maintaining political stability. Evidence on the elite-mass gap in South Korean politics will be presented in Chapter 5, derived from the results of a nationwide survey of elite and mass strata in South Korea in 1973 and 1974.[51]

In view of the basically different orientation of North Korea's political system, none of the survey questions posed to the public in South Korea may be asked in North Korea. Unfortunately, North Korea does not permit outsiders to come in and undertake social science field research and investigation.[52] Different instruments and measures are obviously needed for the study of North Korea's changing society. The identical political culture and tradition that North and South Korea shared up until 1945 does give some assurance that the views of North Korea's elite and mass public may not deviate greatly from the pattern of political attitudes and orientation found among the South Koreans surveyed. North Korea's mass campaign to inculcate the virtue of "absolute loyalty and dedication" to the Great Leader, "generation after generation," reflects the preoccupation on the part of North Korea's ruling elite that Kim Il Sung's charisma may not be institutionalized through the hereditary succession of legitimacy from father to son. The mass campaign of political socialization is therefore a recognition of the problem of elite-mass cleavage in North Korea after long years of Kim Il Sung's rule.

The Politics of Defiance During Acute Crises

Finally, contemporary Korean politics is noted for the ever-present danger of renewed political instability through revival of the old tradition of defiance by the masses. During most normal periods the mass public in Korea is generally deferential toward and in compliance with authority. However, at times of acute crisis the spirit of violent defiance may flare up. This trait is evident when, for example, a breakdown in authority or a change in administration occurs. Popular discontent and disapproval of incumbent leaders is manifested in widespread protests and riots.

Although most antigovernment acts and demonstrations are spontaneous, some of the more serious ones are conspiratorial; these outbreaks often have the explosive power of a volcanic eruption, reflecting the defiance of the masses.

The spirit of defiance and rebellion is rekindled in Korean politics when the governmental authority and policies are perceived by the masses to be arbitrary and unjust. Such volcanic explosions in Korean politics took place during the 1960 Student Revolution and the 1980 Kwangju uprising. Historically, the Tonghak Rebellion of the 1890s led to widespread disorder and discontent in the southwest provinces. The Tonghak Rebellion was quelled only with the help of outside powers and at the heavy price of outside intervention in the domestic affairs of Yi Korea. The Sino-Japanese War of 1894-1895 actually was the result of the failure of Yi Korea's central government to quell the Tonghak Rebellion: asking China for aid led to the Japanese sending troops to Korea as a countermeasure.[53]

The 1919 March First Independence movement was organized by the nationalist leaders as a protest against Japanese rule and harsh colonial policies. This popular protest was a spontaneous and nonviolent protest movement that affected the course of Korea's modern history.[54] There is no guarantee that similar popular movements will not emerge in Korean politics if a spark to ignite the volatile situation of domestic political crisis is provided, by events such as the death of the supreme leader.

Because the Korean people are generally submissive to and deferential toward authority during normal and routine periods, the phenomenon of defiance and rebellion may sound contradictory and incomprehensible. However, the very passive and compliant behavior of the Korean people during times of political normalcy makes acts of defiance and rebellion doubly significant. Usually, anger and frustration accumulated over a period of time underlie the act of defiance. Normally, pervasive corruption and injustice provide the setting for decisive acts of political defiance and rebellion by the Korean people. Because of the high degree of political trust and obedience to the supreme leader during normal circumstances, the infrequent but dramatic turn of events leading to mass defiance seems all the more dramatic. Mass protest behavior takes the form of violence and rebellion, including anarchic behavior such as assassination, arson, hostage taking, wholesale destruction, and mass killing.

Korean political culture, seen from another perspective, is also a high-risk system.[55] The Korean people are highly intelligent, imaginative, and intense in their life experiences and in their search for and pursuit of meaning and stated objectives. Politics in divided Korea is likewise pursued intensely and thoroughly by both elites and the mass public in such a way that politics becomes a high-risk enterprise. Politics in Korea, whether in the communist north or in the capitalist south, is a business of life and death for the participants. A zero-sum political game is applied in the political struggle and competition within each Korean society as well as between the two halves of divided Korea. Under this situation of high-risk politics no compromise or negotiated solution is encouraged or tolerated, with the consequence that the winners and the losers in the cutthroat political competition are clearly distinguishable.

When all five traits of Korea's contemporary political culture and the perspective of a high-risk system are taken into account, the inescapable conclusion is that Korean politics is volatile, full of excitement, energy, and surprises. Korea's adult population, elite and mass public alike, are fully mobilized today—especially in the South—and are conscious of their participatory role in politics. Korea's contemporary politics since 1945 has been influenced largely by the tug of war and contending forces in world politics; domestic political forces have likewise been engaged in push and pull movements in the political arena. The impact of external factors upon the process of Korea's political development in recent eras has been cataclysmic.

Korea's contemporary political history since 1945 has produced a clearly distinguishable pattern of "truncated" politics.[56] This has to a large extent been the inevitable product of a territorial partition of the Korean people and the bifurcation of the Korean nation into two hostile regimes. At the end of World War II in 1945, the Korean people were challenged to embark upon the ambitious task of nation building, liberated by the victorious Allied powers from the yoke of Japan's thirty-six-year-long colonial rule, from 1910 to 1945. Nevertheless, the Korean people fell victim to great power rivalry and hegemonic designs, which partitioned the Korean Peninsula into two zones of military occupation led by the United States and the Soviet Union. Although the spirit of independence and the yearning for self-determination by the Korean people were temporarily crushed, Korea's search for self-respect and identity has revived and will continue. The tasks of Korea's political development, attaining the goals of nation building, state building, and society building, will be carried out in spite of the adverse situation created by the "truncated" pattern of Korea's recent political history.

An Organizational Overview

This book is an attempt to analyze the contrasting political styles and policy performances of the two halves of Korea as a divided nation. The political experience of North and South Korea since 1945 is described and interpreted, but the primary focus of this book is Korean politics of the early 1980s. Chapters 2 and 3 present a broad sketch of the major political developments and issues in North and South Korea prior to 1980: Chapter 2 covers 1945 through 1970, and Chapter 3 covers 1971 through 1980. Important political events and personalities are highlighted separately for North Korea and South Korea and then interwoven throughout the discussion.

Chapter 4 examines political regimes and political stability in the respective Korean states since 1980. The Fifth Republic in South Korea is examined in terms of the transition of power from the Fourth Republic and the political movements and forces of 1980 through 1983. The possible establishment of a hereditary communist state through father-son political succession in North Korea is considered next, in the context of the origin and legitimization of the new political order since the conclusion of the Sixth KWP Congress in October 1980. Chapter 5 examines Korea's political culture in terms of both traditional and contemporary beliefs. It looks at Korea's political leadership, comparing divergent leadership styles, leadership principles, and personal traits of key political leaders. The focus then turns to Korea's supreme leadership, first Kim Il Sung and Park Chung Hee, then Chun Doo Hwan and Kim Jong Il.

The divergent approaches adopted by North and South Korea in their management of and strategy for political economy are presented in Chapter 6, which also looks at policymaking and implementation of major policy tasks. The similarities and differences in the policy performance and carrying capacity of the two Korean states and regimes are highlighted by comparative statistics and data for economic development, the arms race, diplomatic competition, and foreign trade. Chapter 7 analyzes the domestic and foreign policy behavior of the Korean regimes between 1980 and 1983, tracing the development and implementation of specific public policies. South Korea's developmental strategy in political, social, and economic domains and its performance in maintaining external links and handling the security issue are examined first. North Korea's policy of building a "unitary and monolithic system," tied in with succession politics, economic development policies, and diplomatic policy behavior is considered next.

Chapter 8 addresses the important question of the reunification policy and politics of divided Korea. North and South Korea's official unification policies and positions of the 1970s are compared and contrasted. Next, the two Koreas' unification policy documents, Pyongyang's DCRK (Democratic Confederal Republic of Koryo) plan and Seoul's UDRK (United Democratic Republic of Korea) plan, as unveiled in 1980 and 1982 respectively, are scrutinized. The possible motivations and strategic considerations of the two unification proposals are examined. The concluding chapter reviews the salient characteristics of Korean politics in the years of divided nationhood since 1945. After examining several hypotheses aimed at explaining system transformation of Korea as a divided nation, the chapter concludes with a speculation regarding the future of inter-Korean relations and political developments in the two Korean states.

Part 1
Historical Dimensions

2
Divided Korea and Its Political Development, 1945–1970

As the politics of deference and defiance provide the twin motifs of Korea's political culture, so the confrontation between the two rival states—the socialist Democratic People's Republic of Korea (DPRK) in the north and the capitalist Republic of Korea (ROK) in the south—has served as the central historical fact in Korean politics ever since the country was partitioned at the end of World War II. The dominant theme of Korea's political development in the era of divided nationhood since 1945 has been the politics of competing legitimacy between the two Korean states. Nevertheless, what has brought the two antagonistic regimes together, in spite of their mutual animosity and unyielding stance on ideological grounds, has been the driving force of Korean nationalism and the yearning desire for Korea's national reunification.

Korean nationalism began as a modernization movement in the late nineteenth century and became an anti-Japanese independence movement during the colonial period prior to 1945. Its development since 1945 has been decisively influenced by the political reality and historical experience of Korea as a divided nation.[1] Just as the movements toward economic modernization and political independence have remained potent as historical forces, the desire of the Korean elites and masses for national reunification did not abate but instead flourished, capturing the mainstream of Korea's nationalist movement in the post–World War II era.

The path of political development traversed by each Korean state since 1945 has been neither smooth nor straight: it contains many unexpected twists and turns. The three interrelated tasks of political development relevant in the Korean context have been state building, nation building, and society building.[2] The accomplishment of these tasks has invariably been affected by three sets of prevailing conditions: those within each Korea, those between the two Korean states, and those outside the Korean Peninsula in the external milieu of international politics. Whereas the first task of state building was achieved in each half of Korea primarily by exercising political power, the second task of nation building in each Korea entailed a manipulation of political symbols such as national independence and unification through education and socialization of the citizenry. The third task, society building, required the formulation and implementation of developmental plans, such as programs of economic development aimed at improving the welfare and livelihood of the populace.

In a survey of political developments within, between, and outside the two Korean states specific benchmarks are identifiable along the historical path: national liberation in 1945, the Korean War of 1950–1953, and the inter-Korean dialogue initiated in 1971. The history of Korea between 1945 and 1980 has been divided, for our purposes, into three broad eras: (1) the period of national liberation and civil war (1945–1953), (2) the period of estrangement and consolidation (1954–1970), and (3) the period of authoritarian adaptation (1971–1980). Each period will be scrutinized from the perspective of the threefold task of political development mentioned above, but first the origin of Korean partition needs to be discussed in the overall context of divided Korea and its political development prior to 1980.

The Partition of Korea (1945)

The circumstances surrounding the division of Korea are by no means clear.[3] But Korean partition is clearly the result of external forces, i.e., of the great-power rivalry between the United States and the Soviet Union in the Cold War era. The Korean people are naturally distressed over the callousness with which the wartime agreement was reached by the great powers to partition their country into two halves. They rightly claim that Korea was victimized by considerations of political and military expediency among the major powers in World War II. In this respect, little difference of opinion prevails between the official accounts of North and South Korea.

The nationalistic Koreans are almost unanimous in their perception that the decision to partition Korea was both a mistake and a tragedy. It was a mistake because the decision was ill-conceived and hastily made in a way that reflected the national interests of the great powers but not of the Korean people. It was a tragedy because no serious consideration was given to the probable consequences of territorial partition for the Korean people. Korea was sacrificed, so many Koreans believe, upon the altar of major power politics. In this regard the Korean people's distrustful sentiment toward outside powers was clearly expressed by a popular Korean saying right after World War II:

Ssoryon saramege sokchimalko,
Miguk saram mitchimalla,
Ilpon saram ironani,
Choson saram chosimhara!

(Don't be deceived by the Soviets,
Don't count on the Americans,

The Japanese will soon rise again,
So, Koreans, look out for yourselves!)[4]

Why the Koreans arrived at this nationalistic sentiment in 1945 may be seen more clearly if we examine both the circumstances surrounding the decision to partition Korea and the participants involved in that decision.

Divided Korea is a consequence of the Allied powers' wartime agreement in World War II and particularly of the decision to establish separate zones of military occupation along the 38th parallel.[5] In order to receive the surrender of the Japanese army at the conclusion of the war, the United States and the Soviet Union agreed to divide Korea at the 38th parallel north. The matter of what to do with Korea after the war was deliberated at a series of wartime Allied conferences attended by the president of the United States (Franklin D. Roosevelt initially and then Harry S Truman), British prime minister Winston Churchill, Chinese generalissimo Chiang Kai-shek, and Soviet premier Joseph Stalin. The Cairo conference issued a communiqué on November 20, 1943, which stated that the three great powers, the United States, Great Britain, and China, "mindful of the enslavement of the people of Korea, are determined that in due course Korea shall become free and independent."[6] This principle of Korean independence was reaffirmed at the Yalta conference of February 1945 and the Potsdam Declaration of July 26, 1945. The Soviet Union subsequently "adhered" to the Cairo conference provision on the future of Korea by signing the Potsdam Declaration; this was at least the U.S. interpretation.

The decision on divided Korea was part of the Allied wartime agreements that included the terms of Soviet participation in the Pacific war against Japan. It was at one of the military talks between the U.S. and Soviet officials held in Potsdam, for instance, that the Korean problems were discussed, although no explicit statement was made at the Potsdam conference regarding the division of Korea into two occupation zones. The military planners reportedly agreed that there should be a line of military demarcation in the general area of Korea between the U.S. and the Soviet air and sea operations.[7] No decision was made at the Potsdam conference regarding Korean partition because, according to Harry Truman, neither U.S. nor Soviet troops were expected to "march into Korea in the immediate future."[8] Nonetheless, one source indicates that the plan to occupy Korea was formulated unilaterally by the United States in a set of instructions in July 1945 from General George C. Marshall, who was then the U.S. army chief of staff, to Lieutenant General John E. Hull, the U.S. army operations division chief and a member of the military delegation at the Potsdam conference. An eyewitness reports:

> ... General Hull and some of his planning staff studied a map of Korea trying to decide where to draw a line for an army boundary between U.S.

and Soviet forces. They decided that at least two major ports should be included in the U.S. zone. This led to the decision to draw a line north of Seoul which would include the port of Inchon (and Pusan). This line north of Seoul, drawn at Potsdam by the military planners, was not on the 38th parallel but was near it and, generally, along it.[9]

The U.S. decision to divide Korea was prompted by a sudden and rapid deterioration of the Japanese forces in the Pacific. On August 8, 1945, two days after the dropping of the first atomic bomb on the Japanese city of Hiroshima, the Soviet Union entered the war against Japan. On August 12 the Soviet troops had already crossed into northeastern Korea and two days thereafter, on August 14, 1945, the Japanese emperor, Hirohito, announced that he would accept the terms of total surrender, putting an end to the Pacific war. As a result the U.S. strategy changed from an invasion of the islands of Japan to the military occupation and disarmament of the Japanese army. The United States State-War-Navy Coordinating Committee, an intergovernmental agency, was set up with instructions to advise the President about the surrender of the Japanese forces in Korea to the U.S. forces.[10]

Dean Rusk, who subsequently served as secretary of state during the Kennedy and Johnson administrations, was one of the members of the State-War-Navy Coordinating Committee, which was charged by the War Department to draw up the military demarcation line across the Korean Peninsula. Rusk—then a colonel representing the War Department General Staff—reports that on August 11 the War Department asked him and Colonel C. H. Bonesteel III "to come up with a proposal which would harmonize the political desire to have U.S. forces receive the surrender as far north as possible and the [ability of] U.S. forces to reach the area. We recommended the 38th parallel," continued Rusk, " . . . because we felt it important to include the capital of Korea in the area of responsibility of American troops."[11] A decision was also made at this time to place "administration of civil affairs" under "the responsibility of the respective commands of the two zones in Korea" until the completion of the Japanese surrender.[12]

The U.S. policy of dividing Korea along the 38th parallel was formally communicated to the Allies on August 13, 1945. According to Truman, the Allied powers "made no comment or objection."[13] The U.S. directive was also incorporated in General Order No. 1, which was sent to U.S. Army General Douglas MacArthur in Manila to implement as part of the policy of the military occupation of Japan. In defense of the U.S. decision to establish the division along the 38th parallel, President Truman also wrote that it was made "as a practical solution when the sudden collapse of the Japanese war machine created a vacuum in Korea."[14] The initial expectation that the Korean decision was to be "purely a temporary one to facilitate the surrender of Japanese troops in that country," rather than a permanent arrangement, proved to be naive and unduly optimistic.[15]

The official denial of U.S. government leaders notwithstanding, the decision to divide Korea into two halves was prompted as much by political considerations as by considerations of administrative convenience. Obviously, the United States would benefit from the partition of Korea, especially in the rivalry with the Soviet Union anticipated at the end of World War II.[16] Four specific considerations in the U.S. political strategy seem to have underlain the decision on Korea. These were:

(1) to prevent the occupation of all of Korea by Soviet forces, which was considered unavoidable in the absence of such an arrangement, (2) to place the United States in as strong a position as possible to implement the promise of Korean independence, (3) to provide for the security of Japan and of United States forces during the period of the military occupation of Japan, and (4) to limit the area of Communist control.[17]

A similar consideration of expected political gain was also evident in the Soviet acquiescence in the U.S. decision to divide Korea. It seemed clear that the Soviet leaders, like their U.S. counterparts, initially overestimated the war-making potential of the Japanese troops in Manchuria. The real desire of the Soviet leaders probably was to participate in the occupation of the Japanese isles with the U.S. rather than to share the occupation of Korea. Why the Soviet army stopped at the 38th parallel in August 1945, although certainly in a position to march down to Pusan at the time, remains a mystery. It is possible that the Soviet Union, like the U.S., was unprepared to take over the entire Korean Peninsula in the face of the sudden collapse of the Japanese Empire on August 15, 1945. Occupation of Korea north of the 38th parallel proved to be less of a challenge.[18]

In their decision to divide Korea into two parts, the Allied powers were insensitive to the possibility that the Korean people might resist— as they actually did—the decision to partition their country along the 38th parallel. They also failed to involve key Korean groups abroad, such as the provisional government in exile in Chungking, China, in an effort to gain their cooperation in implementing the occupation policy.[19] This mistake later proved costly, as it led to less than enthusiastic cooperation with occupation authorities by certain nationalist groups in both parts of divided Korea.

The decision to partition Korea, although intended initially as a temporary measure of military expediency for receiving the surrender of Japanese forces in Korea, soon became permanent and irreversible. As part of the agreement reached at the Allied Foreign Ministers' Conference on the trusteeship of Korea, held in Moscow in December 1945, a joint U.S.-Soviet commission on Korea was called into session in 1946 to assist in the establishment of a unified Korean government. Unfortunately its efforts proved to be futile because of the ensuing Cold

War, and the attempt was abandoned by the United States in the middle of 1947.[20]

National Liberation and Civil War (1945-1953)

The 1945-1953 period commenced with liberation from Japan, but ended with the national tragedy of an internecine war between the two halves of the divided nation. The Koreans quickly realized how difficult it was to found a new and independent state with the nation split ideologically and the land under foreign military occupation. The fact that Korea was liberated by outside powers naturally raised a host of questions among some observers. Some wondered how capable the Koreans were of achieving political independence by their own efforts and accomplishing the difficult task of state building in the harsh political environment of the postwar era.

Korea Under Foreign Occupation

In 1945 the Koreans were generally unprepared to face the new situation of projected independence and state building. The colonial policy of imperial Japan prior to 1945 had been repressive and self-serving; so the Koreans had not been directly involved in the process of self-governing.[21] Unlike some former colonies of Western nations, Korea generally lacked sufficiently trained officials or administrative personnel to take over the mantle of government power from the governor-general of Japan in Korea without causing some disruption and discontinuity. In spite of this adverse situation many Korean individuals and groups took upon themselves the challenging task of self-governing, maintaining law and order by their own efforts in the jubilant and exciting environment of national liberation.

Some Korean groups—notably that of Yo Un-hyong and his followers—made a serious attempt to prepare and lead the people toward political independence. They established an organization called *konguk chumbiwiwonhoe or konjon* (preparatory commission for the construction of the state) and also proclaimed the establishment of *Choson inmin konghwaguk* (Korean People's Republic) on September 7, 1945, two days before the arrival of the U.S. occupation forces in Inchon.[22] Soon after Korea's liberation, large-scale immigration took place as many Koreans returned home from Japan, China, and other overseas locations where they had been either a part of Japan's war efforts or engaged in anti-Japanese activities.[23] Also, a largely spontaneous movement for self-government was underway throughout the country. This organizational network for self-government in postliberation Korea as a whole, under the name of the People's Committee, was largely inspired by some nationalist and communist leaders, and the network soon started to engage the people and spread throughout the countryside.[24]

In this freer atmosphere the Korean people shared a common environment in founding political systems in North and South Korea, and shared the tasks of state building under military occupation by foreign troops. People in the respective Koreas were radically different, however, in the ideological coloration of their respective political systems. The political forces contending for power in liberated Korea were generally divided into nationalists and communists, although many groups had overlapping membership. This configuration largely reflected the situation that had prevailed in the years of the Korean independence movement under Japanese rule prior to 1945.[25] Eventually the political system of South Korea was created by the conservative wing of nationalist leaders; that of North Korea was the work of the communist and some nationalist leaders. Other nationalists were eliminated in both North and South Korea in the process of state building. Many were either purged, as in the case of nationalist leader Cho Man-sik of North Korea, or bypassed and excluded from political participation, as with nationalist leaders Kim Ku and Kim Kiu-sik of South Korea.

The political system of South Korea was forged out of a bitter rivalry between the rival camps of the right and the left among the nationalist forces. Constant shifts in political alignment occurred among the various groups in South Korea and efforts to bring about right-left collaboration were of no avail. In the long run, the conservative wing of the rightist group, consisting of some nationalist leaders returning from exile abroad and those Koreans who had benefited from Japan's colonial rule, provided the leadership role in founding an independent political system in South Korea. This rightist conservative group, which successfully won the support of the U.S. occupation forces in Korea, was an alliance between the landed gentry of the Korean Democratic Party (KDP) and Syngman Rhee and his followers, who played a decisive role. Other members of the rightist group, such as Kim Ku and his followers in the Korean Independence Party (KIP), were either left out or did not participate because they felt that founding a separate government in the south would make Korea's divided nationhood permanent.[26]

The political system of North Korea, on the other hand, was firmly grounded upon the communist ideology of Marxism-Leninism. North Korea took a policy position of building "a united front" of representatives from divergent political and social groups such as the indigenous domestic forces and those returning from the Soviet Union and China who had fought against the Japanese forces. This policy line of "forging a unity out of diversity," was a success initially, but as time progressed, the "new" communist group led by Kim Il Sung proved to be superior in tactical maneuvers, obtaining the confidence of the Soviet occupation authority. By mobilizing mass support Kim's "new" or "partisan" faction prevailed at long last over other rival groups in the north, including the nationalist and the "old" communist groups.[27]

The divergent philosophy of military governments represented by the U.S. and Soviet authorities proved to be important in stamping the character of the political regimes and specifying the nature and extent of Korean participation in the process of governing in subsequent years. Compared with the U.S. military government in the south, the Soviet authority seems to have allowed more initiative to be taken by the indigenous Korean population. The Soviet authority, for instance, allowed the formation of the North Korean Provisional People's Committee in February 1946, which became the highest administrative organ in North Korea. Kim Il Sung was made committee chairman and Kim Tu-bong vice-chairman. This North Korean Provisional People's Committee was an outgrowth of the People's Committee organized throughout the countryside of North Korea soon after the liberation of Korea in August 1945. Early in 1947, the Supreme People's Assembly (SPA) was inaugurated as the highest legislative body; it created in turn an executive branch called the Central People's Committee, consisting of various ministries and bureaus.[28]

The task of state building in the north was well under way with the active support of the Soviet authorities and participation by all the leftist groups in North Korea. Many returnees from the Soviet Union were employed and encouraged to provide the necessary leadership in administering the People's Committee works. Although nationalist groups such as Christian leader Cho Man-sik's were initially involved in taking responsibility over from the Japanese for maintaining law and order by organizing the People's Committee, rightist leaders were soon replaced in North Korea by returnees from the Soviet Union and China, with the active encouragement of the Soviet occupation authority.

Thirty-three-year-old Kim Il Sung, whose real name was Kim Song-ju but who adopted the name of a Korean legendary hero while fighting against the Japanese in Manchuria, was one of those returnees from the Soviet Union. Recruited as a member of Soviet intelligence during the World War II years, Kim Il Sung returned to Korea with the Soviet Red Army wearing the insignia of captain.[29] Although Kim Il Sung had participated in the anti-Japanese guerrilla fighting in Manchuria near the Korean border in the 1930s, in coordination with the Chinese Northeast People's Revolutionary Army, he spent the World War II years (1941–1945) at a Soviet camp near the city of Barabash, not far from Khabarovsk, along the Ussuri River. He served as a battalion commander in the Eighty-Eighth Special Brigade of the Soviet Red Army, which specialized in the training of paratroopers and intelligence agents to penetrate the rear of the Japanese troops in the Far East. Kim's comrades and followers who later became active members of his ruling circle in North Korea included Kang Kon (battalion commander), Ch'oe Yong-gwon (the brigade's political officer), Kim Ch'ek (vice battalion commander), Kim Il (company commander), and Pak Song-chol (platoon leader).[30]

The returnees to North Korea from China, called the Yenan Koreans, actively collaborated with the Soviet Koreans at the beginning.[31] The New People's Party, founded in Pyongyang in March 1946 and led by

Yenan Korean Kim Tu-bong, merged with the North Korean bureau of the Korean Communist Party, founded in Pyongyang in October 1945, to establish a new North Korean Workers' Party in August 1946. The latter merged in turn with the South Korean Workers' Party in June 1949 to constitute what is known today as the Korean Workers' Party, the ruling communist party in the north. Since 1946 Kim Il Sung has served as general secretary of this party.[32]

The situation in South Korea was strikingly different. A plan for state building was slow to emerge, and the U.S. occupation authority seemed to lack a clearcut policy for governing South Korea until early in 1946.[33]

Although a recent study documents that there was more preemptive U.S. policy involved than benign neglect in making South Korea an anticommunist bastion, such policy directives were not clearly conveyed to the local commander of U.S. occupation forces landing in Inchon in September 1945.[34] When the directive finally arrived from Washington, U.S. policy was to govern South Korea not as a liberated area but as an occupied area, although Korea had not been a party of belligerency during the war. The United States further relied on direct rather than indirect rule, denying sufficiently active participation by the Koreans in the political process of self-governance. What particularly disturbed some nationalist leaders in the south was the practice of keeping the Japanese police infrastructure intact as a means of maintaining domestic peace and order in the initial phase of the U.S. occupation of South Korea. The U.S. forces also reestablished Korean personnel who had taken part in the Japanese administration of Korea prior to 1945.

As the United States Army Military Government in Korea (USAMGIK) found it increasingly diffficult to administer Korea directly, it instituted a Korean legislature to act as an advisory body to the military government. It was the rightist conservative group, however, that succeeded in winning the support of USAMGIK. This group gradually moved to take control of the government bureaucracy and the security forces. Taking advantage of the U.S. occupation policy of reviving and retaining the Japanese colonial bureaucracy in Korea, the rightist group obtained the support of the former Korean civil servants in the Japanese administration, and moved to place their own men as deputies to the occupation forces in charge of government administration. The national police forces were taken over through the appointment of U.S.-educated Cho Pyong-ok (later to become presidential candidate and head of the opposition KDP during the First Republic) as chief of the Korean National Police and Chang Taek-sang, a British-educated aristocrat, as chief of Seoul's metropolitan police. Yun Po-son, another British-educated aristocrat, was made Korean director of USAMGIK's Department of Agriculture and Forestry.[35] Yun Po-son became president of the Second Republic, and after his ouster by military coup in 1961, he unsuccessfully challenged the incumbent in the popular presidential elections of 1963 and 1967.

The Constabulary Forces were also established at this time. In October 1945 the commander of the U.S. army forces in Korea, Lieutenant

General John R. Hodge, decided to establish Korea's military forces as a "backup resource" and as "an auxiliary" for the Korean National Police.³⁶ A military English-language school (*kunsa yongo hakkyo*) was established on December 5, 1945, to train officers destined for the Constabulary Forces. The 60 officers trained at the time, known later as the members of the First Class of the Korean Military Academy, consisted of three groups: 20 from the Japanese army, 20 from the Japanese Kwantung army, and 20 from the Korean Provisional Government's Kuomintang-aligned *Kwangbok kun* (Restoration Army).³⁷ Although not all former military men necessarily took part in this retraining program, many who went through the program later emerged to play key roles in the political development of South Korea. Yi Pom-sok, who was the first prime minister under President Syngman Rhee's administration in 1948, for instance, was a Kwangbok leader and one-time officer in the Kuomintang army, although he refused to participate in the constabulary.³⁸ Others who went through subsequent training programs at the academy include: Chang To-yong (chief of staff during the 1961 military coup and thus its nominal leader), Chong Il-gwon (premier, Third Republic), Park Chung Hee (president, Third Republic), and Kim Jae-kyu (President Park's assassin in 1979).

The U.S. side lost valuable lead time to the Soviet side in its competition for state building in liberated Korea. The USAMGIK instituted the South Korean Interim Legislative Assembly in December 1946. Of the total membership of 85, U.S. General Hodge appointed 44; the remaining 41 were elected members representing various South Korean political groups. In 1946, the U.S.-Soviet Joint Commission on Korea was established to work out arrangements for establishing a unified and independent government for all of Korea. The U.S. hope for the planned establishment of an independent government for all of Korea unfortunately proved to be illusory.³⁹ As the joint commission failed to make any headway, the United States began to entertain alternative plans for the disposition of the Korean question. These included presenting the Korean issue to the United Nations for deliberation and calling for elections to establish a separate government in the south. The U.S. plan was opposed strongly by the Soviet Union and was also criticized by many groups and individuals in the south, including both leftists and some nationalist leaders, as a measure to perpetuate the territorial division of Korea.⁴⁰

Establishing Separate Regimes

The task of state building was completed in both halves of Korea in the course of 1948. In the south, a UN-supervised election took place, a constitution was adopted on July 17, 1948, and a separate government for the Republic of Korea (ROK) was founded on August 15, 1948. In the north, a constitution was adopted early in 1948, and the Democratic People's Republic of Korea (DPRK) was officially proclaimed on September 9, 1948. The rival regimes forwarded conflicting claims for political legitimacy. South Korea, for instance, claimed that the establishment of the ROK in 1948 was "legitimate" because it was based on a UN-supervised election held throughout South Korea and because it was subsequently recognized by the United Nations General Assembly as "the only and lawful government of Korea." The constituent assembly of representatives, elected on May 10, 1948, adopted a constitutional provision stipulating that 100 seats be reserved for North Korea for their possible subsequent participation.

North Korea, on the other hand, claimed that its government was "legitimate" as it represented the interests of all Korea, and that the establishment of the DPRK in September 1948 was based on an election in North Korea and also an underground plebiscite held in the south. North Korea criticized the U.S. decision to refer the Korean issue to the United Nations as ultimately responsible for perpetuating Korean partition. Neither side of divided Korea, therefore, was prepared to recognize the reality of separate political regimes in Korea or to accept the counterpart government as "legitimate."

Apart from the question of legitimacy, however, the two Korean governments proceeded to inaugurate various innovative policy plans and to implement programs that had a far-reaching impact upon society. The subsequent political developments in Korea in the years 1948–1950 represent the phase of consolidation of authority by the ruling groups in the two Koreas. Once the task of state building was completed, the political leadership in North and South Korea busily consolidated their achievements through internal reforms and by conducting the day-to-day business of civil government.

In pursuing the task of society building both North and South Korea were influenced by their separation and by the competitive spirit of excellence that prevailed between them from the outset. The communists in the north were more self-assured and clear about policy direction and were determined to carry out without delay their program of social reform and economic development. Korea was at that time a predominantly agrarian society; so the first order of business in the north was, not surprisingly, land reform. On March 5, 1946, North Korea's Provisional People's Committee proclaimed the Land Reform Act. The implementation of this act, completed in less than one month, affected 54 percent of the total cultivated land in North Korea.[41] Other progressive measures of legislation that soon followed were the Labor Law and the Nationalization Law on public enterprises and properties.

By eliminating landlords as a class and redistributing land to landless peasants and small landowners, the communist regime in the north was able to broaden its base of popular support among the peasants and to embark on new programs of society building. Agricultural surplus generated by the land reform went to support the governmental economic program, with peasants paying the government through agricultural tax in kind what they had previously paid their landlords in rent. The nationalization of industry proclaimed on October 10, 1946, by the Provisional People's Committee was the second of the reform measures. It affected some 1,034 key industrial enterprises comprising 90 percent of all industry in North Korea.[42] These and other reform measures were followed by a series of economic plans—one-year plans for 1947 and 1948 and a two-year plan for 1949–1950—that laid the basis for developing a heavily industrialized economy. Due to the Korean War, no new plan was instituted in 1950.

South Korea was not as efficient or organized as its counterpart in the north in carrying out the tasks of society building. However, a series of land reform programs was also adopted in the south in two separate stages. First, the U.S. military government, soon after its arrival in early September 1945, had taken over all lands formerly owned by Japanese landlords in the Oriental Development Company—now called the New Korea Company.[43] It had also placed a ceiling of one-third of a year's crop on rents to be paid by the tenant farmers, as a preliminary step toward anticipated land reform by the provisional Korean government. As attempts at land reform in 1947 and 1948 failed to pass the Interim Legislative Assembly, however, USAMGIK ultimately proclaimed Ordinance No. 173, which dissolved the New Korea Company and transferred the lands previously owned by the Japanese to the newly established National Land Administration. It also legislated the distribution of land to former tenants under a limit of 2 hectares (4.9 acres) each, with the price of 150 percent of one year's production to be paid over a fifteen-year period. This disposed of some 90 percent of the land (or 606,518 acres) previously owned by the New Korea Company.[44] Although the land affected by this ordinance was less than 20 percent of all the land under cultivation at the time, it significantly improved the distribution of land ownership in South Korea on the eve of its independence in 1948.

The second step of land reform was the Farmland Reform Law enacted by the National Assembly in June 1948. Although this law was not implemented until after the North Korean occupation of South Korea in the summer of 1950, it was a far-reaching and drastic piece of social legislation. The new law authorized the government to redistribute the remaining Japanese holdings as well as all absentee-owned cultivated lands. It outlawed private land holdings in excess of 3 hectares (7.4 acres). About one-third of all farmland in South Korea was redistributed as a result of these measures, and although this was short of the target of about 40 percent of the arable land initially earmarked for redistribution, the land reforms of 1948 and 1949 caused a wholesale transformation of the rural structure in South Korea. They abolished the tenant farmer system and established a small farmer owner-cultivator system in its place.[45] By legislative acts both regimes were thus able to carry out a major structural reform of Korean land ownership that during other periods of Korean history and under more ordinary circumstances would have required more force to bring about.

The withdrawal of foreign occupation forces from Korean soil presented a new situation and new opportunities for both Korean states. However, just as the fate of the Korean people was decided by external forces in 1945—by U.S.-Soviet partition and separate military occupation of Korea, so were subsequent political developments in Korea influenced by outside decisions. The Soviet troops in the north were first to complete their withdrawal, officially announced on December 16, 1948. U.S. troops withdrew from the south as of June 29, 1949. Decisions on troop withdrawal from Korea were made in Moscow and Washington.

Although the opportunity for initiating inter-Korea dialogue and negotiation for reunification was technically open following the troop withdrawal, the two Korean regimes were so self-righteous and secure as to deny the other's legitimacy. The separate regimes, once established, were impossible to dislodge or disband because of the vested interests that had become entrenched. Thus, each Korean regime pursued the hard-line policy of mutual vituperation and provocation that led to an eventual military showdown between North and South Korea in 1950.

The Korean War (1950–1953)

The clash of the conflicting legitimacy claims by North Korea's DPRK and South Korea's ROK resulted in numerous skirmishes and armed clashes along the 38th parallel. It was one such conflict that led to the onset of the Korean War on June 25, 1950.

How to interpret the chapter of the Korean War in modern history of Korea remains tentative and controversial.[46] Historians disagree as to who was responsible for the tragedy of internecine war between North and South Korea. The question of who fired the first shot, however, is important but incomplete unless the character of the war is accounted for.[47] The prevailing consensus seems to favor the right of the Korean people to reunify their divided land unchallenged by outside powers. The 1950 Korean War, above all else, was a "civil and local war" between the two halves of a divided nation, which as a result of intervention by outside powers became a full-blown international war. This tragedy brought about great sorrows and destruction to the Korean people, yet in retrospect, the war taught an invaluable lesson to the Korean people—that peace and "unification by force" were incompatible and that reunification of the country had to be pursued by peaceful means.

North Korea's official view of the Korean War is that it was "a just fatherland's liberation war" and "a civil war" waged "to liberate the southern half of the republic." After the war, Kim Il Sung claimed that North Korea scored a "brilliant victory," although he had mentioned in his address marking the anniversary of Korea's liberation from Japan on August 15, 1952, that North Korea was seeking an armistice that reflected the principle of "neither the victory nor the defeat in the war."

North Korea continued to blame "U.S. imperialism" for causing "a war of aggression in Korea" in 1950. "Who Prepared and Provoked a War of Aggression in Korea," a statement issued by a North Korean spokesman on June 22, 1981, is typical of North Korea's official position on the origin of the war. It charges that, "having occupied South Korea since the end of the Second World War, the United States had hampered the peaceful reunification of Korea and had long prepared armed invasion against the northern part of the republic with a view to turning the whole of Korea not only into a colony but also into a springboard to attack the Asian continent and the socialist countries."[48]

On the question of who initiated the attack, the North Korean position was that "the South Korean puppet regime started a surprise invasion of the north along the whole front of the 38th parallel line at dawn on the 25th" and that its "People's Republic Army succeeded in repulsing the enemy force."[49] The claim that South Korea was responsible is not an accepted view outside the Communist bloc countries, although it was given credence by U.S. journalist I. F. Stone, who questioned the official explanation of the war's start. In *The Hidden History of the Korean War*, Stone argues that Syngman Rhee and Chiang Kai-shek, together with John Foster Dulles and General Douglas MacArthur, had attempted to reverse U.S. Far Eastern policy by forcing a strong U.S. commitment in Asia. According to Stone, Rhee therefore provoked North Korea's attack, which in turn led to a full-scale attack on the Republic of Korea and U.S. intervention. The North Korean statement quoted above cites I. F. Stone as blaming South Korea for the initiation of the war.

This revisionist interpretation of South Korean provocation, however, seems less convincing in light of the contrary evidence. Stone's hypothesis was forcefully denied by observer Frank Baldwin:

> The answer [to the question of a possible South Korean provocation] at present is no. The most interested party, North Korea, has yet to substantiate its allegations with credible evidence. The very term "provocation" is rendered all but meaningless by the nature of the North Korean allegation and the known sequence of events. North Korea did not charge a South Korean intrusion or sustained attack in the spring of 1950, in May or early June. Such an attack might have led to the mobilization of North Korean forces and their deployment along the 38th parallel for an extended counteroffensive if another incident occurred. However, according to the North Korean charge, the South Korean attack occurred on the morning of June 25. Yet overwhelming and indisputable evidence shows that North Korean forces advanced across the 38th parallel at several widely separate points, including a commando landing on the east coast, early in the morning of June 25. Eyewitness reports place the North Korean attack of Kaesong, for example, at 4:00–5:00 A.M., June 25. The coordinated movement of troops, preceded by artillery bombardment, could have been accomplished only after lengthy, careful planning. That such a movement of forces could have been an instantaneous response to a South Korean attack is patently implausible.[50]

Captured documents of the North Korean unit obtained by the U.S. government also provide a detailed account of the shift of North Korean People's Army units to the 38th parallel in mid-June and their preparation for an offensive campaign. The captured documents include a "pre-invasion reconnaissance order from the G-2, General Staff, North Korean Army, to the Chief of Staff, 4th Infantry Division, outlining reconnaissance activities to be implemented both prior to and after the initiation of hostilities."[51]

The question of which side is responsible for the Korean War in 1950 is thus not easy to establish conclusively.[52] It must be reassessed from the perspective of the Korean people trying to accomplish the task of nation building that was frustrated by the tragic division of the land and by the adverse political developments both within and without the Korean Peninsula. Most importantly, the significance of the Korean conflict is seen in a different light depending upon whether one considers the Korean War a "civil war" or an "interstate war" between the two independent political entities in the Korean Peninsula.

The fact remains that in 1950 the political leadership of each half of Korea harbored the design, secretly or openly, of reunifying the divided land, by military force if necessary. President Syngman Rhee of South Korea openly advocated a "march to the north campaign," while Premier Kim Il Sung of North Korea appealed for a "fatherland liberation war" to reunify the country. Intervention by the United Nations, led by the United States and the fifteen other countries that sent a token number of troops on behalf of South Korea, and by the Chinese "volunteer army" on behalf of North Korea, changed the character of the Korean conflict from a civil war to an international war.[53]

The three years of the Korean War not only frustrated the nation-building task of achieving national reunification, but also inflicted deep wounds on the consciousness and memory of the Korean people. The Koreans experienced psychological defeat with the sudden demise of the nationalist cause, which had earlier been expressed in an ardent desire for political independence and sovereignty. By the time the Korean conflict ended in 1953, the human suffering and cost of the three-year Korean War was extensive, as can be seen from the casualty list shown in Table 2.1.

The eight-year span between 1945 and 1953 was a time of both joy and sorrow for the Korean people. The national consciousness of the Koreans, dormant and suppressed during colonial rule, was suddenly awakened by the thrilling experience of national liberation following Japan's defeat in World War II. The national aspiration for political independence and unity was then crushed by the Korean War. Both sides of divided Korea completed the task of state building, between 1945 and 1950, but progress on the tasks of society building and nation building was interrupted by the onset of the Korean War. Efforts toward building a unified nation by force proved counterproductive. The 1945–

TABLE 2.1
Casualties of the Korean War, 1950-1953

	Civilian		Military Personnel		Others	
	North Korea	South Korea	North Korea	South Korea	Chinese Volunteers in North Korea	UN Mil Personnel in South Korea
Killed	406,000	373,599	294,151	227,748	184,128	36,813
Wounded	1,594,000	229,652	225,849	717,083	715,872	114,816
Missing	680,000 a	387,744 b	91,206 c	43,572	21,836	6,198 c
Total	2,680,000	990,995	611,206	988,403	921,836	157,827

Sources: Toitsu Chosen Shimbun, June 27, 1970, as cited in Takehiko Hayashi, Kita Chosen to Minami Chosen (Tokyo: Saimaru Press, 1971), p. 62 and Yoshikazu Sakamoto, Korea as a World Order Issue, World Order Project Occasional Paper No. 3 (New York: Institute for World Order, 1978), p. 6.

a Refugees to South Korea included
b 84,532 of this figure represent those taken to North Korea
c Prisoners of war as reported

1953 period, as a whole, showed that the Korean people were more the victims of political decisions made by outside powers than they were autonomous actors making decisions and shaping their own destiny.

Estrangement and Consolidation (1954–1970)

Between 1954 and 1970 North and South Korea followed separate paths of political development, but they were miles apart insofar as their experiments in institution building and political development were concerned. Following the traumatic experience of the Korean War the two populations remained isolated from each other. Only sporadic efforts at informal contact were made through the infiltration of subversive agents across the Demilitarized Zone (DmZ), which replaced the 38th parallel as the new demarcation line between the north and the south.

The two political systems were basically incommunicado: no official contact between the two capitals was maintained either directly or indirectly, through a third country or international agencies. Each Korean regime acted internationally, in fact, as if the other side did not matter or exist, refusing even to call the opponent by its proper name. The two Korean states were in this sense worse than strangers toward one another.

In the post–Korean War era the separate states of Korea emphasized the consolidation of their respective political systems from within. In the initial achievement of socioeconomic development, the North Korean regime, generally speaking, was ahead of South Korea, but the latter regime was quick to catch up with the north. The politics of North Korea will be examined first.

North Korea

After the Korean War, North Korea pressed on with the tasks of political development. In pursuing the task of state building, Kim Il Sung pushed through a series of bloody political purges of his rivals. The task of society building was approached through a series of economic plans which achieved greater success in the years immediately after the Korean War than in the 1960s. The goal of national reunification was temporarily put aside as efforts were directed toward building socialism in one half of the divided country, what they called "the northern half of the republic."

By the end of the Korean War, five major political factions had emerged to vie for political hegemony in the KWP. As leader of one of these factional groups, Kim Il Sung moved to eliminate his rivals—real and potential—one by one through the skillful use of a united front campaign strategy. The five groups in the KWP hierarchy were (1) the domestic faction, (2) the Soviet faction, (3) the Chinese or Yenan faction, (4) the South Korean Workers' Party faction, and (5) the Kapsan faction.[54] Kim Il Sung was leader of the Kapsan faction, consisting of former members of the anti-Japanese guerrilla units in Manchuria (which Kim had led prior to 1945) and their followers.

The first group to be purged—predating the Korean War period—was North Korea's domestic communist faction. The assassination of a promising North Korean communist leader, Hyon Jun-hyok, on September 28, 1945, as he was returning from a meeting with the Soviet military officials in Pyongyang, was the opening salvo against the domestic faction. The murder of Hyon, who had been a leftist student leader in the 1930s and who was released from jail in 1945 following Japan's defeat in World War II, was generally attributed to Kim's followers, although the possibility that a rightist group was responsible cannot be ruled out. The purge of the respected nationalist leader Cho Man-sik by the Soviet authority, with the backing of leftists in the north, was another step toward eliminating real and potential rivals among the indigenous leadership in North Korea.

Kim Il Sung next moved to eliminate the South Korean communist faction that had joined with the North Korean communists during the war years. Actually, the mainstay of the communist movement in Korea before 1945 had been the leaders of the South Korean Workers' Party (SKWP), which in June 1949 merged with its northern counterpart to form the Korean Workers' Party. On August 7, 1953, the trial of the seven leaders of the South Korean Workers' Party was announced. They were charged, convicted, and sentenced to death for the alleged crime of acting, incredibly, as "spies of U.S. imperialism" during the Korean War years. Included in the list of executed leaders were Pak Hon-yong (vice-premier and foreign minister under Kim Il Sung during the Korean War years), Yi Seung-yop (KWP secretary and minister of state inspection), Yi Kang-kuk (former foreign affairs director of the South Korea's People's Committee) and Yim Hwa (poet and vice-chairman of the Korean Soviet Cultural Association). Pak Hon-yong's execution was not officially announced until over two years later, on December 17, 1955.[55] He had been underground leader of the Korean Communist Party before 1945 and head of the South Korean Workers' Party during the pre–Korean War era.

Underlying the purge of Pak Hon-yong and the SKWP faction was the policy dispute in North Korea over responsibility for the failure to win the Korean War. Kim Il Sung and his followers blamed Pak Hon-yong for misinformation regarding the situation in South Korea on the eve of the war in 1950, misinformation which led Kim Il Sung to believe that the South Korean masses would rise up against the South Korean regime. Pak Hon-yong and others may have blamed Kim Il Sung for his miscalculations, and charged Kim with responsibility for losing the war.

In 1955, Kim Il Sung spoke, during a speech to party propagandists and agitators, of the need not only for "eliminating bureaucracy, dogmatism, and formalism," but also for "further intensifying the class education of the party members," and for "establishing Juche in ideological work."[56] With this statement Kim Il Sung launched his attack on the leaders of the Soviet faction and the Yenan faction. Kim Il Sung complained in the same speech that "many comrades swallow Marxism-Leninism whole, instead of digesting and assimilating . . . [thereby becoming] unable to display revolutionary initiative."[57] Directing his fire at his political rivals, returnees from exile in the Soviet Union and the PRC, Kim Il Sung charged his close associates with being "anti-party sectarian." As Kim put it, "during the war, Ho Gai-i, Kim Jae-uk and Pak Il-u once quarreled stupidly among themselves over the problem of how to carry on political work in the army. Those from the Soviet Union insisted upon the Soviet method and those from China stuck to the Chinese method, so they quarreled, some advocating the Soviet fashion and others the Chinese way. That was sheer nonsense," Kim Il Sung proclaimed, because "it does not matter whether you use the right hand or the left, whether you use a spoon or chopsticks at the table.

. . . No matter how you eat, it is all the same insofar as food is put into your mouth, isn't it?"[58] Laying the groundwork for his Juche idea, which he later used as a weapon against rival factions, Kim continued, "It is important in our work to grasp revolutionary truth, Marxist-Leninist truth, and apply it correctly to the actual conditions of our country. There can be no set principle that we must follow the Soviet pattern. Some advocate the Soviet way and others the Chinese, but is it not high time to work out our own?"[59]

Soon after this speech was delivered, the Soviet faction leaders were purged. This was followed in the summer of 1956 by the purge of the Chinese or Yenan faction leaders, including Kim Tu-bong (chairman of the Supreme Peoples' Assembly) and Choe Ch'ang-ik, whose assistance and support Kim Il Sung had used to carry out earlier purges.[60]

In 1956, the political system of North Korea had faced a serious crisis of intraelite conflict. The source of strain within North Korea was the position of Kim Il Sung. In the Soviet Union, Nikita Khrushchev's secret report to the Twentieth Party Congress of the Soviet Union initiated the de-Stalinization campaign in 1956. In North Korea, several members of the KWP Central Committee criticized Party Secretary Kim Il Sung for encouraging an excessive personality cult. Critics also charged that as premier Kim had failed to bring about the simultaneous development of heavy and light industries.

The severity of intraelite conflict within North Korea led to an attempt at mediation by foreign parties. Soviet and Chinese party leaders Nikolai Mikoyan and Peng Dehuai reportedly made special trips to Pyongyang to mediate the disputes and to mend the differences between Kim Il Sung and the anti-Kim factions.[61] This foreign intervention in the internal affairs of North Korea provided Kim Il Sung with a golden opportunity. He exploited the occasion by waging his "anti-sectarian struggle," which justified the elimination of potential rivals to his supremacy.

Reconstruction of the war-torn society of North Korea was the first priority of society building in 1953. A brief preparatory stage promoting postwar rehabilitation and development lasted for nine months after the conclusion of the armistice agreement in July 1953. This was followed by the inauguration of the Three-Year Plan of Economic Development for 1954 through 1956.

The implementation of the economic development plan in North Korea was accompanied by incessant policy debate and struggle for party hegemony among the top elites.[62] The issue at stake was which sector of the economy would receive primary support: heavy industry or light industry and agricultural development. The North Korean elite decided in 1953 to follow the Soviet model, developing heavy industry first and emulating the pattern of Stalinist "forced" draft strategy. The main task of the three-year plan, according to the official version, was to ensure "priority development of heavy industry, without overlooking the simultaneous development of light industry and agriculture."[63] The three-year plan, fulfilled in two years and four months, was credited by North Korea with having laid a foundation for the construction of socialism and communism in the northern half of the Korean Peninsula.

There was little disagreement over how the economic development projects would be financed. In a closing speech before the plenum of the KWP on August 8, 1953, Premier Kim Il Sung announced that the Soviet Union would donate 1 billion rubles and that other gifts would come from the People's Republic of China and other communist countries that were "demonstrating a true fraternal spirit."[64] It was obvious, however, that the bulk of economic development was to be financed through the sacrifice of the North Korean population, especially the farmers and the workers.

Between 1954 and 1958 North Korea also carried out an ambitious program of agricultural collectivization. As a result, private farms were completely abolished in the north by 1958. Farmers were compelled to join one of three types of cooperatives, progressively moving from type 1 to type 2 and then to type 3 by 1958. The first type was a simple "mutual aid cooperative" in which the land and labor were pooled and the draft animals were shared to make farming easier. The second type, considered to be "intermediate" and "transitional," was a semisocialist farm. The land was privately owned but collectively used, and the distribution of agricultural output was based on the amount of labor and land contributed. The third type was completely socialistic: the land, draft animals, and farm implements were collectively owned by the cooperatives, and the distribution of farm output was based solely on labor contribution. Type 1 agricultural cooperatives—the only kind in existence in 1953—were abolished by 1954; type 2 farms were completely replaced by type 3 cooperatives by August 1958.[65]

The state invested a large sum of money to develop these experimental agricultural cooperatives, which (as claimed by North Korea) "supplied chemical fertilizers, agricultural machinery and building material, loaned food stuffs and seed; advanced funds; cut the tax rate in kind and offered labor assistance."[66] By applying a similar principle of socialist cooperatives to urban handicrafts and capitalist commerce and industry, North Korea claimed that by August 1958 it had achieved "the socialist transformation of the relations of production, in both the rural and urban communities." The significance of this achievement, in the words of Kim Il Sung, was to make "it possible to liquidate the sources of exploitation and poverty which had existed for thousands of years and to improve the material and cultural standards of the people markedly."[67]

Throughout the 1960s, North Korea continued to prepare the foundation for constructing a socialist and communist state and society. As a result of the successful fulfillment of the first five-year plan (1957–1961) one year ahead of the target date, it was said that "North Korea advanced from the period of rehabilitation into a period of technical innovation," laying the foundation "for socialist industrialization and building a base for the development of an independent national economy." The Seven-Year Plan of Economic Development launched in 1961 (1961–1967) was "to equip all branches of the people's economy with up-to-date technology by realizing socialist industrialization, for radically improving the people's living conditions and culture and for achieving socialism."[68] However, the overambitious plan failed to achieve its stated goal, largely because of the lagging capability of the North Korean economy and the diversion of limited resources to purposes other than economic development. At the end of 1966 it was announced that the implementation of the seven-year plan was to be modified to accommodate the need for a defense buildup. Eventually extended for a total of three extra years, the plan was completed in 1970.

The Fourth KWP Congress, held in September 1961, was the occasion for Kim Il Sung to celebrate his victory over his political rivals and to consolidate his position of power in the party. In his report to the party Kim Il Sung claimed that the "historical task was accomplished by bringing about complete unity of the Korean communist movement through liquidating the long-standing factionalism and localism." The revised KWP Bylaws adopted at the time had the following new provision in the Preamble: "The KWP is the direct successor of the glorious revolutionary tradition established by the Korean communists in the anti-Japanese armed struggle."[69] This statement suggested that by 1961, the Kapsan faction led by Kim Il Sung had finally established itself as the dominant political force in North Korea's communist politics.

In spite of these claims, however, it was not until 1967 that Kim Il Sung was really able to lay the basis for the "monolithic" unitary system of the 1970s. Even within the ranks of his own Kapsan faction, for instance, Kim Il Sung had to purge two prominent members, Pak Gum-ch'ol and Yi Hyo-sun, who ranked fourth and fifth respectively. This purge took place in March 1967, over policy disputes regarding North Korea's ineffective policy toward South Korea. By the end of 1967, Kim Il Sung had eliminated all threats to his position and had consolidated his authority in North Korea.

The North Korean economy did not fare well in the 1960s, in contrast with the post–Korean War years of the 1950s. At the KWP representatives conference in October 1966, the first vice-premier, Kim Il, blamed external exigencies for the necessary extension of the seven-year plan. These included, according to Kim Il, insufficient economic assistance from fraternal socialist countries due to the intensified Sino-Soviet confrontation and Soviet "revisionist" policies. The increased threat of war from "U.S. Imperialism," as evidenced by the Cuban missile crisis of October 1962, was also blamed for the necessity to increase defense expenditures and defense preparedness.[70] Nevertheless, the failure of domestic policy must also be pointed out as a contributing factor to the poor performance of North Korea's economy in the 1960s. Shortages of labor, capital, and technical know-how, inefficient management, and the unbalanced sectoral growth that resulted from the isolated command economy were all factors in the failure of North Korea's economy in the late 1960s.

North Korea was not fully prepared to profit from the momentarily chaotic situation that prevailed in South Korea with the collapse of the First Republic in 1960. In spite of rhetoric supporting South Korea's 1960 revolution and its dissident movements, the North Korean government was ill equipped to render material assistance to the antigovernment forces in the south, as it was preoccupied instead with its own sense of threat and insecurity.

Underlying North Korea's failure to provide active support to South Korea was the presence of U.S. military troops in South Korea, which were said to have been equipped with nuclear weapons since around 1957. This acted to deter potential North Korean moves against the south. Since the 1961 military coup in the south was interpreted by the communist leaders as an act engineered and encouraged by "U.S. Imperialism," they perceived the new military regime as a potential threat to North Korea's security. Kim Il Sung decided to double defense expenditures and revise the timetable for the completion of the seven-year plan. As Park Chung Hee's military government gave way to civilian rule in a soldier-turned-bureaucrat fashion, Kim felt increasingly that the security of the north was inversely related to the consolidation of Park's authority in the south. In view of this perceived threat, Kim Il Sung successfully negotiated mutual defense treaties with the Soviet Union on July 6, 1961 and with the People's Republic of China on July 11, 1961.[71]

South Korea

Compared with North Korea, South Korea made slow progress along the path of political development in the post–Korean War years. The government of President Syngman Rhee did not initiate the democratization of the political process, but instead perpetuated Rhee's autocratic rule. No constructive plans for economic development (society building) or reunification (nation building) were formulated, and the tasks of political development in the south were largely ignored until the Rhee government was overthrown in 1960. During the one-year period following the April 1960 Student Revolution the Chang Myon government in South Korea did not have sufficient time to demonstrate its capability for achieving political development, although the democratic orientation of the regime was highly promising. The Chang government of the Second Republic was in fact involved in developing long-range plans for economic development when it was overthrown by the military.[72]

South Korea failed to achieve positive gains in its policy of social reconstruction in the years immediately following the Korean War. The Republic of Korea under President Syngman Rhee's administration depended heavily upon the inflow of foreign aid from the United States and the United Nations, given under the pretext of rehabilitating the war-torn economy of South Korea. The war-afflicted South Korean society was not able to recover fully, however, due to ensuing inflation and mismanagement of the economy. Instead of developing a bold and assertive plan for economic development, the Rhee government relied throughout the 1950s upon a conservative policy of patchwork ad hoc resolutions. It lost precious time and missed opportunities for initiating meaningful economic reforms and inaugurating economic development programs. Due to the close ties between economic and political interests, the Rhee government also suffered from pervasive corruption and rampant favoritism.[73]

The story of South Korea's political development in the post–Korean War years is one of progressive deterioration of the processes of democracy and constitutionalism, leading to the dictatorial assumption of power by President Rhee and his entourage. With the passage of time, the Rhee government became increasingly arbitrary and authoritarian. Constitutional amendments were put through the legislature in 1951 and 1954, first to enable direct popular election of the president and then to remove the ban on Rhee's reelection. The ruling Liberal Party was used to manipulate the allocation of political favors and resources to the party faithful.

The 1954 constitutional amendment removed the two-term restriction on presidential terms of office. This measure enabled President Rhee to stay in power indefinitely by manipulating the electoral process in his favor. Rhee proceeded to restrict the power of the political opposition and the National Assembly. Rhee not only failed to call for the election of the upper house mandated by constitutional provision; he also failed to implement the measures providing for local autonomy.[74] President Rhee's arbitrary rule, which resulted in a fatal blow to the First Republic, was revealed in the presidential election of 1960, which was rigged by government officials faithful to Rhee to return him to office for a fourth term. This flagrant violation of democratic procedure finally led to massive indignation and to mass demonstrations led by university students. The Student Revolution of April 19, 1960, caused the eventual overthrow of the First Republic.[75]

During the year following the Student Revolution—a chaotic and volatile year full of energy and aspiration—South Korea threw off autocratic political rule to become a free and open polity. During the three-month period of interim government under Acting President Ho Chong, the constitution was revised to create the Second Republic. It provided for a responsible cabinet form of government and for the holding of a free and fair election. During the subsequent government of Premier Chang Myon and his Democratic Party, the position of the executive was considerably weakened, the legislature was strengthened, and measures for local autonomy were finally put into effect. The Chang Myon government of the Second Republic was not able to survive the test of the times, however, due to incessant factional strife within the ruling Democratic Party, and due also to the increasing inflationary trends and economic hardships that the government failed to resolve. The students who had tasted political power in the April 1960 revolution also increased the level of their demands and expectations.[76]

The ensuing political chaos and indecision provided the pretext for a small group of army officers, both active and retired, to plan a coup d'etat. Brigadier General Park Chung Hee and his associates, who included retired Lieutenant Colonel Kim Jong-pil, carried out a predawn coup on May 16, 1961, overthrowing the constitutional government and the Second Republic.[77] In the subsequent three-month period the parliament and political parties were suspended and elections were prohibited for at least two years. The military junta under General Park governed South Korea with authoritarian control, suspending civil rights and banning political participation by those "old politicians" whom they considered corrupt. In spite of his earlier pledge to return power to the civilians, Park and his followers had second thoughts, and decided to change their uniforms to civilian clothes to prolong their hold on political power.

Following the 1961 military coup, the establishment of the Supreme Council for National Reconstruction provided a foundation for political development in South Korea in the subsequent years. Although the military regime set back the democratization of South Korea, it concentrated during its year and a half of rule upon the social reconstruction of South Korea. During the Third Republic, inaugurated in 1963, South Korea continued in the task of state building, and initiated the work of society building.

The political institutions of the Third Republic showed signs of vitality and efficiency as the citizenry took part in the electoral process of the country. National elections for the presidency and for the National Assembly were conducted in a reasonably honest manner in the 1960s; the First Five-Year Plan (1962–1966) and the Second Five-Year Plan (1967–1971) of Economic Development were also successfully implemented. No headway in nation building was made, however, during the 1954–1970 years. The policy toward reunification in this period was largely a matter of rhetoric and empty gesture, expressing a pietistic attitude toward the sacred national task.

The instrument of political rule by the civilianized military was the Democratic Republican Party (DRP) founded by Kim Jong-pil in late 1962.[78] Retired General Park Chung Hee ran for president in 1963 as the DRP candidate. In the election, candidate Park narrowly defeated his opponent Yun Po-son, presidential candidate of the Democratic Party. Yun had been president of the Second Republic that Park and his military cohorts overthrew two years earlier. In the subsequent 1963 National Assembly election, Park's DRP succeeded in obtaining the majority of seats in the legislature. The DRP stressed a policy of modernization and also began a drive against corruption. Four years later the incumbent

Park was reelected despite opposition charges of corruption. His party also fared well in the 1967 National Assembly election, increasing its share of seats from 32.4 percent in 1963 to 52.8 percent in 1967.[79]

After its victory in the elections Park's government took a number of bold measures for political reform and economic development in the 1960s. His government initiated the First Five-Year Plan for Economic Development in 1962. It also began negotiations with Japan on a diplomatic normalization treaty, signed in 1965, to end the twenty years of noncommunication between the two close neighbors.[80] The Seoul government immediately received a large monetary payment from Japan as indemnity for the ills and exploitation of Korea during colonial rule by Japan. Park's government used these funds as capital investment for financing its economic development projects. Dwindling U.S. economic aid led Park Chung Hee to allow Japan to reestablish a foothold in South Korea only twenty years after her defeat in World War II and forced withdrawal from the peninsula in 1945. Park's bold initiative toward Japan was met by strong opposition from some nationalist groups, including student activists in the south. The normalization of diplomatic relations with Japan was also vehemently opposed by North Korea on the grounds that it would usher the "Japanese militarists" onto Korean soil.

Park's government also took the bold action of sending ROK troops to South Vietnam in 1966 to assist the U.S. effort there.[81] The move, ostensibly made to repay the debt incurred to the United States during the war, gained hard currency for South Korea in the form of payment for services rendered by the South Korean armed personnel in Vietnam and for the purchase of Korean goods and services there. Park seemed to have won the gamble of the Vietnam adventure, as he successfully quieted down domestic opposition through 1972, when South Korean troops were finally withdrawn from Vietnam after the Nixon administrations' settlement of the Paris peace talks with North Vietnam.

During the 1960s North Korea was anxious to capitalize upon the political dissent in South Korea to create Vietnamese-style revolutionary conditions in the south. Its efforts throughout the 1960s and in the early 1970s, however, did not strike a responsive chord in South Korea. On the contrary, such belligerent actions as the commando attack on the Blue House (Park's presidential residence) in January 1968 and the seizure of the U.S. intelligence ship *Pueblo* off Wonsan Bay a few days later angered and frightened the South Korean public. In fact, the Seoul government was able to turn public opinion in South Korea against the northern communists by presenting a picture of escalated belligerency and enhanced threat from the north across the DmZ.

By the time the international situation shifted following the pronouncement of the Nixon Doctrine in 1969 and the initiation of détente by the Nixon administration, the Seoul government had decided to initiate on its own the bold action of seeking direct contact with North

52   Historical Dimensions

Korea. The Park Chung Hee regime wanted to create a favorable impression of activism and present an aggressive stance on Korean unification, an objective that until then had been pursued only by the North Korean side. As the Kim Il Sung regime had already stated its position of conducting talks on unification with "the democratic forces" in the south—although steadfastly refusing to deal with Park Chung Hee, it was relatively easy for the Seoul government to propose North-South dialogue and negotiations with the Pyongyang authority.[82]

This decision by Park to open a dialogue with Pyongyang seems to have been the result of mixed motivations, including his government's exaggerated sense of self-assurance and confidence that the economic prosperity in South Korea in the late 1960s would impress the population of North Korea and win them over to its side in the long run. It was also triggered by Park's growing insecurity and fear that unless the Seoul government did something positively and quickly the rapidly changing world might sooner or later bypass South Korea, leaving his government increasingly isolated from the world community. In this gamble Park Chung Hee seems to have reaped initial success, although it was not clear whether he could win the ultimate contest with Kim Il Sung of North Korea in the embattled politics of competing legitimacy.

By the time the decade of the 1960s drew to a close it became obvious that both North and South Korea were increasingly to influence and to be influenced by political developments within the other half of Korea. Although North and South Korea were divided territorially by the DmZ, they were linked psychologically in their national will and consciousness, which finally found expression in the initiation of North-South dialogue in 1971.

Concluding Remarks: Divided Nation Politics

The initial act of Korean partition, although externally imposed, became hardened and irreversible as a result of (1) the failure of Korean groups to attain consensus on the unification process and (2) the institutionalization of vested interests in both Koreas. The onset of the Cold War between the United States and the Soviet Union was also internalized by Korean groups within each half and between the two parts of North and South Korea. The internecine war between the two halves, which failed to reunify the land due to external intervention, hardened the national division and led to the emergence of separate and antagonistic political systems. When the 1945–1970 period of Korea's modern history is taken as a whole, it is clear that in both cases political institutions were newly created and constantly modified as time went on, accommodating the changing needs emanating from sources internal and external to Korea. Modernization of the tradition-bound agrarian society of Korea, undertaken in both halves of divided Korea, was by no means an easy task. The North and South Korean leadership devised strategies for planned socioeconomic change by implementing a series of economic development plans and social mobilization.

The changes that resulted from these efforts were often far-reaching and revolutionary in their influences upon society at large and upon the lives of the Korean people. The land reforms are a case in point. During the short lifespan of the postliberation and the post–Korean War generations of Koreans, a remarkable transformation of society and of people's way of life took place in both North and South Korea. In this sense society-building and state-building tasks were far more efficiently carried out in the Korean states than the task of nation building.

The years between 1945 and 1950 saw rapid initial gains in political institution building, only to have them lost again through the Korean War. New political institutions were founded and measures for political participation by the citizens were allowed during the early years. During the post–Korean War era of the 1950s, however, South Korea suffered from political decay as a result of the autocratic rule imposed by Syngman Rhee, who turned the timetable of democratic politics backward and manipulated the constitution through frequent amendments. North Korea, on the other hand, continued along the path of state building as Kim Il Sung busily consolidated his power through efforts at party building and mass-line politics that included bloody purges of his political rivals.

Following the student-led revolution of April 1960 in South Korea, the authoritarian rule of Syngman Rhee was replaced by parliamentary democracy, which in turn was soon crushed by the military coup of May 1961. In the decade of the 1960s both Korean states scored substantial gains in internal political development by institutionalizing political procedures and organizations. Whereas South Korea allowed periodic elections to choose representatives and presidents, North Korea allowed the membership of the KWP to expand, broadening the base of mass political participation in national political life. The ruling elite of North Korea cohered around Kim Il Sung and remained loyally with him throughout, while that of South Korea changed composition in the early years and later cohered around Park Chung Hee in the postcoup era of the 1960s and beyond.

If one test of political development is to harmonize political institutions with pressures for increased political participation, both North and South Korean states appeared to have progressed on the path of political development. Political institutions were adapted commensurate with the demand for political participation by the newly mobilized individuals and groups in society. Political development, as Samuel Huntington observed, is the process that "involves the creation of political institutions sufficiently adaptable, complex, autonomous, and coherent to absorb and to order the participation of these new groups and promote social and economic change in the society."[83]

From the overall perspective of Korean politics in 1945–1970, the creation of new institutions preceded—rather than followed—the expansion of political participation of the population and the mobilization of new groups in society. However, in the later years, the development of political institutions corresponded more closely with the demands and need for political participation. Unfortunately, this trend was not maintained consistently in the decade of the 1970s.

This suggests that Korean politics, whether communist or noncommunist, suffers greatly from the general tendency of what may be called "politics of mobilization." Korean politics has assumed the pattern of political mobilization led from above, rather than evolving from civic and participatory activities initiated voluntarily from below. This hierarchical pattern of authority relationships and centralized direction of political activities from the top is one of the hallmarks of Korean politics. The top-down politics, instead of bottom-up politics in the pre-1970 years, effectively prevented democratic political tradition from taking root in the Korean soil. This failure of democracy in the pre-1970 era, exacerbated by Korea's divided-nation politics, gave rise to "authoritarian" politics in the south and "totalitarian" politics in the north in the 1970–1980s, as the subsequent chapters will show.

3
Authoritarian Adaptation, 1971–1980

As the decade of the 1970s opened, the ruling elites of North and South Korea began to show greater sensitivity toward signs of change in the internal and external environments of Korean politics. Domestically, mounting pressure for social change came from the fact that by 1971 both Koreas had achieved measurable success in economic development and both societies were undergoing rapid socioeconomic transformation due to progress in industrialization, in urbanization, and—especially for South Korea—in communications development. Internationally, the diplomatic situation regarding the Korean Peninsula was unsettled as a result of a diplomatic initiative taken by the United States in pursuit of détente and rapprochement with its superpower adversaries.

Korean Response to Major-Power Rapprochement

The initial reaction to the news of U.S.-China rapprochement was one of shock and dismay. The two Korean capitals reacted with great surprise and disbelief to the July 15, 1971, announcement of U.S. President Richard Nixon's forthcoming visit to the People's Republic of China. The lack of immediate official comment on the news by either Korean regime indicated that both entertained a sense of fear and uncertainty regarding the possible impact of this new development upon the international position of their governments. The Sino-U.S. détente that followed President Nixon's visit to China in February 1972, and the Sino-Japanese rapprochement in September 1972 were interpreted by both sets of Korean leaders as potential threats to their independence and international positions.[1]

In view of North Korea's close alliance with the PRC and uncompromising animosity toward the United States, President Nixon's forthcoming visit to China must have been a source of dismay and embarrassment to Kim Il Sung. Although the news could have damaged North Korea's alliance with China, North Korea soon realized that it had no alternative but to respond positively and adjust to the evolving détente. Of course, China must have forewarned North Korean leaders about the existence of U.S.-Chinese dialogue and negotiations.² A party and government delegation from the PRC, led by Vice-Premier Li Xiannian, who was also a Politburo member of the Chinese Communist Party (CCP), was on an official visit to North Korea from July 10–16, 1971. Although the official purpose of that visit was to commemorate the tenth anniversary of the conclusion of the DPRK-PRC Treaty of Friendship, Cooperation, and Mutual Assistance, the Chinese delegation could have dropped hints about the nature of the ongoing secret discussions between the PRC and the United States. The visiting delegation was officially received by Kim Il Sung on July 13, 1971.

North Korea remained silent on the announcement of Nixon's scheduled visit to China for about three weeks. Its official reaction to the news came in the form of Kim Il Sung's speech at a Pyongyang mass rally in honor of a visit by Cambodia's Prince Nordom Sihanouk on August 6, 1971. Kim Il Sung, claiming that the Nixon Doctrine represented the United States' "desperate attempt to save itself from ruin," declared that Nixon's visit to China "means that the hostile policy towards China . . . has eventually gone to complete bankruptcy and . . . that the U.S. imperialists have at last succumbed to the pressure of the mighty anti-imperialist revolutionary forces of the world." Kim then continued:

> In the last analysis, Nixon is going to turn up in Beijing with a white flag just as the U.S. imperialist aggressors who suffered a defeat in the Korean war in the past came out to Panmunjom with a white flag. . . . Nixon's visit to China is not a march of a victor but a trip of the defeated, and it fully reflects the declining fate of the U.S. imperialism. This is a great victory of the Chinese people and a victory of the world revolutionary people.³

South Korea also expressed initial shock and dismay over the news of President Nixon's announced visit to China. The Seoul government was particularly disappointed that as a close ally of the United States it had received no advance warning as to U.S. intentions and changes in U.S. policy toward China. Although no communiqué was issued, South Korea privately expressed its concern and dismay over the failure of the United States to consult its close ally on this major policy shift. The South Koreans, like the Japanese, felt that they were entitled to know in advance how U.S. policy toward China would change, in view of the geographical proximity and special cultural ties they shared with China.

The impact of the U.S.-Chinese détente on Korea was to help the Korean regimes acquire a more realistic perception of themselves vis-à-vis the external powers and the adversary regimes in divided Korea. It is true that North Korea's perception of the United States as "the archenemy" and as "the principal stumbling block" to Korea's reunification did not change. However, North Korea realized that it had better respond to the U.S.-induced change in world politics. South Korea also acquired a new perception of China as an important country to reckon with, not only in terms of influence on North Korea's behavior but also as a possible factor in a long-term solution to Korea's reunification question. Both Korean regimes grudgingly realized that they had to adjust to and accommodate a fait accompli over which they had very little control. This changed mood brought the two Korean regimes closer psychologically and led to the initiation of North-South dialogue on resolving some of the outstanding issues of inter-Korean relations.

Not surprisingly, therefore, Korean response to the major power rapprochement in 1971–1972 initiated the long-awaited inter-Korea dialogue on divided families and reunification issues. Rapid change in the international milieu provided the pretext for the two Korean regimes to get together. It soon became evident, however, that the two Korean regimes had an additional motivation for their decision to initiate North-South dialogue. The occasion of inter-Korea dialogue was exploited by the Korean leaders to consolidate political rule and control at home. The necessity for carrying out the North-South dialogue on Korean reunification was used by the ruling elites as a convenient excuse for strengthening the authority structure and control mechanisms of the political systems in the two Koreas. Before noting the process of domestic "authoritarian" adaptation, however, we need to examine how the inter-Korea dialogue progressed in 1971–1973.

The preliminary meeting of the Red Cross talks at Panmunjom in September 1971 opened a new era of dialogue in inter-Korean relations. Representatives of the Red Cross societies of both Koreas met to try to help unite families that had been divided and dispersed following the partition of the country in 1945 and during the Korean War years, an ostensibly humanitarian concern but one with political overtones. The Red Cross talks proved to be a smokescreen for the political motives of each Korean regime to probe the intentions and assess the capabilities of its opponent. The real significance of the Red Cross talks, which unfortunately failed to produce any positive and substantive results, was to pave the way toward a political understanding reached between the two Korean authorities in the form of the Joint Communiqué on North South Dialogue announced on July 4, 1972. A considerable degree of elation and commotion was expressed at the time by many observers of Korea in the hopeful expectation that reunification of divided Korea would eventually be achieved. In retrospect, it seems obvious that whatever was worked out between the two regimes of Korea in 1972 was only a marriage of convenience and was not meant to be a lasting relationship. After 1972, both sides of divided Korea continued to face each other not as a pair of trusting compatriots but as distrustful competitors.

A dramatic announcement was made on July 4, 1972, in Seoul and Pyongyang simultaneously, about the agreement reached between the two Korean authorities in the Joint Communiqué on North South

Dialogue. This agreement was no doubt stimulated by a similar joint communiqué issued by their respective allies—the Shanghai Joint Communiqué between the United States and China—on February 28, 1972. In the context of Korea's recent history, the July 4, 1972, joint communiqué truly represented a significant milestone that reflected the strong desire of the Korean people for eventual reunification of their divided country.

The announcement of the joint communiqué was preceded by a series of "unofficial contacts" between liaison delegates from the north and the south since November 1971, including an exchange of secret visits by Director of the Korean Central Intelligence Agency Lee Hu-rak to Pyongyang on May 2–5, 1972, and by Vice-premier Pak Song-chol of North Korea to Seoul on May 29–June 1, 1972. The statement, issued in the names of Kim Yong-ju (younger brother of Kim Il Sung and director of the KWP Organization and Guidance Department) and Lee Hu-rak "pursuant to the intention of their respective superiors," declared that the two sides—not the two governments or the two states—had reached an agreement on the three principles of reunification.

The North-South joint communiqué started with a statement that "the two sides" of North and South Korea exchanged talks "to discuss problems of improving North-South relations and unifying the divided fatherland" and that they "have reached full agreements" as to how to go about putting the negotiated terms into effect. The first point of the seven-point agreement stated the following three principles of Korean unification:

> First, unification shall be achieved through independent efforts without being subject to external imposition or interference.
> Second, unification shall be achieved through peaceful means, and not through use of force against one another.
> Third, a great national unity, as a homogeneous people, shall be sought first, transcending differences in ideas, ideologies, and systems,

The remaining points of agreement were that both sides "agreed not to defame and slander one another; nor to undertake armed provocations against one another" (point 2), "to carry out various exchanges in many areas" (point 3), "to seek an early success of the South North Red Cross Conference" then in progress (point 4), "to install and operate a direct telephone line" between the respective capital cities (point 5), "to create and operate a South North Coordinating Committee . . . in order to implement above-mentioned agreements" (point 6), and to "solemnly pledge . . . to faithfully carry out the agreements" (point 7).

The most important point in the joint communiqué is the agreement of both Korean regimes to accept the threefold principle of Korean unification, based on the commitment that unification be sought through (1) independence, (2) peaceful means, and (3) a greater national unity, "transcending differences in ideas, ideologies, and systems."[4]

This was a noteworthy event in the history of inter-Korean relations. It reaffirmed the unfinished task of nation building and declared the reunification of the divided country to be the supreme mission of the Korean people. It also recognized a basically nationalistic, independent, and peaceful posture to be the only acceptable and workable approach to the task of Korean reunification. By agreeing to issue the joint communiqué on inter-Korean dialogue, both regimes of Korea also demonstrated their flexibility in adapting to the rapidly changing international situation. Although similar perceptions of external change brought the two parties together at the conference table, the Korean regimes varied in their pattern of response and style of adaptation. How did the Korean states respond and adapt to the changing external environment? How was the external pressure translated in terms of internal considerations and the enhancement of legitimacy claims? First we shall examine the experience of South Korea under Park Chung Hee and then turn to that of North Korea under Kim Il Sung.

Park Chung Hee's Yushin Korea

The South Korean response to détente under President Park was the more daring but its effect upon internal politics was damaging to the cause of democracy. As the decade of the 1970s began, President Park's already-firm hold on power at home was strengthened considerably. His success in carrying out the program of economic development was widely recognized, and his victory in the 1971 presidential election also enhanced Park's political stand. As the first and second five-year plans (1962–1971) were successfully implemented the economy expanded rapidly and the standard of living of the average citizen rose.[5] Rapid expansion of the economy was made possible through the government's active investment in key industries and infrastructure-building projects. The government strategy of industrialization through the expansion of export-generating manufacturing concerns also paid off handsomely. The changing economic structure of South Korea became more industrial than agricultural through the decade of the 1970s.[6]

Industrialization of the economy under President Park's leadership was attained at considerable cost, however. Rural needs were neglected in the early years so that the gap between urban and rural life-styles and standards of living widened throughout the 1960s. Continuous large-scale migration of the rural population into the congested urban areas in search of employment led to serious political and social problems. Although rural Korea received increased government support in the early 1970s through the inauguration of the Saemaul movement in 1971–1972, Park Chung Hee's electoral strategy until 1971 was to favor the industrial wage earners and urban dwellers through the policy of keeping the rice price low and other such fiscal measures.[7] Ironically, in spite of Park's one-sided policy favoring the city dwellers, his electoral support throughout his tenure largely came from rural Korea, rather than from the urban areas.

In 1971 Park was reelected for a third term. In July 1969, Park had made it known that he would not oppose a constitutional amendment enabling him to serve a third term as president. In September 1969, an amendment bill was introduced to the National Assembly in a secret predawn maneuver by the ruling DRP, without the presence of opposition party members. In spite of strong criticism of such high-handed parliamentary tactics, the constitutional amendment was subsequently endorsed in a popular referendum held on October 21, 1969. The sense of a security threat from the north perhaps influenced the Korean voters to go along with Park's tenure. The Nixon Doctrine was announced in 1969 and U.S. troop withdrawal from South Korea was much debated in the press and was consequently in voters' minds.

In the 1971 presidential election Park received 51.2 percent of the vote, defeating his main opponent Kim Dae-jung, the nominee of the New Democratic Party (NDP), who received 43.6 percent of the vote. Although slightly less than the previous record of 51.4 percent received in 1967, this figure was still impressive, and far better than the 43.6 percent with which Park was elected in 1963. In spite of this electoral victory Park felt uncomfortable and insecure in his hold on power. In the ensuing National Assembly election of May 1971 the ruling DRP candidates won only 47.7 percent of the seats in the assembly. The DRP gained 86 of the 153 single-member electoral district seats and 27 additional seats based on total votes received by the party. The opposition NDP gained 65 and 24 seats respectively. Although the DRP electoral performance in 1971 was far better than the 32.4 percent won in 1963, its record in 1971 was a decline from the 52.8 percent won by the party in 1967. A more disturbing fact for Park, however, was that in the nine major urban areas, the opposition NDP gained 35 seats compared to 7 seats for the ruling DRP. This poor showing by his party in the urban districts confirmed Park's suspicion that his policy and programs were unpopular in the urban areas.[8]

Park next moved to tighten internal security by declaring a state of emergency on December 6, 1971. His stated reason was to maintain law and order in the face of mounting domestic disturbances, including campus demonstrations, to be suppressed by using military troops against students. Park argued that these emergency measures were necessary because of rapid changes in the international situation and North Korea's "aggressive" intentions to exploit the weakness of South Korea, timed with the initiation of the North-South Red Cross negotiations in August 1971. On December 26, 1971, the National Assembly passed a bill granting emergency powers to the president at a session boycotted by the opposition members. These and similar measures adopted by Park's government in 1971 were only a harbinger of what was yet to come in 1972.

A state of martial law was proclaimed on October 17, 1972, to prepare the stage for executing an amibitious, premeditated "coup in office" that destroyed the Third Republic and replaced it by the new Fourth Republic. The Yushin or "Revitalizing" reform that followed was defended as necessary for promoting the cause of national unification, although Park's desire to stay in power indefinitely was probably one of the motivating factors for his action.[9]

The martial law decrees proclaimed on October 17 to carry out the Yushin program were all-encompassing: they suspended the constitution, dissolved the National Assembly, revoked the freedoms of speech and assembly—including the activities of political parties, and restricted the civil rights of the citizenry. These measures were necessary, as Park's spokesman put it, because "we must have unity in order to have a dialogue with the North" and because South Korea "cannot afford to risk political unity when North Koreans have complete control over everything their people say and do."[10] Park also stated later, on January 12, 1973, that the constitutional revision was necessary to cope with the "great changes" on the international scene, which according to him included such events as the Sino-U.S. rapprochement, the Sino-Japanese diplomatic normalization, the severing of Japan's official ties with Taiwan, the deteriorating situation in Vietnam, and uncertainty in the North-South Korean dialogue. Although Park did not state it outright at the time, his action was probably also motivated by insecurity over the withdrawal of some 20,000 military personnel, the U.S. Seventh Division, in March 1971. This withdrawal was carried out as part of the Nixon Doctrine pronounced in 1969, in spite of Park's strong opposition to the U.S. troop withdrawal plan.[11]

In order to maintain a democratic facade of political participation by the public, and also to legitimize his coup, Park's government had the Yushin Constitution approved by the electorate in an ensuing referendum for the constitutional amendment, with an overwhelming 91.5 percent affirmative vote by those participating. Moreover, Park's government defended its imposition of the Yushin reform as a way of establishing a "Koreanized" democracy, i.e., of adapting democracy to the conditions and situation of South Korea. While destroying the foundation of democratic institutions, Park ironically defended and rationalized his action in the name of assuring "Korean democracy"![12]

On December 23, 1972, pursuant to the new constitutional provision, Park was elected for a six-year term by the electoral college, called the National Conference for Unification. He received near unanimous support, winning the votes of all but two of the 2,359 delegates. The 2,000 to 5,000 members of this new representative institution were to be directly elected by the people for three-year terms. In spite of its official name, the National Conference for Unification functioned not as a deliberative body on South Korea's unification policy but primarily as an electoral college to choose the president, who also happened to be president of the conference. Other responsibilities of this body included approval of constitutional amendments proposed by the National Assembly—to be newly constituted under the Yushin Constitution—and approval of the one-third of the members of the National Assembly that were to be nominated by the president.

Under the Yushin Constitution the office of the president was greatly enhanced in authority, while the National Assembly and the judicial branch were correspondingly weakened. The legislative role of the one-house National Assembly was greatly reduced following the February 27, 1973, election, and the assembly became subject to dissolution by the president. Since one-third of the 219-member body was appointed by the president, this group, named the *Yujonghoe*, constituted the largest single voting bloc in the legislature. When combined with the DRP, the second largest bloc, President Park could be assured of an automatic majority in the legislature. Although the remaining two-thirds of the assemblymen were directly elected for a term of six years by secret ballot, they were almost evenly divided between the ruling party and the opposition party. The independent judiciary also gave way to the presidential appointment of justices in the Supreme Court, whose nine members were to serve for terms of six years each. The authority to rule on the constitutionality of a law, however, was vested in the newly created Constitutional Committee, not in the Supreme Court.[13]

The authoritarian grasp of power by Park Chung Hee in Yushin Korea was attested to by the fact that the president was also empowered to exercise emergency powers. Article 53 of the Yushin Constitution had these provisions: "In time of natural calamity or a grave financial or economic crisis, and in case the national security or the public safety and order is seriously threatened or anticipated to be threatened . . . the President shall have power to take necessary emergency measures in the whole range of the state affairs, including internal affairs, foreign affairs, national defense, economic, financial, and judicial affairs." During emergencies the president could temporarily suspend the basic rights of citizens, although he was required to inform the National Assembly of the measures so proclaimed. The president's actions, however, were not to be subject to judicial review and he was therefore to be the sole authority in determining the legality of any emergency measures undertaken. Finally, the latitude of presidential authority to declare martial law was broad; he could do so "in time of war, armed conflict or similar national emergency, when there is a military necessity, or a necessity to maintain the public safety and order by mobilization of the military forces."[14]

The presidential emergency powers authorized in the Yushin Constitution were exercised several times in 1974 and 1975. Under Emergency Measure No. 1 in 1974, any criticism of the Yushin Constitution or government system was prohibited, as were any forms of unauthorized student political activity. This decree, issued on January 9, 1974, stated that "it shall be prohibited for any person to deny, oppose, misrepresent or defame the constitution of the ROK," and that "any person who violates . . . and . . . defames the present emergency measures shall be subject to arrest, detention, search or seizure, without warrant thereof, and shall be punished by imprisonment" (article 5), and will "be tried and sentenced in the emergency courts-martial."[15] Under these provisions, some 203 persons were tried; 168 were subsequently released, although they were not pardoned. Of the remaining prisoners found guilty of crimes under the emergency decree, 8 were sentenced to death and were executed in April 1975.

Emergency Decree No. 4, proclaimed on April 3, 1974, singled out a specific organization, the National Democratic Youth and Student Federation, for the purpose of suppressing the student activist movement. This organization, according to government charges, spearheaded an anti-Park demonstration in 1973. The emergency decree therefore prohibited any person from organizing such demonstrations or joining the said organization. The vindictive nature of suppression was clear in that the decree not only prohibited anyone from organizing or joining this federation but also forbade citizens to "praise, encourage, or sympathize" with it (article 1), "to publish, produce, possess, disseminate, exhibit, or sell documents, books, photographic records, or any other measures of expression concerning the activities of the said organization or its members" (article 3).[16] Although this notorious emergency decree was subsequently lifted and most of the student leaders released, the Park government rearrested and jailed some of the leaders connected with the student movement to prevent the anti-Park movement from spreading throughout the country. One of the rearrested intellectual leaders was the poet Kim Chi-ha, whose writings were harshly critical of the Yushin dictatorship.[17] One of Kim Chi-ha's poems, entitled "Cry of the People," was published in early 1974.

> The *Yushin* signboard advertisement
> Is merely to deceive the people;
> . . . .
>
> On democratic constitution's tomb
> Dictatorship has been established;
> . . . .
>
> Human rights went up in smoke;
> Now sheer survival is at stake.[18]

Earlier Kim Chi-ha had published other poems—such as "Five Bandits" (1970) and "Groundless Rumors" (1972)—of biting criticism of Park Chung Hee's political rule and policies in the south. For his writings and his participation in the movement for South Korean democracy,

Kim was subsequently court-martialed and imprisoned by a military tribunal on the charge of violating the country's national security law.

Another notorious emergency measure, no. 9, put into effect on May 13, 1975, outlawed any political actions, any calls for constitutional revision, any criticism of the emergency measure itself, any student political activities and any spreading of "false rumors."[19] The Park government justified these restrictions on internal political activity by citing the need to increase national unity in order to defend South Korea against the North Korean threat. These repressive measures adopted by the government were, however, criticized by Protestant and Catholic church groups, students, intellectuals, and some newspaper reporters. The mounting criticism against the harsh measures imposed by the Park government eventually led to an escalated confrontation between the government and the opposition forces. It represented a delayed response on the part of the articulate sector of the society against Park's increasingly arbitrary and repressive measures.

Rapid socioeconomic change, fueled by the drive for increased exports and industrialization, led to higher expectations for a better standard of living for the masses. This also led to an increased demand for political participation on the part of the articulate segment of the population in the increasingly complex and pluralistic society of the south. Under the new leadership of Kim Young-sam, the opposition NDP was increasingly bold and vocal in its criticism of the Yushin system and Park Chung Hee's dictatorship. Kim Young-sam was subsequently expelled from the National Assembly for criticizing government policies, leading to a major riot in Pusan, Kim Young-sam's electoral district. Christian leaders and clergy also actively voiced their sympathy for the hardships of industrial wage earners, especially the young women workers who were recruited from the countryside. The Urban Industrial Mission, which was run by Catholic workers for such purposes as helping organize labor unions, was suppressed and harassed by the Yushin police forces.

The worldwide economic recession and inflation fueled by the second OPEC price hike in 1979 also hit middle-class Koreans hard. The South Korean economy was no longer able to sustain the pace of rapid growth and expansion, and the demand for Korean manufactured products abroad did not grow as fast as in the previous years. On top of this the Park Chung Hee government made a serious policy error, going ahead with its import substitution plan of building heavy industry, including chemical and armaments industries, and in the process incurring a huge external debt to generate investment capital.

The combination of economic hardship and political repression prevalent in 1979 thus created an explosive and volatile domestic situation in Park Chung Hee's Yushin Korea. In September 1979 a spontaneous antigovernment demonstration took place in the country's second largest city, Pusan, and soon spread to the nearby city of Masan. The student-initiated street demonstrations, joined by other citizens, turned into a major riot, with crowds overturning passenger cars and burning the police precinct stations. It was suppressed momentarily by troops following the proclamation of a state of emergency throughout the city. Rather unexpectedly, the stage was thus set for a possible overthrow of the Yushin system in the southernmost city of South Korea, which had traditionally been claimed to be the stronghold of pro–Park Chung Hee political forces.

Yushin Korea under Park thus imposed "repressive adaptation" upon the population to counter the perceived threat emanating from the changing environment at home and abroad. South Korea under Park's Yushin system changed from the hopeful, modernizing, and fairly democratic system of the 1960s to the increasingly arbitrary, repressive, and authoritarian system of the 1970s. Yushin Korea, in spite of its success in achieving an "economic miracle," became a model of political repression and authoritarian rule. The basis of political support of the regime became increasingly narrow, eroding as the decade of the 1970s progressed. The growing alienation of the progressive forces in society, including intellectuals, religious leaders, students, and the press, made President Park's hold on power that much more precarious and vulnerable. The Yushin system finally received a fatal blow on October 26, 1979, when President Park was assassinated by one of his close aides, who professed to represent the voices and cause of democratic restoration in South Korea.

The Land of Kim Il Sung

While South Korea was imposing the measures of "repressive adaptation" domestically, North Korea was pursuing the line of "progressive adaptation" internationally. The response of the Korean regimes to the rapidly changing external environment in the 1970s thus produced different effects: South Korea internalized and North Korea externalized the shocks from the outside. Since North Korea, by 1970, was already firmly controlled by Kim Il Sung and his followers, its pursuit of the policy line of "socialist revolution and construction" was rather routinely projected, although incessant mass propaganda campaigns and mobilization made the theme of continuous revolution even more urgent in the north.

As the decade of the 1970s opened, Kim Il Sung's grasp of power was ever firmer, and his presence as the Great Leader became ever more pervasive. When the Fifth KWP Congress was called into session in November 1970, the composition of the Central Committee membership indicated that a new breed of Kim Il Sung followers had been recruited to leadership positions, together with the hard-core members of Kim Il Sung's inner circle of power. Of the total of 117 full members of the Fifth KWP Central Committee, only 31 were retained from the Fourth

KWP Central Committee; the remaining 86 were newly elected. An overwhelming majority of these new Central Committee members (66) were identifiable as belonging to the "new group" that was the product of North Korea's communist system; 13 others belonged to Kim Il Sung's "partisan group" or "Kapsan faction."[20] Rapid turnover in the membership of the KWP Central Committee between party congresses had been the general rule in North Korea's communist politics. However, the Fifth KWP Congress in November 1970 was still remarkable for the noticeable absence of contending groups such as the Soviet or the Yenan factions. Kim Il Sung was one of two men who had served on all five Central Committees prior to 1970; the other was his close associate Kim Il, who had been Kim Il Sung's right-hand man and comrade in arms since the anti-Japanese guerrilla fighting years of the 1930s.

At the Fifth KWP Congress Kim Il Sung, in his capacity as the party's general secretary, delivered a major policy address in his report to the party on the work of the Central Committee. His five-part report was one of the most comprehensive and revealing summaries of the 1960s and became a blueprint for the 1970s. Kim first reviewed the accomplishments of North Korea's economy in the process of North Korea's transformation into a socialist industrial state, touching upon themes such as the cultural revolution, ideological unity, the defense system, and socialist economic management. He then outlined the basic tasks of the new six-year economic plan, giving particular emphasis to the goals of socialist construction, the cultural revolution, ideological revolution, the strengthening of national defense capabilities, and improvement in people's living standards. He also spoke of the twin themes of the reunification of Korea and the need for revolution in South Korea. Kim then proceeded to discuss the situation of international relations, pledging to increase solidarity with the revolutionary forces of other countries. He spoke last of the need to promote ideological unity with the thought of Juche in North Korea.[21]

During the course of his report, Kim Il Sung boastfully announced the successful completion of the seven-year economic plan. As already noted, this plan failed to reach completion by its initial target date in 1967 and had to be twice postponed before it was completed in 1970. With the achievement of this economic plan Kim asserted that North Korea had now transformed itself from a "socialist industrial-agricultural economy" into a "socialist industrial" state. Despite this exaggerated claim, North Korea's economic difficulties were readily apparent during the course of the party congress.[22] At the same KWP congress, Kim Il, as vice-premier, repeated the same old line, blaming external exigencies such as "U.S. Imperialism" for the less than successful performance of the economy at home. This was clearly meant to divert attention away from the serious internal difficulties of the economy associated with structural problems of the command economy, which led to excessive centralization and bureaucratic control and reduced efficiency in production and management.

On the question of reunification Kim Il Sung made it clear that South Korea's revolution and the issue of reunification were inseparably interrelated. He emphasized that "to unify the divided fatherland is the greatest national task for the entire Korean people at the present stage and the most pressing task, the solution of which brooks no delay."[23] Yet he also stated that South Korea must go through the revolutionary struggle not only against "U.S. Imperialism," as represented by the continued U.S. troop presence in South Korea, but also against the "military fascism" of the Park Chung Hee government.

In spite of these self-righteous pronouncements and hostile attitude toward Park Chung Hee's government in the south, Kim Il Sung's government began to show some flexibility in its tactical moves toward South Korea on the unification issue. Having earlier abandoned the policy of armed infiltration of the south, Kim Il Sung announced in August 1971 his willingness to negotiate with South Korea's ruling Democratic Republican Party. In adopting this posture of flexibility, Kim Il Sung was no doubt influenced by the rapidly changing atmosphere in international politics initiated by the U.S. moves toward improving relations with China. But the new stance of North Korea helped to create the atmosphere through which the North-South dialogue on divided families was initiated through the Red Cross societies. To South Korea's August 12, 1971, proposal on the preliminary Red Cross talks to find separated family members, to be held in Geneva before the end of October, North Korea responded positively with a counterproposal. On August 20, 1971, the first contact was thus established in Panmunjom between "messengers" of North Korea's Red Cross and South Korea's Red Cross to exchange documents containing the two Korean proposals on divided families.[24]

North Korea's response to the evolving détente in 1970–1971 was "a grudging accommodation to a fait accompli."[25] Although North Korea was not wholly sanguine about the changing situation, fearing that it would adversely affect its interests and traditional ties with its communist allies, Kim's government realized that it had no alternative but to go along with China, its ally. The bittersweet nature of Kim Il Sung's reaction to the evolving drama outside North Korea, over which he had little control, was clearly revealed in the August 6, 1971, speech already alluded to.[26] Actually, North Korea was already bent upon improving its ties with China at the time. During the era of China's Cultural Revolution, 1966–1969, the relationship between the two communist countries had been at a low point, but in 1969, Pyongyang had sent a delegation to China's October 1 celebration for the first time since 1965. North Korea's gesture was reciprocated by a state visit to North Korea by China's premier, Zhou Enlai, on April 5–7, 1970. In a joint communiqué North Korea and China expressed their mutual fear of a hostile U.S.-Japanese alliance, which they said was designed to revive Japanese militarism. The leaders of both governments were reacting to the Nixon

Doctrine and the 1969 Nixon-Sato joint communiqué, in which both the United States and Japan expressed the position that stability in the Korean Peninsula was a matter of concern to both countries.

In the spring of 1975, on the eve of the Indochina debacle, Kim Il Sung made an official state visit to China. His trip to China was ostensibly to seek China's support for his grand scheme of inciting revolution in the south and promoting the cause of Korean reunification. Kim reportedly failed to obtain China's approval and active support for his designs on South Korea, although he was successful in extracting China's official endorsement of his policy and stand on Korea's reunification. In a joint communiqué, China and North Korea stated that the DPRK was the sole legitimate government in the Korean Peninsula and that both countries demanded the withdrawal of U.S. troops from South Korea.

At a banquet speech in Beijing on April 18, 1975, Kim Il Sung reiterated his basic stand on Korean reunification and stated that "if the U.S. troops pull out of South Korea and a democratic figure with a national conscience comes into power as its people demand, we will firmly guarantee a durable peace in Korea and successfully solve the question of Korea's reunification among us Koreans by peaceful means." However, he also added that "if revolution takes place in South Korea, we, as one and the same nation, will not just look on it with folded arms."[27] In spite of the Sino-U.S. rapprochement and the cessation of China's anti-American propaganda rhetoric, North Korea thus continued to adhere to its policy line that the United States was "the archenemy" of the Korean people and "the principal stumbling block" to Korea's reunification.

In spite of its anti-American stance, however, North Korea sought to normalize relations with the United States as part of its overall strategy to undermine the position of South Korea. It proposed talks on the possible conclusion of a bilateral agreement that would replace the existing armistice treaty with a new peace treaty formally terminating the Korean War. Although it seemed sensible, Pyongyang's move was interpreted by Seoul as a ploy to isolate South Korea because Pyongyang steadfastly refused to include the Seoul government in the process of diplomatic negotiations.[28] The 1979 proposal for a tripartite conference on the future of Korea between Washington, Pyongyang, and Seoul, advanced by President Jimmy Carter during his Seoul visit in July 1979, did not entice a positive response from Pyongyang. North Korea objected to the Carter proposal on the grounds that South Korea had no legal right or qualification to participate in the U.S.–North Korean bilateral talks. This was interpreted as a politically motivated ploy to isolate South Korea, even if North Korea had legal merit in its case. South Korea had refused to sign the 1953 armistice agreement on the ground that it would perpetuate the territorial division of the country. By refusing to sign the armistice agreement, South Korea had thereby forfeited its right to be represented, according to North Korea.[29]

Domestically, the new six-year economic plan for 1971–1976, revealed during the Fifth KWP Congress in November 1970, was aimed at accomplishing the "three technical revolutions." The policy, as stated by Kim Il Sung, was to "narrow the gap between heavy and light labor and between industrial and agricultural work" as well as to "free women from as many house chores as possible."[30] On September 23, 1975, North Korea announced that it had successfully fulfilled its six-year plan (1971–1976) sixteen months ahead of schedule. There is no way to independently establish the validity of this claim. However, it was clear that, as a result of the purchase of plants from the West, North Korea was making great strides in increasing the production and efficiency of its industries. However, in 1974 and 1975 North Korea also experienced difficulties in making payments on purchases of technology from Japan and Western European countries. In March 1976, North Korea reportedly asked for a two-year moratorium on the payment of trade debts to Japanese firms. Its outstanding debt was estimated to be between $2.1 billion and $3 billion as of early 1977.[31] In this episode, North Korean planners obviously fell victim to the adverse international economic trends in the aftermath of the OPEC oil price hike in 1973–1974. North Korea's exports, needed to earn foreign currency with which to purchase technology from the West, failed to keep up with international inflation. North Korea therefore suffered a large trade deficit in the early 1970s.

Paralleling its economic overtures, North Korea under Kim Il Sung reversed its long-standing posture of diplomatic isolation. The Pyongyang regime adopted a new policy of increased international involvement, belatedly joining various international governmental organizations such as the World Health Organization (WHO) and the UN Educational, Scientific and Cultural Organization (UNESCO), and seeking establishment of diplomatic ties with other countries. It also set up the DPRK Permanent Observer Mission to the United Nations in New York. In retrospect, North Korea benefited more internationally than South Korea did from the favorable impression that both regimes made by opening the North-South dialogue. North Korea succeeded in winning wider diplomatic recognition not only from Third World countries but also from some West European countries that had traditionally been friendly to South Korea. It was vehemently opposed to the idea of "the two Koreas" or "the one nation/two states" formula. This plan, adopted by East and West Germany, would lay a basis for mutual accommodation and rapprochement between the two halves of the divided nation and for maintaining diplomatic cross-recognition by other countries. Therefore, it vehemently objected to the idea of joining the United Nations as two separate governments, as proposed by the Seoul government on June 23, 1973—a plan that Pyongyang criticized as "a scheme for perpetuating the national division."[32]

Internally, North Korea decided to carry out its own plan for political reform at the end of 1972. Kim Il Sung strengthened his already-firm position of authority. Unlike South Korea, which relied on extraordinary means for political reform, including constitutional amendment, the North Korean approach was more or less routine: it adopted a new constitution by following normal and preestablished procedures. Although the regime had not involved the masses in the process of deliberating the draft of the new constitution, the North Korean leaders decided to use the existing means and channels for political change by calling for the election of a new Supreme People's Assembly, North Korea's national legislative body. The Kim Il Sung regime first called in December 1972 for a plenum meeting of the Fifth Party Congress of the KWP, which deliberated and approved the plans for a new constitution in rapid succession. The new constitution was then referred to the newly formed body of the Fifth Supreme People's Assembly, which—again without any modification or dissension—passed the KWP recommendation on the new constitution. The fiction of popular participation in the due process of constitution making was thus maintained in North Korea by the end of 1972.

The 1972 Socialist Constitution of the DPRK, with 11 chapters and 149 articles, was much lengthier than the first constitution of 1948. Although the basic format and some provisions remained the same—especially those dealing with the rights and duties of citizens (Chapter 4), the Supreme People's Assembly (Chapter 5), local assemblies and people's committees (Chapter 9), the court (Chapter 10), and the emblem and flag (Chapter 11)—there were some drastic changes in the new constitution, especially regarding the administrative organs of the state. New provisions included the creation of the new Office of the President (Chapter 6), the Central People's Committee (Chapter 7), and the State Administration Council (Chapter 8). Kim Il Sung assumed the new title of president of the state, and his decisionmaking authority was now buttressed by the Central People's Committee (a kind of supercabinet), of which he was chairman, and the Administrative Council (a cabinet in the conventional sense), to be headed by his prime minister. The basic principles of the constitution were also expanded to incorporate political (Chapter 1), economic (Chapter 2), and cultural (Chapter 3) aspects of the affairs of the republic. The focus of the 1972 Socialist Constitution was clearly to formalize and regularize what had already taken place in North Korea's communist politics, that is, the enhancement of Kim Il Sung's role and status as the supreme leader and the strengthening of his instrument of political rule and control.[33]

The political system of North Korea that emerged in the 1970s had the potential of becoming a sui generis form of authoritarian politics, operating not only as top-down politics extended by the supreme leader but also as bottom-up politics based on the mass loyalty extended to him by his followers. Not only was Kim Il Sung politics in North Korea a case of extreme "command" politics exercised by a supreme leader who extols the virtues of loyalty and dedication in his followers; it was also a case of extreme blind "following" carefully controlled and manipulated through the party instrument. Kim Il Sung's authoritarianism went beyond Stalinism in the sense that masses in the north "venerate their leaders" and give the leaders absolute loyalty and dedication as well. North Korea's authoritarianism thus is based on the dynamics of the leader-follower relationship in the political process.

The KWP after the Fifth Party Congress of 1970 was transformed into an instrument of personal rule by its leader. The iron rule of Kim Il Sung reached the point of surpassing any other examples of totalitarian regimes in modern times. The cult of personality of Kim in the north became pervasive and extreme, to the extent of possibly overshadowing other cases of autocratic rule in the modern era, including that of Joseph Stalin. Kim was praised and worshipped in North Korea as the "sun of the Korean people," "respected and beloved leader," "peerless patriot," "national hero," "great leader produced by mankind," "brilliant revolutionary theoretician," and "ever-victorious, iron-willed genius commander."[34]

"The Land of Kim Il Sung" was literally what North Korea preached and practiced in the 1970s. Kim Il Sung's grip on power was absolute. A body of hagiology was created around him to command absolute respect and loyalty by the masses.[35] In spite of its Marxian vocabulary and secular rituals, the KWP became a quasi-religious body. "Unabashed and unswerving faith in the leader" was expected of the party members and this faith was "refreshed daily by canonical readings."[36] In the words of one noted scholar on North Korean communism, "if President Kim's words constitute the soul of the KWP, the party organizational mechanisms serve as its body, and this body has been forged according to the will of the leader to obey every whim and command from the center."[37] Moreover, the cult of personality of Kim Il Sung has been extended to include his "revolutionary family" members, including his own son, putting into motion the process of deification of Kim Il Sung. No wonder then that North Korea by the 1970s had become "The Land of Kim Il Sung" and that Kim as "the Great Leader" extracted absolute dedication and loyalty from the masses, reigning in the land as if it were his personal kingdom.[38]

Reflecting the enhanced status of the supreme leader, the modified government structure of North Korea enabled Kim Il Sung to amass in his hands all the dictatorial powers in North Korea. He was general secretary of the KWP, president of the DPRK, chairman of the KWP Defense Commission and chairman of the Central People's Committee. Why did this consolidation of authority and concentration of power in the person of a single leader take place in North Korea? How do we explain the fact that in North Korea—as in South Korea—the incumbent leader invariably and jealously guarded his power? Why is this phenomenon of the vortex of power so evident in Korean politics? These questions will receive further attention in Chapters 4 and 5.

Concluding Remarks: Korea's Authoritarian Politics

Neither of the Korean regimes practiced full measures of democracy in the 1970s. No orderly and periodic alternation of political power took place in either of the Korean states. Nor did the Korean regimes allow such essential democratic procedures and practices as broadening the basis of citizen political participation, assuring a freer atmosphere for party competition and development, and tolerating political opposition to regime policies.[39]

In the light of these nondemocratic political trends in the 1970s, many observers in and out of Korea harshly criticized the repressive regimes and policies—particularly those of South Korea. Given that the political system in South Korea professed to be more open, liberal, and pluralistic in its orientation than that of North Korea, critics argued that the antidemocratic tendency of politics in the south under the Yushin system seemed more deplorable, and they subjected South Korean politics to stronger condemnation than the totalitarian and monolithic political system of North Korea. This criticism raises the question of how to interpret Korea's political development in the 1970s, the authoritarian practices in the south, and the totalitarian politics in the north.

In retrospect, it is apparent that the political elites of both North and South Korea abandoned strategies for simultaneous industrialization and democratization as a way of achieving modernization. The Park regime in the south was impatient with democratization as a way of attaining the goals of political development. It criticized the democratic movement, represented by the demands of student leaders and human-rights activists, as inefficient and as obstructing the attainment of industrialization. The Kim regime of North Korea also rigorously pursued the "forced draft" plan of industrialization, and in the process denied the population the democratic rights to criticize the regime and its policy. While slogans such as "building socialism and construction" were inculcated upon the masses, the political elite in the North was busily engaged in the task of consolidating its hold on power.

By the time the North-South Korean dialogue began in 1971, however, the leadership in both North and South Korea was tightening the reins of political control, disallowing the political opposition and prohibiting challenges to the party in power. The adoption of the new constitution in South Korea at the end of 1972 heralded a new era of Korean politics, an authoritarian politics that granted the incumbent ruler a constitutional guarantee for lifelong tenure in office. Challenging the party in power through constitutional means was made practically impossible. The adoption of the 1972 Socialist Constitution in North Korea also strengthened the authority of Kim Il Sung as supreme leader by giving him an institutional basis for exercising dictatorial power. The experience of both North and South Korea in the 1970s discouraged optimism as to the furthering of democratic developments through restoring a proper balance between political institution building and political participation by the Korean people.

In achieving the policy goal of modernization, one of the foremost concerns of the political leadership of North and South Korea was how to strike a balance between the necessity of political stability and the process of continuous socioeconomic change. When the two Koreas' experiences in political development are seen together, the contrast between them is especially noticeable in the area of harmonizing political institution building and political participation. Whereas South Korea experienced discontinuous political change and instability, North Korea experienced a process of continuous, cumulative, and progressive political change and stability. Retarding the timetable of democratic political development stimulated the emergence in the 1970s of a new authoritarian political tradition in Korean politics. This new trend was carried forward to the decade of the 1980s in both North and South Korea.

The experience of political development in divided Korea shows that both Korean societies suffered acutely from disharmony between political institutionalization and political participation and from the growing gap between the two. What are the reasons for this anomaly in Korean politics? Why has the democratic tradition failed to take root in Korean politics? The answers to these questions must take into account Korea's contemporary political culture plus a number of factors including the country's culture, tradition, and value system, and the attitudes and behavior of the Korean people.

4
Regimes and Stability in the 1980s

A series of events took place in 1980 and 1981 that marked a turning point in the political development of the Korean states. In North Korea the Sixth KWP Congress was held in October 1980, after the lapse of a decade since the Fifth Congress in 1970. This congress laid down some important party policies for the decade of the 1980s. In South Korea a new constitutional framework for the Fifth Republic was established in 1981. This followed the sixteen months of political turmoil and uncertainty ushered in by the assassination of President Park Chung Hee in October 1979.

As the civilianization of the military regime was taking place in the south, a system of political succession was being institutionalized in the north. The thirty-nine-year-old son of President Kim Il Sung, Kim Jong Il, was elected on October 10, 1980, by the Sixth KWP Congress to the all-powerful five-man Presidium of the Politburo of the KWP Central Committee in North Korea. His election, announced during the party congress, confirmed the rumor circulating since 1974 that Kim junior might be groomed as Kim Il Sung's heir apparent. In South Korea, a forty-nine-year-old soldier-turned-politician, Chun Doo Hwan, was sworn in on March 3, 1981, as president of the Fifth Republic. As a general he had ordered paratroopers to suppress the bloody Kwangju insurrection that lasted for nine days in May 1980. These events heralded a new era of volatile politics in Korea in the 1980s, with uncertain political implications and significance.

The rise of Chun Doo Hwan in the south and that of Kim Jong Il in the north are obviously of great importance for future political development in Korea. Does the emergence of Chun Doo Hwan and Kim Jong Il signify a period of political stability for both South Korea and North Korea? Will Chun succeed in keeping the military intact and subordinated, and also in restoring the confidence of civilian leaders in and out of government service? Will the death of Kim Il Sung in the future be met by an orderly transfer of power quite unlike the political turmoil that followed the death of Mao Zedong in the People's Republic of China? What impact, if any, will the change of political leadership in both north and south have on Korean relations with the Soviet Union, the PRC, Japan, and the United States? Finally, what effect will it have on future inter-Korean relations and on the prospects for Korean reunification? This chapter will discuss the emergence of South Korea's Fifth Republic first and then turn to the North Korean communist system under the reign of father-son partnership and the possibility of a hereditary communist state.

The Fifth Republic Emerges: The South

The year 1980 was a period of political turmoil and unrest for South Korea after the assassination of President Park Chung Hee. By 1981 South Korea had managed to restore the semblance of political stability and order, occasioned by the rise of former-paratrooper-turned-politician Chun Doo Hwan.

South Korea in 1980 was widely acclaimed as an advanced developing country (ADC) or a newly industrializing country (NIC).[1] Measured by the usual indicators of socioeconomic modernization, such as gross national product (GNP) per capita or the quality of life, South Korea had clearly achieved great strides in its march toward economic development. South Korea's GNP in 1981 was estimated to be close to U.S. $60 billion and its per capita income was close to U.S. $1,500, as a result of the continuous steady growth of the economy at a pace of almost 10 percent a year in real terms in the decade prior to 1979.[2] South Korea thus was no longer the typical poor less-developed country (LDC)—an excolony with less than $100 GNP per capita—it had been prior to 1960. The successful export-led strategy of economic development that South Korea experimented with between 1963 and 1979 had provided inspiration to other LDCs in their search for an appropriate developmental strategy.[3]

In sharp contrast to its remarkable success on the economic front, however, South Korea had failed to make positive strides toward political democracy, as witnessed by the emergence of a "new authoritarian political order" in 1980–1981.[4] South Korea moved backward politically as it moved forward economically. The liberal assumption widely held in the 1960s, that socioeconomic modernization leads to political democracy, does not seem to hold true for this developing East Asian country.[5] How does one account for the emergence of a new authoritarianism in South Korea? The central issue in examining South Korea's politics in 1980 and 1981 is to explain the sudden demise of the old system and the rise of the new political order. What were the circumstances and events that led to this transition of power? How can one account for the process of political change from the old authoritarianism under President Park Chung Hee (1961–1979) to new authoritarianism under President Chun Doo Hwan (1980–)?

The Collapse of the Yushin System

The collapse of the Yushin system occurred with the assassination of President Park Chung Hee by Kim Jae-kyu, director of the powerful

Korean Central Intelligence Agency (KCIA) and one of Park's close associates, on October 26, 1979.[6] Park's assassin, a retired three-star army general, was Park's classmate from the second graduating class of the Korean Military Academy in 1946, and one of his close confidants. Yet in 1979, Kim Jae-kyu harbored a secret plan of political reform and change, acting from within the ruling structure by virtue of his influential position as KCIA director. In the early days of October Kim was engulfed in a policy dispute with Park and especially with Park's bodyguard in the Blue House, Cha Ji-chol, who took a hawkish and uncompromising stance on suppressing the antigovernment mass demonstrations underway in the southern cities of Pusan and Masan.

The antigovernment demonstration of October 1979 took place—as already noted—as a result of public anger over President Park's suppression of opposition leader, Kim Young-sam. The citizens of Pusan waged a mass protest demonstration during the first week of October 1979. As the protest and discontent, which was also stimulated by economic difficulties in the summer of 1979, spread out of control, Park's government declared a state of martial law in the Pusan and Masan area, and Kim Jae-kyu as KCIA director was dispatched to assess the situation.

Whereas Cha Ji-chol, who had been a paratrooper and bodyguard of Brigadier General Park Chung Hee during the May 1961 coup, advised restoring law and order immediately by dispatching a paratrooper Special Forces unit to the scene if necessary, Kim Jae-kyu recommended a more conciliatory and moderate policy of government response to President Park. When Kim's position was overruled during their dinner meeting at a restaurant in the KCIA compound near the Blue House, Kim fired first at Cha and then at Park, killing both men at the scene. This occurred around 7:30 P.M. on October 26, 1979. Kim's KCIA men killed several other bodyguards outside of the restaurant.

Park's assassination was like a political bombshell or earthquake that shook the very foundation of South Korea's political structure. With his death the edifice of the Yushin system, imposed in 1972 to perpetuate Park's personal rule and carefully nurtured during his lifetime, crumbled and collapsed.[7] In retrospect this was inevitable, for Park had amassed almost all political power around himself and left no political successor. His power was sustained by several coercive institutions, such as the army and the security forces, including the Presidential Security Force, whose director, Cha Ji-chol, was also assassinated, and the KCIA, whose director was the assassin. This entangled and bloody assassination, carried out in palace-coup fashion, was a fatal blow to the Yushin system.

Other participants in the Yushin system who were also displaced eventually included the Yujonghoe members who had served in the National Assembly as appointed by President Park. Park's former associates and aides, who had previously made political and financial fortunes and still wielded considerable influence (ex–prime minister Kim Jong-pil, former presidential secretary Lee Hu-rak, ex–speaker of the National

Assembly Kim Jin-man, former chief of the Presidential Security Force Park Chong-kyu, and so on), also felt the demise of power.

An interim government was organized and led by Choy Kyu Ha, who had been prime minister under Park Chung Hee. Acting President Choy was elected president in his own right on December 6, 1979, by the rubber-stamp electoral college of the National Conference for Unification. Unfortunately, Choy had been a career civil servant during all of his political life, after briefly serving as a high school teacher after World War II, and he lacked political experience and leadership qualities. In a conciliatory move, Choy attempted to pacify the anti-Yushin opposition forces by abolishing the much-hated Emergency Decree No. 9. This was the notorious decree of May 13, 1975, which outlawed all forms of criticism against the Yushin constitution. However, concerning the adoption of a new constitution to accelerate the process of an orderly and smooth transition of power, Choy was indecisive, losing valuable time necessary for consolidating his power base and winning over the broad support of the democratic forces. Furthermore, Choy was unable to facilitate interparty dialogue and negotiations between the ruling Democratic Republican Party and the opposition New Democratic Party to pacify mounting student demands for a rapid democratic transition of power and allay the pressure coming from the military for maintaining law and order. This delay and hesitation cost Choy dearly by unleashing the widespread student demonstrations in May 1980, which in turn triggered a military takeover and the Kwangju uprising of May 18–26, 1980. Choy eventually yielded to the military pressure from the right, resigning the presidency on August 16, 1980.[8]

While the civilian politicians were busily jockeying for power in the process of drafting a new constitution, factionalism in the military emerged to influence the course of political development in South Korea. In the months after Park's assassination, South Korea's political atmosphere improved considerably with the abolishment of Emergency Decree No. 9, but South Korea was still under martial law, imposed after Park's death. The investigation of Park's assassination was conducted by the Defense Security Command unit of the Martial Law Command and headed by Major General Chun Doo Hwan, commander of this unit, an army intelligence force charged with preventing internal subversion in the army. This unit, in the course of its investigation, uncovered sufficient evidence to indicate the possible complicity of some senior army officers in a conspiracy to kill Park. As a result, on December 12, 1979, Major General Chun moved against his superiors, carrying out an act of insubordination by placing Martial Law Commander General Chung Seung-hwa (also chief of staff of the army) and his associates under arrest. This power play by Chun and his followers raised the ever-increasing fear of the disintegration of the military chain of command and the specter of political instability resulting from rampant military factionalism.

On the evening of Park's assassination, Army Chief of Staff General Chung was present at the private dinner party hosted by KCIA Director Kim Jae-kyu at a separate restaurant near the scene of the crime. After killing Park and his chief bodyguard, Kim Jae-kyu was in fact driven away in General Chung's limousine to the general's army headquarters. During that fateful encounter between the two, who were intimate friends, Kim Jae-kyu allegedly attempted without success to persuade General Chung to execute a coup to establish a new political order. What actually transpired in the mind of General Chung during those critical moments has not been fully revealed to the public in spite of the subsequent court-martial hearings held in closed session. What became clear, however, was that General Chung did not fully go along with Kim Jae-kyu's conspiracy plan. Instead, Chung was more concerned about the security threat from the north and the maintenance of law and order in his capacity as martial law commander.

The military's rise to power in 1979–1980 was engineered by the eleventh class of the Korean Military Academy, the graduates of 1955, led by Chun Doo Hwan among others. The army's methodical assumption of power was facilitated by the lack of party unity both within and between the ruling party and the opposition parties. South Korea's politics in the winter and spring of 1980 were volatile yet full of aspirations for democratic restoration. Dissident Kim Dae-jung, whose civil and political rights had been restored on February 29, 1980, was looked upon by many as one of the leaders to promote the cause of democracy in South Korea. But Kim Dae-jung was also engulfed in factional strife with the opposition NDP leader Kim Young-sam, whose challenge to the Yushin system in 1979 had precipitated the political crisis that eventually brought the system down. The ruling DRP was also engulfed in factional strife as former prime minister Kim Jong-pil, the new party leader, feuded with his time-honored rival Lee Hu-rak for party hegemony.[9]

Meanwhile, the worsening inflation and recession in 1980, precipitated by the OPEC oil price hike in 1979, was undermining the livelihood of many citizens and wage earners. Sluggishness in the export market abroad led to numerous bankruptcies, including that of Yulsan, a major trading company; social discontent and labor disputes resulted in a miners' riot in Sabuk, Kangwon Province, in April 1980. The climate for military intervention was ripe.

The Birth of a New Political Order

The military moved to consolidate its power by putting a series of measures into effect. On April 14, 1980, General Chun Doo Hwan, who already headed the powerful Defense Security Command, was also made acting director of the KCIA, now renamed the Agency for National Security Planning. This prompted a student demonstration demanding the immediate lifting of martial law and the removal of the "remnants of the Yushin system," including General Chun. Throughout the spring of 1980, escalating campus sit-ins and demonstrations continued, with students demanding the institution of measures of educational reform and democracy on campus and pressing for a speedy restoration of democracy in South Korea. On May 17, 1980, the military reacted by suppressing the student demonstrations.

The military also used the pretext of eliminating political corruption and restoring law and order as an excuse for carrying out a coup against the Choy government that same day. The leaders of the coup—Chun Doo Hwan and his associates, mostly colleagues from the Korean Military Academy—forced President Choy Kyu Ha to proclaim nationwide martial law for the explicit purpose of curbing the escalating student demonstrations.

The classic confrontation between student activists and the government in power thus gave the military its excuse for taking action to usurp political power. As previously described, a similar student-led mass movement in 1960 (protesting the rigging of elections by the officials of President Rhee's government) led to the April 19, 1960, revolution that toppled the First Republic.[10] This was not to be a repetition of that historical confrontation between students and the military, however. Whereas in 1960 the Student Revolution had succeeded in overthrowing the First Republic, thereby facilitating the birth of the democratic political order of the Second Republic, the student protest movement of 1980 precipitated the authoritarian political order of the Fifth Republic. The Second Republic was overthrown by the May 16, 1961, "bloodless" military coup, led by then Brigadier General Park Chung Hee, which, after eighteen months of rule by the military, resulted in the founding of the Third Republic. The interim government of President Choy in 1980 failed to evolve into a democratic system like that of Ho Chong in 1960. Military intervention and usurpation of power destroyed the promise of democratic restoration in 1980.

The new Martial Law Decree No. 10—proclaimed, ironically, on May 17, 1980, one day after the nineteenth anniversary of the 1961 coup—closed down the universities, prohibited demonstrations both indoors and out, imposed prior censorship of the press, outlawed criticism of the incumbent and past presidents, and prohibited the manufacture and spreading of rumors. Chun and his fellow coup leaders went on to arrest the opposition leaders, including dissident Kim Dae-jung and NDP President Kim Young-sam, as well as the Yushin leaders, including former prime minister and DRP president Kim Jong-pil, Lee Hu-rak, and Park Chong-kyu, who had been closely associated with the slain president.[11] The arrest of Kim Dae-jung led to a nationwide protest by Kim's followers and to the bloody riots of Kwangju, the provincial capital of South Cholla, Kim's home province. The former Yushin politicians were subsequently released in exchange for their admission of corruption, for "volunteering" to donate all of their property to the state, and for pledging to retire from public life. However, dissident Kim Dae-jung was court-martialed on the charge of inciting riots and sedition and given the death sentence, later commuted to life in January 1981 and to twenty years on March 1, 1982.[12]

The Kwangju riot started as a campus demonstration by students of Chonnam National University and was later joined by the Kwangju citizens. As the martial law order barring mass demonstrations was challenged, and as the police were unable to control the crowd, troops near Kwangju were dispatched to maintain law and order. In the ensuing clash between the soldiers and the demonstrators, however, the troops used excessive and brutal force, which was said to have been deliberately provoked by some militant student leaders to incite a riot. Seeing the brutality the Kwangju citizenry was angered, and their sympathies turned toward the demonstrators. As the situation became uncontrollable, the military forces were temporarily withdrawn from the city and the rioters were left in control of the city. Some rioters also raided nearby installations where military vehicles and equipment were stored.

In the next nine days, between May 18 and May 27, the Kwangju riot turned into a major insurrection, spreading widely to other areas in South Cholla Province and becoming a serious threat to the central government's ability to govern. Eventually, a paratrooper unit was dispatched into the city to recapture key downtown installations from the hands of rebels. In the process, hundreds of civilians and rebel students were killed. Although the official account placed the estimated casualties at around 183 dead and several hundred wounded, according to eyewitness accounts the actual figures were considerably higher (some accounts were higher by over 2000 dead and wounded).

Once the immediate situation of political crisis due to the student demonstrations and Kwangju riots was under control, the military moved to put its own prearranged plan to consolidate power within the government into effect. On May 31 the Special Committee for National Security Measures was established, ostensibly to assist "the President in directing and supervising Martial Law affairs" and to "examine national policies." The 25-member committee was headed by President Choy himself and included some of his cabinet members as well as chiefs of the military services and other military officers. This was, however, the supreme body in name only. The real power was vested in the 31-member Military Civilian Standing Committee headed by General Chun, which included 18 field-level officers on active duty and 12 high-level government officials. The 4 members of the Special Committee who also served in the Standing Committee constituted the core of the military power group. These were General Chun Doo Hwan himself, General Ro Tae-wu (commander of the Metropolitan Security Command), General Chung Ho-yung (Commander of the Special Forces), and General Ch'a Kyu-ho (deputy chief of staff of the army).[13]

This junta-like Standing Committee now operated through its thirteen separate subcommittees to make all decisions affecting the state. It exercised authority and enacted new laws until the new National Assembly came into being after the passage of the new constitution. It initiated a purification campaign in which some 8,000 government officials and some 840 politicians were purged and barred from engaging in political activities for the following eight years. The Special and Standing committees lasted only until October 22, 1980, however, at which time the committees were reconstituted as the new 81-member Legislative Council for National Security. Council members were appointed from among former committee members and also from the outside, and included former NDP leaders, academics, lawyers, and leaders of social organizations. The council acted as an interim legislature, enacting laws until April 1981, when the new National Assembly was constituted following the March 1981 general election.

While this restructuring of governmental bodies was taking place, Chun Doo Hwan was busy establishing his position of power. Before resigning as acting director of the KCIA on June 2, 1980, General Chun worked to restructure the agency. On August 5, he promoted himself from three-star to four-star general. Upon the resignation of President Choy on August 16, 1980, Prime Minister Pak Ch'ung-hoon was elevated to serve as acting president. General Chun resigned from the army on August 22, and on August 30, 1980, Chun Doo Hwan was elected president by the rubber-stamp electoral college created by Park Chung Hee, the National Conference for Unification. As the only candidate, Chun Doo Hwan received 2,524 of the total of 2,525 votes, with 1 vote declared invalid. He assumed the Presidency on September 1, 1980.

During his inaugural address, Chun pledged to work toward building what he called "a new society where all the corrupt practices of the past would be replaced by justice and mutual trust." For this purpose he pledged that he would remove "old politicians" from the political scene and establish a tradition of peaceful transfer of power, "by reforming the political culture in Korea so that democracy would take root." He also pledged that a new constitution would be drafted soon and adopted by national referendum.[14]

The new constitution, drafted by a government-appointed committee, was announced on September 29, 1980, and subsequently approved by plebiscite, winning 91.6 percent of the votes cast in a national referendum held on October 22, 1980. With the general election for a National Assembly held on March 25, 1981, the process of founding the new political order of the Fifth Republic was completed.

The Nature of the Political Regime

Who governs and who benefits in the Fifth Republic of Korea? What is the pattern of ruling coalition and opposition forces? What specific policies and programs have been put into effect by the government? These are essential questions in determining the character of the political regime that emerged in South Korea in the early 1980s. If one agrees with Guillermo O'Donnell that three basic patterns and types of political rule emerge from the mix of regime, coalition, and policy: i.e., oligarchy, populism, and bureaucratic authoritarianism, the Fifth Republic in South Korea at the outset of the 1980s would fall somewhere between the oligarchic and bureaucratic authoritarian types of political order.[15]

The Fifth Republic of South Korea originally began as a military or predominantly military regime. The military under strongman Chun Doo Hwan controlled and dominated the state institution in the postassassination period from October 1979 to March 1981. The populist impulse and current was present in the Korean political scene, but military factionalism prevailed in the volatile political situation of the winter and spring of 1980. The government used the populist measure of conducting a plebiscite to approve the constitution of the Fifth Republic by national referendum on October 22, 1980. This procedure was largely ritualistic and ceremonial, however, intended to project legitimacy with little substantial meaning. The writing of the constitution itself, for instance, was undertaken by a government appointed–group with no popular participation. The constitutional referendum took place, moreover, under the conditions of national emergency and extended martial law proclaimed on May 17, 1980.[16] The junta-like Special Committee for National Security Measures and the 31-member Military Civilian Standing Committee, led by Chun Doo Hwan, acted as the ultimate decisionmaking bodies for the entire state. Even the 81-member Legislative Council on National Security was appointed by President Chun Doo Hwan rather than elected by the people. As an interim legislative body this council enacted various important bills that were neither "democratic" nor "populist," in substance or in the style of lawmaking employed.

The state as an institution may be defined as an instrument of political rule by a specific class or group in society.[17] In the Fifth Republic of South Korea in 1979–1980, the military clearly controlled and dominated this state apparatus. Because the ruling military faction led by General Chun Doo Hwan attempted to exclude previously active popular sectors, including political parties—both the ruling DRP and the opposition NDP—and student groups, the political regime initially was a military oligarchy or dictatorship.[18] However, with the passage of time, the ruling group attempted to expand its base of political support by activating the popular sector and allowing participation by other political groups. The character of the political regime of the Fifth Republic, therefore, became more inclusive than exclusive and more or less authoritarian in orientation, rather than remaining a military oligarchy as such. To the extent that the military still remained the dominant institution in politics, however, the Fifth Republic of Korea was clearly an authoritarian state rather than a democratic, populist state.

From a historical and developmental perspective, the Fifth Republic is clearly a "successor regime" to the Yushin system it replaced. Because of bad connotations associated with the old regime, however, the incumbent leadership of the Fifth Republic clearly disavowed identification with the Yushin system. In spite of its denials, however, the circumstances and character of the founding of the Fifth Republic resembled that of the Third Republic. The jailing and purging of ex-leaders of the Yushin system, such as Kim Jong-pil and Lee Hu-rak, and the banning of political activities by opposition NDP leaders such as Kim Young-sam were not sufficient to eradicate the old impressions of the remnants of the Yushin political regime. After all, the incumbent leader of the Fifth Republic, President Chun Doo Hwan, was a protégé of slain president Park Chung Hee, and it was through his investigation of Park's assassination that General Chun claimed legitimacy for his coup of December 12, 1979.

What makes the Third, Fourth, and Fifth Republics remarkably similar, in terms of leadership composition and character, is the basically authoritarian orientation of these political regimes. Whereas autocracy and tyranny describe the nature of a single ruler wielding absolute power unrestrained by law, authoritarianism as it prevailed in South Korea was collective rule, characterized by a political regime dominated by the military as an institution.[19] Whereas Syngman Rhee of the First Republic was a kind of autocrat, Park Chung Hee and Chun Doo Hwan were closer to the leadership role evident in the politics of an authoritarian system. Park and Chun have ruled modern Korea through the use of coercive instruments and by monopolizing the state apparatus. One notable distinction between Chun Doo Hwan and Park Chung Hee is the more positive role assigned by President Chun to political parties—at least in terms of professed policy. Also, whereas Park's Third Republic changed from the democratic and constitutional polity of the 1960s to the authoritarian polity of the 1970s, Chun's Fifth Republic may or may not evolve from the authoritarian polity of 1983 to a more democratic polity and populist regime in the years ahead. Whether Chun's public pledge and rhetoric is realized in a long-awaited turn toward democracy remains to be seen.

The Ruling Coalition

What sustains the political regime in an authoritarian system is the strength and character of the ruling coalition. In Chun Doo Hwan's South Korea, the military provides the backbone of the ruling structure. Power in the Fifth Republic, as at the time of Park Chung Hee's Yushin Korea, rests in the hands of the three strategically important institutional positions in the army: (1) the Defense Security Command, (2) the Metropolitan Defense Command, and (3) the Command of the Special Forces. In 1979, at the time of Park's assassination, the Defense Security Command was led by Major General Chun Doo Hwan, who had been personally chosen by the slain president. In view of the strategic importance of these positions of power, one can readily understand why the responsibility for commanding these army units was given to trusted classmates of Chun Doo Hwan soon after the palace coup of December 12, 1979. General Ro Tae-wu and General Chung Ho-yung, Chun's classmates of the 11th class of the Korean Military Academy, were appointed respectively as commander of the Metropolitan Defense Command and commander of the Special Forces.

The commanders of these three important army units, however, were replaced in 1982 by followers of President Chun Doo Hwan from the 12th and 13th classes of the Korean Military Academy. Chun and his followers felt that as president, Chun had to be more than first among equals and that he should not cultivate political rivals and challengers from among his classmates. Chun's dilemma was that without active support by officers of these senior classes, all of whom proudly maintained a high esprit de corps as graduates of the four-year regularized training of the military academy, President Chun's position of power would probably not remain secure for long. It was natural that President Chun preferred to cultivate his power base among the much younger military officer classes, lower than the 15th or 16th classes, for the simple reason that they would pose less of a challenge to his authority than officers of senior classes. Until he was successful in this project of cultivating personal loyalty and a following, however, President Chun had to cope with the difficult problem of both pacifying and courting the active support of the graduates from the senior classes of the military academy.*

The maneuvers taking place in the military hierarchy in 1982 suggested that the factional lineup within the army was about to change from the pattern that prevailed immediately after the December 1979 coup—an ongoing confrontation between the military academy graduates and the non–military academy officers who had become senior generals. The factional makeup within the army in 1982 was divided into the "main current" and the "non–main current." Whereas the main current consisted of the followers of President Chun, the non–main current was made up largely of advocates of military professionalism and military noninvolvement in politics. They favored returning to the army barracks rather than remaining in the political arena after the coup. This position was allegedly shared by two of Chun's close classmates, General Ro Tae-wu and General Kim Bok-dong. When the former was retired in late 1981, the latter followed suit, retiring on January 15, 1982. Until his retirement, General Kim was superintendent of the Korean Military Academy and was reportedly popular among the cadets for his forthright stand.[20]

A 1981 episode involving former Major General Park Se-jik illustrated the intricacy of military factionalism and the potentially serious nature

---

*At the time of this writing in 1983, the mainstay of influence on President Chun Doo Hwan had shifted from the 17th graduating class of the Korean Military Academy to the 12th and 16th graduating classes. The 1982 replacement of Chun's chief aides in the Blue House, Ho Sam-su and Ho Hwa-pyong (both in the 17th class), is often cited as evidence of this shift in power balance among the military.

of staff appointment in the military. General Park, a bright and promising member of the 12th class of the military academy, was relieved of his post in the Metropolitan Defense Command in August 1981 on allegations of impropriety and influence peddling. Park was, however, subsequently appointed as advisor to the Ministry of Energy. Although his position was admittedly inconspicuous, this action was apparently a conciliatory move on the part of President Chun to pacify Park's classmates. Once Park Se-jik, the leader of the 12th class graduates, was removed, President Chun might have felt secure enough, but he also felt it necessary to win the confidence of the remaining classmates of Park. This episode underscored the dilemma of President Chun, and his actions also indicated that the initial charges against General Park in August 1981 were either false or exaggerated.[21]

A serious test and potential threat to Chun Doo Hwan's control of the military took place in November-December 1982, in connection with the rumor of an abortive coup. The story came out with the unexpected resignation of two of President Chun's most influential and closest aides, Ho Hwa-pyong and Ho Sam-su, in December 1982. Both aides, as graduates of the 17th class of the Korean Military Academy, had served in General Chun's army security command as colonels at the time of the 1980 coup, and they represented a hard-line policy in the government. They were implicated in the execution of three-star general Paik Ung-taik, commander of the Second Army Command stationed in Taegu, who was allegedly plotting a coup. Paik was reportedly shot to death during his trip to Seoul in November 1982. According to one unconfirmed report, he was executed on the spot when his coup plans were revealed, and the two aides responsible for Paik's death had to resign in order to restore confidence in Chun among the military.[22] This episode raised the spectre of an ongoing power struggle in the military through similar coup attempts in the future.

Apart from the military, the ruling Democratic Justice Party (DJP) constitutes another member of the ruling coalition, albeit a junior partner. Although the DJP could develop into a major instrument of political rule, so far it has been a secondary actor in the political process of the Fifth Republic. The founding of the DJP as a governing party on January 15, 1981, was preceded by a meeting on November 28, 1980, of 15 charter members and by a general meeting of 105 founding party members on December 2, 1980.[23] The Democratic Justice Party's purpose, as announced on November 28, 1980, was "to lead the way in advancing national goals in the new era, including a democratic and just welfare society and the peaceful unification of the homeland." This founding statement was subsequently incorporated into the party platform, and the party's basic five ideas—national integrity, democracy, justice, welfare, and national unification—were also reflected in the party flag.[24]

President Chun Doo Hwan of the Fifth Republic wished to see the DJP develop into a major instrument of his political rule. He was elected president of the Fifth Republic in his capacity as head of the party, making him South Korea's twelfth president. The DJP also won 151 of the 276 National Assembly seats in the general election held on March 25, 1981. Of the 151 DJP members, 61 were chosen as delegates at large in accordance with the system of proportional representation. In January 1982, one year after the founding of the party, the DJP claimed a membership of 170,000, all of whom had gone through party training programs of one kind or another. A membership of a million and a half was stated as the ultimate goal of the party.[25] The building of a mass-based party was also stated as a party objective that would allegedly make possible successful negotiations with North Korea's KWP on the reunification issue.

In reviewing one year's accomplishments in January 1982, the DJP boasted that it had been instrumental in causing the government to simplify and improve "a total of 256 laws and decrees and 409 administrative forms." The enactment of the Public Servants' Ethics law, made possible because of the party's initiative, the DJP spokesman claimed, would allegedly keep lawmakers and ranking government officials from involvement in taking bribes and in other forms of corruption. The party also prided itself on having revised the contents of the Fifth Five-Year Economic and Social Development Plan and the formula of the government budget for 1982, by paying greater attention to the social development and welfare aspects of the five-year plan.[26]

Other groups in the Fifth Republic that are politically relevant—although less powerful than the military as members of the ruling coalition—include key members of big business, higher civil servants and members of the government bureaucracy, and those intellectuals and trained specialists who might broadly be called technocrats. Although the service and loyalty of these groups are essential, they clearly have been junior partners, subservient to the command of the dominant military group. Whether members of all of these functional groups will become full partners in the ruling coalition of the Fifth Republic under President Chun, as they were under Park's Yushin system, remains to be seen. Considerable time will elapse before the core groups and dominant members of the ruling coalition can be merged and integrated into a single coherent political force. If this development occurs, a bureaucratic authoritarian political structure might eventually evolve in South Korea, sustained by an alliance of the civilianized military, big business and industry, and technocrats in and out of government service.[27] Already by 1983, the technocrat component of the ruling structure of the Fifth Republic had become entrenched. The list of President Chun's cabinet members and aides, including those killed in the October 9, 1983, Rangoon bomb blast and those who replaced them on October 14, is a testimony to this accomplishment under President Chun's rule.

The Opposition Forces

At the opposite end of the political spectrum from the ruling coalition are the opposition party members in the National Assembly and the purged politicians of the earlier period. As members of the counterelite, opposition groups provide an alternative channel for political rule if and when the Chun regime might somehow fail to govern. The opposition parties in the Fifth Republic have been quite different from those of previous years in their composition and character.[28] Instead of there being a single opposition party, as was the rule in the Third and Fourth Republics, several minority parties have been allowed to compete in the Fifth Republic. A multiparty system has in fact been encouraged in place of a single- or two-party system. Political opposition in the assembly allegedly practiced the "politics of confrontation" in the old days. In the Fifth Republic, a new style was to be instituted in the form of the "politics of dialogue" and negotiation.

President Chun Doo Hwan has reportedly warned that "the National Assembly should not be a replica of the old one in which the members . . . with the next elections in mind . . . made political remarks to gain popularity."[29] In spite of this warning, however, Chun as politician could not overlook the reality of electoral politics and party strength as reflected in the National Assembly allocation of seats. Through a clever manipulation of the electoral laws, in 1981 Chun's ruling DJP came to command an absolute majority of 151 out of the assembly's total of 276 seats (184 elected and 92 at large). The way in which this seat allocation was made, in accordance with the political party law enacted by the legislative council in 1980, indicates the somewhat arbitrary nature of political decisions in the Fifth Republic. For instance, in the March 25, 1981, general election, the ruling DJP was successful in winning 90 out of 92 electoral district seats. By virtue of their winning the largest number of district seats, an extra 61 out of the additional 92 seats at large were allotted to the ruling party under the proportional representational system. (Electoral districts in Korea are plural-, not single-, member districts and 92 districts have 2 members each. In addition there are 92 at-large members elected on proportional representation, bringing the total to 276 seats in the National Assembly.) This meant that although the DJP received only 35 percent of some 16 million votes cast nationwide, the electoral law enabled the DJP to control 55 percent of the seats. This also meant that some 65 percent of the voters had supported opposition candidates even though the opposition forces were admittedly fragmented and split.

Of all the opposition parties represented in the National Assembly, only two emerged in 1981 as major parties by capturing a respectable number of parliamentary seats. The first was the Democratic Korea Party (DKP) which received 81 seats (57 elected and 24 at large) in the 276-seat National Assembly; the second major opposition party was the Korea

National Party (KNP) with 36 seats in the assembly (29 elected and 7 at large). In the March 1981 National Assembly election twelve political parties had competed, but only five minor parties, in addition to the two already mentioned, were successful in the election. Together these five parties captured 18.8 percent of the total votes, although their combined strength in the National Assembly amounted to a total of only 8 seats.[30] Because of poor representation in the National Assembly, the prospect for these minor parties of the Fifth Republic becoming major parties was dim unless, of course, the electoral law was amended to make representation more equitable.

The opposition forces in the Fifth Republic lacked strong leadership. With the jailing of opposition leader Kim Dae-jung, and the banning of other former leaders such as Lee Hu-rak, the Chun Doo Hwan government endeavored to clear the way for a new breed of political opposition more amenable to and cooperative with the ruling group. The politicians who were banned from politics would, however, either emerge to form a counterelite to President Chun's ruling coalition or turn into antisystem dissidents, eventually undermining political stability in the Fifth Republic. There was a demand that President Chun do something about removing the ban on political activities by the "old politicians." He was much criticized for inaction on the issue of restoring the political rights of these purged politicians of the preceding era.

An alliance of disaffected groups with the counterelite might produce a successful formula for the overthrow of the Fifth Republic. After all, it was the alliance of 6 million Christians and student activists waging violent street demonstrations in 1979 that had challenged Park's Yushin system and led to Park's eventual downfall after eighteen years in power. This was why an alliance between students and labor or between labor and the Christian groups was very much feared by the Chun government, which also worried about labor unrest and the possible explosion of regional grievances into riots such as the Kwangju uprising of May 1980.

Student activism did not abate but briefly resurged in the fall of 1981. Because of the government's strong-arm tactics, student demonstrations were largely confined to campuses rather than spilling over into the streets. The on-campus disturbances became radical in late 1981, challenging the political legitimacy of President Chun's rule and condemning him as a "fascist dictator." During September and October 1981, some fifteen instances of university student disturbances and demonstrations reportedly took place, involving more than a dozen separate schools in Seoul and other regions. The number of students involved in these demonstrations ranged from 50–100 to as many as 2,500 students.[31]

Several activist students involved in one of these protests set fire to the United States Cultural Center in Pusan in March 1982. The arsonists poured a can of gasoline in the library wing of the building and set fire to it; two students using the facility were burnt to death. The shock of the arson attack drew attention to the radical turn of the antigovernment movement, and strategies became a matter of serious concern to the policymakers. The anti–Chun Doo Hwan movement had found a new pretext for waging an anti-American campaign, U.S. support of Chun's policy of repression. Although the arsonists were subsequently apprehended, the fact that Catholic priests had protected the suspects after the burning of the cultural center indicated the potentially serious nature of the controversy and the possible joining of anti-Americanism and the antigovernment movement. In the subsequent trial the two student leaders were sentenced to death, but their sentences were commuted to life by presidential pardon on March 1, 1983. On September 22, 1983, another U.S. cultural center was burned, in Taegu, the third largest city, taking the life of one student and injuring five others. The second bombing was believed to have been the work of North Korea's saboteurs sent to the south.

The new labor law passed by the Legislative Council on National Security in 1980 prohibited Protestant missionaries from working for the welfare of industrial workers. The Urban Industrial Mission carried out by the Protestant churches to enhance the status of textile workers and female wage earners had led to clashes between the church workers and the Park government in the preceding years. The Chun government was determined to put into effect as of January 1, 1981, a new labor law, called the Labor-Employer Council Law. It also drastically modified and revised the four other existing labor laws: the Labor Standard Law, the Labor Union Law, the Labor Dispute Settlement Law, and the Labor Committee Law.[32]

Under the new labor legislation, the conduct of labor-employer relations became the responsibility of the Labor-Employer Council, instead of using the labor union mechanism of the old system. The Federation of Korean Labor Unions and Industrial Labor Unions now became ineffective. The professed purpose of the Labor-Employer Council was to improve productivity, promote the welfare of the workers, carry out the education and training of workers, prevent labor disputes, and handle the workers' grievances. The underlying purpose of this legislation, however, was to exclude outsiders or third parties from labor disputes and bargaining, so that only the government would take part in settling labor disputes between workers and their employers.[33]

The adoption of this law changed the character of the labor union system in South Korea from an industrial labor union system to a business enterprise labor union system. The Chun government intended for this measure to weaken the power of labor unions and the labor movement, cutting off the unions from solidarity with outside supporting forces. The law was also intended to strengthen the position of business groups and the power of a government agency to influence the labor movement.[34]

Many intellectuals continued to criticize the Fifth Republic's repressive character and policies, although they were deprived of the opportunity to freely express their opposition. The suppressed intellectuals in the Fifth Republic included many college professors, journalists, civic leaders, and Protestant and Catholic church leaders. Some 800 Presbyterian ministers, for instance, met on October 25, 1981, and resolved to hold prayer meetings as they sought the release of about 168 students and the reinstatement of 83 professors who had been ousted from their jobs for political reasons.[35] They also demanded that the National Assembly revise the new labor law to lift the ban on Protestant missionaries working for better treatment for factory wage earners. Some 19 dissenters, including a young editor with a publishing firm, were charged in late 1981 by the police with plotting to infiltrate trade unions, allegedly to cause labor disruption and foment a student-led revolution to topple the government and to set up a communist regime in South Korea.[36] The 3 students who had turned themselves in for setting the U.S. Cultural Center in Pusan on fire were subsequently tried in open court. Two of these students were sentenced to death by the Pusan court on August 11, 1982, on the charge of violating the National Security Law. Their terms were subsequently commuted to life imprisonment by a special act of presidential amnesty, as previously noted, and this was largely in response to mounting pressure both within and outside of Korea.

The Son Also Rises: The North

North Korea's political development in 1980 was not as dramatic or disruptive as that of South Korea. The Sixth KWP Congress in October 1980, however, was significant because policy decisions arrived at during the congress would have some far-reaching effects and implications for Korea's political future throughout the remainder of the 1980s. By 1982 North Korea's president, Kim Il Sung, who had ruled communist Korea since 1945, had become one of the longest-tenured communist leaders, surpassed only by Albania's Enver Hoxha. Under his rule North Korea has been transformed into a fiercely proud socialist country, pursuing the policy line of Juche (translated as "independence" or "autonomy"). The considerable material gains and achievements of socialist Korea under the KWP policy line of "constructing socialism in the northern half of the republic," has been impressive. This is especially notable when the wholesale devastation and destruction left by the Korean War is taken into account.

In contrast with the progress in material construction and the building of socialism, the political practices and preachings of the DPRK have remained an enigma to outside observers. North Korean politics has centered around the personality cult of its supreme leader, Kim Il Sung, who has been exulted and praised as a hero and worshipped as a demigod. Kim's grasp of power has been absolute. Ironically, in spite of the rather archaic practice of hero worship that a personality cult entails, Kim Il Sung has preached and taught the mass-line principle in politics.[37]

The personality cult and adulation of a leader is a widespread practice in many socialist countries: Stalin's Russia and Mao's China are obvious examples. In fact, North Korea shares the tendency for a personality cult extended over generations with the European communist countries of Rumania and Bulgaria. What is rather unusual in North Korea, however, is the attempt to institutionalize a father-son hereditary succession. This resembles the practice of Kuomintang Taiwan. In order to cope with the thorny issue of political succession, Kim Il Sung has designated his eldest son, Jong Il, as his heir. Kim junior will thus continue the unfinished task of "socialist revolution and construction" beyond the lifetime of his father.

Like his father, Kim junior has been praised in the north as "the hero of the DPRK," "the great instructor comrade," and "beloved leader." If the effort to build up a personality cult around Kim Jong Il and establish Kim Il Sung's own son as his political heir is successful—a practice reminiscent of the feudalistic hereditary system of bygone eras—North Korea would be the first communist dynastic state in history.[38] The two central issues of North Korea's communist politics in the early 1980s are to explain (1) the longevity of Kim Il Sung as the communist leader and also (2) the emergence of the seemingly archaic system of father-son leadership. The issues of personality cult and political succession are therefore closely intertwined in North Korea.

The Cult of Personality and Hereditary Succession

"The Land of Kim Il Sung" is a highly organized and efficient system, perhaps more regimented and controlled than any other communist system in history. What has held it together up to now is the popular loyalty and trust preached, demanded, and, it seems, enjoyed by the KWP and its "Great Leader Comrade," Kim Il Sung. "No other communist party in the world appears to have cultivated as strong a faith in its leadership," according to Chong-Sik Lee. "Unlike the CCP [Chinese Communist Party] or the CPSU [Communist Party of the Soviet Union], the KWP does not permit self-doubt, self-ridicule, cynicism, or mild dissension, even in a humorous vein. President Kim's words must be followed in relentless and dead seriousness."[39] Moreover, "a body of hagiology has been created around the leader and his family to command the present and to define the future."[40]

In 1982, at the age of seventy, Kim Il Sung joined the ranks of the aging leaders of the Communist bloc countries, side by side with President Leonid Brezhnev of the Soviet Union and Vice-chairman Deng Xiaoping of the People's Republic of China. Septuagenarian leaders are by no means confined to communist countries. President Ronald Reagan is one example, and President Syngman Rhee of South Korea's First Republic was eighty-two in 1960 when he stepped down after twelve years in office. But communist leaders once in power are difficult to remove, and many of them retain lifetime positions, such as Ho Chi Minh in Vietnam and Mao Zedong in China. Moreover, the rule of septuagenarian leaders tends in communist systems to inspire a series of political maneuvers, policy adjustments, and potential succession struggles. In the 1980s, North Korea therefore faces the challenge of assuring an orderly and smooth transition of political power beyond the Kim Il Sung era.

Although apparently in good physical health, Kim Il Sung's advancing age has become a matter of great concern to him and to his associates. Under the pretext of assuring the continuation of the revolutionary task, "generation after generation," the North Korean elite has adopted an ingenious method for assuring the orderly transition of political power. The Sixth Congress of the KWP elected Kim Jong Il—then thirty-nine years old—as a ranking member of the newly established five-member Presidium of the Politburo during its October 1980 session. He was also elected at that time to join the party's five-member Military Commission as the third-ranking member, next to his father and his father's seventy-one-year-old defense minister, General O Jin-u. In the early summer of 1981, Kim Jong Il was made the second-ranking member of the presidium, with his father as first-ranking member.

The elevation of Kim's son to a position of leadership in North Korea was a carefully planned and executed act, prepared long before its official announcement in 1980. In pursuing this path the North Korean elite was undoubtedly motivated by the failure of smooth political transition in the Soviet Union after Stalin's death in the 1950s and in the PRC after Mao's death in the late 1970s. North Korea was determined not to repeat the errors made by other socialist countries in solving the question of political succession. Yet why did the North Korean elite choose the particular method of father-son succession? Does this unusual method have a realistic possibility of being implemented in North Korea when Kim Il Sung dies? An answer to these questions necessitates an analysis of the preparatory work executed prior to the 1980 announcement of Kim Jong Il as designated heir.

The plan for father-son succession in North Korea had been in progress for a long time, possibly since 1973.[41] In October 1980, Kim junior was already in firm control of party affairs. As director of the Organization and Guidance Department of the KWP since around 1974, he ranked second in the ten-member secretariat, next to his father, as general secretary. Moreover, Kim Jong Il was involved extensively in recruiting followers from the new generation, especially the young intellectuals, party cadres, and government functionaries of his age group. Kim Jong Il was credited with organizing and launching the Three Revolutions Teams (TRT) movement in 1973. Members of the TRT, which consisted of twenty or thirty young party cadres, technicians, and intellectuals, were dispatched to cooperative farms and factories to carry out revolutionary works like the "speedy campaigns" for implementing the six-year economic plan.

To keep the preparatory work for political succession confidential, however, the name of Kim Jong Il was not mentioned openly in party publications before October 1980. Instead, a code word for Kim Jong Il, "the Party Center," was employed.[42] The preparation for smooth leadership succession took at least three directions. First, Kim junior was given an important position in the KWP bureaucracy. As the second-ranking member of the secretariat, Kim Jong Il served as a kind of chief of staff in the party, while his father, the general secretary, was the elder statesman. Second, after 1973 Kim junior was given the task of mobilizing the masses through the TRT movement. Kim Jong Il's base of political support was broadened as team members became "the vanguard" of the revolution. Between 1970 and 1980, KWP membership increased from approximately 2 million to 3 million, with most of the recruits coming from the younger age group.

Most important was Kim junior's position as the third-ranking member of the KWP Military Commission. This military position and its support was considered essential for Kim Jong Il's rise to power and ability to stay in power. Of the 34 members of the politburo, at least 11 were serving as generals or had a military background, and at least 20 percent of the 248-member (145 full and 103 alternate) Central Committee were military officers at the time of the Sixth KWP Congress in October 1980. The only other leadership positions that Kim junior required for absolute control of North Korea were in the Supreme People's Assembly, to which he was elected as a deputy in February 1982, and the Central People's Committee, the highest state organ.

Legitimizing the Succession

The charisma of President Kim Il Sung was used to justify the legitimacy of Kim Jong Il as successor to his father. In view of the loyalty and affection that Kim Il Sung apparently commanded in North Korea, the communist leadership planned to allow Kim junior a period of political apprenticeship and learning under the tender care of his father. This political tutorial was undoubtedly intended to assure stability and to prevent any possible breakdown of law and order in socialist Korea after the death of Kim Il Sung.

Whether the emergence of Kim Jong Il will mean continued stability or potential instability in the politics of North Korea in the 1980s is not clear at the time of this writing in 1983. A widespread campaign in North Korea continues to glorify the immortality of the "revolutionary family" of Kim Il Sung, and to praise the "genius" and "artistic talents" as well as the "absolute loyalty" of Kim junior. On the occasion of the seventieth birthday of his father on April 15, 1982, Kim junior was awarded the title, "Hero of the DPRK." The North Koreans believe the succession of Kim Jong Il after the passing of his father will be a natural and easy transition. As with any well-laid plan, however, unforeseen circumstances may cause the whole edifice to crumble. Much will depend, of course, on how well the present North Korean leadership handles pressing issues of domestic and foreign policy during the remaining years of Kim Il Sung's reign.

Whether Kim Jong Il will be as efficient and successful as his father in institutionalizing the KWP's rule and in commanding the trust and loyalty of the populace remains to be seen. His youthful age—forty-two years old in 1983—is an asset and so is his extensive experience of holding posts with major responsibilities for policy and administration. At the same time, Kim Jong Il is much younger than many potential rivals to power, the veterans of earlier struggles for independence and prosperity in North Korea.

Members of the North Korean elite are confident that they have resolved the coming succession crisis, unlike other communist states such as the Soviet Union and the PRC. North Korea's political arrangement of father-son succession, however, demonstrates that succession is an open and potential thorny issue. The very fact that President Kim found it necessary to appoint his own son as a successor is an admission of the failure of his earlier plans. The "immortality" of Kim Il Sung and his "revolutionary family" is a reflection of the weakness, not the strength, of the grand design for institutionalizing Kim Il Sung's political legitimacy.

On the occasion of announcing the choice of Kim Jong Il as Kim Il Sung's successor, the KWP spokesman presented a set of formal explanations that have been adhered to since then.[43] First, the revolutionary cause of the Great Leader could not be completed in a single generation. "It is the historical task that can be completed only through the efforts of succeeding generations." Second, the successor to the leader had to emerge from the new generation, not from the present generation. Third, it was deemed necessary for a successor to the Great Leader to go through a preparatory period of learning and absorbing from the leader the thought, theory, and art of leadership. Fourth, the successor should be a man who was boundlessly loyal to the leader and who embodied the leader's ideology and leadership qualities.[44]

Applying the preceding specifications for the successor to the choice of Kim Jong Il was an easy and self-evident process. It was claimed that only one person in North Korea could meet all of these criteria. This was, needless to say, none other than the Great Leader's eldest son, Kim junior! Kim Jong Il's loyalty to the Great Leader was and still is beyond question. Kim junior was said not only to have "embodied" (*ch'ehyon*) all the lofty virtues and leadership abilities of his father but—more importantly—to have also personally "formalized" (*chongsik-hwa*) the idea of the Great Leader into "Kimilsungism."[45] Moreover, Kim Jong Il was said to be a genius with artistic talents and with an impressive record of achievements in the cultural, theoretical, and political fields.

In order to promote the myth of Kim Jong Il's extraordinary virtue and talents, North Korean propaganda tracts began to cover a large number of episodes and examples of Kim's alleged accomplishments. Most of these statements are presented as personal anecdotes and testimonies.[46]

The buildup campaign for Kim Jong Il in the 1970s concentrated on both the media and the person-to-person level. It was the person-to-person buildup, according to one observer, that provided the background, the context, that made the media campaign comprehensible.[47] If the person-to-person campaign was "concrete, direct, open, and blunt, yet visible only to the North Korean populace," the media campaign was clearly "abstract, indirect, and highly secretive."[48] Between 1974 and 1977 the term "Party Center" (*tang chungang*) was used by North Korea's mass media to hide the identity of Kim Jong Il while revealing the activities and qualities of the person Kim Jong Il. Although this term was a long-standing abbreviation for "Party Central Committee," the North Korean regime succeeded in using this familiar term to communicate with the populace directly and yet hid its intentions from the outside world for several years.

The media credited the Party Center in various publications with "setting forth" various "guidelines" (*pangch'im*), with "wise guidance," "embody[ing] the teachings of Kim Il Sung." These publications included the party daily *Nodong Sinmun* and the KWP Central Committee theoretical journal *Kulloja*, but the campaign was more prominent in youth and artistically oriented publications such as *Choson Yesul* (Korean Art), *Choson Munhak* (Korean Literature), and *Nodong Ch'ongnyon* (Working Youth), the organ of the Socialist Working Youth League. In these media the Party Center was reported as busily engaged in writing lyrics for songs, helping actresses with their dialogue, going into the pits to provide guidance to miners, sending helicopters to rescue maidens stranded on ice floes, and so on.[49]

A university professor by the name of Hyon Ho-pom, former dean of the faculty of political economy at Kim Il Sung University, recalled, in an article written in February 1976, Kim Jong Il's student days at the university in the early 1960s. "No sooner had the Beloved Comrade Leader . . . who has extraordinary intelligence, arrived on our campus than he discerned that our (the faculty's) outlook lagged behind the times and showed us how the situation could be rectified in a patient and benevolent way." More revealingly, Kim Jong Il was credited with helping his nominal instructors, including Hyon, restructure the entire university curriculum in political economy. The previous practice of blindly following foreign concepts and terminologies was replaced because of Kim Jong Il's "wide guidance" by a Juche-oriented curriculum based on "the economic ideas and theories of the Great Leader." Kim Jong Il was credited with having written numerous scholarly papers while attending the university and setting forth "original ideas" including one on the nature of "modern imperialism."[50]

In addition to the familiar themes of Kim Jong Il's alleged "intellectual brilliance" and "artistic talents," the North Korean media promoted Kim's alleged traits of "absolute loyalty" and "boundless benevolence." Kim Jong Il is unquestionably portrayed as the most "loyal" and "trustworthy" person in North Korea. Not only is he called "endlessly loyal to the Great Leader, perfectly embodying the ideas, outstanding leadership, and noble traits of the leader, and brilliantly upholding the grand plan and intention of the leader at the highest level," according to a statement made at the Sixth KWP Congress in October 1980; he is also said to possess "bright wisdom, deep insight, strong sense of revolutionary principles of strong will."[51] In spite of these rhetorical claims, the fact remains the Kim Il Sung could find no one other than his son to trust as his successor.

Grant that Kim Il Sung has charisma and commands absolute loyalty from the North Korean masses (a premise that will be proven true or false after Kim's death). Even if this assumption is valid, it is uncertain whether Kim's legitimacy can be transferred to anyone else, especially when the successor happens to be his own son.

Some of the obvious questions that President Kim must answer, in defending his choice of Kim junior as his successor, are as follows. Why could he not permit the Central Committee of the KWP to select a leader from among themselves, as Chong-Sik Lee has asked?[52] Are there no others equally loyal and able as his son? Also, despite the high praises of Kim Jong Il, his leadership ability remains to be proved, and will not be truly tested until after the death of his father. What assurances are there that the next generation of the North Korean elite will treat Kim Jong Il the same way his father was treated by the present generation? Will Kim junior be able to contain potential conflict among the top leaders after his father's death? Kim Il Sung's consolidation of power was not complete until he had waged an intraparty campaign and struggle that culminated in a purge of his political rivals in the 1950s and again in the 1960s.[53]

The experience of Kim Yong-ju, younger brother of Kim Il Sung, in 1973 may demonstrate the difficulty in North Korea's familial approach to the political succession issue. It appears that initially Kim Il Sung had selected his younger brother as his successor, but the gradual rise and sudden demise of Kim Yong-ju in the KWP hierarchy indicates Kim's subsequent abandonment of that plan. In 1961, at the Fourth KWP Congress, Kim Yong-ju was elected as a member of the Central Committee with a rank order of 47, and subsequently climbed up the ladder to 24 in 1966 and 16 in 1967. By 1970, at the Fifth KWP Congress, he was made a member of the Political Committee (Politburo since 1980) and of a party secretariat in charge of the powerful Organization and Guidance Department, emerging as number 6 in the rank order. In July 1972, Kim Yong-ju was appointed cochairman of the North-South Coordinating Committee, as a counterpart to South Korea's KCIA director, Lee Hu-rak. Sometime in 1973, however, possibly timed with the emergence of Kim Jong Il, Kim Yong-ju suddenly dropped out of the picture, although he was made a vice-premier and served briefly in that capacity in 1974-1975. In 1980, at the Sixth KWP Congress, Kim Yong-ju was completely removed from the roster of the 248-member Central Committee, and also dropped from the Politburo. Many of Kim Yong-ju's associates and followers were also dropped from the roster of the Sixth KWP Central Committee in 1980.

In 1972, at the time of the North-South dialogue and negotiations, Kim Yong-ju was described by the North Korean authority as being in ill health. He was therefore represented at the North-South Coordinating Committee meetings by Pak Song-chol, Kim Il Sung's trusted aide and one of the vice-premiers in 1972. However, Kim Yong-ju's subsequent removal was obviously based not on his health but on the new party policy of selecting a successor from "the new generation." Despite poor health, other ailing figures in North Korea, such as Ch'oe Yong-gwon and Kim Il, have been kept and until recently honored as political committee members.

The rise and fall of Kim Yong-ju epitomizes the dilemma of the North Korean approach to the succession issue. Kim Yong-ju, initially judged to be a suitable successor to Kim Il Sung, was subsequently disqualified. This reversal demonstrates that the "immortal revolutionary family" can sometimes be erroneous in judgment, and that assigning political legitimacy based on criteria other than suitability as a political successor is incompatible with the administration of modern government, whether in North Korea or anywhere else.

During the change of political leadership in China occasioned by the demise of Hua Guofeng—Mao Zedong's designated successor—and the rise of Deng Xiaoping, who carried out the de-Maoization campaign, the *People's Daily* carried an article entitled "The Leader and the People," on September 18–19, 1980.[54] Although addressed to a Chinese audience, urging them to cope with China's problem, it had broad implications for communist politics generally. Appearing less than three weeks before the Sixth KWP Congress, this article was not reprinted or reported in North Korea. In defining the nature of the relationship between the leader and the people, the writer indicated that the relationship was one of equality rather than one of personal dependency: "The people can select the leader but the leader cannot select the people." The leader's practices of "lifelong tenure" and "designating his own successor" are remnants of feudalism, a practice that even bourgeois societies have done away with and that is unacceptable in socialist countries where the people are the master, the *People's Daily* claimed. For a socialist system to rely on passing the mantle of political leadership through father-son succession is unheard of in the annals of international communism. For this reason, the rise of Kim Jong Il, so laboriously and painstakingly managed, may very well prove to be the Achilles' heel of the North Korean socialist state.

Praising the "Earthly Paradise"

The North Korean masses are led to believe that the DPRK is an "earthly paradise," thanks to the brilliant leadership of "the Great Leader

Comrade Kim Il Sung." Visitors to North Korea from outside are always escorted to the Mangyongdae Shrine, in the outskirts of Pyongyang, which marks the birthplace of Kim Il Sung and is the mecca of all tourists from within and without North Korea. During the course of a stay in North Korea the visitor will generally be taken to the Mansudae Art Theatre in downtown Pyongyang to see one of the musical plays. In recent years the opera called "The Song of Paradise" has been shown to foreign visitors. This musical extravaganza attempts to convey the theme that North Korea has been transformed into a modern country and that it is the most beautiful place on earth. This musical play, with much fanfare and with some technical innovations, was allegedly produced under the guidance and direction of Kim Jong Il.[55]

Foreign visitors to North Korea are also taken to the Youth Palace in downtown Pyongyang as well as to various nurseries, kindergartens, and elementary and secondary schools. In these educational institutions one will witness a familiar sight that is repeated daily all over North Korea. The schoolchildren sing their praise of the Great Leader Kim Il Sung and his "revolutionary family"—including the "Beloved Leader Kim Jong Il"—to which the youngsters are giving their "eternal loyalty" and "thanks" for the happiness that the people of North Korea are enjoying. The teenage chorus at the Youth Palace sang a song for some recent visitors containing the refrain: "We are eternally happy under the bosom of the Great Leader Comrade Kim Il Sung. There is nothing to envy in the whole world. We are living in the paradise on earth."[56]

In recent years, many Western visitors to North Korea have noted widespread, large-scale construction projects completed and under way throughout the country.[57] Particularly noteworthy are the rebuilding of the city of Pyongyang, with its elegant public buildings, high-rise modern apartments, and subways, and the transformation of the villages in the countryside. As North Korea was almost destroyed during the Korean War, this is a remarkable achievement.

Literally thousands of plaques are displayed in public buildings and scenic spots across North Korea noting visits by Kim Il Sung. These commemorate the occasions of "on-the-spot-guidance" by Kim Il Sung, and increasingly, by Kim Jong Il as well. On the steps inside the entrance of the Central Museum of History in downtown Pyongyang, a larger-than-life-sized statue of Kim Il Sung overwhelms the visitor and reminds one of the presence of his spirit throughout the museum tour. On top of a hill overlooking the city of Pyongyang is the Museum of Korean Revolution that extols the record of Kim Il Sung's anti-Japanese resistance stands. This huge and extravagant building of some 95 exhibition rooms covering 240,000 square meters, with a 20-meter statue of Kim Il Sung in front, was dedicated in 1972, timed with the sixtieth birthday of "the Great Leader Comrade Kim Il Sung."[58]

The Tomb of Patriots, which boasts statues of 100 independence fighters personally chosen to be memorialized by Kim Il Sung, stands in the open air on a hill overlooking the city of Pyongyang. The modern maternity hospital in Pyongyang, which contains the latest automated equipment imported from Western Europe, was constructed in 1980 under the personal guidance of Kim Jong Il, according to a North Korean guide. In 1982, to commemorate the seventieth birthday of the Great Leader, a huge tower called "Juche" was built along the Taedong River facing downtown Pyongyang. An archway, more elaborate than the Arc de Triomphe in Paris according to an eyewitness account, was also erected in 1982, timed with Kim Il Sung's seventieth birthday celebration. The public restaurant Okryukwan, the public recreation center Changkwangwon, the Great People's Cultural Palace (the public library), and an indoor ice hockey hall were also completed in time for Kim Il Sung's birthday celebration.

Based on official accounts and observations made by outside visitors, North Korea seems to have successfully resolved the age-old problem of satisfying the three basic human needs: clothing, food, and shelter. Although the price of clothing in the stores is still high, children's clothing is subsidized by the state, and the people in the street are relatively well-clad. North Korea is self-sufficient in food production. The government claims that in 1979 North Korea's total grain production reached 9 million tons and that some of its rice was exported to other countries. The prices for food and housing are relatively low due to heavy subsidies by the state. With an average monthly salary of 70–120 won (approximately U.S. $35–60 based on North Korea's official exchange rate in 1981) per worker, the typical North Korean family of two working adults and two children spends about 10 won (about $5) for monthly rent. The state-subsidized price of rice is only 7 chon (3 1/2 cents) per kilo. North Korea also boasts that it is the first country in modern history to have abolished tax systems.[59]

True to the ideology of socialism, the wage scale in North Korea is reasonably equitable, especially compared with China or the Soviet Union. The ratio between lowest and highest wages, in terms of basic monthly salary, is small in North Korea. A five-point grade system for classifying positions and wages is usually followed. In the Taean heavy machinery plant outside Pyongyang, for instance, industrial workers started in 1981 at the monthly pay scale of 70 won ($35); the highest wage, for first-grade engineers, was 130 won ($65). This wage ratio of 1:1.9 between the highest and the lowest salary compares favorably with that in a typical Chinese industrial plant, where, according to one source, 1981 pay scales ranged from 40 yuan ($24) to 150 yuan ($88).[60] Faculty salaries at Kim Il Sung University reportedly ranged from 100 won ($50) for a beginning instructor in 1980 to 250 ($125) for a first-grade full professor, as compared with Shanghai's Fudan University, where salaries ranged from 80 yuan ($47) to 325 yuan ($191). New medical doctors in a Pyongyang hospital reportedly received 120 won, with their senior colleagues earning up to 250 won. Government functionaries generally begin at 90 won, and their first-grade superiors (cabinet ministers) receive 300 won.[61]

Salaries alone, of course, do not tell the whole story. North Korean wage earners are given a variety of supplies, benefits, and "gifts" in kind. The quantity and quality of these items naturally vary according to status, grade, and occupation. The government provides school uniforms, books, and other supplies to schoolchildren of all ages. Even the teachers at Kim Il Sung University are given basic educational supplies. Full professors with doctoral degrees can use government-supplied cars for transportation. According to a North Korean driver, car assignment is decided by rank in terms of particular models. High government officials are provided with Mercedes-Benz sedans. Members of the ruling establishment in North Korea, such as high party officials, government leaders, and senior military officers, are known to have access to special shopping centers, imported goods, new apartment assignments, free travel, and generous rice and meat rations.[62]

Artists are also treated well in North Korea in terms of wages and fringe benefits provided by the state. Actors and actresses, musicians, dancers, acrobats, painters, and other artists enjoy high social prestige and standing, and the best artists are recognized and decorated. They are often excused from Friday labor obligations. Those who are designated as "people's actors" and "people's artists" are highly rewarded with cars and other privileges. Understandably, competition to enter colleges of music and fine arts is very tough—about eighteen applicants for each open position, according to one source.[63]

To achieve this standard of living, the masses in North Korea have worked diligently, and the price they have paid includes sacrificing freedom of movement and knowledge of the outside world. North Koreans are not free to travel from place to place without permission, let alone to change jobs or to move to another location. For traveling, each North Korean citizen carries a domestic passport, which is always inspected by officials at the various checkpoints established throughout the country for security reasons. The regime's ironclad control keeps the population in a state of complete isolation. The North Korean masses, therefore, are either uninformed or misinformed about world events. North Koreans blame their isolation on outside powers, like "U.S. Imperialism," but isolation is also imposed by the North Korean leadership. North Korea has basically became a socialist "Hermit Kingdom."

North Koreans also pay high prices for commodities other than "basic necessities." The decision as to which commodities fall into which category is itself made subjectively by party and government officials. Nonetheless, the North Korean masses are far from benefiting from common goods that are readily available to people in other countries. The prices of goods available in ordinary department stores and other shops tend to have a two-tiered structure. Although the items that are widely needed on a daily basis are reasonably priced, any personal goods deemed to be luxury or nonessential are expensive.

For instance, a person's average monthly wage (90–100 won) can buy only 2 meters of high-quality silk fabric, and is not enough to pay for a man's ready-made suit (116 won). "When all schoolchildren receive a package of personal gifts—uniforms, coats, sweaters, stationery, caps, bags, shirts, etc.—from President Kim on his birthday, they and their parents unashamedly cry not only because they are grateful to his 'loving care and benevolence,' but also because the value of each child's gifts can easily surpass an average wage earner's monthly salary."[64]

The daily necessities of modern living, including such items as radio, telephone, and television, are either nonexistent or priced beyond the reach of the ordinary worker. Radios are not sold in stores nor are they installed in ordinary homes. Only a public speaker connected with and controlled from a central location in the apartment or village center is made available. A black-and-white 19-inch television set (500 won) requires savings equal to one half of the average industrial worker's annual cash wages. Telephones are rarely seen in ordinary houses and are available only at official or public places. Processed items such as canned meat, cosmetics, fountain pens, handbags, medium-heeled shoes (no high-heeled shoes are sold), and bath towels are highly priced. Art objects such as paintings, embroidery, ceramics, and lacquered boxes are also very expensive.

North Korea in the 1980s is a country that has attained great material progress in exchange for political regimentation and the sacrifice of personal freedom. Whether North Korean society is indeed a "Paradise on Earth" is debatable. What is important in understanding the political development of North Korea in the 1980s is that the myth of paradise has been projected by the leadership as an article of faith and common belief by the masses. One reason that the North Korean leaders exaggerated the vision of North Korea as "paradise" is to present a stark contrast to the situation in South Korea, described as the embodiment of living "hell."[65] In the following chapter the contrast between North and South Korea will be drawn more clearly in terms of their conflicting political systems, states, and societies.

Concluding Remarks: Regimes in Contrast

The governing regimes of the two Koreas have become firmly established in the 1980s. Whereas the father-son partnership characterizes the regime in socialist North Korea, the civilianization of the military regime typifies capitalist South Korea. Both Korean regimes have emerged since 1945 as authoritarian political systems; yet "authoritarianism Korean style" is different not only from authoritarian regimes elsewhere in the world but also between the two Korean states. If capitalist South Korea resembles the authoritarian regimes and praetorian states commonly found in many Third World countries, socialist North Korea closely resembles the totalitarian system of the Soviet Union, and even, some would argue, prewar Germany and Italy, which were highly controlled and regimented. Since the North Korean regime consciously promotes its image as a Third World country, and identifies closely with the nonaligned nations movement, this characterization is quite astounding.

As a communist socialist state, the North Korean regime shares many features with the prototype of totalitarianism. The distinguishing characteristics of a totalitarian political system, as explicated by Friedrich and Brzezinski, are:

1. an official ideology
2. a single mass party led by one man
3. a system of terrorist police control
4. technologically controlled monopoly of communications
5. monopoly of all means of coercion
6. central control and direction of the economy through bureaucratic means.[66]

When these criteria are applied to North Korea, some features fit very well and others do not.

North Korea's totalitarianism, for instance, is equipped with an official ideology called *Juche Sasang* or *Kimilsungism*, described as an application of Marxism-Leninism to the Korean experience. North Korea's ruling party, the Korean Workers' Party, is a communist party that practices the Leninist principle of populism and adheres to the principles of party discipline and leadership. Even if the North Korean regime claims that other political parties coexist and elect deputies to the nominal legislature, for all practical purposes socialist Korea is a single-party state. No parties other than the communist party have any realistic chance of winning power.

The North Korean regime also seems to fit well with the remaining characteristics of totalitarianism, given certain modifications. Although the system of public safety in socialist Korea is not well understood by outside observers, it is widely believed that there are numerous detention centers for dissident groups and a system of close surveillance of citizens' activities by the secret police. In the name of maintaining security, North Korea has—like South Korea—turned into a garrison state in which personal freedom is severely restricted. The means of coercion and communication are monopolized by state agencies, and the economy is centrally controlled and directed through the state planning commission. On matters of surveillance and control of the masses, the North Korean regime tends to utilize more psychological techniques of persuasion and pressure, inculcating the virtue of loyalty, than is the case with other totalitarian systems. Also, the leadership advocates the mass-line principle of management as an antidote to the centralized direction of the economy. In the light of these totalitarian features and tendencies discernible in North Korean politics, it is no wonder that some students have called socialist Korea under Kim Il Sung a "monocracy" or a Stalinist regime.[67]

As a civilianized military regime and praetorian state, South Korea also shares many features with other authoritarian political systems. In terms of close ties between the armed forces and the technocratic elites, coopted by the military into a ruling coalition, South Korean authoritarianism has become identifiable in recent years with a type of polity called bureaucratic authoritarianism. This form of government occurs in several Latin American countries, including Brazil and Mexico. The prototype of the bureaucratic authoritarian state, as specified by O'Donnell, includes these defining characteristics:

> high government positions . . . occupied by persons who come to them after successful careers in complex and highly bureaucratized organizations— the armed forces, the public bureaucracy, and large private firms;
> political exclusion . . . through the imposition of vertical (corporatist) controls by the state on such organizations as labor unions;
> economic exclusion . . . that . . . reduces or postpones indefinitely the aspiration to economic participation of the popular sector;
> depoliticization . . . that . . . pretends to reduce social and political issues to "technical" problems . . . and
> transformation in the mechanisms of capital accumulation . . . that are a part of the process of a peripheral and dependent capitalism characterized by extensive industrialization.[68]

When these criteria are applied to South Korean authoritarianism, some features fit well and others fit with some modifications. Generally, political economy considerations provide the justification for the military to impose authoritarian rule in the first place. Having seized power through a coup d'etat, the military regime pursues a policy of coopting certain civilian sectors, such as technocrats and bureaucrats, but excluding populist civilian groups that are critical of the regime—opposition parties, student activists and intellectuals, labor union leaders. In this respect, South Korean authoritarianism is close to what exists in many Latin American bureaucratic authoritarian states. There are some differences, however. The South Korean regime in the 1980s is more civilianized, has a closer government-business partnership, has more confrontation between students and armed forces, is more repressive and manipulative of opposition forces in politics, is more export-oriented in development, and is industrializing and urbanizing more rapidly than other bureaucratic authoritarian states.

Likewise, North Korean totalitarianism differs from that of other totalitarian states. Under the rule of Kim Il Sung and his son, North Korea in the 1980s is more familistic, more socialistic in ideology, more focused on autonomy, more rapidly industrializing, more monolithic and unitary in culture, and more hierarchical in its authority relations than other socialist countries in the Third World. North Korea may be called a Confucian communist state or a familistic communist state insofar as the leadership style and pattern of politics is concerned. In the intensity and thoroughness with which Koreans pursue their political tasks, both North Korea and South Korea stand out as distinct from the respective prototypes of totalitarianism and authoritarianism that they basically follow.

In spite of structural differences, the North and South Korean regimes of the 1980s are similar in many ways because of their shared political culture. Both Korean regimes are nondemocratic in leadership style and orientation, despite the rhetoric of "democracy" often invoked and utilized by the political elites of both societies. Politics in both Korean states basically follows a "top-down" rather than a "bottom-up" approach. The directives always flow down the hierarchy rather than travel up the ladder. Both Korean societies are highly exposed and vulnerable to the pressures of centralization. Authority inflation, to borrow Ilchman and Uphoff's expression, seems to characterize the arena of Korea's "vortex" politics.[69] New styles of authoritarian politics are operative and a new tradition of totalitarian politics is about to take root in the soil of Korea. In the subsequent chapters some of these dominant features of Korean politics will be examined in more detail, in terms of specific policy patterns and processes. We turn next to an examination of Korea's political culture and leadership style.

Part 2

Policy Patterns and Processes

5
Political Culture and Leadership

The two states that have emerged in divided Korea since 1945 have been engaged in a cutthroat, zero-sum political game of competing legitimacy. In this atmosphere the very survival of society is at stake, and the welfare of the people depends on the outcome of the competition between the two antagonistic political systems. Whatever is a positive gain to one side of divided Korea is interpreted automatically as a negative loss by the other side. Seen from a larger perspective of promoting Korea's national interest, this situation of prevailing hostility between the two Korean societies is unfortunate but inevitable given the nature of the existing political regimes. Korean politics is a high-risk system in which the stakes of political conflict are very high; the winner takes all and the loser takes nothing.[1]

The high-risk nature of Korean politics is not necessarily a modern phenomenon. Korean politics has traditionally been prone to contention and factionalism.[2] However, the fact of divided nationhood seems to have accentuated the conflicting elements of Korean political culture. Korea's political culture, both traditional and contemporary, will be examined in terms of the competing hypotheses and evidence available. This discussion will be followed by an analysis of political leadership in the two Korean states, in terms of leadership style and principles, political elite composition, and comparison of supreme leadership.

Korea's Political Culture

Traditional Beliefs

As North and South Korea share a common culture and tradition, with a continuous record as a unified and homogeneous nation since the seventh century A.D., the present generation of Koreans may consider the territorial division of the country since the end of World War II in 1945 as a transitory phase in the longer historical perspective of the Korean people. The sources of inspiration and interpretation for the analysis of present political developments may therefore be sought in the cultural heritage and past experience of the Korean people. This approach to the comparative politics of divided Korea may be illustrated by the examples that follow.

The Confucianism of Yi dynasty Korea (1392–1910), the official ideology of the state, was initially a revolutionary doctrine that replaced Buddhism as the official ideology of Koryo dynasty Korea (918–1392). With the passage of time, Confucianism in Yi Korea brought about a rigid conservative ideological bias that emphasized the principles of hierarchy in human relations and dependence on outside powers (*sadaechuûi*). The modern leadership of North and South Korea since 1945 has generally reacted critically to the negative aspects of Confucianism, rejecting and modifying some of its tenets to suit present needs. In a way, Kim Il Sung's preaching of Juche and criticism of dependence on outside powers is his personal reaction to the *sadaechuûi* (serve the great) tradition of the Confucian past. This is especially evident in Kim's pursuit of an independent line of foreign policy in relations with Moscow and Beijing.[3] Recently, the virtue of the Confucian heritage, with its emphasis on education and learning, has also been given a fresh interpretation by some Western observers. They credit it with stimulating the rapid socioeconomic modernization of Korea, especially in the south. Confucian mores and culture are believed to have a status equivalent to the Protestant ethic, generally believed to have led to the rise of capitalism in the West.[4]

Another interpretation of Korean politics in terms of traditional political culture pertains to the origin of authoritarianism and totalitarianism in Korean politics. Both Yi Song-gye, who founded the Yi dynasty, and Park Chung Hee, president of the Republic of Korea between 1961 and 1979, came to power through a military coup. Following their assumption of political power, both former generals used official ideology to rationalize and legitimize their political rule. Just as Confucianism was adopted as the official ideology of Yi Korea, nationalism, anticommunism, and economic performance were used to justify the rule of Park Chung Hee in South Korea. Kim Il Sung also used an appeal to nationalism, anti-Japanese guerrilla fighting, and communism as the basis for his claim to legitimacy in North Korea. Just as Confucianism in Yi Korea was an alien ideology, borrowed from China, so communism in North Korea was a foreign ideology, which subsequently became Koreanized in the form of Kimilsungism in North Korea.[5] In the name of neo-Confucianism, Confucian scholars in Yi Korea adopted a "holier than holy" posture toward their adopted ideology. In North Korea today, Kim's Korean communism is oftentimes more radical and revolutionary than the communism practiced in China or the Soviet Union, both in rhetoric and in practice.

Some scholars trace the origin of factionalism and authoritarianism in Korean politics to Yi dynasty practice and to the colonial experience of Korea under imperial Japanese rule during the totalitarian mobilization era prior to 1945. One scholar who undertook a study of the literary purges in seventeenth century Yi Korea found a tradition of Korean factionalism stemming from aristocratic rivalry and struggle among degree holders and Confucian scholars.[6] Others argue that under Japanese colonial rule many Koreans tasted the ruthlessness of totalitarianism and police rule, so that it was an easy matter for older Koreans to emulate the Japanese method of political control.[7] Korea not only became a police state under Japanese rule; it also turned into a forward base of the Japanese militarists in their expansion into China during World War II. Under the circumstances of wartime mobilization, the state institution was strengthened at the expense of the traditional institutions and culture of Korean society. The industrialization of Korea under Japanese colonial rule on the eve of World War II inspired liberated Korea, especially North Korea, to emulate the Japanese method of mobilizing and utilizing human power and limited resources in the most efficient and effective manner.

This linking of present political phenomena and trends in divided Korea with the historical experience of Korea, although interesting, should not be carried too far. One also needs to guard against the temptation to draw an overly simplified analogy between Korean developments and the experiences of other countries, especially when the analogy is based on theories derived from Western history. A case in point is the dispute over the vortex phenomenon in Korean politics, which scholar Gregory Henderson has explained by applying the theory of mass society politics to Korea. Cultural homogeneity and the centralization of power are described as the "apeiron of Korean political culture," which somehow led to the rise of mass society tendencies in Korea.

> In Korea . . . the imposition of a continuous high degree of centralism on a homogeneous society has resulted in a vortex, a powerful, upward-sucking force active throughout the culture. This force is such as to detach particles from any integrative groups that the society might tend to build—social classes, political parties, and other intermediary groups—thus eroding group consolidation and forming a general atomized upward mobility.[8]

This metaphorical explanation of Korean politics, derived from the application of William Kornhauser's political theory of mass society, is certainly interesting and illuminating.[9] But to conclude that traditional Korea was a mass society is both misleading and inaccurate.[10] The notion of Korea as a mass society, as Bruce Cumings points out, "does not derive as much from a careful analysis of Korean social conditions . . . as from an imposition of a model drawn from a particular frame of reference, a model with a long intellectual history sustaining a basically elitist approach to social analysis."[11] Although he correctly depicted the pervasive phenomena of centralization and homogeneity in Korean society, Henderson was not justified in postulating the existence in traditional Korean society of "mass" conditions, which are more or less the product of modern and Western societies.[12] The political culture analysis of divided Korea must go beyond explanations based on a mechanical application of theories derived from Western experiences or based solely on Korea's historical heritage. We must also apply contemporary theory and data on the changing political attitudes and behavior of the elite and the mass public.

Contemporary Beliefs, Attitudes, and Behavior

The political attitudes and beliefs of contemporary Korean society may be ascertained by analyzing some of the opinion surveys conducted in South Korea. Although no survey data are readily available on North Korea's elite and masses, one may conjecture that North Korea is no better off than South Korea as far as democratic orientation and public attitudes are concerned.

Table 5.1 presents the pattern of South Korean political participation as revealed in a 1973-1974 study of community notables (*yuji*) and adult citizens throughout South Korea.[13] The findings have broad implications relevant to the 1970s and the 1980s as well. The community notables in South Korea, as compared with the mass public, were more interested in and knowledgeable about politics, more active in politics, and also belonged to more secondary groups or organizations. The urban elite and mass public are more active politically than rural residents. Urbanization and industrialization seem to have affected the political consciousness of South Korea's adult population and their willingness to participate more in politics. However, elite status seems to be a more influential factor than urban or rural residence upon the degree of participation by South Korea's adult population in politics.

One consequence of the rapid socioeconomic change associated with industrialization is the ever-widening gap in the perception of political issues between the elite and masses in Korean society, north and south. Although not a problem unique to Korea, this elite-mass gap will continue to widen. An analysis of the world view and trust level shared by the elite strata and mass public may illustrate this aspect of political culture in South Korea.

Tables 5.2 and 5.3 present evidence for the elite-mass cleavage in South Korean society. The level of political trust and the world views held by the public in Korea are not only important indicators of the degree of consensus and conflict; they also have some broad implications for future Korean politics. When a gap exists between elite beliefs and mass opinions, for instance, the potential disruption is greater in a country like Korea, whose political culture is noted for a high degree of hierarchy and centralization in authority relations. When the elite-mass gap in perception and preference on conflict issues is smaller, the possibility of maintaining political stability is greater.

What is striking in Table 5.2 (derived from a 1973-1974 nationwide opinion survey in South Korea) is the considerable gap between elite

TABLE 5.1
Political Participation of South Korea's Adult Population
(in percentages)+

Questions	Community Notables		Citizenry	
	Urban	Rural	Urban	Rural

Q: How interested are you in political affairs around us?

Very much	38.1	31.6	10.0	9.3
Somewhat	45.5	49.8	35.9	35.7
Not at all	17.4	18.6	54.1	55.0
Total	100.0	100.0	100.0	100.0
(N)a	(247)	(215)	(1150)	(1019)

Q: Speaking of your political leaders, would you by any chance know the name (or names) of your assemblymen?

Know two names	89.8	79.4	35.5	44.0
Know one name	8.9	16.8	30.2	29.6
None	1.2	3.7	34.3	26.4
Total	99.9	99.9	100.0	100.0
(N)	(246)	(214)	(1149)	(1027)

Q: During the last election campaign, did you attend any political rallies or meetings?

Many times	37.1	45.4	20.5	17.0
Once or twice	38.4	37.0	47.6	44.4
Never	24.5	17.6	31.9	38.6
Total	100.0	100.0	100.0	100.0
(N)	(245)	(216)	(1146)	(1028)

TABLE 5.1 (Continued)

Questions	Community Notables		Citizenry	
	Urban	Rural	Urban	Rural

Q: Have you thought of some public issues about which you wanted to do something?

Frequently	62.0	63.4	15.8	13.3
Few times	24.9	27.7	25.2	30.1
Never	13.1	8.9	59.1	56.6
Total	100.0	100.0	100.1	100.0
(N)	(245)	(213)	(1116)	(1007)

Q: Do you belong to any organization, such as social clubs, unions, church, cooperatives, political groups or others?

Two or more	34.4	15.7	3.0	2.6
One	30.8	31.9	15.4	16.9
None	34.8	52.3	81.6	80.5
Total	100.0	99.9	100.0	100.0
(N)	(247)	(216)	(1157)	(1035)

Source: Young Whan Kihl, "Political Roles and Participation of Community Notables: A Study of Yuji in Korea," in Chong Lim Kim, ed., Political Participation in Korea: Democracy, Mobilization, and Stability (Santa Barbara, Calif.: Clio Press, 1980), pp. 98, 99, 102, 107.

a. N = number surveyed.

+Totals of other than 100% result from rounding errors.

TABLE 5.2
World Views Shared by South Korea's Elites and Mass Public, 1973 (in percentages)

	Legislators (119)	Local Notables (468)	Mass Public (2276)

Q: What is your view on the following statement: "Conflict is basic to human nature, society, and politics."

Agree	90.0	62.0	25.0
Disagree	9.0	0	4.0
DK, NR	1.0	48.0	71.0
Total	100.0	100.0	100.0

(Comparable data of those who agreed with the statement)

Turkey	60.0	63.0	71.0
Kenya	80.0	28.0	20.0

Source: Chong Lim Kim and Young Whan Kihl, "The 1973 Korean Survey of the Constituents and Local Notables," University of Iowa Comparative Legislative Research Center, Iowa City, Iowa, 1974.

beliefs and mass public opinion as far as world view is concerned. Whereas 90 percent of the legislators and 62 percent of local notables interviewed agreed with the statement, "Conflict is basic to human nature, society and politics," only 25 percent of the public agreed. Although this gap was also noted in Kenya, South Korea was sharply in contrast with Turkey, where an identical survey question was used.[14]

Table 5.3 shows a much smaller gap in the trust level of South Korea's public and elite. Fifty-eight percent of higher civil servants, 77 percent of local leaders, and 82 percent of the mass public agreed with the statement, "Most people cannot be trusted and therefore you cannot be too careful in dealing with them." A more even division between trust and distrust is evident in the response to the second questionnaire item, the statement that "Most of the people would try to take advantage of you if they have the chance."

Unfortunately, a similar survey could not be conducted in North Korea, which is closed to outsiders conducting field research. However,

TABLE 5.3
Level of Trust Among South Korea's Elites and Mass Public, 1973
(in percentages)

	Higher Civil Servants (225)	Local Notables (468)	Mass Public (2276)
Questions: What is your view on the following statements:			
1. "Most people cannot be trusted and therefore you cannot be too careful in dealing with them."			
Agree	58	77	82
Disagree	42	22	15
DK, NR	0	1	3
Total	100	100	100
2. "Most of the people would try to take advantage of you if they have the chance."			
Agree	48	57	44
Disagree	51	40	49
Dk, NR	1	3	7
Total	100	100	100

Source: Chong Lim Kim and Young Whan Kihl, "The 1973 Korean Survey of the Constituents and Local Notables," University of Iowa Comparative Legislative Research Center, Iowa City, Iowa, 1974.

the eyewitness accounts of North Korea's politics provided by political refugees and visitors from the outside world reveal that many similar characteristics exist between Korean politics in the north and those found in the south. These include a highly elitist style of politics, a top-down approach to leadership, extreme loyalty and dedication of the masses to the supreme leader, and a widening gap between party cadres and ordinary people.[15]

Leadership Style and Traits

A study of divided Korea yields a unique opportunity for undertaking systematic research on the interaction between politics and socioeconomic development. Whatever divergence exists between North and South Korea today may be attributed to the influence of political factors in the two separate states and societies of Korea. The difference in political orientation may be attributed in turn to the role of the political leadership in shaping and directing the course of political development. For this reason, a discussion of political leadership—its nature, character, and style—is important in the study of comparative Korean politics.[16] The Korean state has become the prime mover in the process of planned political and socioeconomic change. The character and composition of the ruling elites that occupy and control the positions of authority in the respective Korean societies are, therefore, a key to understanding the nature of political process and dynamics.

The Composition of Political Elites

As the composition of elite structure changes, so do the characteristics and orientation of the members of both North and South Korean elites. In the 1970s, political leadership in the two Koreas shifted from those whose outlook was "revolutionary" in the north and "entrepreneurial" in the south to those who were more "task-oriented" and "technocratic" respectively.

Although North Korea's political leadership is no longer staffed exclusively by revolutionary elites, as was the case prior to 1970, the newly recruited elites are thoroughly trained and indoctrinated to continue the legacies of Kim Il Sung's anti-Japanese guerrilla fighting. South Korea's leadership, in contrast, is recruited from members of the technocratic elite who have the skills and training to perform the tasks of a rapidly industrializing state. In the early 1980s, North Korea's first generation of leadership under Kim Il Sung is still intact, but South Korea has seen the emergence of a new generation of leadership, a generation that is the product of post–World War II and even post–Korean War socialization.[17]

A study of the composition of the KWP Central Committee (based on the social background data of all members for the five party congresses held between 1945 and 1970) shows that some important changes have taken place in the communist party leadership of North Korea. These changes include the appearance of a large number of newly recruited young leaders trained by the communist system, who are replacing the "old" communists, and the disappearance of factional groupings through the purging of rivals to Kim Il Sung, carried out in the name of party unity and party spirit.[18] The generational change and the disappearance of anti-Kim factions are a natural result of Kim Il Sung's prolonged rule.

A similar study, based on an aggregate analysis of the KWP's top party leaders, shows "a trend toward functional specialization among the top elites in North Korea" and "the compartmentalization of the North Korean elite into military, party, and state functionaries."[19] About fifteen of Kim Il Sung's close followers dating back from the anti-

Japanese guerrilla era constituted "the inner circle of power and the top echelon elite in North Korea" in 1972.[20]

A pattern of change is also noticeable in South Korea in terms of elite orientation toward the future. A study by Hahn-been Lee, based on his personal experience of government service in South Korea prior to 1966, shows that the political and administrative elites in the Third Republic became more future-oriented and development-oriented than those of the First Republic (1948–1960) and the Second Republic (1960–1961).[21] This shift toward greater task- and program-orientation has been corroborated by other studies on the perception of the legislative, party, and bureaucratic elites in South Korea in the 1970s.[22]

Apart from the change in composition of political elites and leadership groups, it is important to examine the top political leader in North and South Korea respectively if the dynamics of Korean politics is to be grasped. The values of loyalty to the leader, consensus, and harmony are extolled in Korean political culture rather than those of intergroup bargaining, competition, conflict, and consultation; and this affects the leadership principle as subscribed to by both old and new political leaders.[23]

Leadership Principles

Both Korean regimes practice authoritarian leadership, although the North Korean leadership puts greater emphasis on corporatism and on the cult of personality. North Korea's communist politics is centered around its leader, and political ideology and organization in socialist Korea revolves around and embodies the personal life history of the Great Leader. The idea of Juche (Chuch'e) is proclaimed as the symbol of the Korean nation that reflects the creative genius of Kim Il Sung's leadership.[24] The KWP, moreover, is said to provide the core of the organizational structure necessary for carrying out the socialist revolution and construction and for translating the idea of Juche into specific policies and programs in North Korea.[25] "The Juche idea," according to Kim Il Sung, "is based on the philosophical theory that man is master of everything and decides everything."[26] Juche, Kim continues, "constitutes the quintessence of the revolutionary ideas of our Party" and "the monolithic ideological system of our Party."[27] On the substance of the leadership principle, Kim Il Sung asserts that "what is important in applying the Juche idea is to carry out the principles of Juche in ideology, independence in politics, self-support in economy, and self-defence in guarding the nation."[28] A more thorough explanation of the idea of Juche was presented by Kim Il Sung during a lecture at the Ali Archam Academy of Social Science of Indonesia, on April 14, 1965.

> To establish Juche means holding fast to the principle of solving for oneself all problems of the revolution and construction in conformity with the actual conditions of one's country and mainly by one's own efforts. . . . While resolutely fighting in defense of the purity of Marxism-

As a more practical approach to solving the problems of increasing agricultural and industrial production levels, Kim Il Sung also inaugurated the Chongsanri method (derived from the agricultural cooperative in Chongsanri, Kangso County, South Pyongan Province) in 1960 and the Taean work system in 1961.[34] The Chongsanri method, formulated by Kim Il Sung during his "on-the-spot guidance" in February 1960, was to serve as a guide for planned management of agricultural cooperatives by placing priority on farm planning, mechanization, and team work among various local level organizations. These included the *ri* party organization (*ri* is the village-level administrative unit), the county party committee, the management board, and the county people's committee.[35] "The essentials of the Chongsanri method," according to Kim Il Sung, "are that the higher organ helps the lower, the superior assists his inferiors . . . lives [with] priority to political work with people."[36]

The Taean work system, modelled after the Taean electrical machinery plant, was an industrial counterpart to the Chongsanri method in agriculture. This work system was to embody the mass line in economic control, to eliminate over-centralization, individualism, and capitalism and bureaucracy in economic management. The Chongsanri method was incorporated into the 1972 Socialist Constitution as Article 12, which stipulated that "The State applies the Great Chongsanri spirit and its method in all its work to guarantee the higher bodies help the lower, the masses' opinions are respected and her enthusiasm is roused by priority given to political work with people."[37]

South Korea's politics is also leader-centric, but it is less structured and regimented than North Korea's. As authoritarian leaders, both Syngman Rhee of the First Republic and Park Chung Hee of the Third Republic practiced the art of highly centralized and authoritarian decisionmaking. They amassed power at the center without delegating authority or paying due consideration to local interests. In arriving at policy decisions these leaders did not bother to consult with related interests in the periphery.

Yushin Korea under President Park established a system of executive dominance and presidential government whereby the president amassed dictatorial powers in his hands and in the Blue House, the presidential mansion. As military men both Park Chung Hee and Chun Doo Hwan favored the leadership principle of "follow me." Both Park and Chun were fond of making unannounced surprise visits to government ministries and project sites, a reflection of habits cultivated during military service.

Although Park generally preferred to rely on bureaucratic procedures for decisionmaking, especially on matters of economic development policies and programs, he also attempted to mobilize the public through waging a mass campaign. The Saemaul movement was launched in 1971 along with the third Five-Year plan (1971–1976) to solve the nagging problem of the urban/rural gap by increasing rural household income and improving the stagnant and backward farm villages. The Saemaul

Leninism against revisionism, our Party has made every effort to establish Juche in opposition to dogmatism and flunkeyism towards great powers. Juche in ideology, independence in politics, self-sustenance in economy and self-defense in national defense—this is the stance taken by our Party.[29]

This idea of Juche was enshrined as basic state and party policy in North Korea. The 1972 Socialist Constitution, adopted by the Fifth Supreme People's Assembly on December 27, 1972, stipulated in Article 4 that "The DPRK is guided in its activity by the Juche idea of the KWP which is a creative application of Marxism-Leninism to our country's reality." The 1972 KWP rules adopted by the Fifth Party Congress also stipulated in its preamble that "The KWP is guided in its activity by the great Juche idea which is a creative application of Marxism-Leninism by comrade Kim Il Sung."[30]

What makes North Korea's monolithic and unitary system, which is basically leader-centric and authoritarian, more democratic and progressive in appearance is Kim Il Sung's preaching of the mass-line principle in politics. Paradoxically, although Kim Il Sung practices an ironclad dictatorship in socialist Korea, his leadership is defended in the name of promoting and protecting the cause of the working masses. Reminiscent of Mao Zedong's teaching, Kim Il Sung claims that "the masses of people are masters of the revolution and construction and it is they who carry them out."[31] Actually, Kim's mass-line doctrine is borrowed from the Leninist and Maoist populist principle of "serving the masses." What distinguishes Kim's approach to the mass-line principle from that of Mao Zedong, however, is Kim's emphasis on indoctrinating the masses and giving the cadres a more positive role in guiding the masses. Thus, if the Maoist mass-line doctrine extols the slogan of "from the masses to the masses," Kim's mass-line principle preaches "to the masses, from the masses, to the masses," according to Bruce Cumings.[32] The typical leader-centric, top-down approach of Korean political culture is reflected in Kim's preaching of the Leninist principle of participatory mass democracy.

Kim Il Sung's leadership style is best known for his so-called "on-the-spot guidance" to inspire the masses and solve difficult problems in the socialist revolution and construction in North Korea. He has given literally tens of thousands of moments of such "on-the-spot guidance" all over the country. As a way of increasing the level of economic production in North Korea through exaltation and mobilization of the masses, at the December 1956 plenary meeting of the KWP's Central Committee Kim launched the Chollima (Flying Horse) movement, similar to Mao's "Great Leap Forward" of 1957–1958. This mobilization campaign, timed to coincide with the initiation of the five-year economic plan for 1957 through 1961, stressed "continuous advance" and "uninterrupted innovation" to speed up production and other areas of socialist construction.[33]

movement was an attempt to initiate a self-help program for village development in rural Korea with an initial government provision of financial and material assistance.[38] The Saemaul movement was subsequently extended to urban areas to encompass residential settlements and industrial enterprises as well.

Park Chung Hee also preached the spirit of *jaju* and *jarip*, meaning independence and self-reliance,[39] although his government was dependent on foreign sources for the input of technology and capital needed for the industrialization of the economy. He also emphasized the virtues of cooperation and national harmony. It was in the name of promoting national harmony, called *ch'onghwa*, that he suppressed political dissension and opposition.[40] Park despised partisan bickering and interparty disputes. It was in the name of injecting a new spirit of cooperation and harmony that he pressed for the inauguration of the Yushin system (the revitalizing reform) in October 1972.[41] He was also determined to initiate what he and his supporters called Korean democracy or Koreanization of democratic institutions and procedures to suit the condition and needs of Korea.[42] Ironically, in the name of building the foundation for Korean democracy, his regime imposed harsh repressive measures and abused the human rights of many dissidents opposed to his dictatorship.

In a larger sense, Park Chung Hee was preoccupied with building a modern and prosperous society in South Korea. He considered it his mission to carry out the program of rapid industrialization of the economy for South Korea. He was obsessed by achieving an economic miracle for Korea to enhance the wealth and power of the nation. In this way Park attempted to legitimize his authoritarian rule by economic development and by promoting the welfare of the nation.[43] His assassination in October 1979 left his lifelong mission unfulfilled.

The accomplishments of the Park era in attaining an economic miracle through practicing political authoritarianism is a subject the successor government of President Chun Doo Hwan is reluctant to discuss. Although Park Chung Hee was his benefactor, Chun Doo Hwan tries to dissociate himself from Park Chung Hee's Yushin Korea in the belief that the Fifth Republic should not repeat the errors of the Fourth Republic. He wants to make a clean break in the hope of avoiding the mistaken policies of the past, such as prolonged dictatorial rule, in favor of allegedly promoting the peaceful transfer of power. By drawing a sharp contrast between the authoritarianism of the Park era and the self-proclaimed "new politics" of the 1980s, the Chun government is obviously trying to disavow the legacy of Yushin Korea.

Supreme Leadership

What makes the political leadership of North and South Korea similar is that the top leader (called *suryong* in the north and *taet'ongryong* in the south) is invariably in a position to command and to expect the obedience of the population. Whereas in the north the cult of personality of Kim Il Sung is extolled, in the south the presidency is occupied by a military strongman who, like his predecessor President Park Chung Hee, is accustomed to the military outlook and manner of command and following. The incumbent leaders of political office are expected to be much revered by the general population in both North and South Korea. Korean political culture encourages the supreme leadership in the north as in the south to expect the unopposed political support of the population. The supreme leader at the apex of the political system takes it for granted that the masses will be receptive to commands from the top.

The cult of personality of political leadership in North Korea is especially extreme. The political leadership in the south generally attempts to appeal to the public and solicit their support for policies and programs. However, their repressive practices are defended in the name of maintaining national unity and harmony and promoting the welfare of the people.

In the south, political leadership has passed from Park Chung Hee to Chun Doo Hwan; in the north, power has shifted, or is about to shift, from Kim Il Sung and his comrades to Kim Jong Il and his followers. To accentuate the contrast between the old and the new leadership, the following analysis will begin with a comparison of Kim Il Sung and Park Chung Hee and end with a comparison of Chun Doo Hwan and Kim Jong Il.

Kim Il Sung and Park Chung Hee as Political Leaders

Kim Il Sung and Park Chung Hee were dramatically different in their upbringing, career pattern, and leadership principles. As first generation political leaders, however, both Kim and Park were basically "men of swords" rather than "men of letters."[44] As former soldiers, both men were heavily influenced by the military way of thinking. This feature is a departure from Korea's historical pattern; in Yi dynasty Korea only civilians were recruited as political leaders.

Kim was an anti-Japanese guerrilla leader based in Manchuria and the Soviet Far East in the years prior to 1945, and Park Chung Hee served in the Japanese army after receiving officer's training from military academies both in Japan and in Manchukuo, Japan's puppet state in Manchuria in the 1930s. After Korea's national liberation, Kim Il Sung returned to North Korea with the Soviet occupation troops, wearing the insignia of a Red Army captain; Park Chung Hee returned to South Korea as a lieutenant of the Japanese Imperial Army. Park resumed his military career in the south by joining the U.S.-established Constabulary Forces, graduating from the officer's training program as a member of the second class in 1946. Kim Il Sung made himself marshall of the Korean People's Army following the Korean War; Park Chung Hee, after carrying out a successful coup as brigadier general in May 1961, made himself a full general before retiring from the military in 1962. Both men thus had predominantly military careers, reaching the apex of the military hierarchy and establishment. However, as political and military leaders they could survive only with the active support and following of subordinates. In this regard Kim's followers, who dated back to the 1930s and 1940s, proved to be more dependable. Park "lacked do-or-die comrades in arms" and his followers were "dispensable in times of political crises."[45]

Both leaders embodied in their leadership styles the basically authoritarian feature of Korea's political systems. If Kim Il Sung was a totalitarian, Park Chung Hee was more or less an authoritarian. Kim was totalitarian because "he and his regime virtually control private lives, economic management, and political participation" in North Korea. Despite the mass-line principle that proclaims the masses to be "the master of the revolution and construction, Kim Il Sung was the Master of the Masses in reality," as one astute observer noted.[46] In spite of the Juche idea extolling independence and self-reliance, Kim Il Sung was the source of legitimacy and wise leadership to whom the masses gave their loyalty and dedication.

Park was authoritarian because "he and his regime interfered moderately with people's private lives and with the socioeconomic sectors," a fact that Sung Chul Yang has characterized as following a "Fascist syndrome." Park's Japanese military training undoubtedly enhanced his emphasis on order, authority, and obedience. His political behavior, according to Yang, revealed these characteristics: conventionalism, rigidity, intolerance of ambiguity, desire for certainty, dogmatism, and toughmindedness.[47] Park emphasized command in lieu of compromise, duties and disciplines before rights and freedoms, and national ethos over individual human dignity.[48]

Apart from their similar leadership styles, Park and Kim were basically different types in personality and life-orientation. Yang argues that both Kim and Park had "low self-images," although their negative self-images took radically different forms. Both men tried, Yang explains, to compensate for their low self-image, Kim by promoting a personality cult around himself, Park by worshiping past historical figures. Kim Il Sung has permitted the erection of many statues and monuments that celebrate his accomplishments all over North Korea. Park Chung Hee, although less extreme and more or less a modest man, was concerned with preserving the past heritage of Korea by restoring historical monuments and reviving historical scholarship. These different life-styles indicate to Yang that "Kim was *narcissistic*, making himself his hero, and Park was *obsessional*, making historical figures his heroes."[49]

> His (Kim Il Sung's) hero is himself. He has constructed his own monuments, museums, and memorials, not only to demonstrate his "monumental" achievements during his anti-Japanese revolutionary past but also to overshadow his Chinese (and Russian) connections. In contrast, Park . . . was not his own hero although the cult of Park was not entirely

absent in South Korea, especially in the last years of his rule. Park's heroes were historical figures: King Sejong, Admiral Yi Sun-sin of the Yi Dynasty, General Yon'gesomun of the Koguryo Dynasty, and Kim Ch'un Ch'u of the Silla Dynasty. Park restored shrines, historical sites, and sanctuaries for these figures not only to bolster the national ethos of the Korean people but also to bury the guilt arising from his past association with colonial Japan.[50]

Kim and Park also differed in their attitudes toward foreign powers in general and toward Japan and the United States in particular. Their different backgrounds and life experiences were reflected in Kim's anti-Japanese and anti-American stance and in Park's pro-Japanese and pro-American policy positions. This divergence prompted Yang to identify Kim as essentially a *xenophobe* and Park as basically a *xenophile*. Kim's "xenophobia" is "marked by his bent for stiff resistance against adversity, acquired during his anti-Japanese guerrilla years in the Manchurian front" and reinforced by the defeat in the Korean War. Park's "xenophilia," in turn, "was largely the product of his successful life encounters during the Japanese colonial period in Korea," such as attending the Japanese Imperial Military Academy, which "set in him the inclination toward stiff compensation for advancement . . . and his essentially positive images of Japan and the United States."[51]

This difference in personality traits was partly responsible for Park and Kim's dissimilar approaches to the realization of self-reliance. "Kim attempts to achieve his Juche idea by restraining North Korea's foreign entanglements while Park attempted to realize his Jaju (self-reliance) spirit by increasing South Korea's foreign transactions."[52] Although these contrasting orientations toward the outside world may result in the extremes of either isolation or dependency, the two Korean leaders were more or less aware of the practical limits of their postures and the need for attaining a middle ground in politics. Thus—at least in theory—"Kim's Juche stresses economic autarchy, political independence, self-defense, and ideological purity, while Park's Jaju emphasized economic interdependence, political alignment, military safe-guards including foreign shields, and de-ideologization."[53]

Chun Doo Hwan and Kim Jong Il: Biographical Sketches

Assessing the true leadership potential and style of the new generation of leadership in North and South Korea in the 1980s, headed by President Chun Doo Hwan of the Fifth Republic in the south and the KWP Secretary Kim Jong Il in the north, is difficult and premature at the time of this writing in 1983.[54] First and admittedly superficial impressions of the two leaders nevertheless reveal some interesting contrasts and differences in their personality characteristics and socialization experiences.

Chun Doo Hwan, as a former army general, is an action-oriented man of the sword. He is said to have a more gregarious and outgoing personality than his predecessor, President Park Chung Hee. Kim Jong Il, in contrast, appears to be a man of artistic bent and orientation. The Western hairstyle he wore some years ago was quite revealing of his state of mind in the otherwise austere and rigid atmosphere that generally prevails in the land of Kim Il Sung. Although his life is shadowed by the awesome presence and protection of his father's charisma, Kim Jong Il appears to be somewhat intellectual and innovative in his experiments with new art forms and activities.

Chun and Kim junior also have quite dissimilar qualifications and backgrounds for attaining leadership roles. Chun Doo Hwan has had a large following of military academy graduates. Chun's continued support by the military largely depends on his performance as president in fulfilling his initial pledges to usher in a "New Just and Welfare Society" and achieve a second economic takeoff for South Korea. Nevertheless, he has managed to keep the military in line and has continued to receive its support. Kim Jong Il as a leader has no military experience. Instead, he has consolidated his leadership position by successfully organizing and leading the Three Revolutions Teams movement, which consists largely of youthful party cadres and intellectuals though not necessarily excluding military officers. To compensate for his deficiency in military experience, Kim Jong Il was appointed at the Sixth KWP Congress in October 1980 to membership in the National Defense Commission. In serving as party secretary and as director of the powerful Organization and Guidance Department, Kim Jong Il has acted as a gatekeeper and has recruited his own followers in the party hierarchy among the youthful cadres and technocrats.

The two leaders attained their present positions of authority under very different circumstances. Chun's assumption of power after the assassination of the incumbent president was rather sudden and dramatic. Kim's political succession has been gradual and carefully prepared. Chun was rather inexperienced when he initially assumed the position of the highest office in the country, and he had to learn about the leadership role on the job. Kim, on the other hand, has had a long period of political apprenticeship under the care of his father. Chun's political rise was unexpected; Kim's emergence as a leader was anticipated.

The two leaders, finally, had different childhood experiences and went through dissimilar socialization processes. Chun was born the son of a poor farm family in a remote region in South Kyongsang Province. His schooling was irregular; the military academy that Chun attended for four years during most of the Korean War period was the first regular and thorough training he received. Kim Jong Il's childhood, in contrast, was protected and privileged.

How these different childhood and socialization experiences will affect the leadership style and philosophy of the two political leaders is difficult to say and remains to be explored in the future. Instead of continuing this line of comparing the two political leaders, this analysis of the two

Koreas' political leadership will conclude by presenting a brief biographical sketch of the two Korean leaders: President Chun Doo Hwan in the south and Party Secretary Kim Jong Il in the north, in that order.

Chun Doo Hwan. Chun Doo Hwan was born in 1931 in a remote mountainous farm village, Naech'onri, Yulgok Myon, Hapch'ongun, South Kyongsang Province. He was the third child in a family of four children.[55] He studied the Chinese classics at an early age but started his formal primary school rather late. In 1940, at the age of nine, his family migrated to Manchuria in search of a better life. Chun entered Horan primary school in Pansok-hyon, Jilin Province, where his father worked at a clinic of Chinese medicine operated by a Chinese; his mother was a farm hand. After one year and three months, his family moved back to Korea and settled down in Taegu, the third largest city in Korea.

Following a period of irregular education, Chun Doo Hwan was finally admitted to Hido Primary School in Taegu as a fourth grader in April 1944. His exposure to the Japanese school system in Korea, unlike his predecessor Park Chung Hee, was brief and inconsequential. Park Chung Hee had been admitted to the elite Taegu Normal School as a scholarship student after graduating from the primary school near his home village as an honor student. It is interesting, however, that both Park and Chun received their early schooling in Taegu, although at different times and under different circumstances. It is said that Chun earned part of his school expenses as a newspaper delivery boy to help his father, who continued in the Chinese medicine trade he had picked up in Manchuria. In 1947 Chun was admitted to the six-year Taegu Technical Middle School, only to have his education interrupted by the onset of the Korean War in June 1950.

Chun Doo Hwan passed the competitive entrance examination to the newly inaugurated four-year course at the Korean Military Academy in December 1951. For the next four years, from 1952 to 1955, which included part of the Korean War years, Chun Doo Hwan spent his days as a cadet at the academy. He was more athletically than intellectually oriented, serving at one time as captain of the academy's soccer team. Chun had ample opportunity to display his leadership abilities as a cadet. The close classmates who would later play an important role in assisting the military coups led by Chun in 1979 and 1980, including Ro Tae-wu and Kim Bok-dong, were more intellectually minded than Chun. In 1955, Chun was commissioned as a second lieutenant upon graduating from the eleventh class, the first class to receive four years of training at the Korean Military Academy.

In December 1958 Captain Chun Doo Hwan married Lee Soon Ja, the daughter of retired general Lee Kyu-dong, who once had served as G-4 (General Staff in Charge of Logistics and Supply) at the Korean army headquarters and was also a military academy classmate of former president Park Chung Hee. His wife's two uncles, Lee Kyu-seung and Lee Kyu-kwang, were also army officers. Lee Kyu-seung was a colonel and Lee Kyu-kwang became a brigadier general after serving as chief of the Army Military Police. At the time of his wedding, Captain Chun Doo Hwan had been recruited as a founding member of the Paratrooper Special Forces stationed at a base in Kimpo, outside of Seoul. In 1959 Captain Chun went to the United States for a five-month training program on psychological warfare at the United States Special Combat School at Fort Black in North Carolina.

In April 1960 Chun was made G-3 (General Staff in Charge of Combat Planning and Operations) of the Special Forces. He was on U.S.-ROK joint maneuvers in Okinawa when the April 19, 1960, Student Revolution took place in South Korea, resulting in the overthrow of President Syngman Rhee's government. On May 16, 1961, when Brigadier General Park Chung Hee and his followers led the military coup, Captain Chun took the initiative to contact General Park to offer him his allegiance and service. Chun was credited with having persuaded the cadets of the Korean Military Academy to stage a procoup march through the Seoul streets in support of General Park Chung Hee. During the junta rule in the following months Captain Chun was appointed as one of Park's senior secretaries in charge of civilian petitioning affairs.

The subsequent career pattern of Chun Doo Hwan in the military was smooth and rapid. Although he served at various posts, including the KCIA and the army headquarters as G-2 (General Staff in Charge of Intelligence), he spent most of his army days as a paratrooper. It is said, in fact, that Chun took part in the paratrooper's skydiving exercises over 500 times.[56] As lieutenant colonel, Chun served as deputy commander of the First Paratrooper Special Forces in 1966, and as battalion commander of the Metropolitan Defense Division in 1967.

In 1966 Lieutenant Colonel Chun received an important boost from the graduates of the Korean Military Academy that later would prove to be the key to his success in conducting military coups. In that year he was elected president of the North Star Club, an alumni association for Korean Military Academy graduates of the four-year regularized course of education. As a graduate of the first regularized class, Chun was one of two candidates nominated for the position. The first ballot was close, with Chun receiving only a few votes more than his challenger. However, when his competitor withdrew from candidacy, Chun Doo Hwan was unanimously elected to serve a four-year term, receiving all thirty votes of the class representatives. Each class of graduates from the eleventh class to the twenty-fifth class was represented by two delegates. Four years later, in 1970, Chun Doo Hwan was elected to serve a second four-year term.[57]

In November 1969, Chun Doo Hwan, now a full colonel, served in army headquarters as senior aide to the army chief of staff. He was the first in his class to be promoted to full colonel, and later general, although academically he had been mediocre, ranking in the middle range of his class of 156 graduates. In November 1970, Colonel Chun volunteered to serve in Vietnam and was made commander of the Twenty-ninth Regiment of the Republic of Korea Ninth Division. After one year's field experience in combat, Colonel Chun returned home to assume the position of commander of the First Paratrooper Special Forces. While in Vietnam, Chun Doo Hwan allegedly suggested in a letter to President Park the idea of establishing "democracy Korean style." President Park responded favorably, later writing to Chun that he had made an address on this theme before to the graduating class of the Korean Military Academy in 1971.[58]

On January 1, 1973, Chun Doo Hwan was made brigadier general and appointed to serve in the Blue House Protective Forces as assistant deputy chief. On February 1, 1977, he was promoted to major general, and in 1978 he was appointed commander of the Republic of Korea First Division. On January 10, 1978, during his tenure with the First Division, his unit was credited with having uncovered North Korea's third invasion tunnel along the DmZ near Panmunjom. On March 5, 1979, Major General Chun Doo Hwan was appointed to a key position, commander of the Defense Security Command, which subsequently enabled him to successfully plot coups in December 1979 and in May 1980. It was as commander of the Defense Security Command that Chun was placed in charge of the investigation of President Park's assassination on October 26, 1979.

Kim Jong Il. Kim Jong Il was born on February 16, 1941, in the Soviet Union, as the first son of Kim Il Sung and his first wife, Kim Jong-suk, now deceased.[59] His childhood Russian name was Yura. His younger brother, two years his junior, drowned at the age of two in Pyongyang. Kim Jong Il attended the Mangyongdae Revolutionary School, set up to educate the descendants of Kim Il Sung's comrades in arms during the anti-Japanese guerrilla years and to train future political leaders in North Korea. He also briefly attended a primary school in Jilin, China, from 1950 to 1952 during the war. Kim graduated from Namsan Middle-High School in Pyongyang in 1958, then attended the Air Academy in East Germany from 1960 until he transferred to Kim Il Sung University in 1962. In 1963 he graduated from Kim Il Sung University with a major in political economy.

In 1964, Kim Jong Il began his career in the KWP Secretariat Organization and Guidance Department under the tutelage of his father and his uncle Kim Yong-ju, who was then in charge of the office. He rapidly climbed up the ladder of party hierarchy. In 1970, Kim Jong Il became director of the Culture and Art Department of the KWP Secretariat. In that capacity he was credited with having directed the production of five major operas, including "The Flower Selling Maiden" and "The Song of Paradise."

By 1973, Kim Jong Il had organized and directed the Three Revolutions Teams movement as preparatory work for political succession to his father. His birthday, February 16, has been designated as a holiday in

North Korea since 1975. The code word of "Party Center" began to appear in order to keep the identity of Kim Jong Il secret while his mystique was enhanced and perpetuated. Kim junior also acquired such honorific titles as "beloved leader," "leading star," "the sun of communist future," and so on. Although Kim Jong Il's family life is shrouded in mystery, he is believed to have two children. This information was inadvertently revealed by Kim Il Sung to a visiting dignitary, the chairman of Japan's Socialist Party, when he spoke of having two grandchildren.

Concluding Remarks: The Politics of Contestation

The politics of divided Korea is in many ways the outcome of a contest between the leaders of North Korea and South Korea, and of the clash of their political will. In this situation of contest between political leaders, the masses generally are supportive of their government. They play the role of passive rather than active followers, especially during times of normalcy. This political passivity of the Korean mass public is manifest in Korean voting behavior.

In countries like North and South Korea, which are small and poor in natural resources, political leadership undoubtedly affects the welfare of the masses and the citizenry in society. The two Korean states began as new ventures in 1945. Political institutions were newly established and citizen participation in politics was greatly enhanced. As the two Korean societies were experiencing rapid economic development with the deepening process of industrialization, new policy issues and new agenda evolved that demanded the regimes' attention. For instance, as the number of people living in rural areas decreased, a new policy on urban settlement and population migration had to be designed. As more people were mobilized socially through better education, urban living, and an industrial way of life, policies of social welfare and cultural enrichment had to be devised and promoted. The Korean people are increasingly exposed to new ideas and expectations for a better future, both in the open society of South Korea and the closed society of North Korea, which is under pressure to become more open.

At a time of rapid socioeconomic change it is no wonder that the two Korean societies are experiencing a clash between the weight of traditional beliefs and the demand for modern values and ideals. The political behavior of both leaders and followers in divided Korea naturally reflects this hiatus between modern values and traditional beliefs, and political perceptions are invariably influenced by the tension between traditional and modern ways of thinking.

Deference and hierarchy in authority relations, for instance, are traditional Korean traits. Kim Il Sung's designating his own son as successor, although repugnant to modern ideas of democracy, has not received public outcries of protest and opposition in the north thus far. This may be because a father-son partnership in politics is more Confucian than communist, and the family-centered or familistic behavior of the supreme leader has not gone against Confucian cultural mores that still linger on in the popular mind.

Taiwan presents one example of a father-son partnership political succession, from Chiang Kai-shek to his son Chiang Jing-kuo. This precedent in Taiwan raises the possibility that the Confucian state of North Korea—albeit communist—may also successfully achieve this transition. Likewise, a traditionally compliant attitude toward authority may explain why thus far the civilianized military regime in South Korea has been largely tolerated and heeded by the mass public. Despite the repressive policy measures adopted by the military regime, the mass public—with the exception of small articulate segments of the population such as intellectuals and student leaders—has stayed outside the political arena of antiregime protests and demonstrations.

Korea's truncated political experience in recent history has made the political culture of Korea more complicated. The territorial bisection and political division of Korea make Korean politics potentially disruptive and explosive. This predicament is manifested in the tension between the reality of deference and the potential of defiance.

The usual deference of the masses toward authority and the ever-present potential of mass defiance must be delicately balanced for Korean society to stay intact. This tension and hiatus between the two opposing forces propel Korea's day-to-day politics. Cognizant of the tension and the possibility for defiance, the leadership of the respective Korean states is determined to manipulate the political process to reinforce its own position of authority and thereby to prolong its hold on power.

The mass public in Korea has been a pawn in the political game plan of the supreme leadership in both Korean states. The active or tacit support of the masses is sought and utilized in promoting the interests of the regime. While North Korea takes an ideological approach, invoking the rhetoric of Marxism-Leninism and Juche, South Korea is more pragmatic in orientation and pluralistic in social structure.

Although the future vision of the ideal society entertained by the ruling elites in the respective Koreas is presented with zeal, the fact is that the masses do not live by ideological exultation alone. They cannot lead life puritanically and always be expected to give their full devotion to the supreme leader and his commands. People must also carry out the mundane but necessary tasks of daily living associated with food, clothing, and housing. On the matter of raising the material standard of living, both socialist North Korea and capitalist South Korea appear to have done reasonably well.

When and if the expectations of the masses are not met adequately, however, both in terms of spiritual needs and material conditions, one may witness the rise of mass revolts in Korea. The streak of defiance and rebellion is firmly ingrained in Korea's political culture, and can erupt in violence and rebellion during times of acute crisis and rapid socioeconomic change.

Mass revolt could therefore upset the political stability and the delicate balance that now exists in the two Korean societies. Disruptive acts of violence could be fueled by the demands for political participation that are increasingly felt in society with the progress of modernization and development in the Korean states. A discussion of the political economy and performance of divided Korea will show how the two Korean societies have changed under the pressure of modernization.

6
Political Economy and Performance

In the years the two Korean states have remained isolated from each other, different economic policies and measures have been put into effect in the two Korean societies. The consequences of these policy choices and different developmental strategies in the early years are apparent in the 1980s in the striking contrast between the two Korean states and societies. During the period of divided nationhood the progress of industrialization has affected both Korean societies measurably, introducing new policy agendas and adding new conflict issues. The political economy and policy analysis presented in this chapter will provide a comparative perspective for ascertaining the nature of the two competing political economy systems that have emerged in the Korean Peninsula.[1]

The performance of the two Korean states in formulating developmental policies and implementing specific programs needs to be examined comparatively. The data thus generated would help us to identify the policy goals and capabilities of the respective Korean regimes and also to evaluate whether or not policies and programs have been carried out efficiently and effectively.[2] In the absence of systematic data that are readily accessible and comparable across the two divergent political systems, however, the present chapter will instead highlight the obvious structural differences between the two economic systems of socialist North Korea and capitalist South Korea. This will be followed by a discussion of the policy choices and strategies of the respective Korean regimes and the consequences of these decisions, as manifested in the overall pattern of economic performance and resource distribution. Finally, we will examine sectoral policy issues and performance in various functional domains, including overall socioeconomic development, military defense, diplomatic activities, and foreign economic relations.

Economic Systems in Contrast

The contrast between the economic systems of North Korea and South Korea is derived from the different ideologies and principles of economic management pursued by the two states. In the socialist North Korean economy the means of production and distribution are publicly owned and operated; in the capitalist economy of South Korea they are privately owned and operated.[3] Within this overall structure, however, each Korean state has modified its basic ideology and economic principles to suit specific needs and conditions. The contrasting patterns and processes of North and South Korea's economies may be illustrated by focusing on three key aspects.

The first is the role of the central government in the operation of the market, i.e., in the production and distribution of resources and in the exchange of goods and services. The second is the performance of the national economy during a given period of time as influenced by government policies. The third is the nature of external links established with the world economy—the dependent or independent orientation of the national economy.

The government's role in managing the national economy obviously varies between the north and the south. The role of the central government is all-pervasive in North Korea and limited in South Korea. Whereas the North Korean government makes all decisions on allocating resources and determining economic policy, the South Korean government makes key decisions regarding economic policy but shares the responsibility for resource allocation decisions with the private sector. By using the criteria of (1) government role in the economy and (2) locus of allocation decisions and ownership of capital, we are able to obtain a "two by two scheme" of the political economy model applicable to comparative Korean politics (Figure 6.1).

North Korea generally conforms to "comand-type socialism." It maintains the principle of centralized state planning of the economy, which is also followed in the Soviet Union.[4] North Korean socialism is somewhat different from the "market-oriented socialism" evident in some East European countries. In these countries the market process of supply and demand is monitored by the government and is in turn accommodated by state planning of the economy. Command-type socialism tends to operate instead according to the policy directions and guidelines set up by the party congresses. There is thus less flexibility in accommodating market forces in the command-type socialism practiced in North Korea.

South Korea does not have a pure system of "market capitalism." Instead, South Korea's economic system is closer to "command" or "guided capitalism." Because the central government owns and operates key industries such as utilities, steel production, and tobacco manufacturing, South Korea's economy has often been labeled as "state capitalism" or "guided capitalism." It basically has a "mixed economy," in which the central government intervenes in the market through the policy instruments of subsidies and foreign exchange controls. The market's determination of productive activities is tempered by central government planning and guidance.

The mixed-economy model best approximates South Korea's situation in the 1960s and 1970s during the Park Chung Hee era.[5] The situation has changed somewhat with the new "economic reform" policy of

FIGURE 6.1
The Political Economy Model Applicable to North and South Korea

		Locus of Resource-allocation Decisions and Ownership of Capital	
		Public	Private
Government Role in the Economy	Market	Market-oriented Socialism	Market-Capitalism (So. Korea since 1980)
	Command	Command-type Socialism (No. Korea)	State (or Mixed) Capitalism (So. Korea)

Note: The figure represents a two dimensional space only, although a third dimension of time may be introduced to the picture. Thus, whereas North Korea's economic system remained as command-type socialism through the years, South Korea's economic system moved away from state (mixed) capitalism in the late 1960s and the 1970s toward market-capitalism in the 1980s.

President Chun Doo Hwan. In 1981 President Chun's government undertook some drastic "reform" measures, gradually giving up control of key industries such as banking. In 1981 the government relinquished its majority equity shares in all five of the leading commercial banks.[6] It also adopted new policy measures to liberalize imports by giving greater weight to the market forces of supply and demand than to government intervention in the market process. The South Korean economy in the 1980s is therefore moving closer to market capitalism.

An important aspect of the government directed economies of the two Korean states has been the series of economic development plans. Since 1946 North Korea has had one-year, three-year, and seven-year plans, and since 1962 South Korea has had a series of five-year economic plans. Both Korean states are "hard states," not only in their adoption of specific economic plans but also in the sense of implementing these development plans and programs rigorously and forcefully.[7] The economic bureaucracy in both Korean states—the Economic Planning Board (EPB) in the South and the State Planning Commission in the North—are highly efficient and capable, working closely with other government agencies in mobilizing energy and resources to achieve development goals.

The economic performance achieved in implementing these state plans shows that both Korean societies have been successful in attaining the policy goals of economic development, in most cases exceeding planned targets. North Korea's economic performance shows, for instance, that industrial production in 1965 was nineteen times greater than in 1953; agricultural production also increased significantly during the same period (see Table 6.1). Likewise, industrial production in 1978 was more than ten times greater than in 1960,[8] while agricultural production again was about double. Between 1947 and 1965, North Korea's overall GNP expanded at an annual growth rate of 7 percent: agricultural production grew at an annual rate of 5 percent and industrial production at a rate of 22 percent. Between 1966 and 1978, North Korea's GNP increased at an annual rate of 6 percent; agricultural production at a rate of 5 percent; and industrial production at a rate of 14 percent (see Table 6.1).[9]

South Korea's economy showed an annual GNP growth rate of about 4.1 percent during the 1953–1962 period, in terms of 1970 constant prices.[10] However, in 1962, when the first five-year plan was inaugurated, the GNP growth rate accelerated, with the economy expanding at an annual rate of 9.6 percent in the 1962–1976 period. In the early years of 1953–1962, the primary (agriculture, forestry, and fisheries), secondary (mining and manufacturing), and tertiary (social overhead and services) sectors of the economy recorded 2.5 percent, 10.8 percent, and 4.3 percent growth rates annually; in the 1962–1976 years the growth rates increased to 4.5 percent, 17.9 percent, and 9.4 percent respectively. Commodity exports expanded most dramatically in these periods: from a 7.6 percent growth rate in the 1953–1962 years to a 36.8 percent rate in the 1962–1976 period.[11]

South Korea's overall economic performance since 1962 has been dramatic: during the first three five-year plan periods of 1962–1976, the target GNP growth rate was 7.1 percent for 1962–1966, 7.0 percent for 1967–1971, and 8.6 percent for 1972–1976. The actual GNP growth rates surpassed these targets with 7.8 percent, 9.7 percent, and 10.1 percent respectively.[12] Although the GNP increase for the fourth plan period, 1977–1981, fell far short of the planned target—5.6 percent instead of 9.2 percent—the performance record was still respectable in the light of the worldwide economic recession and domestic political turmoil of those years (see Table 6.2).[13] These economic performance

TABLE 6.1
North Korea's Economic Performance, 1947-1978, by Major Sectors:
Aggregate Indicators and Growth Rates(a)

	GNP (in bil. U.S. $)	Per Cap.GNP (U.S. $)	Agricultural Production	Industrial Production
Index: 1953=100				
1946			87	46
49			131	156
53			100	100
56			139	285
60			195	972
63			233	n.a.
65			193*	1900
Index: 1970=100				
1960	2.9	270	85**	30
65	4.6	380	90	59
70	6.1	430	100	100
73	8.3	540	107	160
74	9.3	580	140	188
75	10.0	610	154	225
76	9.7	570	160	248
77	9.7	550	170	276
78	10.4	570	170	323
Growth Rates:				
1947-65	7.0%		5.0%	22.0%
1966-78	6.0%		5.0%	14.0%
1961-70	n.a.		n.a.	12.8% (18.1%)***
1971-76	n.a.		n.a.	16.3% (14.0%)
1978-84	n.a.		n.a.	n.a. (12.1%)

Sources: Joseph Chung, The North Korean Economy; Structure and Development (Stanford: The Hoover Institution Press, 1974); US CIA, Handbook of Economic Statistics, 1979, 1980 (Washington, D.C.: 1979, 1980); Gordon White, "North Korean Juche: The Political Economy of Self-Reliance," in Manfred Bienefeld and Martin Godfrey, eds., The Struggle For Development: National Strategies in an International Context (New York: John Wiley & Sons, Ltd., 1982): 337-338; Frederica M. Bunge, ed., North Korea: A Country Study, Area Handbook Series of the U.S. Department of the Army (Washington, D.C.: Government Printing Office, 1981), p. 252.

a. based on official statistics and gross value in 1978 U.S. $.
* Grains only.
** Figure derived from author's estimate.
*** Figures in parentheses are those targeted in the seven-year and six-year plans; otherwise, they are actual achievements in the plan period.

TABLE 6.2
South Korea's Economic Performance, 1962-1986, Growth Rates by Major Sectors: Achievements versus Targets (in percentages)*

	1st Plan 1962-66	2nd Plan 1967-71	3rd Plan 1972-76	4th Plan 1977-81	5th Plan 1982-86a
GNP &	7.8 (7.1)	9.7 (7.0)	10.1 (8.6)	5.6 (9.2)	5.4 (7.6)
GNP PC	5.0 (4.2)	7.3 (4.7)	8.2 (7.0)	4.0 (7.5)	n.a.(5.9)
Agriculture, Forestry & Fishery	5.6 (5.7)	1.5 (5.0)	6.1 (4.5)	-0.7 (4.0)	4.5 (2.6)
Mining & Manufacturing	14.3 (15.0)	19.9 (10.7)	18.0 (13.0)	9.2 (14.2)	3.9(10.8)
Manuf. Only	15.0 (15.0)	21.8 n.a.	18.7 (13.3)	9.4 (14.3)	11.2(11.0)
Social and Other Services	8.4 (5.4)	12.6 (6.6)	8.4 (8.5)	6.0 (7.6)	4.7 (7.3)
Foreign Trade:					
Exports	38.6 (28.0)	33.8 (17.1)	32.7 (22.7)	10.5 (16.0)	5.0(11.4)
Imports	18.7 (8.7)	25.8 (6.5)	12.6 (13.7)	10.3 (12.0)	0.7 (8.4)
Population Growth	2.7 (2.8)	2.2 (2.2)	1.7 (1.5)	1.5 (1.6)	n.a.(1.5)
Fixed Investment	24.7 (14.6)	17.9 (10.2)	11.1 (7.6)	10.5 (7.7)	11.5 (9.0)
Employment	3.2b (4.7)	3.6 (3.3)	4.5 (2.9)	2.3 (3.2)	n.a. (3.0)

Source: Economic Planning Board, as cited in Korea: Executive Guide (New York: Citibank, 1982): 13-14; For 1982 statistics, see: Kim Kihwan, "Korea's Economic Reforms," a speech by President of the Korea Development Institute before the U.S.-Korea Society for Business and Cultural Affairs in New York on March 22, 1983, as reprinted in Korea's Economy, Vol. 2, No. 4 (May 1983) (Washington, D.C.: Korea Economic Institute, 1983).

* Figures in parentheses are those targeted in the five-year plans. Otherwise, they are actual achievements (i.e., average annual growth rate) in the plan period.
a. The figures for achievement are provisional. Percentages for 1982 are shown to represent the fifth five-year plan period.
b. 1963-1966 annual average only.

statistics reflect the degree of efficiency and effectiveness of the economic policies and their implementation by the economic bureaucracy of the respective Korean states.

The contrast between the economies of North and South Korea in the 1980s may also be interpreted as the logical result of contrasting developmental policies and strategies. These strategies differ especially in terms of their emphasis on growth and equity, on the one hand, and on establishing links with the world economy, on the other. Whereas North Korea, in line with its socialist ideology, gives greater emphasis to equity and distribution—without necessarily overlooking the growth of the economy as a policy concern, South Korea has steadfastly pursued the policy line of rapid economic growth and expanded production, and has given lesser emphasis to the equity and distribution aspects of the economy. North Korea's Juche economy has pursued an independent posture, shying away from entanglement in the international market; it has resisted pressure to join the Soviet system of COMECON (Council of Mutual Economic Assistance).[14] South Korea has instead pursued a developmental strategy of dependency and interdependency by actively participating in the world economy; it specialized in the export of labor-intensive commodities to gain comparative advantage in world trade. Although in terms of income distribution South Korea is considered more or less an egalitarian society compared with other less-developed countries, it is decidedly less egalitarian than North Korea.

Finally, both Korean states are situated in the periphery of the world economy. Whereas South Korea depends heavily on the world market, thereby exposing itself to fluctuations in the world eocnomy, North Korea generally emphasizes independence and autarky. South Korea has pursued an export-led strategy of industrialization; until 1971, North Korea experimented with an import-substitution strategy of industrialization. Both Korean states are thus more enmeshed in the world economy in the 1980s than they were in the 1960s and 1970s.

Policy Choices and Consequences

The political economy and policy analysis approach to comparative Korean politics, as applied in this study, is based on the assumption that choice and decisionmaking are central to the exercise of political leadership and are therefore the key to understanding the process of modern government.[15] How to allocate limited resources in society more "efficiently" and "effectively" has always been a challenge to political leadership in all ages and places. The question of "rational choice" for the efficient utilization of limited resources has therefore been a central focus of attention for students of political economy and policy analysis. This concern is derived from what economists call the "scarcity assumption," which assumes that resources are always insufficient to go around. This is why rational choice and decisionmaking are both important

TABLE 6.3
Strategic Choices for Development: Policy Emphasis as Indicated by
Allocation Decisions, 1953 and 1971

Strategic Choices	North Korea 1953	North Korea 1971	South Korea 1953	South Korea 1971
Developmental Goals:				
Growth	X		X	
Equity		X		X
Product:				
Light Industry		X	X	
Heavy Industry	X			X
Marketing:				
Domestic	X	X	X	
Export				X
Sectoral Support:				
Urban/Industrial	X	X	X	
Rural/Agricultural				X

and imperative. The political leadership of any state is responsible for the effective allocation of finite resources.

The efficiency and effectiveness of the policies pursued by the respective Korean states may also be evaluated in terms of impact on specific sectors of the economy, such as agriculture, industry, and foreign trade, to ascertain the political consequences of choosing particular policy goals and implementation strategies. Likewise, how a regime copes with demands and support by sectors such as functional groups and regional constituencies is important in determining the overall success and failure of the political regime.[16]

The heart of political economy is choosing from the set of alternative courses of action and policies open to the political leadership. The strategic policy choices available to the North and South Korean regimes have ranged from basic economic development policy decisions, such as production and market decisions, to sectoral support policy decisions, such as a price support policy for agricultural goods or subsidies for food prices for the urban and industrial sectors. Table 6.3 is a schematic presentation of policy choices made by the two Korean regimes in 1953 and 1971.

The years of 1953 and 1971 were chosen because of their importance for subsequent political and socioeconomic developments in the two Koreas. In 1953 the Korean War ended, and the regimes of divided

Korea put measures for rehabilitation and economy building into action, with heavy doses of foreign assistance from their respective allies. In 1971 a new era started, with détente and with shifts not only in the relationships between the two Korean regimes, but also between each Korean regime, its allies, and the other countries of the world.

Both Korean states opted for the development strategy of economic growth in 1953 and then shifted policy emphasis to equity by 1971. Their means of achieving these development objectives, however, varied, with the north building heavy industry first and light manufacturing later, and the south building light industry first and heavy industry later. In terms of market processes, the north continued throughout to concentrate on the domestic market; the south moved from concentrating on the domestic market to exporting its manufactured goods to earn foreign currency for further investment in the economy. While North Korea has relied on an import-substitution strategy, South Korea has moved toward an export-led strategy of industrialization.

In terms of sectoral support policies, the north has consistently given priority support to both the urban and industrial sectors. The south initially supported only the urban and industrial sectors but soon expanded its support to include the rural and agricultural sectors of the economy to stem the deterioration of the agricultural economy in trade and the slide of farm household income vis-à-vis urban household income. The inauguration of the Saemaul movement in 1971 reflected this change in the sectoral policy in South Korea. Meanwhile, the continued emphasis on heavy industrialization in North Korea demonstrated its policy of preferential support for the urban and industrial sectors over rural and agricultural sectors.

The consequences of policy choices and decisions made at critical times in the past are subsequently revealed in performance data. Table 6.4 presents comparable data on the North and South Korean states for 1960 and 1980.[17] These data, although crude, indicate the relative standing of North and South Korea on the three key policy dimensions of (1) human resources (population growth and the labor force), (2) urbanization, and (3) education. The data for 1960 and 1980 seemed particularly pertinent in assessing the success and failure of the policies of each Korean regime that, as shown in Table 6.3, were put into effect in 1953 and 1971. After a lapse of seven to nine years, the impact of policy choices and decisions adopted in the earlier period should be clearly reflected in the pattern of policy performance, as indicated in Table 6.4.

The performance data in Table 6.4 show that despite the structural differences of their economies both North and South Korea have made remarkable progress toward achieving the policy goal of modernizing society. Over a period of two decades, from 1960 to 1980, Korean society has become more industrial, more urban, more educated, and more developed. When the data are contrasted with the strategic choices

TABLE 6.4
North and South Korea's Policy Performance in Three Key Sectors, 1960 and 1980

	North Korea		South Korea	
Indicators	1960	1980	1960	1980
Human Resources				
Population Growth Rate	2.9	2.6	2.5	1.7
Fertility (per thou.)	42	31	43	24
Mortality (per thou.)	13	7	9	6
Labor Force				
%Pop Working Age(15-64)	53	56	54	62
% Labor Force in:				
Agriculture	62	49	66	34
Industry	23	33	9	29
Services	15	18	25	37
Urbanization				
Urban Pop as % total	40	60	28	55
Annual Growth Rate	5.1	4.4	6.4	4.7
% Urban Population:				
in largest cities	15	12	35	41
in cities over 50,000	15	19	61	77
# cities over 500,000	1	1	3	7
Education and Welfare				
No. Enrolled in as % of the age group:				
Primary Schools:				
Male	n.a.	115	99	112*
Female	n.a.	112	89	111*
Total	n.a.	113	94	111*
Secondary School	n.a.	n.a.	27	76
Higher Education	n.a.	n.a.	5	12
Adult Literacy Rate	n.a.	n.a.	71	93
Life Expectancy (years)	54	65	54	65
Infant Mortality Rate per thous.(aged 0 - 1)	78	34	78	34
Child Death Rate per thous.(aged 1 - 4)	9	2	9	2

Source : The World Bank, World Development Report 1982 (Washington, D.C.: The World Bank, 1982), pp. 143, 145, 147, 149, 151, 155.

*Due to universal primary education, the gross enrollment ratios exceed 100 percent; some pupils are above the official primary school age.

for development made in the earlier periods, as shown in Table 6.3, one can readily see the results of specific policy choices and decisions. For instance, the fact that both Korean states gave priority to growth over equity in the 1950s but reversed the emphasis in the 1970s probably explains the decline in the mortality rate and the improved life expectancy statistics between 1960 and 1980.

The expansion of the industrial and service sectors of the economy during this period was much greater in South Korea than it was in North Korea, again reflecting a delayed response to South Korea's decision to pursue an industrialization policy in the late 1960s and the 1970s. North Korea had already pursued a policy of heavy industry in the 1950s, and did not emphasize the production of consumer goods until the 1970s, while South Korea did not focus on heavy industry until the late 1960s. The service sector of the economy in South Korea was expanding more rapidly with the deepening of industrialization than was that sector in the North Korean economy.

Table 6.4 also indicates the differential pattern of urbanization in divided Korea. Although both North and South Korea became more urbanized between 1960 and 1980, the pace of urbanization in South Korea was much faster. Whereas the urban population of the north is scattered throughout small and medium cities, city dwellers in the south are concentrated in large metropolitan regions. Seventy-seven percent of the urban population in South Korea live in cities over 50,000, but only 19 percent do so in North Korea. North Korea had only one city with a population of over 500,000 in both 1960 and 1980, although the size of the city—Pyongyang—more than doubled during that time. South Korea in 1980 had seven cities with a population of over 500,000, more than double the number of such cities in 1960. Seoul's population was estimated at 8.9 million in October 1982, and 9.4 million a year later. Pyongyang's population was estimated at 2 million in 1982.

Caution is obviously needed in interpreting the performance data for North and South Korea. The question of equity, for instance, cannot be ascertained fully without accounting for the ideological variations between socialist North Korea and capitalist South Korea. It is one thing to employ quantitative measures to compare the standard of living for ordinary people in the two halves of divided Korea. It is another matter, however, to establish the quality of life for both elites and masses in the two Korean societies that have developed in isolation from each other.

Comparative Data: Endowment and Performance

In divided Korea, cutthroat competition has been going on between the capitalist south and the socialist north. This competition is multidimensional in scope, ranging from the arms and economic races to diplomatic maneuvering bilaterally and multilaterally. Both regimes are bent on showing the world that they are not only excelling in the tasks of governance and policy performance but are also superior to the rival Korean political system. By looking at several comparative statistics and data in different functional domains, we should be able to acquire an overall picture of the two Korean societies in terms of resource endowment and also see how capable they are in managing these resources and achieving the modernization of society. A socioeconomic profile of North Korea and South Korea, as shown by several socioeconomic indicators, will be followed by a discussion of the contrast between the two Korean regimes in the arms race, diplomatic competition, and foreign economic relations in the world arena.

Economic and Social Contrast

The features of divided Korea become much sharper when we draw a comparison of North and South Korea in terms of their physical endowment and socioeconomic characteristics. By capitalizing upon existing resources and capabilities, the political leadership in both Koreas has steadfastly pursued programs to build a modern and prosperous society once the task of organizing power and structuring authority was under control. As a result of the successful management of developmental tasks for more than a generation, each Korean society has come to have a set of distinctive features and attributes. Table 6.5 gives an overall profile of North and South Korea as socioeconomic systems.[18]

Although the aggregate statistical data shown in Table 6.5 are not always an accurate reflection of true socioeconomic capabilities, in the absence of hard comparative data this surrogate information may be useful as evidence for the underlying economic capability and performance of the two competing Korean regimes. The assumption here is that these aggregate data, especially when they are contrasted over time, may capture the overall pattern and the underlying trends of socioeconomic transformation and also that government policies play a determining role in influencing the nature, direction, and outcome of these changes. Before examining the table in detail, some general observations are called for.

North and South Korea as separate entities are relatively small compared with the giant neighboring East Asian countries of China, the Soviet Union, and Japan. Nonetheless, the combined population of the two Koreas—an estimated 60 million in 1980—is sizable enough that a unified Korean nation would be one of the larger countries in the world, ranking among the first twenty. The combined economies of North and South Korea, with an estimated gross national product of some U.S. $70–80 billion in 1981, would also make a unified Korea one of the economically strongest and most viable nations in the world among the developing countries. Although Korea is relatively small in territorial size and poor in natural resources, the Korean people are very industrious. The Confucian cultural legacy that makes a virtue out of learning has enabled the Korean people to stress scholarship and to achieve a high

TABLE 6.5
Socioeconomic Profile of North and South Korea: A Comparison

Characteristics	North Korea	South Korea	Ratio (N/S)
Resources: Physical and Human			
Total Area (1000 km sq)	120.5	98.4	1.11
Population, 1980 (in Mil.)	18.3	38.2	0.46
Population Growth (in %)			
Annual Rate, 1960-1970	2.9	2.5	1.21
Annual Rate, 1970-1980	2.6	1.7	1.50
Population Density, 1978	141.7	372.4	0.38
(persons per km sq.)			
Economic Indicators:			
GNP at Market Prices (U.S. $ Mil.)			
1978	17,040a	48,000	0.35
1977	11,680	29,440	0.39
1976	10,810	25,280	0.42
GNP Per Capita (US $)			
1978	1,000a	1,310	0.76
1977	700	810	0.86
1976	670	700	0.95
PC GNP Growth (in %)			
Annual Rate, 1960-1976	5.2a	7.3	0.71
Annual Rate, 1970-1976	6.8	8.7	0.78
Cultivated Land in 1975b			
(in thousand hectares)			
Total	2,071	2,241	0.92
Paddy Field	697	1,263	0.55
Dry Field	1,374	978	1,40
Social Characteristics:			
Communications c			
No. Vehicles, 1976	92,000	200,521	0.46
No. Radio Stations, 1976	13	56	0.23
No. Television Stations, 1976	2	12	0.17

Sources: World Bank Atlas for 1978, 1979 and 1980, Published by the World Bank, Washington, D.C.; World Development Report 1982, (World Bank, Washington, D.C., 1982); Economic Comparison Between South and North Korea, 1977 (Seoul: Research Center for Peace and Unification, 1977); A Statistical Comparison Between South and North Korea (Seoul: Korean Overseas Information Services, 1978).

a. Estimates of GNP, per capita GNP and its growth rate for North Korea are tentative.
b. Estimates by South Korea.
c. Estimates by South Korea.

educational standard for the population at large. With their well-trained human resources, the Korean people are capable of building a prosperous modern nation and maintaining a reasonably high standard of living for the people as a whole.

Korea is, however, a resource-poor country. The country is 100 percent dependent upon foreign petroleum, for instance, as a source of energy to implement its ambitious program of industrializing the economy. The bill for imported oil in South Korea alone ran as high as U.S. $3.6 billion in 1980; North Korea's bill was estimated to be $17.5 million that year.[19] Within the confines of this overall resource scarcity, the two Korean regimes have nonetheless done remarkably well in building dynamic and expanding industrial economies.

The scarce resources that do exist are not divided evenly between the two halves of divided Korea. North Korea, generally speaking, is better endowed than South Korea. North Korea contains 80 to 90 percent of all known mineral deposits in the Korean Peninsula, with some 300 different types of minerals. The deposits of some of these minerals, such as coal, iron ore, lead, zinc, tungsten, barite, graphite, and magnesite, are considered significant by world production standards.[20] The iron ore and coal reserves in the north—estimated to be about 2 billion tons and 8 billion tons respectively—are not of high quality, however. Access to these abundant minerals enabled North Korea's leadership to launch an ambitious program of heavy industrialization.

South Korea, in contrast, lacks large or numerous deposits of basic minerals. Only tungsten and amorphous graphite, located mainly in the south (along the central east and inland coast), are available, so South Korea relies heavily on imported raw materials, including fuels needed for its project of export-generating industrialization. Most reserves of coal in South Korea and North Korea are anthracite; bituminous coal to run the steel mills must be imported from abroad. Both North and South Korea manufacture cement in large quantities, however, by utilizing the abundant limestone deposits available throughout the land.

North Korea also has abundant timber forests, especially in the northern interior. The south generally lacks natural forest, although almost two-thirds of the land area in South Korea is officially classified as forest.[21] Both North and South Korea have developed an extensive fishing industry to benefit from the rich marine resources readily available along the coastal waters. Recently, the two Korean regimes have been competing over ocean fishing in the high seas away from the coastal waters.

Some of the recent trends in economic competition between North and South Korea can be seen from the data in Table 6.5. Economic indicators using aggregate statistics only are often misleading, however, especially when the two divergent political and social systems across the ideological line of socialism and capitalism are subject to comparison. Nevertheless, some trend lines are discernible in the direction and rate of change over time. One can say that the two halves of divided Korea are almost evenly matched in terms of total area and amount of cultivated land. Population density is much higher in the south, which has over twice the population of the north, although the rate of growth is much higher in the north than in the south.

The wealth of the two sides of divided Korea, in terms of the size of the economy, was quite evenly matched until the early 1970s, when the south started to outdistance the north. The aggregate GNP of South Korea in 1974 was approximately twice that of North Korea, although the GNP per capita was almost evenly matched between the two Korean societies in the same year. Throughout the 1970s, however, South Korea's economy grew at a much faster rate than North Korea's, so that the GNP ratio for the two halves in 1980 was estimated to be almost 3 to 1 in favor of South Korea.[22] Whereas the GNP per capita in the north grew at an average annual rate of 5.2 percent between 1960 and 1976, South Korea maintained a rate of 7.3 percent during the same period. In South Korea, GNP per capita increased from U.S. $590 in 1975 to $810 in 1977 and $1500 in 1981; in North Korea it changed from $620 in 1975 to $700 in 1977 and $950 in 1981.[23]

The economies of both North and South Korea underwent major structural changes in the 1970s. Both Koreas, for instance, advanced from a largely agricultural economy in the 1960s to a semi-industrial economy in the 1970s. In the south the share of agriculture declined from 40 percent of the GNP to 20 percent between 1965 and 1976, while industry's share increased from 16 percent to 36 percent.[24] Although the details are unknown, trends in the north are believed to have followed a similar course.

Many reasons are given as to why the GNP has grown faster in South Korea than in North Korea in the 1970s. According to a U.S. government study, three factors were responsible for the south outperforming the north in the decade prior to 1976.[25] First, the south spent proportionately much less on defense than the north; second, the south, by importing more efficient technology, had a much higher return on industrial investment; and third, the south developed a dynamic, export-oriented economy that generated the foreign exchange necessary to finance rising levels of capital imports.[26] The study also noted the structural contrast between the two Koreas. North Korea is "a tightly closed society with a planned economy with many elements of the bureaucratic Soviet model of the 1940s and 1950s," and "its educational system spends about as much time imparting the ideology of Kim Il Sung as instilling more practical knowledge."[27] The technical competence of North Korea's labor force and bureaucracy suffers as a result, and it remains inferior to that in the south. The economic planners and top businessmen in South Korea are not only well-educated, many with advanced degrees from foreign universities, but are providing extensive training facilities for upgrading the technical skills of a diligent labor force. "Firms with more than 200 employees, for example, are required to provide training for

15 percent of their employees."[28] In the communications field, the south is way ahead of the north. The number of vehicles, radio stations, and television stations is much larger in South Korea.

These aggregate statistics are too crude as measures to be useful for comparing the divergent socioeconomic systems of North and South Korea. To be more accurate in analyzing the respective Koreas' economic performance, the pattern of policy performance needs to be contrasted on at least two additional dimensions. The first would be to examine the data for two or more time periods, or for the periods preceding and following a given year. The second would be to do this for specific sectors of the economy, such as agriculture, industry, education, health. Reliable data on socioeconomic performance in specific sectors of the economy and society are either totally absent or unavailable to outsiders for South Korea and especially for North Korea, which has had a policy of not releasing statistical information to the outside world. For this reason, the information shown in Table 6.5, although useful for reference, is not an accurate reflection of reality in the respective Korean societies. In the absence of hard empirical data, only qualitative statements have been presented in the comparative study of North and South Korea.

The Arms Race and Military Postures

The Korean Peninsula is probably one of the most heavily armed spots in the world in the early 1980s. A precarious military balance has prevailed between North and South Korea for more than thirty years since the conclusion by armistice of the Korean War on July 27, 1953. More than a million soldiers under arms and combat ready confront each other along the military demarcation line that cuts east-west across the Korean Peninsula. The demilitarized zone, 248 km long and 4 km wide, is a symbol of the tragedy of Korea's territorial partition since 1945. Armed with the latest military equipment and weapons, inlcuding nuclear weapons in the south, and the entangling military alliances that each Korean regime has entered into with its respective allies, the Korean Peninsula in the 1980s continues to be a powder keg that might explode at any time. The U.S. military presence in the south, with some 38,000 ground troops and air support units in 1981, has made the military balance between North and South Korea more than a matter of inter-Korea rivalry. The situation is one of international concern and great-power strategic calculations.[29]

The heavily armed society of Korea has naturally caused a heightened concern about security on the part of Koreans. It has also led to an enhanced role of the military in the civil affairs of the state. Military security has become the number one preoccupation of the ruling elites in both Korean states, with the unfortunate result that Korean society in the 1980s has become literally an armed camp or security state manned by military generals and managed by the military bureaucracy. The heavily fortified garrison states of divided Korea in the 1980s are ironically in

TABLE 6.6
Military Expenditures: North and South Korea (in millions of U.S. $)

Years	Current		Constant a	
	N.Korea	S.Korea	N.Korea	S.Korea
1971	758	719	1296	1229
1972	1030	822	1692	1350
1973	1080	764	1678	1187
1974	1370	1078	1945	1531
1975	1080	1461	1399	1893
1976	1310	2160	1615	2663
1977	1250	2577	1453	2997
1978	1310	3262	1423	3544
1979	1320	3385	1320	3385
1980	1300	3846	1178	3486

Source: Reprinted from U.S. Arms Control and Disarmament Agency, World Military Expenditures and Arms Transfers: 1971-1980 (Washington, D.C., 1983), p. 55.

a. 1979 is used as the base year.

sharp contrast with the civilian society that prevailed for more than 500 years during the Yi dynasty. At the time of Korea's annexation by Japan in 1910, only 5,000 ill-equipped poorly trained soldiers tried vainly to defend the country against the Japanese military takeover.[30] The nonmilitaristic tradition of Korea was in a way a reflection of the thoroughly Confucianized character of Yi Korea's civilian society, in which the role of the military and the martial arts was subordinated to that of scholarship and learning.[31]

Now, North and South Korea typically spend a large amount of money on the military and the arms race. Some 15 to 20 percent of the GNP, on average, is believed to be spent for defense by North Korea; 6 to 7 percent of the GNP goes to defense in South Korea. As Table 6.6 shows, up until 1974 North Korea's military expenditures were much higher than South Korea's. Since around 1975, however, South Korea's military spending has outstripped that of North Korea, according to a U.S. government study, although the estimates for North Korea were subsequently upgraded in 1978, based on a new U.S. defense intelligence report. In 1979, U.S. intelligence data showed a rather rapid increase in North Korean military strength since 1971, indicating that the north might have spent as much as 15 percent of its GNP on military expenditures during these years.[32]

This pattern of military spending in North and South Korea reflects the changes in the defense policy orientation and posture of the Korean regimes. Since 1962, North Korea has pursued a parallel policy of economic construction and defense buildup. The "Four Great Military Policylines" adopted at the Fourth KWP Congress in 1962 contained the slogans "arm the entire population," "fortify the entire country," "cadetify the entire army," and "modernize the entire army."[33] Under the first policy the working masses in North Korea were trained to bear arms in addition to the regular forces, by establishing units like the Worker-Peasant Red Guard units. The second policy helped to strengthen defense all over North Korea, fortifying the front lines and building underground supply storages. The third policy was intended to enable all Korean People's Army (KPA) soldiers to assume the task of leadership, if necessary, so that military units might constantly be replenished and combat ready during wartime. Under the fourth policy, the KPA was to be given the latest advanced training as well as the latest weapons and equipment, to be domestically produced or purchased from abroad if necessary.[34]

South Korea's increase in military spending was stimulated by the 1969 Nixon Doctrine of gradual U.S. military disengagement from Asia and by the withdrawal of the U.S. Seventh Infantry Division from Korea in 1971–1972. It was also a response to the now-suspended Carter policy of U.S. ground troop withdrawal from Korea, first officially announced in 1976. As a way of enhancing its own defense capability and preparedness, South Korea first adopted the Five-Year Force Modernization Plan in 1971 and then the second Force Improvement Plan in 1976.[35] To finance these defense efforts the Seoul government had the National Assembly adopt a 10 percent defense surtax bill in May 1975, although its purchase of arms from the United States was benefited by the Foreign Military Sales Credit extended by the U.S. Congress to South Korea.[36] Table 6.7 shows the size of the military in North and South Korea in terms of personnel and weapons for each of the three service branches.

South Korea's military capability in 1981 consisted of an army of 520,000 soldiers with 2 tank divisions of some 1,000 tanks; a navy of a single marine division, 2 marine brigades, and 118 vessels (82,000 total tonnage), including 11 destroyers; and an air force of some 380 combat planes, including F-4 and F-5 fighter planes.[37] The army is broken into three field armies of 20 infantry divisions, with the first and second field armies assigned near the DmZ and the third army in the rear. The South Korean navy, although separated by two seas in the east and the west, will be able to combine the combat efforts of the separated parts of the navy and assist each other. The air force fighter planes are believed to have a high combat capability. South Korea also maintains 1,215,000 reservists and a national guard of 3.3 million.[38]

TABLE 6.7
Comparison of Military Postures: North and South Korea, 1982

	North Korea	South Korea
Population, 1981	18,600,000	38,900,000
Total Active Forces	784,000	601,600
Total Reserve Forces	300,000	1,215,000
Para-military Forces**	798,000	3,300,000
Army	700.000	520,000
Armored Divisions*	2	0
Mechanized Divisions*	3	1
Infantry Divisions*	35	20
Infantry Brigades	4	2
Commando/Airborne Brigades	20	5
Armored Brigades	5	3
SAM and SSM Brigades(Battalions)	4 (5)	2 (7)
Tanks	2,675	1,000
Artillery Pieces	4,100	3,004
Rocket Launchers	1,000	0
Frog Launchers	39	6***
Mortars	9,000	5,300
AA Guns	5,000	1,000
SAMs	250	93
Navy	33,000	49,000
Submarines	19	0
Destroyers (Frigates)	0 (4)	11 (7)
Subchasers (Escorts)	33	28
Missile Patrol Boats	18	8
Gunboats & Torpedo Boats	331	36
Landing Ships (Crafts)	24 (75)	28
Naval Bases	2	7
Air Force	51,000	32,600
Combat Aircraft	602	380
Airlift Aircraft	230	38
Helicopters	40	56
Trainers	0	220

Sources: The International Institute for Strategic Studies, The Military Balance 1982-83, London, 1982, pp. 88-89; Jane's Fighting Ships, 1976-77, London, 1976, pp. 197, 301-304; Young-Ho Lee, "Military Balance and Peace in the Korean Peninsula," Asian Survey 21-8 (August 1981), pp. 852-864; Vernon Guidry, "How the Two Koreas Stack Up Militarily," Washington Star, May 27, 1977, p. 3.

* North Korean divisions are modeled after USSR/PRC divisions, and number about 10,000 men, about 65% of the strength of South Korean division. The latter follows U.S. division organization. Most of the manpower differences lie, however, in combat support and logistics troops and they are roughly equivalent to the combat strength of a South Korean division.

** Para-military forces include security forces, border guards, militia, etc.

*** Honest John.

North Korea's military capability, in contrast, consists of an army of some 700,000 soldiers organized into 35 infantry divisions, 2 armored and 3 mechanized divisions, including 2,675 tanks; a navy of 480 vessels (67,000 total tonnage), including 19 submarines, 4 frigates, and 18 high-speed missile launchers; and an air force of 602 combat planes, including IL-28, MIG-21, and MIG-19 fighter planes. North Korea's ground forces are believed to be superior in firepower and mobility to those of South Korea and are thought to have acquired extensive capability and added mechanization in recent years. The KPA possesses a special unit, the Eighth Special Corps, of some 100,000 men, which can be dispatched to the south for conducting guerrilla warfare. The navy is primarily oriented to defending the coasts, although it is believed to possess the capability for conducting amphibious operations. Most of its vessels are smaller than those of the South Korean navy, although many are also faster. Unlike the south, the North Korean navy is handicapped by having to wage a two-sea operation in time of war. North Korea's air force, although almost twice as large as South Korea's in the number of planes, is believed to be using older models and to be behind South Korea in fighter capability. North Korea also possesses 300,000 reservists and 2.5 million Worker-Peasant Red Guards who in time of war can be fully mobilized to carry out combat duties.[39]

The military balance between North and South Korea is influenced by geography and terrain, apart from the number of men under arms and the weapons count. The location of the respective capitals of North and South Korea makes an important difference in terms of strategic concern and force deployments. Whereas Seoul, South Korea's capital, is only 50 km (31 miles) from the DmZ, North Korea's capital city, Pyongyang, is 145 km (90 miles) from the DmZ. With 9.4 million (1983 estimate), more than 20 percent of the total population, concentrated in it, Seoul is highly vulnerable to a possible surprise attack by the north, and the defense of the capital city is the foremost concern expressed by government leaders.[40]

For these and other reasons, North Korea would have a significant advantage in the initial days of fighting, provided it achieved tactical and strategic surprise. North Korea has the capability to produce its own weapons, such as tanks and artillery, but it has to rely on outside supplies for strategic items such as fuel. Depending on the duration and intensity of warfare, therefore, North Korea is said to store enough supplies to continue fighting for approximately thirty to ninety days without being resupplied by the Soviet Union and China. The U.S. command in Korea insists that the military posture of the north is offensive, and cites the forward deployment of troops and the discovery of three "invasion" tunnels as evidence for North Korea's war preparedness.[41]

South Korea's military posture is described by Washington as defensive, with U.S. troops playing the role of a deterrent or "tripwire" for a possible North Korean attack.[42] Tactical nuclear weapons deployed by U.S. troops in South Korea provide a bulwark against potential aggressive moves by the north, although the danger of the United States becoming a hostage in an armed conflict in Korea has led some critics of U.S. Korea policy to urge the removal of nuclear weapons and eventual U.S. troop withdrawal from Korea.[43] Until South Korea achieves self-reliance in defense and full control in command, however, the current defensive force deployment and forward strategy under the U.S. supervision is unlikely to change. In view of South Korea's rapid progress in building its defense industry and its desire to obtain a nuclear capability of its own, the future military balance between North and South Korea may shift to favor the south, largely owing to the superior performance of the South Korean economy over the North Korean economy.[44]

As both North and South Korea continue to expand their defense capability, the danger of a renewed military conflict in the Korean Peninsula may also increase. However, in view of the changing pattern of military power relations in the early 1980s, any future North-South conflict in Korea is less likely to involve the outside powers and more likely to be confined to the two Korean states. During the Cold War era Korea provided a focal point of ideological contention between the Communist bloc and the United States. With the détente of the early 1970s, the Korean Peninsula no longer serves as a focal point of East-West conflict. The major powers surrounding the Korean Peninsula have now come to share a desire for stability on the peninsula, lest they are forced into the awkward situation of having to side with either Korea as hostages in an inter-Korean conflict, thereby risking the provocation of a major global and regional confrontation.

Diplomatic Competition

North and South Korea compete intensely on the diplomatic front, usually through bilateral or multilateral diplomatic efforts. The act of establishing diplomatic relations with a foreign country is typically regarded by both Korean states as a matter of international recognition and prestige. They also consider this act as a strategic way of undermining the international position of the opposing Korean state. Both Korean regimes are also engaged in "invitational" diplomacy, whereby foreign political leaders and guests are lured to pay a visit to the capital city. The Korean governments send numerous diplomatic envoys and missions abroad to improve diplomatic ties and to establish commercial and cultural relations. At the multilateral level, both Korean governments are engaged in the diplomatic struggle for participation in international conferences and to win the support of the international community for their respective policy positions, most typically on the Korean reunification issue. Sometimes this competition takes place in the arena of the UN General Assembly and the various specialized UN agencies or functional bodies. The diplomatic forum of the non-aligned nations conferences

TABLE 6.8
Countries Maintaining Diplomatic Relations with North and South Korea

	With South Korea	With North Korea	With both Koreas
March 1974	91	63	32
December 1976	94	90	46
January 1978	102	92	53
April 1980	112	100	61
May 1982	117	104	67

Source: Reprinted from U.S. Department of State, "Diplomatic Relations of Republic of Korea and Democratic People's Republic of Korea," Unclassified, May 26, 1982, p.2.

has received greater attention by both Korean regimes in recent years. Although both North and South Korea applied, only North Korea was admitted to the membership of the Non-aligned Nations Conference at Lima in 1976.

In terms of the competition for bilateral diplomatic support, South Korea was far ahead of North Korea at the onset of the 1970s. However, North Korea has made a strenuous effort to catch up with the South on the diplomatic front, so that at the onset of the 1980s, the two Korean states were almost evenly matched in their diplomatic relations with other countries. The North-South Korean dialogue initiated in 1972, but suspended in 1973, seems to have benefited North Korea more than South Korea in terms of generating a favorable impression and providing an occasion for opening diplomatic relations with foreign countries.

As Table 6.8 shows, the number of countries maintaining diplomatic relations stood at 117 for South Korea and 104 for North Korea as of May 1982. The number of countries recognizing both Korean regimes was 67; the number of countries maintaining diplomatic relations with only South Korea was 50; and the number for North Korea alone was 37 (for a list of these countries, see Appendix A).[45]

The contrast between North and South Korea in the changes over time is revealing. A dramatic shift occurred in North Korea's diplomatic relations in the 1970s. Between 1974 and 1976, the number of countries that opened relations with North Korea increased by 32 percent; the increase for South Korea was only 11 percent. Both Korean states continue to intensify their campaigns for increasing the number of diplomatic ties, and therefore more changes are likely in the years ahead. South Korea's focus is on broadening diplomatic ties with the Third World and with Communist bloc and socialist countries, while North Korea is concentrating its energy on establishing relations with Western European and Latin American countries. North Korea, for instance, reportedly pressed for the exchange of ambassadors with France under President Mitterrand's socialist government. To date France had retained a North Korean trade mission in Paris, but had not reciprocated by placing its own mission in Pyongyang. Both Korean states view the diplomatic struggle as critical to the outcome of discussions on Korea in various international forums, such as the United Nations and the non-aligned nations meetings. Seoul's successful bid to host the 1986 Asian Games and the 1988 Olympics is regarded by South Korea as a positive development. Meanwhile, the Pyongyang government is waging an all-out campaign to dissuade others from participating in the 1988 Seoul Summer Olympics Games.

In the two-year period between 1980 and 1982, both North and South Korea made only marginal gains in their diplomatic competition for increased international recognition. Only two additional countries, Antigua and the United Arab Emirates, recognized South Korea exclusively. The Seychelles broke diplomatic relations with South Korea but not with North Korea. Four countries that had recognized only one Korea established relations with the other Korean state, namely Lesotho, Mexico, and Nauru with North Korea, and Libya with South Korea. Two other countries, Lebanon and Vanuatu, recognized both Koreas during the period under review. In addition, two countries established diplomatic relations with North Korea but only consular relations with South Korea, namely Egypt and Pakistan. There is also one country—Iraq—that has consular relations with South Korea but no full diplomatic relations with either North or South Korea. Iraq broke off relations with North Korea during this period. Two countries received resident North Korean trade missions but had no diplomatic relations with North Korea nor trade missions in Pyongyang: Kuwait and Peru. Finally, the Palestine Liberation Organization maintained an office in Pyongyang during this period.[46]

Foreign Economic Relations

The contrast between the two Korean states is most clearly shown in the area of foreign economic relations. The North and South Korean orientation and approach toward establishing external links with the world economy are radically different. The South Korean economy heavily depends on the condition of growing interdependence in the world market, exposing itself to the risks and opportunities associated with the world economy. The North Korean economy is more nationally oriented, relying on the principle of Juche (self-reliance) in its approach to the outside world. This independent orientation of North Korea makes its economy less vulnerable, at least in theory, to fluctuations in the world economy.

The contrasting orientations toward and linkage with the outside world are the result of divergent strategies of economic development. South Korea is more receptive to direct foreign investment in its economy, whereas North Korea is totally opposed to the infusion of foreign capital in its domestic market. The foreign economic performance of the two Korean states can be measured through available statistics in the areas of foreign trade, aid, loans and investments, and debts prior to the 1980s.

Both Korean regimes are actively expanding their trade ties with the outside world. Whereas South Korea adopted a policy of trade expansion around 1963, North Korea adopted a new posture of trade expansion that included some Western European countries and Japan in about 1971. The structure of foreign trade varies between the two Koreas in terms of total volume and composition of commodities, direction of trade, and trade partners.

As shown in Table 6.9, the ratio of total foreign trade volume in 1979 between the two Korean states was more than 12 to 1 in favor of the South. In 1979, North Korean exports amounted to U.S. $1,536 million, while South Korea's exports reached some U.S. $15,052 million. The overall trade balance in 1979 was more favorable to North Korea than to South Korea. Whereas North Korea registered a trade surplus of $181 million in 1979, South Korea had a record trade deficit of $5,244 million in that year. Although the South Korean economy was able to absorb some of this deficit through such invisible trade factors as the earnings from construction works in the Middle East, its growing external debt has become a matter of serious concern in the 1980s. Although the North Korean economy seems to be in better shape in foreign trade, it also suffers from an unpaid debt to Western European and Japanese banks for the purchase of plants and equipment from these countries in the early 1970s.

The direction of foreign trade is shown in Table 6.10. Prior to the 1970s, the Communist bloc countries were North Korea's only trade partners. Since around 1971, however, North Korea has expanded its trade ties beyond the Soviet Union and China to include Japan, Western Europe, and more recently, the non-aligned nations. South Korea concentrated heavily on the markets of the United States and Japan prior to 1970, but it has made some progress in diversifying its trade beyond these two countries in the 1970s.

Although in 1971 North Korea's trade with the Soviet Union and China accounted for 76 percent of its total imports and 61 percent of its total exports, its trade dependence on these two countries declined by 1977 to 45 percent of imports and 42 percent of exports. Its imports from Japan and its exports to Third World developing countries have

TABLE 6.9
North and South Korea's International Trade, 1970-1980
(in millions of U.S. $)

Year	North Korea			South Korea		
	Import (1)	Export (2)	Balance (2)-(1)	Import (1)	Export (2)	Balance (2)-(1)
1970	396	365	- 31	1983	835	-1148
71	576	333	-243	2394	1068	-1326
72	636	386	-250	2522	1624	- 898
73	855	522	-333	4240	3225	-1015
74	1301	704	-597	6852	4460	-2392
75	1122	805	-317	7274	5081	-2193
76	987	565	-422	8764	7715	-1049
77	860	784	- 76	10803	10016	- 787
78	997	1207	210	14966	12695	-2271
79	1355	1536	181	20296	15052	-5244
80	n.a.	n.a.	n.a.	22228	17483	-4745

Source: Frederica M. Bunge, ed., North Korea: A Country Study (Washington, D.C.: U.S. Government Printing Office, 1981): 255-56; 1980 Yearbook of International Trade Statistics (New York: United Nations, 1981): 557-58.

dramatically increased between 1971 and 1979, to 23 percent and 34 percent respectively. South Korea's dependence on the dominant markets of Japan and the U.S. also declined somewhat throughout the 1970s. Whereas in 1971 South Korea's imports from Japan and the United States were 40 percent and 28 percent respectively, by 1979 the share of total imports dropped to 33 percent and 23 percent. More dramatically, South Korea's exports to the United States decreased from 50 percent in 1971 to 29 percent of total exports in 1979. Its exports to Japan remained more constant.

Both Koreas have benefited from the infusion of capital from abroad through foreign assistance, loans, and investment. Although self-reliance has been its principle of economic development, North Korea has received considerable economic assistance from its allies, especially after the Korean War in the 1950s. It is estimated that between 1946 and 1960 North Korea received the equivalent of some U.S. $1.8 billion in foreign assistance, of which $700 million was from the Soviet Union, $600 million from China, and the remaining $500 million from Eastern European countries.[47] An additional U.S. $1 billion is estimated to have

TABLE 6.10
North and South Korea's Direction of International Trade, by Principal Countries, 1971-1980 (% of total trade)

Country	1971	72	73	74	75	76	77	78	79	80
North Korea's Imports from:										
Soviet Union	64	48	35	20	23	25	26	26	27	
China	12	17	16	13	16	13	19	n.a.	n.a.	
Japan	6	17	13	21	18	11	16	20	23	
W. Germany	1	1	5	7	7	5	3	4	3	
Developing coun.	1	2	9	6	6	19	14	10	14	
Others	16	15	32	33	30	27	22	n.a.	n.a.	
Total Imports	100	100	100	100	100	100	100	100	100	
in US $ mil.	576	636	855	1301	1122	987	860	997	1355	
South Korea's Imports from:										
Japan	40	41	41	38	33	35	36	40	33	26
U.S.	28	26	28	25	26	22	23	20	23	22
Saudi Arabia	2	4	4	10	8	8	10	9	8	15
Kuwait	3	4	2	4	8	8	5	5	6	8
W. Germany	3	3	3	2	3	3	3	3	4	3
Australia	2	2	2	2	3	3	3	3	3	3
Others	22	20	20	19	19	21	18	20	23	23
Total Imports	100	100	100	100	100	100	100	100	100	100
in US $ Mil.	2394	2522	4240	6852	7274	8764	10803	14966	20296	22228

been sent to North Korea between 1961 and 1978: $700 million from the Soviet Union and $300 million from China.[48] Of the total of U.S. $2.8 billion in foreign aid received by North Korea between 1945 and 1978, approximately $2,050 million was in the form of economic assistance, with the remainder in the form of military assistance.[49] South Korea has received even more substantial amounts of economic assistance from its allies. Between 1946 and 1975 South Korea reportedly received a total of U.S. $12.6 billion from the United States alone, of which approximately half was estimated to be in the form of military assistance.[50] An additional U.S. $2.8 billion was received by South Korea during the 1946-1975 period from Japan ($1 billion) and from other countries and international agencies ($1.8 billion).[51]

More recently, economic development projects in both Korean states have been financed not only by domestic savings but also by credits and

TABLE 6.10 (continued)

Country	1971	72	73	74	75	76	77	78	79	80
North Korea's Exports to:										
Soviet Union	41	40	35	28	26	28	24	25	25	
China	20	25	22	17	14	17	18	n.a.	n.a.	
Japan	8	10	13	14	7	12	8	8	9	
W. Germany	3	2	3	3	6	7	3	4	4	
Developing Coun.	3	3	4	13	21	15	30	33	34	
Others	25	20	23	25	26	21	17	n.a.	n.a.	
Total	100	100	100	100	100	100	100	100	100	
in US $ Mil.	333	386	522	704	805	565	784	1207	1536	
South Korea's Exports to:										
U.S.	50	47	32	34	30	32	31	32	29	26
Japan	25	25	39	32	25	23	21	21	22	17
Saudi Arabia	.1	.3	.4	.6	2	3	7	6	5	5
W. Germany	3	3	4	5	6	5	5	5	6	5
Hong Kong	4	5	4	3	4	4	3	3	4	5
U.K.	1	2	2	2	3	3	3	4	4	3
Others	19.9	17.7	18.6	23.4	30	30	30	29	30	39
Total	100	100	100	100	100	100	100	100	100	100
in US $ Mil.	1068	1624	3225	4460	5081	7715	10016	12695	15052	17483

Source: Trade statistics on North Korea are estimates reported in U.S. Department of the Army Area Handbook Series on North Korea, DA Pamphlet No. 550-81: Frederica M. Bunge, ed., North Korea: A Country Study (Washington, D.C.: Government Printing Office, 1981): 255-56. Trade statistics on South Korea are based on the United Nations survey: 1980 Yearbook of International Trade Statistics (New York: United Nations, 1981): 557-58.

loans from allies and multilateral development agencies such as the United Nations. Private loan sources, such as commercial banks abroad, have also been tapped by South Korea in order to meet the growing need for investment capital. North Korean economic projects are in theory self-supporting, but in 1983 North Korea agreed to receive a project loan from the United Nations Development Program (UNDP) amounting to U.S. $18.4 million.[52] The UNDP funds, to last from 1983 to 1986, are earmarked for a comprehensive "integrated country program" for North Korea, to acquire the capability for upgrading national industry, science and technology, agriculture, transport and communication, and natural resources development. North Korea's foreign debt was estimated to be somewhere between U.S. $1.8 and $2.1 billion as of 1980, of which some $1.3 billion was owed to Western European countries and Japan.[53] By the end of 1982, South Korea's external debt had reached a staggering $36.2 billion, with $23.5 billion in long-term and $12.7 billion in short-term debts.[54] South Korea's total and net debt-to-GNP ratios of 54 percent and 38 percent respectively, and its debt service ratio of 14.9 percent in 1982 raise serious doubts as to whether or not South Korea's export earnings are sufficient to meet payment requirements in the future.[55]

The South Korean economy also depends on direct foreign investment in firms operating in South Korea. At the end of 1976, for instance, the number of such firms was 865, and the total value of direct foreign investment on approval basis (rather than arrival basis) amounted to U.S. $953.7 million.[56] The U.S. share amounted to a total of 139 projects with a total investment of $214.8 million; the Japanese share amounted to 835 projects and $621.1 million in the 1962–1976 period. The year 1968 was a turning point in the pattern and direction of direct foreign investment in South Korea, shifting from import-substitution, U.S.-dominated investment to more export-oriented investment in which Japan's share rapidly increased. Between 1962 and 1968, the United States and Japan accounted for 81.7 and 7.9 percent respectively of the total value of direct foreign investment, but during the 1969–1974 period, the U.S. share constituted 21.2 percent and the Japanese share 72.3 percent of total foreign investment in the South Korean economy.[57] Interestingly, although 682 of 733 foreign firms operating at the end of 1974 were joint-venture companies, the wholly-owned subsidiaries were largely concentrated in the electronic industry.[58] In 1974 the share of foreign investment firms in the total output of the mining and manufacturing sector was only about 10 percent, although the share in total exports accounted for about 28 percent of Korea's commodity exports and about 31 percent of manufactured exports.[59]

Concluding Remarks: The Dynamics of Competition

Between socialist North Korea and capitalist South Korea, a herculean struggle for survival and fierce competition has been in progress ever since the rival regimes were established. The dynamics of competition in divided Korea takes the form of each regime trying to excel in the task of policy performance, and also to outperform the opponent regime in various policy domains.

Inter-Korean conflict and rivalry are a legacy of the Cold War era, whose ideological values the Korean people have internalized. Yet despite the ideological bifurcation of the Korean nation, the Korean states have successfully adapted to the changing requirements of the outside world.

They have borrowed foreign institutions and ideas and applied them successfully and efficiently to suit their internal needs. The socialist north, after adopting the idea of command economy, excelled in managing the economy and economic development, and the capitalist south excelled in achieving rapid economic growth and modernization after adopting the Western system of market economy. The North Korean economy has performed well compared with other socialist countries that have similar economic systems, such as China and some Eastern European countries; South Korea stands out above other market-economy Third World countries in its rapid economic growth and industrialization.

Students of comparative politics and history became curious about why and how the economic takeoff took place in the two Korean states, whose economic systems and ideologies are so dissimilar. Among the many explanations given, the cultural theory of Confucianism has been the most interesting and widely held hypothesis.[60] According to this view, both North and South Korea belong to the East Asian cultural sphere where Confucian traditions and belief systems still linger on, encouraging the work ethic and frugality so basic to the modern way of life.[61] This culture also encourages secularism, rationalism, and respect for learning and education. Although this interpretation of Korean economic success as based on Confucian cultural mores and tradition is interesting, it may not explain fully the peculiar circumstances and unique situation of Korea as a divided nation among other East Asian Confucian nations.

What has made the two Korean regimes both efficient and effective in their policy performance and mangement of the economy is the dynamics of inter-Korean competitive pressure. The zero-sum game of competing legitimacy, in which the very survival of political systems and the viability of society is at stake, gives both Korean regimes an additional incentive to work harder, and an occasion to prove to the world that its own system is superior to the opponent's system. Both Korean states had no other recourse than to excel in economic performance and economic development.

Whereas conflict entails direct contact and communication, competition need not.[62] The two Korean states have been in competition ever since they were established in 1945. During the 1950–1953 Korean War era, the violent conflict between the two rival political systems involved direct contact and communication. In the postwar era, however, the two Korean states pursued their policies of internal consolidation in isolation from one another. In the 1970s, with the initiation of the North-South Korean dialogue on unification, the two Korean states became aware of each other's strengths and weaknesses through a brief but intense direct encounter in 1972–1973. Inter-Korean competition in the 1970s and the 1980s subsequently acquired a new intensity and seriousness.

The competition between the two Korean states took several forms in the 1980s. Different sets of policy choices and developmental strategies adopted in the preceding era led to different levels of performance in policy areas. Whereas North Korea stressed autonomous development, self-reliance, and economic independence, South Korea pursued its strategy of industrialization through establishing external links and participating actively in the world trade system. Both Korean states were remarkably successful in achieving the policy goals of economic development as measured by the rapid rate of economic growth. South Korea's economic development was made possible by the rapid increase in exports of manufactured goods and by measures to diversify its external economic ties, such as overseas construction projects in the Middle East and elsewhere since 1974.

The dynamics of inter-Korean competition are also evident in the areas of military preparedness and diplomacy. A keen arms race and diplomatic competition have been going on between the two Korean states throughout the 1970s and the 1980s. The arms race in the Korean Peninsula is an unfortunate legacy of the Cold War era, when divided Korea was a proving ground for the ideological supremacy of communism and democracy. The diplomatic competition betwen North and South Korea in their search for allies and supporters is a duplication of effort and a waste of energy. This is also true in the area of foreign economic relations. Yet given the competitive pressure under which the two Korean states operate in the international arena, it is understandable that the Korean regimes are embarked upon the task of winning friends at one another's expense.

As long as the competition between the two Korean states does not escalate into armed conflict, a modicum of competitive spirit between the two Korean states may not be as deplorable as it sounds at first. One could argue that the dynamics of inter-Korean competition is the driving force that continues to motivate the rival Korean regimes to excel. As long as Korea remains a divided nation—and there is no indication that this situation will change radically in the immediate future—the two Korean regimes are well advised to continue their present courses and policies, maintaining the posture of mutual admonition and stimulation in a healthy and open competition for survival and excellence, rather than through violent conflict and war.

7
Domestic and Foreign Policy Behavior

Korean politics in the remainder of the 1980s will continue to be affected by how the respective Korean states adjust to pressures in the domestic environment, in international relations, and in inter-Korean relations. Whereas internal policy matters pertain to such issues as political, social, and economic development, external policy matters relate to such issues as security, alliance, and unification. An analysis of each Korea's policy behavior and performance in attaining its stated policy goals in specific sectors or issue areas will give us some clues about the character of the regimes and political elites of the respective Korean states. What policies and programs are planned for the 1980s? How realistic and feasible are the proposed policy measures? Are the strategic goals of the respective Korean regimes designed to allow for political participation by the masses or to enhance the power of the ruling elite? How are the interests of the ruling elite and the welfare of the masses likely to be reconciled, if at all?

Of particular relevance to Korea's political future is the balance of power in East Asia. The interests of four major powers converge and conflict in Korea, namely the United States, Japan, the PRC, and the Soviet Union. In spite of the oft-invoked rhetoric of independence and self-reliance, this geopolitical reality makes it imperative for the leadership in each Korea to pay particular attention to domestic political developments in the PRC and Japan as well as to developments within and between the two superpowers of the United States and the Soviet Union. The very survival of Korea's two political systems in the 1980s may depend on how well the regimes of divided Korea are able to adapt to the changing international political environment and to volatile domestic political pressures.

Consolidation and Development: South Korea

Following the birth of the Fifth Republic in 1981, President Chun Doo Hwan first emphasized the tasks of consolidating his position of authority and developing specific socioeconomic programs and policies.

In the name of founding a "just and democratic" society, President Chun relied on a subtle policy of stick and carrot to punish and reward the public. The Chun government and the DJP continued to carry out the "purification campaign," intended to purge the "old politicians" and also to eliminate what it considered to be corruption and malpractice by government officials. In 1981, a new five-year plan for social cleanup was drawn up on special instructions from President Chun Doo Hwan. The government intention was to cause "a drastic turnabout from its previous policies, which were [allegedly] focused on investigating cases involving irregularities and corruption," to a more rational and scientific approach such as renovating administrative procedures for civil petitions, personnel management, etc.[1]

As if to make a New Year's resolution, in the first week of January 1982 President Chun announced the appointment of a new team of key advisors and cabinet members. These included a new prime minister and a new deputy prime minister, both selected from the business community.[2] The move was clearly timed with the implementation of the Fifth Five-Year Plan of Economic and Social Development (1982–1986) and intended to convey a positive signal to the public—the business constituency in particular. Although President Chun was forced to replace his prime minister and other economic ministers six months later, in the aftermath of a financial scandal, his determination to press on with the administration of progressive policy measures did not slacken. Instead, with each new crisis or challenge to his leadership Chun seemed to gain renewed determination to survive and persist with his programs. President Chun apparently desires to put an end to the legacy of the discredited Yushin system of Park Chung Hee, whose protégé he once had been, and to inaugurate a new style of politics and a new political and social order for the present and the future. Chun's determination to be master of his own political destiny has been shown in the type of public policies projected and pursued by the Chun government in coping with domestic politics, socioeconomic development, and foreign affairs.

Strategy for Political Development

In order to bring about the vision of a "just" and prosperous "democratic" society for South Korea, President Chun Doo Hwan outlined a series of specific policy measures and programs in his New Year address on January 22, 1982. The linchpin of his 1982 policy statement was the "new unification formula" in which he proposed the adoption of a "constitution of a unified Korea." This would be accomplished (as detailed in Chapter 8) through the convocation of a Consultative Conference on National Reunification, with participants from both South and North Korea, for the purpose of drafting the constitution. Given the importance of the Korean unification issue for the Korean people, it was fitting that Chun used the unification theme to highlight his theme of "new politics" for the 1980s.[3]

Chun's pledge "to expedite political modernization" was one of the more interesting and important statements in his address. Chun said that the Koreans can attain modernization in politics by "achieving greater political maturity," and more specifically by obtaining "a clear understanding of the function and role of politics in a democracy" and by ensuring that "politicians accept due responsibility for political activities." These commitments on the part of the public and the politicians, according to Chun, were two preconditions for the effective functioning of politics and for maintaining political stability, which he said was "the nerve center for stability in all other areas."[4]

To assure democratic and responsible politics, President Chun pledged that he would promote the cause of "party politics" and especially a close relationship between his government and his own ruling Democratic Justice Party. He categorically stated that "democratic politics are equated with party politics" and that "political parties and the government must develop cooperative relations in formulating and implementing public policies, rather than estranging each other by jockeying for a dominant position."[5]

This statement of President Chun on political modernization, although somewhat simplistic and exaggerated, was a welcome development. His pledge to expedite party politics was also a positive step for the cause of restoring democracy and activating the democratic political process in South Korea. Chun appears to have made a reasonably valid assumption regarding the root cause for the failure of democracy in South Korea. He observed, for instance, that "a look at our political history shows that, regardless of the form of government, political parties were always pushed to the sidelines and the executive branch alone ran the show."[6] This is the practice that Chun said he would try to put an end to. President Chun also asserted that "only when [cooperative party-government] relationships are developed will it be possible not only to energize the National Assembly but also to rid public administration of rigid bureaucratism and expedite the development of energetic, positive, flexible and devoted civil service."[7] Finally, he described the abovementioned measures as "a short-cut to a peaceful change of government" and as an effective way of developing Korea into a "new politically advanced democracy," just as South Korea successfully developed into a newly industrializing country in the 1970s.

President Chun expanded upon his foreign and domestic policies in the remainder of his address. He pledged to work toward easing tension and securing a lasting peace on the Korean Peninsula, and also to maintain solidarity with allies and improve diplomatic ties with friendly and adversary nations. Other measures to promote his stated goal of building a "just and democratic" society included ambitious programs and projects for strengthening defense, revitalizing the economy, promoting the work of welfare and social development, and encouraging developments in culture and education. Chun also pledged to revitalize the Saemaul movement for both urban and rural development.[8]

Underlying the political policies reflected in President Chun's 1982 New Year address were two important new developments. The first was his accent on party politics and party government. This was significant not only as a departure from Park Chung Hee's disregard and contempt for party politics, but also as a recognition of the political reality of the party movement in Korea.[9] After all, it was the dynamics of interparty conflict in the National Assembly in 1979 that triggered political crisis and the eventual collapse of the Fourth Republic. Opposition New Democratic Party leader Kim Young-sam's demand for the resignation of President Park Chung Hee and the abolishment of his Yushin system led to the adoption by the ruling DRP and the Yujonghoe group of a resolution to expel Kim from the National Assembly. This prompted the resignation en masse of the opposition NDP assemblymen. The resultant political crisis culminated in widespread antigovernment street demonstrations in Pusan and Masan, initiated by students but later joined by civilians. This set the stage for Park's assassination by KCIA Director Kim Jae-kyu, allegedly to prevent a bloody confrontation between the government forces and the demonstrators.[10]

In the light of this history, the real challenge to President Chun's regime is not only a question of promoting close relationships between the government and the ruling party, as emphasized in his address, but also of dealing fairly with opposition political parties and groups in and outside of the National Assembly. Perhaps deliberately, President Chun omitted any reference to the matter of promoting interparty relationships between the ruling and opposition parties during his address to the National Assembly.[11]

The second important aspect of the speech was the very fact of Chun's personal appearance before the legislative body to deliver this major policy pronouncement. This was a positive step forward, as the gesture reflected his willingness to give a more prominent role to the legislative process. Whether the style and rhetoric of presidential politics in the Fifth Republic will match the substance, however, remains to be seen in the days ahead.

Corruption, Repercussions, and Reform

Since politics is more than rhetoric, we need to examine the actual political process in South Korea in the years 1982 and 1983. What counts in politics is as much the performance of the leaders as their manipulation of political symbols. Having usurped power by military coup, President Chun Doo Hwan was determined to keep political power at any cost. As an authoritarian regime the Fifth Republic under President Chun was governed by the principle of realpolitik: power determines justice. Chun follows the Machiavellian dictum that political ends justify political means—and staying in office justifies any and all means available. Like other authoritarian leaders in history, Chun uses his power to reward his friends and to punish his enemies. To retain the power he usurped, Chun has utilized several tactics: (1) a well-publicized campaign to eliminate corruption and carry out political reform, (2) political appointments to reward power aspirants and implement frequent cabinet changes, and (3) token gestures of concession to woo real and potential enemies. In overcoming the domestic political challenges of 1982 and 1983, Chun proved himself to be a skillful and efficient realpolitik politician.

Before Chun's blueprint for political development had a chance to go into effect, a major financial scandal broke in the spring of 1982. Because Chun's relatives were implicated, the scandal tarnished Chun's public pledges to root out irregularities and corruption. Although public confidence in Chun remained low throughout the year, his government moved quickly and decisively to investigate the scandal and to carry out a series of financial reforms.

The "Kerb" loan scandal in May 1982 was one of the most serious challenges to President Chun's pledge to build a "just" society. Socialite and financier Chang Yong-ja, whose husband was a former deputy director of the KCIA, was one of the big lenders in Seoul's private credit market. Chang loaned U.S. $79 million in cash to six industrial companies in return for $361 million in bank-guaranteed promissory notes, then sold more than half of the notes for cash in a thirteen-month period ending in April 1982. This private credit granting, called the Kerb market, has been popular in Korea because of the shortage of investment capital available to businesses through regular bank channels. Chang's unorthodox transaction led to the bankruptcy of two major companies—Kong Yung Construction and Ilshin Steel—and several other medium-sized companies.[12] At one point, Chang and her husband, Lee Chol-hi, reportedly manipulated nearly $980 million worth of notes, equivalent to more than 17 percent of South Korea's entire money supply in 1982, estimated at $5.7 billion.[13]

The most devastating element of the scandal for Chun's reputation as president was the involvement of his wife's uncle, Lee Kyu-kwang. Lee allegedly used influence peddling to arrange a loan through commercial banks (then partly controlled by the government) for Chang Yong-ja, who was his sister-in-law. Also implicated was the ruling DJP and its secretary-general, Kwon Jong-dal, who was a close confidant and associate of Chun Doo Hwan. The impression of an attempted cover-up initially conveyed to the public by the state prosecutor's announcement of the case exacerbated public feeling, and the credibility of the government's much publicized anti-corruption and clean-government campaigns was severely damaged.

When the case was tried in August, the court convicted thirty-two people on charges of fraud, bribery, and violations of foreign exchange control laws. The convicted included two bank presidents, Chang, and Chang's husband. The latter two were both sentenced to fifteen years; Mrs. Chun's uncle received a four-year sentence.

This scandal led to a cabinet reshuffling in May 1982 that involved half of its twenty-two members. In June, Chun also replaced prime minister Yu with Kim Sang-hyop, president of Korea University and a former education minister. Because Kim had some opposition support, his appointment was expected to restore a measure of credibility to Chun's government. Chun also appointed Kwon Ik-hyon, a former businessman and his classmate at the Korean Military Academy, as the new secretary-general of the ruling Democratic Justice Party. Under its new leadership the DJP evolved into a more moderate party, abandoning its initial purification campaign and allowing internal democracy and compromise.

With a new prime minister and a new team of economic ministers in the cabinet, President Chun Doo Hwan carried out drastic measures to reform the financial market. In June 1982 the Chun government announced a series of sweeping economic measures, slashing lending interest rates to 10 percent from a 13.5 percent bank prime rate and cutting corporate taxes to 20 percent from the existing level of 33 to 38 percent. These government actions expanded credit, taking the heat off thousands of business firms that were in danger of going under during the difficult time of economic recession. It was reported that about 28,000 medium and small companies, plus a large number of consumers, had turned for financing to the Kerb loan market. It was also announced that the government would urge the National Assembly to pass legislation prohibiting all anonymous bank transactions—which had been legal up until then. These economic measures were designed to rescue small business enterprises while carrying out a reform of the financial market.[14]

President Chun's own ruling DJP, however, failed to pass the proposed Real Name Deposit Law in the National Assembly. This loophole contributed to another business failure in August 1983. One of South Korea's business conglomerates, the Myongsong group, which invested heavily in tourism and the leisure industry, was indicted on charges of tax evasion and illegal fundraising through the Kerb market. The Myongsong group's Kerb-market loans, during the fifty-one months of its spectacular expansion, were estimated to total 106 billion won (U.S. $135 million), of which the company president took 51.2 billion won (U.S. $65.2 million) in principal. The rest was paid out as interest on the loans, with interest rates ranging from 25 to 32 percent a year.[15] Sixteen people were arrested on bribery and embezzlement charges connected with this business scandal, including a former cabinet minister, eight government officials, and four bank officials. The repeated financial scandals, and the many arrests involved, reportedly made the entire business community uneasy.

Once the economic difficulties associated with the Kerb scandal and continuous recession were reasonably under control, President Chun moved to put his programs for political development into effect. The overriding objective that Chun pursued in 1982 and 1983 was to consolidate his position of authority as the unrivaled leader and founder of the Fifth Republic. To achieve this goal Chun moved skillfully and efficiently to recruit a new group of party politicians, government leaders, and technocrats, drawn from key segments of Korean society, including the military, the business community, academia, and the government bureaucracy.

The appointments of Kim Sang-hyop as prime minister in June 1982 and his replacement by Chin Iee-chong in October 1983 were typical of President Chun's skillful moves. Whereas Kim was a respected educator and a former university president, Chin had been an opposition NDP lawmaker in the National Assembly in the early 1970s, subsequently becoming chairman of the ruling party's policy committee in May 1982, after winning a seat in the National Assembly in 1981 on the DJP ticket. Speaker of the National Assembly Chae Mun-shik, elected in 1983, was also a former NDP member turned DJP politician in the Fifth Republic. One of Chun's cabinet members without portfolio, Oh Se-ung, had been a veteran NDP leader in the National Assembly in the 1970s. The appointment of these former opposition NDP members to key posts is evidence of Chun's powers of persuasion and his political skill.

In recruiting former opposition leaders to serve in his cabinet, however, Chun drew a clear line between what he called the new and the old politicians. Chun Doo Hwan was determined to bring about a new style of politics by promoting a younger generation of party and government leaders into leadership positions. He resolved to keep the old politicians out, refusing to lift the ban on political activities by certain politicians of the earlier era.

On March 1, 1981, timed with his inauguration as president, Chun had announced amnesty for 5,221 people. This measure, obviously intended to pacify the government's critics, did not however include the release of prominent dissidents or opposition leaders. The move was followed one year later, on March 1, 1982, by the announcement that amnesty or reduced sentences would be granted to 28,862 additional prisoners. Of these, 297 were said to be "political offenders," including the dissident Kim Dae-jung, whose prison term was reduced at this time from life to twenty years.[16] By releasing Kim Dae-jung from prison in December 1982 and allowing him to travel to the United States for a "medical checkup," Chun in fact sent Kim into forced exile, thereby eliminating one of the root causes of possible political instability and challenge to his rule. When Kim Young-sam carried out a 21-day fast in May 1983, demanding restoration of democracy and an end to the ban on political activities by the purged politicians, Chun responded by ordering Kim Young-sam's house arrest lifted and emergency treatment administered to save Kim's life.[17]

Timed with the celebration of South Korea's August 15 National Day in 1983, the Chun government announced that it was releasing 134 political prisoners, mainly university students arrested for their antigovernment campus demonstrations, and restoring full civil rights to 551 other dissidents already freed.[18] However, Chun refused to lift the ban on the 303 former politicians (out of a total of 835 on the initial purge list in 1980) who still remained blacklisted. It was reported in June that a total of 116 college students were arrested nationwide during the academic year just ending for having allegedly staged antigovernment demonstrations and illegal gatherings while distributing leaflets on campuses and for violating the government law prohibiting assembly and demonstrations. This figure, according to the government report to the National Assembly, represented a threefold increase over the figure for the 1980-1981 academic year. Of the total of 116 arrested, 110 were reportedly convicted. Of those convicted, 82 were allowed to join the armed services, 23 were being put on summary trial, and 5 were still at large and sought by the police.[19]

In the attempt to reinvigorate the activities of the ruling party, Chun as party president appointed one of his classmates in the Korean Military Academy, retired army general Kwon Ik-hyon, as new secretary-general of the DJP. Former speaker of the National Assembly and ex-defense minister Jung Nae-hyok, a retired army general, was made chairman of the DJP in October 1983, while Chun retained his position as DJP president. Chun also strengthened his Blue House team of advisors, appointing U.S.-educated technocrats as his chief aides and policy advisors. Harvard-educated scholar-diplomats, first Kim Kyung-won and then Hahm Pyong-choon, were made chief of staff in the Blue House in 1980 and 1982 respectively. A Stanford University Ph.D. in economics, Kim Jae-ik, became Chun's chief economic advisor. In July 1983, 45-year-old technocrat Suh Suk-joon was appointed deputy prime minister, and Suh was also named EPB (Economic Planning Board) minister, together with other competent technocrats with academic experience.[20] These measures were intended to erase the negative image of Chun's regime and to enhance both the prestige and respect of his government in the eyes of the public at home and abroad.

In order to dispel the rumor of a constitutional amendment to allow a second term of office beyond 1988, President Chun stated on June 1, 1983, that the rumor was "totally groundless" and that he was committed to a peaceful transfer of power. Although President Chun did not actually say, "I will not amend the constitution during my term of office," his determination to safeguard the constitution was clear, according to a *Choson Ilbo* commentary on June 2, 1983. The idea of not "linking the ability of a certain leader with the development of a state" was welcomed by many observers in South Korea, including the opposition DKP spokesman.[21] Chun reaffirmed his stand on a single presidential term during a press conference at the Blue House on August 25, stating that "the peaceful transfer of political power was the core of the process to firmly root democracy" and that it was time for the

Korean people "to implement democratization, rather than to demand it." He also pledged to work toward making Korea "an advanced country," which he said represents "the one in which all citizens live in happiness by virtue of spiritual growth as well as material growth with full enjoyment of their liberties and rights as decent human beings."[22]

Economic Development Plans and Achievements

The public will ultimately judge President Chun's government policies by how well he and his government can implement the program for socioeconomic development. Chun's blueprint for achieving this goal is contained in his ambitious Fifth Five-Year Plan of Economic and Social Development (1982–1986). It is true that the Chun regime inherited many economic ills and difficulties from the Park regime, including uncurbed inflation, business recession, and a heavy defense burden. But after its two years of honeymoon, the Chun government could no longer depend on the residue of goodwill and the "wait and see" attitude displayed by the public toward Chun as a newcomer to the political scene. It was time for the Chun regime to stand on its own feet.

The new five-year plan was designed to achieve the "second economic miracle for Korea" or the "second economic takeoff," and it reflects Chun's policy direction for the 1980s. The strategy for achieving the fifth five-year plan's ambitious goals consists of three key measures: maintaining price stability, liberalizing the economy through lessened government control, and increasing social development benefits. Apart from the possibility that these measures may work against one another, every one of the proposed policies entails both costs and benefits. Less government direction of the economy, advocated in favor of more private and business initiative, is clearly a reversal of past practices of economic development. Although popular among certain business circles, the proposed laissez-faire policy is not without its own risks and uncertainties, as these measures are very new and unfamiliar among the Korean circles responsible for planning and executing economic policy. What made the South Korean economic miracle possible between 1962 and 1979 was, in part, the government-guided strategy for economic development.[23] The Chun government in 1982 proposed the abolition of certain measures of centralized control and participation in the economic development projects. This posture, which reflects the Reaganomics emphasis in the United States, would certainly benefit the business and financial community, but perhaps at the expense of the broad interest of the public.[24]

The fifth five-year plan projects an average annual GNP growth rate of 7.5 percent over the five years covered (1982–1986). It envisions the GNP rising from the current level of U.S. $60 billion in 1981 to $90 billion by 1986, with per capita GNP rising from the current U.S. $1,500 in 1981 to $2,000 by 1986. It also envisions "a shift toward increased social development and improved income distribution." The population is scheduled to increase to 41 million by 1986 from 37 million in 1980. Merchandise exports, which financed South Korea's drive for economic development in the Park era, are expected to jump from about U.S. $20 billion in 1981 to $53 billion (1982 prices) in 1986, based on a projected annual growth rate of 11.4 percent for exports and 8.4 percent for imports.[25]

Developments so far indicate that the projected increase in the economy was too optimistic. The growth of South Korea's economy is contingent upon the health of the world economy and the export demand for South Korea's manufactured products, and South Korea has failed to keep up with its export target. In 1982, exports registered a total of U.S. $23 billion, a meager 1.8 percent increase over total exports in 1981. The demand for Korea's manufactured goods abroad was just not expanding as rapidly in the 1980s as in the 1970s.

Because South Korea depends heavily on the dominant markets of the United States and Japan for both imports and exports, the continuous purchase of South Korea's manufactured products by these two countries is essential to achieve the projected export figures. However, South Korea's exports to these countries as a proportion of the total had declined steadily in the 1970s. In 1980, South Korean exports to the United States and Japan were 26 percent and 17 percent respectively of total exports, a decline from the early record of 50 percent and 25 percent of total exports in 1971. In light of mounting protectionist pressures and the economic recession in these countries, South Korea needed to diversify its markets, away from heavy reliance on the United States and Japanese markets, and to penetrate the Western European, Eastern bloc, and Third World markets in Asia, Africa, and Latin America. What made South Korea's development look brighter in 1981–1982 was the continuous success of South Korea's construction industries abroad, especially in the Middle Eastern countries, which generated a huge sum in invisible service trade earnings.[26]

An analysis of South Korea's 1981–1982 economic performance is instructive. Its overall economy in 1981 and 1982 was fortunately in better shape than it was in 1980. GNP growth was 6.4 percent in 1981 and 5.4 percent in 1982, as against 5.6 percent negative growth in 1980. But the unexpectedly favorable GNP growth in 1981 was not so much the result of the Chun government's policies as of the fortunate circumstances that South Korea enjoyed toward the end of the year. The 1981 harvest was better than that of 1980, which meant that the agricultural sector accounted for at least 5 percent of the overall 6.4 percent growth. Stable crude oil prices also contributed to the successful GNP growth rate in 1981. Also not to be overlooked was the relative stability of wages for the year, which rose by an average of 17–18 percent as compared to 28 percent in 1980. Business recovery in 1981 was actually quite slow; the growth rates for the manufacturing and mining sectors improved by only 1 and 2 percent respectively.[27]

Although the South Korean economy recovered enough to achieve a better performance than most other industrialized economies in 1982, it fell far short of the projected target of the fifth five-year plan, which envisaged a 7.6 percent annual growth rate. World trade in 1982 did not expand as anticipated, and South Korea's export trade was stagnant, with a 4.8 percent growth rate in 1982. Expansion in the domestic market, especially in housing construction—which benefited from a reduction in interest rates, and the rapid decline in inflation proved to be the main sources of the better-than-expected performance of the economy in 1982. As South Korea's external debt continued to rise (estimated at U.S. $37.3 billion in 1982 and projected to reach between U.S. $64.5 and U.S. $49 billion by the end of 1986), its debt service ratio in 1982 reached a record 14.9 percent.[28] South Korea's foreign debt in 1982 was the largest in Asia and the fourth largest in the world.

The less than sanguine economic performance and the worldwide economic recession forced the Chun government to reassess its major policy goals and to readjust the targets of the fifth five-year plan. Some of the assumptions in the original plan, such as a 10 percent annual increase in world oil prices and a 5 percent growth rate for global trade volume, proved to be erroneous. Instead, world oil prices dropped 15 percent during the first half of 1983, and world trade volume contracted by 1 percent in 1982. To reflect these and similar changes, the EPB set up a task force, consisting of eighteen separate teams working within different areas of the government, to reevaluate the plan goals. This was one of the first of the important measures put into effect by the new deputy prime minister, Suh Suk-joon.

As a result of this reassessment the Chun government adjusted the priorities and projections of economic performance for the plan's remaining three-year period to 1986. The government announced that the 1984 budget would be frozen at the 1983 level, about U.S. $13.5 billion, forcing the cancellation or delay of some major public works projects that are considered inflationary (except those related to the 1988 Olympics). The government also lowered its projected estimates for merchandise exports in the five-year plan, from U.S. $53 billion to the more realistic level of U.S. $36.7 billion for the terminal year of 1986.

Chun's economic development program benefited in 1983 from another good performance of the economy for the year. In 1983 GNP grew a reported 9.3 percent in real terms. This was largely attributed by the Korean Development Institute, the government think tank, to rising domestic spending in the service industries and to the construction boom. The government was also successful in controlling inflation, which fell from the projected target of 14 percent to 4.2 percent in 1982. Even more dramatic was the drop to about 1 percent in the first half of 1983, as against the original assumption of about 10 percent inflation for 1983.[29] A historical low of 2.9 percent in inflation was thus registered in 1983. With the bumper harvest in 1983 the Chun government finished the year with a better-than-average economic performance.

The guideline of President Chun's economic development policy for 1983 was "economic recovery with price stability." This realistic policy adjustment was made necessary by economic difficulties at home and abroad, triggered by the financial crash due to the 1982 Kerb scandal and the slow recovery of the world economy. Moreover, the fifth five-year plan was drafted in 1981 amid political chaos and uncertainty following the launching of the Fifth Republic. As President Chun celebrates the third anniversary of the republic, he is more self-confident and assured, believing that the measures for economic reform can be carried out.

With the help of his key advisors and the technocratic elite, President Chun's government is pressing for reform measures to modernize the economic structure, to make the economy more efficient and more responsive to the free market. More specifically, his government is pursuing programs of banking-sector modernization, technological innovation, and development of high technology. This will be a change from the past growth pattern of the economy in the 1970s, which was characterized by high inflation, high international borrowing, and strong government initiatives.[30]

Social and Educational Policy

The Chun government also adopted numerous populist measures in 1981 and 1982. These included abolishing a thirty-six-year-old curfew system and liberalizing overseas trips by the citizens. These measures were meant to show the government's determination in the "new era" to remove all causes of inconvenience to people in their daily lives.[31]

In the area of government educational policy, numerous innovative measures and a detailed implementation plan have also been put into effect. The proposal for reforming the long-standing educational system and practices is controversial, but if the government plan is fully carried out, its effects on the public welfare will be far-reaching. Innovative measures have included a ban on tutorial and extracurricular class lessons for schoolchildren, a change in the primary school entrance age from six to five years old, a reduction in the total years of primary school from six to five, and the institution of a new education tax to improve and expand educational facilities and increase salaries and benefits for teachers.[32] The required school uniform for middle school pupils in South Korea was also abolished in 1982 in favor of street clothes.

The establishment of the new Korea Scholarship Foundation was made possible by an act reorganizing three existing private scholarship foundations. These were dismantled by the government on the alleged grounds that they had been the product of corrupt politicians, namely former prime minister Kim Jong-pil and ex-lawmakers Kim Jin-man and Lee Hu-rak. These Yushin politicians were arrested in 1980 on charges of amassing wealth by abusing their power while in office. The total confiscated assets (including scholarship funds and other assets, mostly in the form of real estate and shares) were evaluated by the Ministry of Education to be worth about 8,950 million won (about U.S. $13 million).[33]

Following the freeing of 131 imprisoned students in 1983, President Chun announced the release of 48 additional students in February 1984. He announced on March 1, 1984, that the political ban would be lifted for 202 politicians. The ban had already been lifted for 250 politicians one year earlier. (Still remaining on the roster in 1984 are 99 opposition leaders of the original 835 blacklisted politicians.) These measures were deemed necessary and expedient for President Chun in order to accommodate the ever-increasing number of jailed dissidents and student activists. On the other hand, the Chun government announced a new experimental policy of encouraging campus self-government for university students, and even delegating decisionmaking authority to the universities. This policy may eventually bring about local autonomy in South Korea. Whether such liberalization measures will bear the intended fruit of enhancing political stability remains to be seen.

External Links and Security: South Korea

In the foreign policy area, the Fifth Republic under President Chun Doo Hwan has pursued since 1981 an activist foreign policy vis-à-vis its major power allies and adversaries. Changes in the Asian strategic environment in the 1980s will cause major fallout both domestically and also in the area of inter-Korean relations in the 1980s, and the diplomatic strategy of the Chun government is designed to deal with these changes. Chun's foreign policy has three key elements: (1) the strengthening of bilateral ties with the major allies, (2) the securing of "cross-recognition" or "cross-contacts" with the major power adversaries (i.e., the Soviet Union and China) as a way of restraining North Korea and stabilizing the Korean Peninsula, and (3) the widening of diplomatic contacts and trade relations with Third World countries in Asia, Africa, and Latin America. Underlying these efforts is the government's concern over the growing security threat from North Korea and the stalemate in the inter-Korean dialogue on unification. The South Korean posture is that peaceful coexistence with the north, not confrontation, is the preferred option, and the quest for unification should be based on that premise. This position is derived from the assumption that time is on the side of South Korea in its competition with North Korea because of the south's larger population base and more dynamic economic growth.

Strengthening Ties with Allies

Acceptance of the Chun Doo Hwan government by the South Korean people has been enhanced by the extent to which the regime has been able to generate support from its key allies, the United States and Japan. For this reason the Chun government has wished to strengthen its external links and to manipulate them for domestic political purposes. South Korea's strategy (not officially acknowledged) has been to establish a de facto tripartite alliance involving both the United States and Japan to maintain stability in the Korean Peninsula. During the 1983 "Team Spirit" exercise, which involved the troops of the United States and the ROK, an invitation was issued to the Japanese Self-Defense Forces to observe the military exercise. Since the early 1970s, cabinet-level security consultations have been held between the United States and South Korea on an annual basis. A similar interministerial conference between Japan and South Korea is also planned.

In January 1981, President Ronald Reagan invited President Chun Doo Hwan to visit Washington, D.C., as the first head of state to be so honored by the new administration. This symbolic gesture improved Chun's status immensely. Visits to South Korea by several high U.S. officials in 1982—Vice-president George Bush, Defense Secretary Caspar Weinberger, and Secretary of State George Shultz—also enhanced the prestige of the Chun government.

President Reagan's official visit to South Korea in November 1983 boosted the sagging confidence of Chun's government following the Soviet downing of the KAL007 flight on September 1 and the Rangoon attack on South Korea's visiting delegation on October 9. In his address to the National Assembly, President Reagan reaffirmed U.S. commitment to defend South Korea against the North Korean threat of attack, stating: "Let every aggressor hear our words because Americans and Koreans speak with one voice. . . . People who are free will not be lost in the Republic of Korea. . . . Let me make one thing plain: you are not alone, people of Korea, America is your friend and we are with you."[34] This is a kind of endorsement that will boost the morale of the South Korean population, and particularly the prestige of President Chun.

South Korea is vehemently opposed to unilateral moves on the part of the United States to open dialogue and establish contact with North Korea. Pyongyang's overtures to the United States are interpreted by Seoul as a strategy to weaken South Korea by loosening its ties with the United States, so that North Korea could unify the peninsula on its own terms after U.S. troops withdraw.

South Korea is also anxious to strengthen its ties with Japan, which shares a common interest in preserving stability and reducing tension on the Korean Peninsula. Japanese opposition to U.S. troop withdrawal from Korea during the Carter administration is often cited as an expression of the shared interest of both countries in preserving the status quo. Because of constitutional restrictions and public opposition to rearmament in Japan, South Korea realizes that a security treaty with Japan is unlikely. However, the Seoul government argues that Japanese dependence on the United States for security in Korea is accomplished through the U.S.-Japanese security pact.

The successful conclusion of negotiations, following Japanese prime minister Yasuhiro Nakasone's visit to Seoul in January 1983, of an economic agreement with Japan for a seven-year, U.S. $4 billion aid package, certainly gave President Chun much-needed support. His government plans to use the funds as capital for executing the programs of the fifth five-year plan. The loan from Japan will provide a needed boost to South Korea's economy, strengthening Chun's ability to cope with the stagnant economy and providing the necessary funds for social development programs. As a result of the visits by Nakasone and Reagan, Chun is now a world-class leader in the eyes of many Koreans at home.

Following their summit meeting, consultation between Nakasone and Chun increased considerably. Nakasone called Chun on June 3 to brief him on the 1983 economic summit of the seven industrial nations in Williamsburg, from which Nakasone had just returned; this call (lasting 23 minutes) was the fifth between the two leaders since Nakasone became prime minister in November 1982.[35]

President Chun's government policy has thus been to strengthen its ties with the United States, its principal ally, and with Japan by invoking the U.S.-Japan Security Pact. The Chun government argues that a firm U.S. commitment to defend South Korea militarily is the key to stability in the Korean Peninsula, which in turn is in Japan's national interest. It has also argued that Korean security is the precondition for continuous economic growth and development in South Korea, which contributes in turn toward the prosperity of the Pacific Basin countries, of which Japan and the United States are leading members.

Cross-recognition

South Korea's second strategy in its foreign policy for the 1980s is to promote cross-recognition as a way of institutionalizing peace in the Korean Peninsula by freezing the status quo. The Seoul government believes that through reciprocal diplomatic recognition by the respective allies of the two Korean governments, the chances of an outbreak of armed conflict and renewed war will be minimized. This cross-recognition plan, initially presented by U.S. Secretary of State Henry Kissinger in 1975 and reiterated in 1976, calls for the United States and Japan to recognize North Korea diplomatically in exchange for China and the Soviet Union's opening of diplomatic relations with South Korea.

The cross-recognition formula has not been implemented due to North Korea's vehement opposition, on the grounds that it would perpetuate the condition of divided Korea. Pyongyang denounces the cross-recognition plan as "a criminal two-Koreas plot" to deny the Korean people the right to seek independent reunification of their country.

Although the cross-recognition formula is deadlocked, the Seoul government has nevertheless moved ahead to establish "contacts" or "cross-contacts" with the Soviet Union and China on an unofficial basis. Although some contacts were already established before 1980, official diplomatic relations were not established because of North Korea's strenuous opposition and pressure on its allies. Given the delicate Sino-Soviet rivalry and competition for North Korea's allegiance, South Korea's strategy for obtaining cross-recognition with North Korea's allies has not been successful.

Contact with the PRC was made unexpectedly in 1983. A Chinese air force pilot flew to South Korea in a MiG-19 in October 1982, followed by another defection in August 1983 by a Chinese air force test pilot in his MiG-21. Both sought asylum in Taiwan. In May 1983, a Chinese civil airliner was hijacked on a domestic flight by five men and one woman and forced to land in a military base near Seoul upon crossing the DmZ from North Korea. A delegation of Chinese officials, led by the chief of the Civil Aviation Administration, was dispatched to Seoul to negotiate for the return of the aircraft and the release of ninety passengers and six crew members, enabling the Seoul government to establish its first official contact with the Beijing government.

In August 1983, Chinese officials in Beijing issued an entry visa to a South Korean government official, allowing him to attend a month-long seminar on aquaculture technique sponsored by the UN Food and Agriculture Organization. A new air route linking Tokyo and Shanghai through the Korean flight information region was also to be opened in August, shortening the flight time by 21 minutes and reducing the flight distance by 276 km.[36] The six Chinese nationals who hijacked the plane to South Korea in May were tried and convicted, although their light jail terms—six years each—were criticized by Beijing as being too lenient. Because of these and other situations South Korea and China seem to be headed toward a de facto rapprochement despite the absence of official ties between the two countries. The Chun government certainly benefits from this evolving relationship with China.

The episode of the ill-fated KAL007 flight from New York to Seoul, shot down by a Soviet fighter plane over the Sea of Japan on September 1, 1983, was a serious blow to South Korea's image and reputation. The sympathy expressed over the 269 victims, including passengers of several different nationalities, was overwhelming and spontaneous, and worldwide indignation was aroused by the arrogant Soviet behavior. Although this outpouring of emotion was helpful in regaining lost confidence, the South Korean leaders were basically angered and frustrated over their inability to deal directly with the Soviet government to demand restitution for injuries and compensation for the loss of lives and property.

An obvious casualty of this unfortunate episode was the lingering hope for possible rapprochement between South Korea and the Soviet Union. Since the early 1970s South Korea had worked strenuously and patiently to improve its ties, both official and unofficial, with the Soviet Union. There were some signs of improvement in relations between the two countries, such as the granting of visas to South Korean government officials to attend an international conference in the Soviet Union. Soviet citizens likewise attended meetings in Seoul. The Korean Airlines incident put an abrupt end to this process of nurturing relations between the two countries, as anti-Soviet rallies and demonstrations swept over the country. Additional protests were staged by Korean residents and by people friendly to South Korea throughout the world.

Diplomatic Offensives

South Korea also moved in the early 1980s to strengthen its diplomatic relations with Third World countries in Asia and Africa. Thus, President Chun's tour of the five ASEAN (Association of Southeast Asian Nations) countries in June 1981 was much publicized and praised. It was instrumental in enhancing Chun's image abroad and at home, and was interpreted as a bold initiative, a display of active leadership on the diplomatic front. For two weeks in August 1982, Chun also paid state visits to Canada and to four African countries—Kenya, Nigeria, Gabon, and Senegal—in an effort to improve diplomatic ties and to promote mutual trade with these countries. His overseas trip in 1982 was reciprocated by official state visits to Seoul by Indonesian president Suharto in October 1982, Turkish president Kenan Evren in December 1982, and Malaysian prime minister Datuk Seri Mahathir Mohamad in August 1983.

The hosting of the Seventieth Inter-Parliamentary (IPU) meeting in Seoul, from October 4 to October 13, 1983, was the centerpiece of the Seoul government's strategy for conducting diplomatic offensives. From the total of 98 countries to which invitations were issued, delegates from 67 countries, as well as representatives from 20 international organizations, took part in the Seoul meeting. Because of the KAL007 episode, however, the Soviet Union and its allies in Eastern Europe, as well as some pro-Soviet Third World countries, abstained from attending the Seoul meeting.[37] The Chun government's desire to use the IPU meeting as an occasion to invite the Communist bloc countries to Seoul and to work toward establishing possible diplomatic relations fell victim to the Korean Airlines disaster.

With the national shock of the KAL downing barely over, the Chun government moved ahead with its third foreign policy strategy, i.e., the widening of its diplomatic contacts and trade relations with countries in Asia and Africa. On October 8, 1983, while the IPU sessions in Seoul were still in progress, President Chun embarked upon an ambitious eighteen-day official tour of six South Asian and Oceanic countries including Burma, India, Sri Lanka, Australia, New Zealand, and Brunei, a British protectorate emerging to become independent. This tour would have been a major diplomatic accomplishment for President Chun; it would have established friendly official relations with non-aligned Asian countries and with two western countries in the South Pacific. Unfortunately for Chun, his six-nation tour—meant to be the high point in his pursuit of an active and positive diplomacy for 1983—ended abruptly in disaster. The significance Chun attached to this particular diplomatic tour was clear; he was accompanied by his wife, by a twenty-member official entourage consisting of several cabinet members and his key advisors, and by other supportive personnel such as the press.

Tragedy befell the South Koreans on the very first day, at the first stop of the diplomatic tour. On October 9 Chun was the target of an assassination plot in Rangoon, Burma, at the Martyr's Mausoleum, where he planned to participate in the wreath-laying ceremony. The powerful explosion at the Martyr's Mausoleum killed 16 South Koreans, including 4 cabinet members, and 3 Burmese journalists. It wounded 48 people, including 2 Burmese cabinet members and 15 South Korean officials at the scene. These people were waiting for Chun, who escaped the bomb blast simply because his motorcade was delayed a few minutes in a traffic jam on the way to the site of the ceremony.

Among the 17 dead in Chun's party (1 of the wounded died later) were the deputy prime minister, the foreign minister, and several high-ranking officials, including the secretary-general, the secretary for economic affairs, and other technocrats such as the energy minister, the trade and industry minister, and the vice-ministers for finance and for science and technology. The reputation of these government members for competence and academic achievement was widely recognized; they had helped Chun to chart a new course of political and socioeconomic development and move toward moderation in politics. Their loss was a serious blow to Chun's ability to govern effectively. Chun cancelled the rest of his trip and headed back immediately to preside over his government at home.[38]

Upon his arrival in Seoul, Chun described the bombing as a "tenacious provocation by the band of communists in North Korea," although no hard evidence was at hand at the time of his charge. Subsequently, the Burmese authorities apprehended two North Korean nationals; a third killed himself and several Burmese policemen as he tried to escape. President U San Yu of Burma condemned the bombing as a "premeditated and dastardly act" by terrorists. It was suspected that those arrested were North Korean commandos sent to Burma to assassinate Chun Doo Hwan.[39] North Korea responded to Chun's accusation as "preposterous and ridiculous," denying any responsibility for the Rangoon blast.[40] The Burmese government issued the final report of its investigation on November 4, announcing at the same time the severance of diplomatic relations with North Korea. The report established the fact that the Rangoon attack was carried out by North Korean commandos—an army major and two captains—sent to Burma to assassinate the visiting South Korean president.

On a more positive note, winning the site for the 1986 Asian Games and the 1988 Summer Olympics was perceived by the general public in South Korea as enhancing the prestige of Korea in the international community. Although these sport festivities were criticized by certain dissident groups as both ill-timed and ill-advised, the publicity payoffs and public relations benefits have already added to South Korea's image and status in the world community. President Chun naturally exploits these accomplishments by claiming a lion's share of the credit, and he is determined to make a success of these sports festivals. In March 1982, Chun's government announced the establishment of a new cabinet ministry in charge of sport affairs, in preparation for the forthcoming Summer Olympics in 1988.

Inter-Korean Relations

What helped the Chun government to stay in power in 1982 and 1983 was the North Korean factor. As a military man, Chun knows how to deal with the communist threat from the north, and he also knows how to use the security issue to his advantage, as a political weapon to silence his domestic opposition and critics. In the name of preserving national security, Chun's regime has justified the imposition of authoritarian rule and the repression of dissident forces both at home and abroad. The determination and strategy of the Chun government in using the unification issue as a political weapon became clear in the early months of 1982. In January 1982, President Chun appointed Lee Bum-suk, an anticommunist refugee from North Korea and former minister of national unification, as his new secretary-general in the Blue House. Lee was subsequently made foreign minister in July 1982.[41] Chun promised to be more active and aggressive on inter-Korean dialogue and competition, especially dialogue with North Korea on the unification question.[42] On January 22, 1982, Chun put forward a new unification formula (examined more fully in Chapter 8) as part of the overall package included in his New Year's policy statement before the National Assembly. This new unification policy was in turn followed by more concrete and specific measures proposed by Chun's minister of national unification on January 30, 1982.

Tying the unification question to the security issue gave Chun a new formula for enhancing his claim to legitimacy. This strategy of linking issues is expected to be rewarding to Chun because Korean unification is an important issue for the Korean people and thus he can readily manipulate and exploit the theme of unification to his political advantage. Although it was not altogether clear whether Chun's initiative on the unification question would bear its intended fruit, the ball was now thrown back to Pyongyang's court, and North Korea had to respond and come forward with a more positive and aggressive plan for unification. Through proclaiming his intention to be more positive and aggressive on the question of unification vis-à-vis his northern counterpart, Chun managed to upgrade the south's basic stance on the North-South dialogue. By pressing for the resumption of inter-Korean dialogue on unification, the Chun government also managed to exploit this opportunity to enhance its prestige at home and abroad. It succeeded in 1982 in creating the image of seeking a "rational solution" of promoting "peace and unification through dialogue," instead of seeking "unification by force or war."[43]

Following the October 9, 1983, Rangoon bomb blast, Chun moved quickly and decisively to recoup his losses. He announced a major cabinet shuffle on October 14, one day after the mass state funeral for the 17 deceased aides. On the grounds of moral responsibility for the Rangoon bombing (due to his government's failure to take adequate precautionary security measures) Prime Minister Kim Sang-hyop and other cabinet members tendered their resignation. A new prime minister (Chin Iee-chong, chairman of the ruling DJP) was appointed, as were 14 out of 22 cabinet ministers and 3 top aides.

On October 20 President Chun warned North Korea, speaking on a nationwide television, that any future "provocation" against South Korea would be answered by "a corresponding retaliation in strength." He said that the Rangoon incident was "an attack upon me as head of state, tantamount to a declaration of war" and that "we are near the end of our patience. I now serve a stern warning to the Kim Il Sung clique of North Korea that this is the last point of endurance.... Should such a provocation ever recur, [North Korea] shall expect, without fail, a corresponding retaliation in strength." He also appealed to all nations that maintain diplomatic relations with Pyongyang to break official ties with the communist government there.[44] Since this was the first time since Syngman Rhee and the Korean War years that a South Korean president had pledged to use force in response to such attacks, the seriousness of this declaration was clear. Tension in the Korean Peninsula has escalated, once again, to the point of a threat to peace and a renewal of armed conflict along the DMZ.

Mobilization and Revolution: North Korea

After the Sixth KWP Congress in 1980, President Kim Il Sung, with his son Jong Il now in a leadership position, pressed forward to attain "socialist construction and revolution" (meaning development) at home and diplomatic gains abroad. Under the new slogan of "modelling the whole of society on [the] Juche idea," Kim Il Sung continued to mobilize the population in the north while keeping it under rigid control and regimentation. The masses were urged to redouble their energy and efforts to achieve a "brilliant victory in the three revolutions," that is, the ideological, technical, and cultural revolutions. These themes were explicated in Kim Il Sung's report to the Sixth KWP Congress on October 10, 1980, and also reiterated in his policy statement before the joint meeting of the KWP's Central Committee and the DPRK's Supreme People's Assembly on April 14, 1982, one day before the celebration of his seventieth birthday in Pyongyang.

In its foreign policy, the North Korean regime continued in the early 1980s to maintain its precarious position of independence and autonomy between the two feuding communist giants, the Soviet Union and China. It also actively maintained diplomatic ties with Third World nations, sought new diplomatic and trade relations with some western countries, and actively participated in the non-aligned nations movement. Under the guise of promoting the campaign to "strengthen the unity of the ti-imperialist, independent forces," the Pyongyang government also continued to preach Kimilsungism and export the rhetoric of revolution, primarily to other Third World countries. Under the idea of Juche, the North Korean regime continued to subscribe to the policy line of political independence by opposing what it called "imperialism" and "dominationism." In spite of its rhetoric of "economic self-reliance and self-help in defense"—also components of the idea of Juche, Kim Il Sung's government experienced some difficulties in maintaining this posture in its foreign trade and alliance relations with China and the Soviet Union.

Building a "Unitary System"

The inauguration of the Three Revolutions Teams early in the 1970s, under the aegis of Kim Jong Il and with the blessing of his father, was the first step in a mass campaign to transform North Korea into a monolithic society practicing the "unitary thoughts" (*yuil sasang*) of Kim Il Sung. What Kim Il Sung urged in 1975 remained valid in 1982. "The Three Revolutions Teams of 20 to 50 members were charged with the task of lending our cadres good help so they may discard conservatism, empiricism, and other outdated ideas and successfully carry out their work as required by the party and thus to develop our economy at a faster pace and more satisfactorily."[45] Kim also proclaimed at that time that "mysticism about technology, conservatism, empiricism, revisionism, and the remnants of capitalist thought and feudalism have not been totally eradicated. The result we attained in the ideological war is analogous to only the first weeding in agriculture. Although it looks good outwardly after the first weeding, the roots of outmoded thoughts are still remaining. Therefore, unless ideological war is relentlessly and powerfully pushed through, they can come alive again."[46] This was a clear warning to the party cadres, both old and new, who might resist pressure by the TRT members under Kim Jong Il's leadership.

Under the overall slogan of "modelling the whole society on the Juche idea," Kim Il Sung stated in his report to the Sixth KWP Congress on October 10, 1980, that North Korea "must wage a vigorous struggle to revolutionize, working-classize and intellectualize all members of society." This was a clarion call to carry out a continuous revolution. Although the meaning of the formalistic rhetoric employed is not always clear, Kim's resolve was clearly to indoctrinate the new generation of the postrevolutionary era. For instance, Kim pointed out the urgent need for "revolutionizing intellectuals" in these ways:

> By intensifying ideological education and organizational life, party organizations should educate and temper the intellectuals in the revolutionary way and induce them to make contact with reality at all times and learn from the ideology, organization and discipline of the working class through practical work. . . . We should also pay profound attention to the revolutionary education of the youth and children. . . . Party organization must intensify the class and revolutionary education of youth

and children, so that without forgetting about the bitter past of our people, they will all bear implacable hatred for imperialism and the exploiter system and resolutely fight on to crush class enemies of all hues and achieve the ultimate victory of the revolution."[47]

This slogan of "revolutionization and working-classization" of the whole country has become the dominant theme of KWP policy in the 1980s, although the phraseology had already been used in the late 1960s. The speech reflected Kim's reaction to the change in North Korea's social structure due to rapid industrialization and the rise of technocrats and intellectuals in society. Although exact statistics are not known, a new generation of trained and educated personnel, scientists, engineers, functionaries, and office workers has arisen in North Korea. President Kim Il Sung boasted that the number of technical personnel increased from 497,000 in 1970 to 1 million in 1976, and would be considerably higher by 1982.[48] These technocrats will never be the same as the first-generation revolutionaries in their outlook, orientation, and style of problem solving. Despite the regimentation and indoctrination with the "unitary thoughts of Kim Il Sung," these intellectuals would tend to be more resistant to mass campaigns and pressures for conformity.

The Kim Il Sung regime has been preoccupied with institutionalizing KWP work beyond the life span of its Great Leader. Ever since the KWP was molded as an instrument of personal rule by its Great Leader, Kim Il Sung and his associates have been concerned about how to preserve and perpetuate his rule beyond his lifetime. With all its boastful accomplishments in socialist revolution and construction, and in transforming the "Land of Kim Il Sung" into "Paradise on Earth," the ruling circle in North Korea could not rest assured of the continuity of the political system after Kim Il Sung. This is why the virtue of "loyalty and dedication" to the Great Leader was extolled and demanded of the masses in North Korea. According to Chong-Sik Lee, a noted student of North Korean communism, "the selection of his son as his successor was Kim Il Sung's answer to the vexing problems he encountered simultaneously pursuing the goals of modernization and maintaining revolutionary order." "More specifically," Lee continues, "it is the leader's attempt to prolong the KWP's role as the mainstay of the revolution in ideology in the face of the strong currents of modernization that might smother the revolutionary order. In short, it is an attempt to assure Kim Il Sung's revolutionary immortality."[49]

The issues of political succession and the change to a new generation of leadership were therefore at the very heart of North Korea's communist politics in the 1980s. The father-son succession announced in 1980 was preceded by almost a decade of preparation, and reflected the underlying social and political forces in motion. Kim Jong Il's rise to power was more than a "degeneration" into a "thoroughly personalized family affair built around a personality cult" of the Great Leader.[50] A more thorough probing of the sociological trends and forces will allow us to give a fuller explanation of succession politics in communist North Korea.

The issues of political succession and generational change in North Korea reflect the law of political dynamics and the transformation of the communist system over time. Tension inevitably arises between the revolutionary tradition and heritage of the past and the newly emerging forces of the postrevolutionary era. This tension between old and new generations is reflected in the political succession issue in North Korea. The first-generation revolutionaries, to which Kim Il Sung belongs, were not at ease with changes in society. Kim Il Sung and his close associates, as first-generation revolutionaries, were molded by their previous experiences as anti-Japanese guerrilla fighters and influenced by the practical experience of carrying out the revolution and building socialism in North Korea. This generation was anxious to leave the tradition and heritage of revolutionary struggle to the succeeding generation in communist North Korea. This led to Kim Jong Il being certified by the Great Leader and his revolutionary comrades as the only acceptable candidate to continue the revolutionary work.

Implementing the Three Revolutions

How is the building of a "unitary system" (*yuil ch'aeje*) in North Korea to be explained? How is Kim Jong Il's leadership style manifested in North Korean politics? The gist of Kim Il Sung's rationale for the policy of building a unitary system in North Korea may be found in a policy address delivered before a joint meeting of the KWP Central Committee and the DPRK Supreme People's Assembly on April 14, 1982.[51]

At the outset of his address, Kim Il Sung asserted that "modelling the whole of society on the Juche idea is the general task of our revolution and the historical mission of the Government of the Republic. This Government must fulfill its historic mission with credit by building a communist paradise in this land as quickly as possible. To build this communist paradise," Kim continued, "the revolution and construction should be vigorously pushed ahead under the banners of the people's power and three revolutions. Communism is the people's power plus the three revolutions." Under the slogan of the three revolutions—ideological, technical, and cultural, Kim intends to "transform people, society and nature and provide the popular masses with complete social equality and happiness. The three revolutions are a struggle to eradicate the survivals of the old society in the ideological, technical and cultural spheres, and to create new communist ideology, technology and culture," which Kim claims is "the content of the continuous revolution in socialist society." The address presents the mass mobilizational campaign to establish a unitary and monolithic system as a natural and comprehensible act of transition.

Kim Il Sung seems to have a realistic grasp of politics, although his conception is decidedly elitistic and authoritarian. According to Kim, "politics is a social function to organize and direct people's activities in a coordinated way in keeping with common class or social interests. Without politics, there can be no collective lives and joint activities of people, nor can society be maintained and developed. Therefore, politics exists in any society, and only when the masses of the people become masters of politics, can they become true masters of society."[52] The rationale for Kim's unitary and monolithic system is reflected in his classic view of politics.

> Politics is conducted by a definite form of political organization, and the character and role of this organization differ with social systems. In a society where the people have common interests and unity and cooperation constitute the basis of social relations, the political organization represents the common social interests and becomes a means of realizing them. However, in a class society where people have conflicting interests, the political organization serves as a means for protecting and meeting the interests of a class.[53]

Juche Korea, as Kim Il Sung envisions it, is a society where there is no class antagonism and where the working masses have emerged to become the master. Thus, Kim claimed, "our people's power is a political organization which represents the interests of the working class, farmers, working intellectuals and the rest of the laboring masses; it is a political weapon which serves the working people."[54] With the successful "transformation of man, society, and nature, all members of society" will become "communist-minded," "the class distinctions, the differences in the working conditions, and material standards" will be "completely eliminated," and "complete social equality for the working people" will be realized. Politics, especially the mobilizational campaign that Kim misleadingly calls the mass-line principle, is a means to attain this utopian communist society. This is why, according to Kim, the imposition of a unitary and monolithic system was both necessary and unavoidable.

The strengthening of Kim Il Sung's "unitary thoughts" was the first and foremost mission in life for Kim Jong Il in the 1970s. He was credited with having the KWP Central Committee adopt a policy document entitled "The Ten Principles for Firmly Establishing the Party's Unitary Ideology System." A unitary system in North Korea will be established, according to Kim Jong Il, by "dyeing the entire society with the revolutionary thought of Kim Il Sung,"[55] that is, by making the people and society of North Korea over according to the standard of Kim Il Sung's thought and by creating a populace loyal to him and willing to give their lives to achieve his goals. "To dye the society with Kim's thought it is necessary first to root out all outmoded ideas from the society by launching an 'ideological battle' (*sasang-jon*), which is 'the speed battle in the ideological field.' This is done by radically improving Party and ideological work."[56]

Kim Jong Il was thus credited with having instituted the "speed battle" (*sokto-jon*) as a means of accelerating the process of attaining economic development goals. The speed battle, resembling the Ch'ollima (Flying Horse) movement instituted by his father in the late 1950s, was intended to "carry out all tasks so as to achieve optimum success quantitatively and qualitatively, with the shortest span of time."[57] In 1975 Kim Jong Il organized the "Speed Battle Youth Shock Brigade" to take part in the concentrated construction projects, such as railroad electrification.[58] As a spin-off of the speed battle, Kim junior also inaugurated, in December 1975, the "Campaign to Capture the Red Flag of the Three Revolutions," a mobilizational program to double efforts for attaining the production quota.

The question of Kim Jong Il's leadership principle and style revolves around the Three Revolutions Teams (TRT) movement. The TRT movement was described by a Korean Central News Agency report in June 1982 as "a new form of implementing the revolutionary leadership principle." It was allegedly "the most revolutionary and scientific leadership principle" that combined "political ideological guidance" with "scientific and technical guidance." The TRT movement led by Kim Jong Il was an instrument to build a unitary system in North Korea. It not only "served as the cutting edge of Kim Jong Il's power consolidation," it also served Kim Il Sung's purpose of uncovering and rooting out "assorted demons," such as revisionism, bureaucratism, formalism, conservatism, "expedientialism," and departmentalism.[59] In this sense the TRT movement was a political weapon for consolidating the power of both Kim senior and Kim junior.

In many ways, North Korea's TRT movement resembled the Red Guards campaign carried out during Mao Zedong's Great Proletarian Cultural Revolution in China, but some contrasts are noticeable. Whereas Mao inaugurated the Great Proletarian Cultural Revolution over a three-year period (1966–1969), Kim Il Sung instituted the three revolutions—ideological, technical, and cultural—simultaneously. Whereas the Red Guards were mobilized in China in the periphery, with participation at the grass-roots level, to wage a campaign against what they called party bureaucratism at the center, the TRT members were led from the top by the Party Center, and were dispatched to the cities and countryside to uphold the new party directives. Finally, the Cultural Revolution and the Red Guards campaign have been discredited in China since the death of Mao. Whether the three revolutions of the TRT movement will face a similar fate upon the death of Kim Il Sung remains to be seen.

The cause of Kim Jong Il as designated heir was aided by the celebration of his father's seventieth birthday on April 15, 1982, which was attended by many heads of state, party leaders, and dignitaries from all over the world. Just before this extravaganza, Kim junior was awarded a medal as the "Hero of the DPRK" in recognition of his outstanding achievements in all works of life. His own forty-first birthday was also celebrated widely in North Korea on February 16, 1982. Cultural and sport activities and tournaments were held by youths all over North Korea. Kim Jong Il was also elected as deputy to the Supreme People's Assembly in late February 1982. Although he did not get elected to one of the three vice-president positions, as anticipated, his position in the SPA has made his grasp of power that much firmer. Kim Jong Il is on the way to becoming a replica of the Great Leader, although his claim to power may not be as widely accepted by the masses as his father's is, at least for some time to come.

Institutionalizing the Succession

The cult of personality, so pervasive in North Korea, has extended beyond Kim Il Sung to encompass his son Jong Il. It is now public knowledge that the North Koreans take the birthdays of their leaders seriously, perhaps a reflection of Confucian cultural legacy. Kim Il Sung's birthday was declared a national holiday in 1972, when he became sixty; the period from February 16, Kim Jong Il's birthday, to April 15, his father's birthday, has been designated as the "Loyalty Festival Period" since 1976.[60] Although Kim Jong Il's emergence as the political leader was officially proclaimed during the Sixth KWP Congress in 1980, in 1983 he has become the undisputed de facto leader in charge of the day-to-day administration of the party and the state. In 1983, Kim junior's birthday was celebrated as a public holiday as in past years; his portraits appear in public buildings and schools together with his father's. Kim junior has also initiated a series of "on-the-spot guidance" tours, a technique his father had used frequently as a means of control and inspection.

To advance his claim for legitimacy, Kim Jong Il is credited with having authored a number of "immortal classics." Following the publication of a treatise entitled "On the Juche Idea" in 1982 Kim Jong Il published two additional works: "The Workers' Party of Korea Is a Juche-type Revolutionary Party Which Inherited the Glorious Tradition of the DIU," on October 17, 1982, and "Let Us Advance Under the Banner of Marxism-Leninism and the Juche Idea," on May 3, 1983. The DIU (Down-with-Imperialism Union), allegedly formed by Kim senior in 1926, was claimed by Kim Jong Il to have been "a fresh start of the Korean communist movement and the Korean revolution."[61] By stating that the second essay marks the occasion of the 165th birthday of Karl Marx and the centenary of his death, Kim Jong Il has promoted himself to the ranks of Communism's founding fathers. This hidden agenda item is clearly shown in the introductory statement issued by Pyongyang's Foreign Languages Publishing House.

> The dear leader Comrade Kim Jong Il is working denying himself sleep and rest to inherit and complete brilliantly the revolutionary cause of Juche started by the great leader Comrade Kim Il Sung. He is the outstanding thinker and theoretician who has fully mastered the great leader's revo-

lutionary ideas; he is the sagacious leader of our Party and people who is possessed of brilliant wisdom, unusual insight and refined art of leadership; and he is the real leader of the people who has unboundedly lofty virtues.[62]

Obviously a campaign is under way to transfer charisma from father to son by establishing a personality cult of Kim Jong Il.

China played a role in promoting Kim Jong Il's claim for legitimacy. On June 10, 1983, the Japanese wire service Kyodo reported from Beijing that Kim Jong Il had visited China, indicating China's official recognition of Kim junior as Kim Il Sung's successor. The Chinese party leader, Hu Yaobang, confirmed Kim Jong Il's "invited but unannounced visit to China" from June 2 to June 12 to a North Korean delegation in Beijing, led by the Supreme People's Assembly chairman, Yang Hyong-sop, on July 7.[63] The next day Pyongyang Radio, in reporting Yang's meeting with the Chinese leader, confirmed Kim Jong Il's PRC visit officially for the first time. The belated announcement of Kim Jong Il's "unofficial" PRC visit shows that China, although disavowing a hereditary system in the communist world and prohibiting personality cults of its leaders in the post-Mao era, extended indirect recognition of the father-son succession plan that North Korea has worked out.

In 1983 there were some changes in the North Korean leadership. With the death in January of Kang Yang-uk, one of the three vice-presidents, Pak Song-chol moved up the ladder from the third to the second vice-president, and Yim Chun-chu was elevated to become the third vice-president. Yim's previous position, secretary of the Central People's Committee, was filled by Yi Yong-ik. Yang Hyong-sop, as noted was elected chairman of the SPA, together with Son Song-pil and Yo Yon-ku as vice-chairmen respectively. The Seventh Plenary of the Sixth KWP Congress, June 15–17, 1983, approved new appointments for 5 spots on the 10-member secretariat. The first 3 positions remained intact, i.e., Kim Il Sung (1), Kim Jong Il (2), and Kim Jung-rin (3); 2 were promoted: Yon Hyong-mok (4) and Hwang Chang-yop (6); and the remaining 5 were newly appointed: Hyon Mu-kwang (5), Ho Jong-suk (7), Son Kwan-hi (8), An Seug-tak (9), and Ch'ae Hi-chong (10). Among those replaced were Kim Yong-nam, Kim Hwan, and Yun Ki-bok.[64] Although the reasons for the demotion of 5 veteran party cadres are not clear, the newly appointed members are believed to be technocrats with economic expertise.

If there is any policy dispute among the North Korean leadership, it is not known to the outside. Some unconfirmed rumors circulated that Pyongyang purged 10–12 generals who had allegedly defected to China in April–May 1982. It was reported that Kim Jong Il had to take a "forced" visit abroad (he went to Malta) in 1982.[65] The fact that at least three defections to South Korea took place in 1983 shows that all is not well in North Korea.

A power struggle between "pragmatists" more concerned with economic policy and "ideologues" loyal to Kim Jong Il, however, resulted in 1983 in the political "ideologues" dominating over the economic "pragmatists."⁶⁶

In late January 1984 a change in key government personnel was announced. Kang Song-san replaced Yi Jong-ok as prime minister; Yi became the fourth vice president of the DPRK, replacing the ailing Kim Il, who died in March 1984. Kim Yong-nam succeeded Foreign Minster Ho Dam, who after many years of continued service resigned to become a politburo member in the KWP Secretariat. Following the repercussion of the Rangoon bombing of October 9, 1983, which was reportedly the work of hard-liners among Kim Jong Il's followers, the government change was thought to be unavoidable. The significance of this change in terms of North Korea's ruling elite composition remains to be assessed in the days ahead.

Pressing for Economic Development

North Korea, like some other communist countries in the Soviet bloc, does not publish economic statistics, which are considered state secrets. All economic data are therefore estimates based on fragmentary information made available periodically by the North Korean authorities. In his report to the Sixth KWP Congress on October 10, 1980, President Kim Il Sung stated that the basic task facing his country was "to speed up the Juche-orientation, modernization and scientization of the national economy" so as to lay "the firm material and technical foundations of socialism and communism." This economic policy of North Korea, reflecting the Juche or self-reliance idea, seeks to solve "the problems of raw materials, fuel and power . . . by using our domestic resources." It also seeks "mechanization and automation of production" and modernization of the economy through science and technology.⁶⁷

In 1981, North Korea passed the midpoint of its second seven-year economic plan for 1978–1984. As initially unveiled in December 1977, at the Sixth Supreme People's Assembly, the overall objective of the plan was to almost double the economic production of North Korea for ten specific items by 1984. The target goals included (1) 56–60 billion kilowatt hours (kwh) of electricity from the 1977 level of 28 billion kwh, (2) 70–80 million tons of coal from 53 million tons, (3) 7.4–8 million tons of steel from 4 million tons in 1977, (4) 1 million tons of nonferrous metals, (5) 5 million tons of engineering products, (6) 5 million tons of chemical fertilizer from 3 million tons in 1975, (7) 12–13 million tons of cement from the current level of 8 million tons, (8) 3.5 million tons of fishery products from 1.8 million tons in 1977, (9) 10 million tons of grain from 8.5 million tons in 1977, and (10) 100,000 chongbo (approximately 245,000 acres) of reclaimed land from the sea.⁶⁸

There was no assurance, of course, that these ambitious goals would be fully met on time in the light of poor past performance and the international economic situation. The first seven-year economic plan of

1961–1967 was eventually extended for another three years, and the six-year economic plan of 1971–76 was also extended for one year. Although North Korea follows the Juche principle, it is not completely immune to the impact of the global economy and recessions abroad. Foreign trade, for instance, adversely affected North Korea's domestic economy in the years 1974 to 1976.[69] Moreover, the seven-year plan has the ambitious goal of simultaneously strengthening industrial output and increasing the production of consumer goods. In formulating the latter goal, North Korean planners were undoubtedly motivated by the rapid economic growth in South Korea between 1962 and 1978.

Kim Il Sung's New Year message sets the tone each year for the policies and programs of North Korea. In 1983, after reviewing the accomplishments of the preceding year, Kim stressed the need for "efforts on struggles to revolutionize and intellectualize whole members of society" by achieving the current seven-year economic plan "ahead of schedule" and attaining the ten economic goals for the decade of the 1980s, as laid down during the Sixth KWP Congress in October 1980. What made the 1983 message noteworthy compared with other years was Kim's emphasis on economic problems and correspondingly lesser stress on political, social, and diplomatic issues. He did not mention the unification issue.[70] Kim stated that industrial growth in 1982 showed a 16.8 percent increase over the previous year. He gave particular emphasis to the increase in mining, coal mining in particular, and in the production of nonferrous metals. North Korea uses imported fuel to power its economy, and zinc, lead, and copper are still the major sources of North Korea's foreign exchange earnings.[71] Kim also made an appeal to augment transportation systems—conveyer, container, and pipeline, to manufacture more locomotives and freight cars and to carry out timely repairs.

In 1983 North Korea pressed toward achieving its economic growth targets by launching a nationwide campaign of mass mobilization to "speed up" production.

The workers were exhorted to double their efforts to achieve the targets of the second seven-year plan (1978–1984) "ahead of the schedule." Commemorating the one-year anniversary of the mass campaign, North Korea's party organ *Nodong Sinmun* carried an editorial on July 20, 1983, entitled "Let Us Further Fan the Flames of the Movement to Create the 'Speed of the Eighties.'" It claimed that workers responded to the challenge of "Let Us Create the 'Speed of the Eighties' with the Spirit of a Great Chollima Upsurge!" by "effect[ing] great upsurges in production in all fields . . . including the fields of ferrous metals, coal, and the electric industry . . . thereby providing a firm guarantee for attaining the goals for the production of 15 million tons of grain, 1.5 million tons of nonferrous metals, and 15 million tons of steel." It cited the Kumdok general mining complex, the Nampo lockgate, and the Tanchon smeltery as examples of model enterprises. The editorial claimed that "the struggle to create the 'speed of the eighties' is a mass advance movement based on the workers' extraordinarily high revolutionary zeal and resolve . . . and is the most powerful weapon in carrying out the great tasks of socialist construction in the 1980s."[72] The wishes of Kim Il Sung, as stated earlier, are met by means of exultation and zeal, according to an official source.

To enhance industrial production, however, North Korea needs to purchase technology from abroad. For this reason, North Korea has promoted foreign trade, and has increased the volume of imported machinery and equipment from Japan and other Western countries, although its foreign trade has generally been with the Soviet bloc countries in Eastern Europe and with China. To finance its purchase of technology and plants from abroad, North Korea had to increase its volume of exports. Most North Korean exports have been minerals, manufactured metal products, and grain. The problem of balancing trade favorably led to a temporary default in 1975; North Korea's debts were estimated to be about U.S. $2 billion in 1976. It subsequently rescheduled its debts, however, and it has continued to receive credits from Western countries and Japan, although specific amounts are not made public. North Korea also announced, in January 1984, a new policy of expanding trade ties with the capitalist countries in the West, inviting them to invest in North Korea's economy.

Another source of difficulty for the North Korean economy has been the ever-increasing ratio of military spending. North Korea maintains a huge military force; an estimated 15 to 20 percent of its GNP was spent on the military in the 1960s, and an even higher percentage in the 1970s.[73] As long as military tension in the Korean Peninsula continues, the prospects of North Korea cutting its defense budget to invest in peaceful purposes are slim. Since North Korea depends on the Soviet Union and China for the latest weapons and fuel, however, it is doubly handicapped, for it must depend on the good graces of its communist allies.

Manipulating Foreign Relations: North Korea

The basic objective of North Korea's foreign policy, according to *Minju Chosun,* is independence, friendship, and peace. This represents Kim Il Sung's "far-reaching strategic plan . . . to defend the interests of our people, strengthen international solidarity for our revolution, oppose imperialism and colonialism and accelerate the victory of the world revolution."[74] These claims cannot be fully met in actuality due to world political forces over which North Korea has little control. North Korea's foreign policy behavior in the 1980s continued its familiar path of promoting relations with the major powers and with Third World countries. Apart from its desire for survival and independence, North Korea's foreign policies were also designed to isolate the south internationally and promote its claim for legitimacy in attaining national unification on its own terms.

North Korea's Relations with the Major Powers

North Korean–Soviet Relations. North Korean–Soviet relations improved, at least outwardly, in the 1980s. Although Pyongyang initially joined Beijing in criticizing the Soviet invasion of Afghanistan in December 1979, this was followed by indications that North Korean–Soviet relations were becoming friendlier. In April 1980, the Pyongyang government sent a cable to express its solidarity with the Soviet-backed government in Afghanistan. Premier Yi Jong-ok led a North Korean delegation to Moscow in late February 1981, and delivered a speech at the Twenty-sixth Congress of the Communist Party of the Soviet Union on March 2, 1981.

An analysis of media statements in 1981 and 1982 also indicates that both Pyongyang and Moscow were engaged in efforts to improve bilateral relations. While North Korea praised the "fraternal" ties and cooperation between the two countries, the Soviet media also used positive expressions to celebrate the anniversary of the conclusion of Soviet–North Korean economic and cultural agreements, including the signing of the 1961 Treaty of Friendship, Cooperation and Mutual Assistance with North Korea. The Soviet media also widely publicized the fact that Soviet economic assistance to North Korea in the past had been substantial—a fact North Korea prefers to downplay in the light of its claim for self-reliance in economic development. Radio Moscow reported on May 11, 1983, that North Korea and the Soviet Union traded a total of 4 million tons of cargo in 1982, the Soviet Union using Najin port as a forward base for the shipment of cargo to such littoral countries in the Pacific region as Vietnam and Cambodia.[75] A Soviet economic delegation to North Korea in May 1983 led to the signing of a North Korean–Soviet commodity delivery protocol.[76]

Radio Moscow also announced on September 7, 1983, that "the Soviet Union has helped North Korea build or reconstruct sixty-two major factories, including power stations in Pyongyang, Pukchang, and Unggi, an oil-processing factory in Unggi, and a synthetic ammonia factory in Aoji." It also claimed that four other major factories are being expanded with Soviet technical aid, which made possible the increase of the steel production capacity of Kim Ch'ek ironworks from 1 million to 2.4 million tons a year.[77] In total the Soviet role in North Korea's economic development was said to be extensive, in that North Korea depended on Soviet aid for 63 percent of its electricity, 50 percent of oil derivatives, 42 percent of steel products and 38 percent of rolling products in 1982. It also revealed that about 3,000 Soviet technicians are assisting in the manufacturing of tractors and trucks and in the shipbuilding industry.[78] These statements present a very different picture from North Korean assertions that its Juche-oriented national economy is single-handedly achieving the targets of the second seven-year economic plan.

Sino–North Korean Relations. Although North Korean–Chinese relations had been "correct and proper" for a while, they became "close and warm" in the 1981–1983 years, highlighted by Kim Il Sung's state visit to China in September 1982. The earlier "properness" in Pyongyang's relationship with Beijing stems from the fact that in the post-Mao era since 1976 the North Korean leadership was not wholly sanguine about Deng Xiaoping's domestic policy of de-Maoization and foreign policy of Sino-U.S. diplomatic normalization. The downgrading of Mao Zedong's personality cult in the post-Mao era was an ominous sign to Kim Il Sung of possible damage to his own cult after his death. Moreover, North Korea's efforts to improve its relations with the United States by using China as an intermediary have not proven successful.

Nonetheless, a surprising turn of events occurred at the end of 1981. In December the Chinese premier, Zhao Ziyang, paid a state visit to Pyongyang. This was followed six months later by the official visit of a Chinese military delegation to North Korea, led by Defense Minister Geng Biao. In September 1982, Kim Il Sung made a fifteen-day visit to the PRC, soon after the completion of China's Twelfth Party Congress meetings. Although the details and the reason for Kim's visit, the first since 1975, were not known immediately, the ostensible purpose was to acquire more economic assistance and the latest military weapons from the PRC. During the banquet in honor of Kim Il Sung in Beijing, it was reported over the news wire service that the Chinese Communist Party general secretary, Hu Yaobang, had revealed a hitherto unannounced trip that he and Vice-chairman Deng Xiaoping had made to Pyongyang on a previous occasion.

While in China Kim Il Sung received a royal welcome. He was escorted by Deng Xiaoping on a train ride to Chengdu, the capital of Sichuan Province, and joined by General Secretary Hu Yaobang in Xian, the capital of Shaanxi Province, on their return trip to Beijing. Kim's visit to China was officially characterized by North Korea as "a historic event which raised to new heights the traditional Korea-China friendship . . . sealed in blood and tempered and cemented in all trials of history."[79] Whether Kim's 1982 visit to China "will further strengthen the bulwark of socialism in the East" and "the solidarity of the anti-imperialist independence forces," as claimed by North Korea, remains to be seen.[80] Underlying the exchange of visits in 1982 was the desire on the part of the North Korean and Chinese leaders to become better acquainted with each other in the altered environment of the post-Mao era. If, as reported, China indeed agreed to provide North Korea with the latest model MiG-23 fighter planes as a result of Kim's trip, North Korea scored an important gain strategically. Kim Jong Il's unannounced ten-day visit to China in June 1983 (revealed by Hu Yaobang on July 7) was another indication of improved North Korean–Chinese relations in 1983.

China's foreign minister, Wu Xueqian, paid a five-day visit to Pyongyang on May 20, 1983, in the wake of the hijacking of a Chinese airliner to South Korea by six Chinese nationals on May 5. The airliner crossed the DMZ from North Korea to the south either undetected or without being stopped—an embarrassment to the Pyongyang regime. In July the twenty-second anniversary of the signing of the Treaty of Friendship, Cooperation and Mutual Assistance with China was faithfully observed in Pyongyang. In Beijing, on July 4, 1983, a protocol was signed following the twenty-third meeting of the Korea-China Inter-Governmental Committee for Scientific and Technical Cooperation. The document appears to have focused primarily on forestry matters.

Following Chinese defense minister Geng Biao's visit to Pyongyang in June 1982, North Korea may very well have received considerable military assistance from China in 1983. China supplied North Korea with over 20 A-5 jets (an improved MiG 21-type fighter), according to *Sankei Shimbun* reports.[81] North Korea also reportedly agreed in 1982 to make the port of Chongjin available for facilitating trade between Japan and China, thereby allowing China to secure a foothold on North Korea's eastern coast, hitherto dominated by the Soviet Union.[82]

Although a close working relationship between North Korea and China seems to have evolved following Kim Il Sung's 1982 visit, the matters of mutual concern were not always settled smoothly or harmoniously. The Western press reported an unconfirmed rumor of a secret trip by Kim to Beijing to meet with Chinese leaders in early November 1983. Kim allegedly made a similar trip to a seaside resort town near Dairen in August.[83] Unlike his earlier official visit, these clandestine trips might indicate North Korea's growing concern over the evolving situation surrounding the Korean Peninsula. Pyongyang vehemently opposes the recent unofficial contacts established between the PRC and South Korea. It is also possible that Kim's second China trip in 1983 was motivated by his desire to defend North Korea's position vis-à-vis Burma, which broke diplomatic ties with Pyongyang after announcing that North Korea was responsible for the October 9 Rangoon bombing.

North Korean–U.S. Relations. The presence of U.S. troops in South Korea continues to be a matter of grave concern to North Korea. The 1979 cancellation of President Carter's plan for U.S. troop withdrawal from South Korea by 1982 was obviously a serious blow to Pyongyang.[84] It was a setback for Pyongyang's timetable for achieving the reunification of Korea, perhaps in the lifetime of President Kim Il Sung.

Pyongyang obviously wants to improve bilateral relations with the United States, but it has been unable to achieve a diplomatic breakthrough. When Congressman Stephen J. Solarz (D, N.Y.) was invited to visit North Korea in July 1980, for instance, Kim Il Sung reportedly told the congressman that North Korea would favor "cultural and other kinds of exchange with the United States," even in the absence of official diplomatic ties between the two countries. At this meeting, Kim also expressed his willingness to "trade with South Korea without preconditions" and declared that North Korea no longer insisted that the anticommunist law in South Korea be repealed as a precondition for the union of separated families and the exchange of mail.[85]

North Korea also used foreign sources to send messages to Washington. In September 1980, Kim Il Sung reportedly told a visiting Japanese delegation, the Afro-Asian Study Group of the ruling Liberal Democratic Party, led by Fujii Katsushi, that North Korea was "prepared to cancel its defense treaties with the Soviet Union and China in exchange for a direct peace treaty with the United States."[86] During the presentation of his report to the Sixth KWP Congress in October 1980, Kim Il Sung also proposed establishing normal relations with the United States, if the United States would withdraw 40,000 troops from South Korea and not obstruct the reunification of the Korean Peninsula. These comments, timed carefully with the U.S. presidential election campaign and South Korea's political adjustment following the Kwangju uprising of May 1980, did not produce a favorable response from the United States.

With the decision of President Ronald Reagan to support President Chun Doo Hwan's government in South Korea, the Pyongyang leadership appears to have abandoned for the time being any hope of resuming the inter-Korea dialogue and negotiations on unification. Also abandoned was the idea of bilateral talks on peace agreements with the United States without involving South Korea in the process, an idea already dismissed by previous U.S. administrations.

As a gesture to woo the interest of the United States, Kim Il Sung made a new proposal to hold tripartite talks on the future of Korea, in a clear reversal of North Korea's earlier position. He conveyed the message to President Ronald Reagan via China's prime minister Zhao Ziyang, who visited Washington in January 1984.

North Korea's policy toward the United States in 1981–1983 may best be characterized as one of intense anti-Americanism. In 1983 Kim Il Sung denounced the "Team Spirit 83" joint military exercises as "a very dangerous military provocation pushing the situation on the Korean peninsula to the brink of war."[87] Timed with this event North Korea placed the country under a quasi-war state between February 1 and May 15, 1983. This was followed by its annual "Month for the Joint Anti-U.S. Struggle" from June 25 to July 27, 1983, commemorating the thirtieth anniversary of the "victory in the war for the liberation of the fatherland." Mass rallies were held all over the country, including one in Pyongyang on June 25 that was attended by more than 100,000 people. Not surprisingly, President Reagan's official visit to Seoul in November 1983 was denounced by the North Korean regime, which compared it to John Foster Dulles's 1950 visit, blamed by Pyongyang for precipitating the outbreak of the Korean War in June 1950.[88]

Despite this anti-American fervor, North Korea continued to entertain the notion of establishing official ties with the United States. In April 1983, when President Mohamed Hosni Mubarak of Egypt paid an official visit to Pyongyang as he was returning from his trip to Washington, D.C., North Korea reportedly proposed bilateral talks with the United States. U.S. Secretary of State George Shultz ordered relaxation on some restrictions on contacts with North Koreans, but this directive was rescinded early in November 1983 in reaction to the Burmese government announcement of North Korea's responsibility for the October 9 Rangoon bomb blast.[89]

A total of 64 U.S. citizens are reported to have visited North Korea from 1972 to 1983, and 23 North Koreans entered the United States from 1977 to April 1983, according to South Korea's foreign ministry report to the National Assembly Foreign Affairs Committee.[90] North Korea, according to the U.S. ambassador to Seoul, Richard Walker, is after U.S. "high technology," and establishing U.S.–North Korean trade will not, in his opinion, ease tension in the Korean Peninsula.[91]

North Korean–Japanese Relations. North Korea also wishes to improve its bilateral relations with Japan. However, no diplomatic normalization between Pyongyang and Tokyo is likely in the foreseeable future because North Korea objects to Japan's support of the South Korean government. It insists on the abrogation of the Japan–Republic of Korea Treaty of 1965, which established diplomatic relations between the two countries, as a precondition for the establishment of diplomatic relations with Japan. In view of the close ties between South Korea and Japan, the conservative government in Tokyo is unlikely to accede to Pyongyang's demand for the time being. Not surprisingly, Japanese prime minister Nakasone's visit to Seoul in January 1983 was criticized by Pyongyang as "a criminal junket to further coil up the tensions in and around the Korean peninsula and increase the danger of war." It also denounced what it called "the fabrication of the triangular military alliance" between the United States, Japan, and South Korea.[92] The party organ *Nodong Sinmun* asserted that Nakasone's subsequent visit to the United States was to carry out this "triangular alliance" as part of the overall U.S. Asian strategy.[93]

In early July 1983, a pro–North Korea Japanese parliamentary delegation, consisting of Chuji Kuno (Liberal Democratic Party) and Togo Yoneda (Japan Socialist Party), visited North Korea to arrange for a new fisheries agreement to replace the one that had expired.[94] Although they discussed the possible establishment of trade missions in Pyongyang and Tokyo, the opening of a new air route linking Tokyo and Beijing that would pass over North Korea, and the exchange of journalists between the two countries, these measures were not officially endorsed by Nakasone's government. However, Japanese foreign minister Abe Shintaro received a visit by a North Korean delegation visiting Tokyo in May 1983, and a senior official of the Japanese foreign ministry stated that the Japanese government was willing to issue an entry visa to Hyon Chun-kuk, vice-chairman of North Korea's external cultural affairs committee, to negotiate the renewal of a nongovernmental fisheries agreement between Japan and North Korea. These developments prompted South Korea to lodge a protest with Tokyo over what it called signs of Japan-DPRK rapprochement. Tokyo notified Seoul that its government would not interfere with "private level" contact, such as the visit by Chuji Kuno, who, although heading the Japan–North Korea Friendship Parliamentary League, acted in a private capacity.[95]

A North Korean soldier defected to Japan in September 1983, aboard a Japanese cargo vessel leaving Nampo port near Pyongyang. North Korea retaliated in late November 1983 by holding hostage a Japanese freighter and its four crewmen as the ship arrived at Nampo port, and by pressing the Japanese government to return the soldier, who had been granted political asylum.

In spite of its rhetoric of self-reliance, North Korea continued to depend upon Japan as a source of technology and as a trade partner. A total of 246 North Korean citizens visited Japan between June 1982 and June 1983 to inspect Japanese plants and schools or to attend to business or trade.[96] Their visas are issued at the Japanese embassy in Beijing, and their personal references are cleared by the "Korea-Japan Trade Co."[97]

Following the Burmese government's announcement of North Korea's involvement in the October 9 Rangoon bomb blast, the Japanese government condemned North Korea's role in the terrorist acts and imposed measures to restrict its trade with North Korea and its officials' contact with North Koreans in third countries. Pyongyang, in turn, criticized the Japanese government's stand and announced its own restrictions against Japan, including a suspension of the fishery agreement talks with Japan.

North Korea and the Major Powers. North Korea professes to pursue an independent foreign policy vis-à-vis the Soviet Union and China. However, as Sino-Soviet relations remain hostile, the posture of North Korea toward its allies is a matter of serious concern. The Pyongyang leadership has successfully avoided entanglement in the Sino-Soviet dispute by refusing to side with either party and maintaining independence from both.[98] However, the geopolitical position of North Korea, which shares a common border with China and with the Soviet Union, and its dependence on military and economic support from each of these states has made North Korea's diplomatic balancing act precarious. Caught in the cross fire between Moscow and Beijing, North Korea's efforts to maintain equidistance between its two communist allies have become increasingly difficult. Although North Korea issues many pro-Soviet or pro-Chinese statements depending on circumstances, it is unable to take explicit anti-Soviet or anti-Chinese lines in its diplomacy.[99]

During the late 1970s, North Korea had been courted by its communist neighbors. In January 1978, for instance, Soviet Politburo member D. A. Kunayev visited Pyongyang to present Kim Il Sung with an "Order of Lenin" medal, one of the Soviet Union's highest decorations. In May 1978, Chinese Communist Party chairman Hua Guofeng led a delegation on a state visit to North Korea, the first of its kind by the top Chinese leadership. Nonetheless, considering North Korea's situation, including its economic difficulties and its need for military hardware, North Korea may be compelled to ask for continued support from its great-power allies. The possibility of a deteriorating power position of North Korea vis-à-vis its communist neighbors is therefore a matter of increasing concern to the North Korean leadership.

From a military and economic standpoint, the Pyongyang government cannot afford to antagonize either the Soviet Union or China. Only the Soviet Union can provide North Korea with modern military weapons and equipment. Petroleum is also provided by China and the Soviet Union. North Korea recently improved the port facility of Najin, which lies in the northeastern corner of the country next to the Soviet border.[100] With the help of the Soviet Union, it had already improved the railway and highway that connects Najin with the Soviet border. North Korea's Najin port, unlike the Soviet port city of Vladivostok, is free of ice during the winter months, providing an important alternative means for the logistic support of Soviet fleet operations in the Far East. An oil refinery was built in Unggi, another port town, halfway between Najin and the border.

Chinese economic assistance to North Korea, although not widely publicized, has also been considerable. While the Soviets were completing North Korea's first aluminum factory in Pukch'ang, north of Pyongyang, in June 1978, the Chinese were helping North Korea build the Ponghwa chemical plant in Shinuiju, a border town in northwestern Korea. It was reported that the Chinese also built a pipeline connecting the oil fields in China's northeast to a North Korean town along the border.

The North Korean leadership seems to be well aware that its international position is vulnerable to the changing configuration of major power relations in northeastern Asia. Its primary concern, therefore, has been to maintain its independence and security without antagonizing allies or provoking adversaries. From Pyongyang's perspective, the Sino-Japanese peace treaty of September 1978, and the Sino-U.S. diplomatic normalization of January 1, 1979, were potential sources of serious disturbances and threats to its diplomatic standing. The Chinese military attack on Vietnam in February 1979, and the Soviet invasion of Afghanistan in December 1979 also alarmed North Korean leaders, raising the specter of a potential threat from their communist allies.

Because of a possible United States/Japan/China entente vis-à-vis the Soviet Union, Pyongyang was determined not to be caught in the middle of major power rivalries. The North Korean leadership realized that the Soviet Union was anxious to keep North Korea's support as a bulwark in the event of a possible anti-Soviet coalition. Since 1981, the Pyongyang leadership has also been concerned about the possible revival of a cold war confrontation between the United States and the Soviet Union under the hard-line policy of the Reagan administration.

Third World Diplomacy

North Korea's Third World diplomacy is motivated by its desire to win the support of these countries on unification issues and to isolate South Korea from the rest of the world. In its policy of identification with the cause of the Third World non-aligned nations movement, North Korea received a series of state visits by government and party leaders from these countries, and also dispatched its officials to the capitals of various Third World countries. North Korea expanded its role as a supplier of arms and military expertise to countries in Africa and Latin America. Arms sales to wealthy countries like Iran were an important source of foreign currency. Along with signing formal bilateral treaties of friendship and cooperation with Libya in November 1982 and with Ethiopia in October 1983, North Korea reportedly agreed to send U.S. $12 million worth of military supplies to Grenada on April 14, 1983.[101]

North Korea was actively engaged in the diplomatic activities of inviting foreign leaders to North Korea and sending its own officials to foreign countries. Visiting heads of state and government leaders invited to North Korea in the twelve-month period between November 1982 and November 1983 included dignitaries from Libya, Central African Republic, the People's Republic of Congo, Upper Volta, Nicaragua, Egypt, Grenada, Seychelles, Lesotho, Rwanda, Guinea, Iran, and Ethiopia.

North Korea professes to be the leader of the non-aligned nations movement, and Kim Il Sung has made it his mission to lead the world struggle against imperialism. During a banquet arranged in honor of Egyptian president Mubarak, Kim Il Sung assessed the non-aligned nations movement thus: "The present situation urgently demands that the non-aligned countries wage the struggle to establish a new international economic order by achieving economic independence and realizing south-south cooperation, along with the struggle to check and frustrate the aggressive and belligerent policy of the imperialists and preserve peace and security in the world."[102]

North Korea was first admitted to a non-aligned nations conference in 1976 in Lima, Peru. North Korea participated in the Non-Aligned Summit Conference in Havana in 1980 and in New Delhi in 1983, sending Vice-president Pak Song-chol. In 1983, Pak reportedly conferred with leaders of various Third World countries in Asia, Africa, and Latin America, including Angola, Benin, the Congo, Ethiopia, Grenada, Guyana, Madagascar, Nepal, Pakistan, Zambia, and Zimbabwe.[103]

North Korea's military role throughout the world also increased in the early 1980s. Arms sales and training missions earned scarce foreign currency to compensate for economic stagnation. North Korea reportedly sold some U.S. $800 million worth of arms and ammunition to Iran in 1982, representing 40 percent of Teheran's military purchases, and also delivered U.S. $640 million worth of arms on credit to Zimbabwe in 1983.[104] North Korean military instructors were sent to more than a dozen countries, including Brunei, Grenada, Libya, the Seychelles, Somalia, Uganda, and Zimbabwe.

In 1981 Pyongyang sponsored a non-aligned nations conference on food production. In July 1983 North Korea also hosted the World Conference of Journalists Against Imperialism and For Friendship and Peace, held in Pyongyang and attended by 169 delegations, including delegates from 118 countries and 18 international organizations. Kim Il Sung gave a grand banquet in honor of the conference participants, and delivered a speech entitled "Let Us Shatter Imperialist Moves Toward Aggression and War and Safeguard Peace and Independence."[105] At the First Conference of Ministers of Education and Culture of Non-aligned and Other Developing Countries, held in Pyongyang in September 1983, Kim made another speech, entitled "For the Development of National Culture of Newly Emerging Countries."[106] North Korea's attempts to lobby the non-aligned nations to endorse its position on Korean unification and request U.S. troop withdrawal from the south have thus far been unsuccessful.

Diplomatic setbacks for North Korea in 1983 included the March expulsion of the DPRK envoy to Finland on the charge of attempted bribery, Burma's severance of official ties with North Korea in November, following an investigation of the Rangoon bomb blast, and in July, the forced departure from the United States of a secretary of the DPRK mission to the United Nations, due to a criminal charge of assault.

Inter-Korean Relations and Reunification

In his 1983 New Year's message Kim Il Sung did not highlight the unification issue, contrary to long-standing practice. He used other occasions, however, to reiterate North Korea's basic position that "democratization and independence of South Korea is the key to reunification." Kim insisted that North Korea has no intention to invade the south, repeated that the "main obstacle to reunification is the presence of the U.S. forces in the south," and blamed Japan for its "helping perpetuate the division of Korea" by supporting "the two-Koreas policy."[107]

It took twenty-three days for North Korea to react officially to the September downing of KAL007 by the Soviets. Pyongyang merely reiterated the Soviet statement that its fighter plane had "to stop the flight" of the intruder plane, which was on "a deliberate preplanned action" and on "an espionage mission for the U.S."[108] Perhaps supporting the Soviet position was an easy way out for North Korea, but its policy stance on the issue was clearly influenced by the desire to embarrass South Korea's Chun government.

Concerning the October 8 Rangoon bomb blast, North Korea responded promptly to President Chun Doo Hwan's allegation that it had master-minded the assassination plot, calling the charge "preposterous and shameless."[109] The subsequent revelation by Burmese authorities that the bombing was carried out by North Korean commandos was damaging news to North Korea. Burma's severance of diplomatic relations and expulsion of North Korean embassy personnel was a serious blow to North Korea's image and its scheme for undermining political stability in South Korea.[110] Pyongyang's foreign ministry criticized the Burmese action as "unjustifiable and unreasonable"; the *Nodong Sinmun* carried a commentary stating that "the bomb blast in Burma was, in fact, a product of the conspiracy" of the United States and South Korea in the attempt to isolate North Korea internationally.[111]

With the intensification of inter-Korean rivalry, peaceful reunification has remained as elusive a goal in the 1980s as ever. Whether North Korea will be able to establish diplomatic relations with other Western countries—socialist France, for example—remains to be seen. It depends, among other factors, on North Korea's flexibility, its willingness to modify self-righteous stands and to improve relations with South Korea. Whether North Korea will be able to stay outside the strategic entanglement caused by major-power rivalry in northeastern Asia is also uncertain. These problems of diplomacy, together with the succession crisis and economic difficulties at home, remain to be resolved during the 1980s.

Concluding Remarks: Linkage Politics

Some students of history and politics have seen a pattern of interactive linkages between domestic politics and international politics. Incidences of domestic disorder and violence, for instance, may lead to violence in the international system, and vice versa.[112] Appropriate examples to validate this hypothesis are numerous in Korea's recent history. The Sino-Japanese War of 1894–1895 and the Russo-Japanese War of 1904–1905 were triggered by domestic disturbances and political instability within the hermit kingdom of Yi dynasty Korea. Korea's predicament as a divided nation since 1945, on the other hand, is a consequence of external circumstances dictating the pattern and process of domestic political developments within Korea and between the two halves of divided Korea.

From the perspective of linkage politics, the domestic and foreign policies of the two Koreas may be understood as a response by the political elites and regimes to outside pressures. Korean policy behavior since partition in 1945 has been notable for the influence of external forces upon domestic policies, and not for the effects of internal forces upon foreign policy. Lately, attempts have been made to restore a proper balance between foreign and domestic influences, although in the Korean context, external pressures have remained the determining factor in the development of public policies.

One explanation might emphasize the potency of "national attributes" of the respective Korean states. The fact that North Korea shares a common border with the Soviet Union and with China has determined the orientation of North Korea's domestic and foreign policy. Pyongyang's diplomatic position is decidedly pro-Soviet and pro-Chinese; its domestic policy, politics, and economics are structured after the pattern of the communist party and state. South Korea's geographic proximity to Japan and close alliance with the United States certainly affect its diplomatic status and posture. South Korea is not only pro-American and friendly toward Japan in diplomacy; its economic system has also been largely patterned after the market economic systems of the United States and Japan.

Both Korean states have lately pursued a policy of relative independence and autonomy vis-à-vis their respective allies. Thus, as North Korea treads cautiously between Moscow and Beijing to retain its independence, South Korea is attempting to reduce its military and diplomatic dependence on the United States and its economic dependence on Japan. The Seoul government has taken the approach of diversifying the sources of its foreign economic and trade relations with countries in the Third World. This change in the pattern of South Korea's foreign policy behavior may be the economic expression of increasing maturity and the deepening of the industrial structure.

Despite their common quest for independence, the policies of the North and South Korean states are radically different. Whereas North Korea is inner-oriented, South Korea is outer-oriented in policy behavior. North Korea has become an isolated society, and South Korea has become a society relatively open and exposed to external influence. Whereas North Korea is a socialist "Hermit Kingdom," South Korea is vulnerable to the dangers of external domination and dependence. From the perspective of cultivating the fine art of governing, neither extreme of policy orientation is defensible. North Korea's Juche, if carried to an extreme, for instance, might become an expression of political inadequacy and insecurity about coping with the outside world. If a country is truly strong and self-assured, it need not fear outside forces provided the regime knows how to manipulate and control the diplomatic process.

Neither approach toward policymaking is good or bad as such. Reliance on internal sources of strength at the expense of external opportunity has the virtue of improving the chances for survival at times of external disturbances and instability. At the same time, this posture of self-reliance tends to keep a nation relatively isolated from the world and provides fewer opportunities for beneficial participation in a growing world economy. At the other extreme, heavy dependence on external sources at the expense of internal and indigenous resources may bring momentary success to the economy, yet involves the risk of a tradeoff between independence and autonomy on the one hand and possible control by outside powers on the other. Both extremes—the posture of full independence or that of complete dependence—must be avoided if a country wants to remain politically viable. What kind of policies are best depends on the ability of the leadership to cope with the immediate situation. What is crucial is the managerial capability of a regime to adapt to changing situations in the midst of a world environment that is constantly fluctuating.

National adaptation and adaptive behavior, as Rosenau argues, counts for more than a rigid or doctrinaire stand.[113] The excessive rhetoric of the Maoist developmental strategy during China's Cultural Revolution in 1966–1969 has now been abandoned by the post-Mao leadership in the name of promoting pragmatic policies. Realizing the limits of self-reliance in spite of its rhetoric, after 1970 North Korea under Kim Il Sung also began to interact more aggressively with the outside world through trade with noncommunist nations such as Japan and the countries of Western Europe.

Socialist North Korea has never abandoned the policy of increasing trade with the outside world, as the rhetoric of a self-reliant and independent economy might lead us to believe. Likewise, capitalist South Korea under Park Chung Hee never traded its independence and self-reliance for foreign loans and investments, which would have made South Korea's economy completely dependent upon and dominated by external sources. Rather, the national government worked closely in alliance with the big business enterprises to foster industrial giants such as the Daewoo, Hyundai, and Samsung business groups, patterned after Japan's general trading companies. These trading companies are national bourgeoisie groups that play a vital role in leading the process of South Korea's industrialization and economic growth.

Finally, the role of government in the economic modernization and transformation of society in the Korean states should not be overlooked. Whereas in socialist North Korea the party and party cadres provide leadership in modernizing the economy and mobilizing the masses, in capitalist South Korea it is the business enterprises and technocratic elites in and out of government that provide the motivating forces for socioeconomic development. Whereas North Korea depends on party directives and decisionmaking in managing its command economy, South Korea has a close government-business partnership that cooperates in controlling the forces of the market. A group of party cadres loyal to Kim Il Sung controls an economic bureaucracy in the north; an army of expertly trained technocrats runs the economy in the south. It is these varying styles and approaches to political economy that account for the different policy agenda and issues in the respective Korean societies.

Part 3

Future Prospects

8
Unification Policy Issues

In 1971, the Korean politics of competing legitimacy involved a struggle for supremacy in the arena of inter-Korean relations, with the initiation of the short-lived North-South dialogue on unification. As the decade of the 1980s opened, both Korean regimes intensified their rivalry through the proclamation of new measures for socioeconomic and political developments, and also of new policies for national reunification.

Korean unification is an important issue for both socialist North Korea and capitalist South Korea. The Korean people long for reunification of their divided country, irrespective of their social standing, place of residence, or ideological persuasion. Korean unification is a highly emotional and cherished issue for the Korean people, and is not to be dismissed lightly. Many Koreans feel they were victimized by outside forces and believe that it was great-power rivalry that brought about the territorial division of the country in 1945. It is therefore natural that many "nationalist-minded" Koreans advocate reunification as a matter of right and justice.[1] This perception, shared by many thoughtful Koreans, is a psychological reality to be reckoned with in the equation of Korean politics. To dismiss the issue of Korean unification as too "dogmatic" and the goal as too "unrealistic," as some critics have, is to overlook the importance attached to the issue by the Korean people themselves.

As the Korean people entered the 1980s, competitive pressure intensified between the two political systems and regimes in divided Korea. In 1972, a European scholar observed that North and South Korea were in a rather fortunate situation for learning from the opportunity for creative mutual interaction. Although the experience of inter-Korean dialogue in the 1970s was less than what was desired, the essential point of Johan Galtung's observation on divided Korea in 1972 is still valid. "Far from being a tragedy," Galtung argued, "divided nations are actually better off . . . because of the diversity at their disposal" and because "free competition between the systems may enrich both."[2] Due to competing claims for legitimacy, however, this potential for creative interaction has not been fully explored by the two Korean regimes. Instead, the two rival states are hopelessly stalemated, and the issue of Korean reunification has been used as a symbol by the incumbent political leadership to advance political interests.

The Basic Premises of Unification Policies

Throughout the 1970s, the authorities of North and South Korea were completely in agreement as to the desirability and basic principles of attaining national reunification. They agreed not only that national unification of the Korean people was "a just cause" but that reunification should be achieved through independent, peaceful, and democratic methods. This threefold principle of national unification, as set forth in the North-South joint communiqué of July 4, 1972, stipulated that unification should be achieved through (1) independent Korean efforts "without being subject to external imposition or interference," (2) peaceful means, that is, "not through the use of force against each other," and (3) a greater national unity, "transcending differences in ideas, ideologies, and systems."[3]

Despite "official" policies and "verbal" pledges to seek Korea's "national unification," the respective Korean regimes were nevertheless unwilling to make mutual concessions or to accommodate mutual interests, essential for a political solution to the Korean unification question. Instead, the interests of the two political regimes were placed ahead of the national interests of the Korean people. The Korean regimes perceived the situation of inter-Korean relations from the narrow vantage point of the current government, rather than from the broader perspective of Korea as a divided nation.

The underlying motives and strategic objectives of the two Korean regimes posed an irreconcilable obstacle to attaining the national aspiration for Korean reunification. The South Korean government typically took the position, for instance, that the ultimate goal of North Korea was to incite a communist revolution in South Korea and that Pyongyang's unification proposals and plans were merely camouflage to hide their true intention. North Korean leaders took the position that the South Korean regime was dragging its feet and scheming for "the perpetuation of the nation's division" and "the two Koreas conspiracy."

It is almost impossible to determine what the "real" and "true" intentions of the leaders and the strategic goals of the governments were. What can be ascertained, however, are the basic assumptions, premises, and hypotheses that underlie the policy process. These may be validated ex post facto in the light of the subsequent actions and behavior of the decisionmakers. Using this approach, we can identify several key assumptions and premises of the unification policy of the two Korean regimes in the 1970s.

South Korea's Unification Policy

The South Korean unification policy in the 1970s rested upon three basic premises, namely (1) the institutionalization of relaxed tension in the Korean Peninsula, (2) a gradual, functional, and step-by-step approach to solving the unification problems, and (3) the use of the unification issue as political capital by the incumbent leadership.[4]

"Peaceful" Unification. South Korea's pre-1980 unification stance began with the premise that a relaxation of tension in the Korean Peninsula had to be attained and institutionalized before any effective and meaningful measures for unification could be put into effect. It was with this strategic goal in mind that the Park government, for example, proposed to conclude a nonaggression agreement between the south and the north pending the reunification of the country. In his New Year's press conference on January 18, 1974, President Park stated the following three points for the conclusion of a nonaggression agreement: (1) both sides shall explicitly announce to the world their promise never to wage armed aggression against each other; (2) both sides shall refrain from mutual interference in the internal affairs of the other side; (3) under all circumstances, the existing armistice agreement shall remain effective.[5] These points for concluding a nonaggression agreement were subsequently incorporated as the "three basic principles for peaceful unification" announced by President Park on August 15, 1974, in his commemorative address marking the nation's independence day.[6]

A strategic move to institutionalize the peace process in the Korean Peninsula was taken by the Seoul government in the summer of 1973. The Seven-Point Declaration for Peace and Unification, issued on June 23, 1973, stated, inter alia, that South Korea would reaffirm its commitment to "peaceful unification" by pursuing South-North dialogue based on the July 4 Joint Communiqué, that "South Korea would not object to its admittance into the United Nations together with North Korea, provided that it would not cause hindrance to national unification," and that it "will open its doors to all nations of the world" urging "peace and good neighborliness" as the basic principle of South Korea's foreign policy.[7]

This basic stance by South Korea, of "unification preceded by peace," was understandable in view of its perception that the tragic internecine war of 1950–1953 had been promoted and initiated by North Korea as "the fatherland unification war." The South Korean leaders were determined not to repeat the error of resorting to an act of war to achieve reunification, and they were as much preoccupied with the question of security and the maintenance of peace as with the question of attaining reunification. For this reason, South Korean leaders were not impressed by the North Korean argument that a nonaggression agreement or a peace treaty should be concluded "only with the external powers, not between the two halves of the divided nation." They also rejected the North Korean insistence that reunification of Korea as a national issue needed to be solved "internally by the Korean people themselves" without involving "outside forces."

Incrementalism. South Korea's earlier unification policy also stressed the need for mutual psychological readjustment between the peoples of South and North Korea prior to attaining reunification. It advocated a gradual, functional, and step-by-step approach to solving the numerous outstanding problems of South and North Korean relations, to culminate in the eventual reunification of the country. According to the thinking of the South Korean authorities, many in-between stages would need to be traversed before the ultimate destination of a unified Korea could be reached. Incrementalism as an approach to Korean unification was articulated by President Park during his 1973 New Year's press conference.

> The current South-North dialogue should progress steadily with mutual patience and sincerity, seeking the settlement of easy questions first. North and South Korea should first of all exert efforts to remove long-standing distrust and misunderstanding. Mutual trust and promotion of understanding are short-cuts to the achievement of peaceful unification.[8]

This incrementalist approach was defended in the name of realism. Less controversial issues of inter-Korea relations, such as the promotion of cultural and economic exchanges, were "comparatively easier problems" to settle, according to those who subscribed to this position. They argued that negotiations on political and military issues were more "difficult" and thus "premature" for the time being. In taking this pragmatic stand, the South Korean government exposed itself to stringent criticism by the North Korean regime, which took a more aggressive, "once-and-for-all" approach to the unification question. North Korea proposed to deal with all issues relative to national unification "simultaneously."

The South Korean approach of incrementalism, promoted in the name of realism, was criticized by North Korea as "less-than-seriously motivated for unification." One perceptive observer characterized South Korea's dilemma thus:

> In a way, realism has been South Korea's Achilles' heel as far as unification policy is concerned. From the standpoint of what can be realistically achieved between North and South Korea, a gradualist and incrementalist approach is well justified. Given the mutual distrust and vast differences in political and social system between the two, the most that can be realistically expected are quite rightly small steps. But by taking such a realistic position South Korea has exposed itself to the unjustified but seemingly plausible accusation that it was less than seriously motivated for unification.[9]

The criticism by North Korea of incrementalism follows the rationale that national unification is a most urgent task of the Korean people and therefore must be achieved as speedily as possible. They argue, understandably but perhaps with a certain exaggeration and with self-serving motives, that the division of Korea has caused "unbearable misfortune and suffering on their compatriots in the south," and constitutes "a national calamity for the entire Korean people, impeding unified development of Korean society."[10]

Unification as a Political Symbol. South Korea's unification policy in the 1970s reflected a posture of "unification through dialogue," a shift from the earlier position of "no dialogue" with communist North Korea. In the 1970s, the rigid, uncompromising, and self-righteous stand toward the northern regime that followed the Korean War gave way to a more flexible, sophisticated, and positive policy. On August 15, 1970, President Park declared that his government was "prepared to make an epoch-making and practical proposal concerning measures for the gradual eradication of artificial barriers between the South and the North," to contribute to the cause of unification. At the same time he appealed to North Korea to "remove its ambition to unify the country by means of force" and to "accept open competition between the South and the North" to prove to the people "which of the two systems can better serve their well-being."[11] This new progressive stance subsequently led to the Red Cross preliminary talks begun in August 1971, and to the secret negotiations with North Korea to arrange for the historic announcement of the North-South joint communiqué of July 4, 1972.

In taking this positive step toward unification, the Park government was undoubtedly influenced by the mounting demands of the people at home, whose aspirations for national reunification remained undiminished. The move was also stimulated by the great-power rapprochement and the fear that international decisions would adversely affect the interests of the Korean people.[12] Finally, the Park government was also using the unification issue to strengthen its grip on power and to consolidate its position of authority at home. The Yushin reform of October 1972 was defended as meeting the challenge of North Korea to carry out the South-North dialogue on unification. The creation of the National Conference for Unification and the Yujonghoe were justified as allegedly presenting a unified South Korean stand under the strong executive leadership of Park, to match the unified position of Kim Il Sung's North Korea.

Obviously, the issue of Korean unification was exploited for political purposes in South Korea as well as in North Korea.[13] In view of the saliency of unification as an issue, the respective leaders of Korea were motivated to appeal to the public for their unswerving support and acquiescence. The theme of Korean unification gave the incumbent leaders a useful symbol and issue that could be manipulated to advance the interests of their respective regimes.

North Korea's Unification Policy

North Korea continued throughout the 1970s to subscribe to the three basic principles of Korean unification put forward in the North-South joint communiqué of July 4, 1972. Its emphasis was slightly modified, however, to accommodate the changing perception and experience of inter-Korean dialogue and negotiation on unification in the 1970s. North Korea's basic stance on national unification cannot be fully understood, however, apart from the larger question of North Korea's political and strategic objectives for inter-Korean relations. Chief among these were forcing U.S. troop withdrawal from South Korea and promoting "democratic" revolution in South Korea. In fact, North Korea's unification policy in the 1970s was part and parcel of Pyongyang's overall strategic objectives regarding the future of Korean politics.[14]

"Independent and Peaceful" Unification. Pyongyang's "basic position" (*kibon ipchang*) on Korean unification prior to 1980 consisted of three principles: independence (*chaju*), democracy (*minju*), and peace (*pyonghwa*).[15] These principles, although basically similar to those set forth in the North-South joint communiqué of July 4, 1972, differed slightly in nuance and emphasis. Independent unification, first of all, meant that reunification had to be attained by the efforts of the Korean people themselves without relying upon external forces. In this North Korea's earlier and later stands were identical. The North Koreans have consistently held the view that Korean unification is an internal problem for the Korean people to solve and that the Korean people possess both the capability and the determination to bring about reunification by their own efforts.

Democratic unification meant that Korean reunification had to be attained through broader participation by the masses in the unification process.[16] Although this position may appear to differ slightly from the earlier principle of seeking "a great national unity" and transcending differences in "ideas, systems, and ideologies," it is in fact consistent with Pyongyang's interpretation of that principle as revealed during the North-South dialogue. The North Koreans cite two reasons for advocating broad participation in the unification process. First, unification is a "national issue" that affects the welfare of the entire Korean people rather than the interests of a particular stratum or class in the society. Second, the Korean people as a whole truly desire to participate in the unification process. This means that the unification talks should not be confined to a dialogue between the "responsible authorities" of North and South Korea—the position that the South Korean government prefers as the initial step, but be opened up to broader participation by the representatives of all political parties and social organization. This measure, the North Koreans insist, is the way to assure that democracy will prevail in the unification process.[17]

Finally, peaceful unification means that Korean reunification must be attained through nonviolent means. Since, as the North Koreans see it, reunification is an internal problem, they insisted that the Korean people would demand a peaceful approach to unification. "Nowadays even international problems are frequently settled through nonbelligerent means. If so, why can't we solve the problem of Korean unification through peaceful means?"[18] In advocating peaceful unification, the North Koreans curiously enough refrained from referring to "dialogue and negotiation" as the peaceful alternative to war. This reluctance to identify a proper channel of dialogue was obviously politically motivated. Even in the 1980s the current Pyongyang government has so far refused to deal with the Chun Doo Hwan government of South Korea, although the latter has repeatedly urged the resumption of the now stalemated North-South dialogue on unification.

(Following the Rangoon episode and the change of government in Pyongyang, North Korea proposed to open a North-South dialogue on unification. After proposing tripartite talks on Korean unification on January 10, 1984, North Korea sent a message to South Korea in the form of a letter from Premier Kang Song-san of the DPRK to Prime Minister Chin Iee-chong of the ROK. The letter reiterated the earlier proposal of holding tripartite talks on the future of Korea, including discussion on U.S. troop withdrawal from the south and on a declaration on nonaggression between North and South Korea.)

U.S. Troop Withdrawal. The North Koreans have consistently held the view that U.S. troops must be withdrawn from South Korea. Pyongyang correctly perceives the presence of U.S. troops in the south as posing a formidable obstacle to the attainment of their strategic objectives in the Korean Peninsula, including reunification. The U.S. military presence in South Korea is, they argue, not only an infringement of Korea's "independence" and "sovereignty," which must be rectified; it is also no longer justifiable from the standpoint of changing strategic relationships.[19] The U.S. military role in South Korea, according to a North Korean official, was established not so much to guarantee peace in the Korean Peninsula or to resist a possible *namch'im* (North Korean attack against South Korea) as to promote the strategic self-interest of the United States in East Asia. The North Koreans believe that the rationale for the U.S. military presence in South Korea has changed from deterrence of an invasion by North Korea to deterrence of Soviet expansion in Asia. Why, they argue, should Korean soil be used to deter the Soviet southward movement?[20]

In this regard the Pyongyang government has been very bitter over former U.S. president Carter's change of policy on U.S. troop withdrawal from South Korea by 1982. This policy, initially announced in 1977, was abandoned in 1980. Pyongyang was especially critical of the reasons Carter gave to justify his action—an error in earlier estimates and the upgrading of North Korea's military preparedness and capability. At the same time North Korea has insisted upon bilateral talks between Pyongyang and Washington, D.C., to sign a peace treaty terminating the state of war on the Korean Peninsula and replacing the existing armistice agreement concluded in 1953. This treaty is urgently needed, they argue, to ease tensions in the Korean Peninsula and to prevent future war. This stand is obviously meant to undermine the rationale for U.S. troop presence in South Korea and to lessen U.S. support of South Korea as an ally and as a client state. The primary aim of U.S. troop presence in South Korea has always been to deter a possible North Korean invasion of South Korea by acting as a "tripwire."

The North Koreans have attached two preconditions for the attainment of national unification that serve as a stumbling block for resuming any North-South dialogue on Korean unification: the withdrawal of U.S. troops from South Korea and the demise of the government of President Chun Doo Hwan. They are realistic enough to recognize that the presence of U.S. troops in South Korea impedes their timetable for a speedy achievement of Korean reunification. Whether the North Koreans are equally realistic in expecting the demise of the Chun government, however, is disputable.

Democratization in South Korea. The North Koreans insisted throughout the 1970s that the democratization of South Korean society (as they conceived it) was necessary before the goal of Korean reunification could be achieved. This "democratization" entails replacing the "fascist military regime" of South Korea by "democratic and patriotic personages with a nationalist conscience" who genuinely promote the cause of national reunification. The South Korean government should not practice anticommunism, they insisted, because North Korea does not (officially, that is) practice anticapitalism.[21] The North Koreans demanded that South Korea adopt instead a policy of tolerating communism. When asked why North Korea, with this proposal, interfered in the internal affairs of South Korea in violation of the spirit of the North-South joint communiqué, the North Koreans responded in an evasive and self-righteous manner: "Even if one can transcend differences of systems to achieve unification, how can one ignore violations of the human rights of patriotic people?"[22]

Differences in the respective Koreas' basic positions on national reunification, according to the North Koreans, account for the failure of North-South dialogue, attempted twice prior to 1980, in 1971–1972 and in 1979. The Seoul government has used the reunification issue, they charge, as a means of perpetuating the partition of the Korean Peninsula, and the Chun Doo Hwan regime is therefore considered ineligible for participation in the unification talks. This self-righteous stand by North Korea is defended as "just and right." As North Korea has consistently advocated extending participation in the unification process to Koreans of all strata, including representatives of various political parties and social organizations in both halves of Korea and abroad, designating the Chun government as ineligible for participation because of its alleged criminality seems arbitrary and capricious. This self-serving posture denies any possible modus vivendi and effectively destroys any basis for holding a meaningful inter-Korean dialogue and negotiation on unification between the two "respective authorities," as proposed by the Seoul government.

Unification Policies in the 1980s

The decade of the 1970s was eventful for establishing North-South Korean dialogue on the unification issue. Although the momentum established in 1971, initiating the process of inter-Korea negotiation on unification, was not carried through the rest of the decade, the fact that both Korean regimes decided to sit together at the conference table was a memorable occasion in the history of divided Korea. The Red Cross talks to help unite 10 million families dispersed since the Korean War, begun in 1971, were suspended in 1973 for all practical purposes, although working-level meetings were still held as late as December 19, 1977, the twenty-fifth and last such meeting to take place at Panmunjom. The North-South Coordinating Committee, agreed upon in the July 4, 1972, Joint Communiqué on North-South Dialogue, held three plenary meetings in 1972 and 1973, but it was boycotted by Pyongyang for all practical purposes in August 1973. The operation of direct telephone lines between the Red Cross officials in Seoul and Pyongyang, agreed upon in the July communiqué, was also suspended by Pyongyang on August 30, 1976.

In 1979 and 1980 both North and South Korean governments made some gestures to restore the inter-Korean dialogue and negotiations on unification. In response to the January 1979 proposal of South Korea, to resume the discussion on all issues pending for the two sides "without any preconditions," North Korea's Democratic Front for the Reunification of the Fatherland (a front organization for the KWP) proposed a meeting in Panmunjom. Although a series of meetings continued in 1979 in Panmunjom, South Korea's call for a dialogue between the "responsible authorities" of the two sides did not elicit North Korea's approval, and the inter-Korean dialogue was again deadlocked. With the political turmoil in the south in 1980 following President Park's assassination on October 26, 1979, North Korea came forward with a proposal for holding a prime ministers meeting of North and South Korea. As a result, working-level contacts were made in Panmunjom in 1980, but the process did not come to fruition because of the May 1980 coup and the suppression of the Kwangju uprising, of which North Korea disapproved. The plan for holding a prime ministers meeting was thus abandoned indefinitely.

The proposal on unification advanced by North Korea on October 10, 1980, and that presented by South Korea on January 22, 1982, were welcome and positive developments. The lukewarm response and outright rejection of these unification proposals by the respective Korean regimes, however, was very unfortunate, although understandable.[23] The Pyongyang regime's October 1980 plan for the establishment of the Democratic Confederal Republic of Koryo (DCRK), was received unenthusiastically by the Seoul government. The Seoul regime reciprocated by presenting its own "unification formula" on January 22, 1982, during President Chun's New Year's address before the National Assembly. This plan was rejected outright by the Pyongyang authorities four days later.

The quest for eventual reunification of divided Korea—however utopian and idealistic this may sound for the time being—demands that any or all constructive plans, proposals, and formulae be given serious, careful consideration. To move the debate on the unification question to a higher plane, what was called for was not a continued exchange of mutual vituperation between the two sides of Korea, but the initiation of a process of rational debate and interchange of creative ideas.

The DCRK Plan: North Korea

North Korea's unification policy in the 1980s is centered around its proposal for founding a Democratic Confederal Republic of Koryo. This proposal was contained in the report delivered by Kim Il Sung to the Sixth KWP Congress on October 10, 1980. Although confederation proposals had been put forward by North Korea in the past, the 1980 proposal was somewhat unusual in the minute, specific detail of its explication. The DCRK plan therefore deserves a careful analysis.

The 1980 Proposal. In his report to the Sixth KWP Congress, Kim Il Sung reiterated North Korea's basic position on the issue of Korean unification, stating that "to win the cause of national reunification" is "the most important revolutionary task of our Party."[24] Kim emphasized how central the unification question was to Korean politics by stating that "division is the road to slavery and national ruin; reunification alone will lead us to independence and prosperity" and that "for our nation today nothing is more precious than reunification and there is no more pressing task than reunifying the country."[25] His strategic thinking toward South Korea as part and parcel of his government policy on Korean unification, however, was not diminished in the least. "We must do away with the colonial fascist rule of the U.S. imperialists and their stooges in south Korea and reunify the country, and thus end the distress and tragedy of our fellow countrymen and open up a bright future for our nation," Kim declared.[26] "If reunification does not come quickly and division continues," he insisted, "our nation will remain bisected forever, and the south Korean people will be unable to cast off the yoke of colonial slavery."[27]

The DCRK proposal contains concrete and detailed steps deemed necessary to bring about "the unified state of a confederal type." These include (1) a supreme national confederal assembly comprised of an equal number of representatives from the north and the south and an appropriate number of representatives of overseas nationals, and (2) a standing committee of the assembly that would guide the existing governments of North and South Korea, which would become regional governments and which would administer all the affairs of the confederal state. Although the regional governments would be allowed to follow independent policies, the confederal republic would be a neutral nation, carrying out specific programs such as mutual troop reduction, the abolition of the military demarcation line, and the repeal of military alliance treaties already concluded, among other actions. The newly established DCRK would abide by a ten-point program that in many ways resembles the professed foreign policy lines of the DPRK. According to Kim Il Sung, the DCRK would do the following:

(1) adhere to independence in all state activities and follow an independent policy;
(2) effect democracy throughout the country and in all spheres of society and promote great national unity;
(3) bring about economic cooperation and exchange between north and south by ensuring the development of an independent national economy;
(4) realize north-south exchange and cooperation in the spheres of science, culture, and education by insuring uniform progress in the country's science and technology, national culture and arts, and national education;
(5) reopen the suspended transport and communications between north and south, by ensuring free utilization of the means of transport and communications in all parts of the country;
(6) ensure a stable livelihood for the entire people including the workers, peasants, and other working masses by promoting their welfare systematically;
(7) remove military confrontation between the north and the south by forming a combined national army to defend the nation against invasion from outside;
(8) defend and protect the national rights and interests of all Koreans overseas;
(9) handle properly the foreign relations established by the north and the south prior to reunification, by coordinating the foreign activities of the two regional governments in a unified way; and
(10) as a unified state representing the whole nation, develop friendly relations with all countries of the world by pursuing a peaceful foreign policy.[28]

The DCRK proposal was defended by North Korean officials as "rational and realistic." According to them, the plan reflects the changing realities, including (1) the ever-widening systemic differences between the north and the south, (2) the ever-heightening aspirations of the Korean people for national reunification, and (3) the constant change in the international environment, notably the intensified struggle for power among the big nations and the growing demand for national independence and sovereignty by people all over the world.[29] They described the formula of "one nation/two autonomous regions" under the DCRK scheme as the most practical solution to Korea's unification problem. The confederal scheme was said to be different from the formula of "one nation/two states" (the German solution) or "one state/two regimes" (the Vietnam solution). People who hold different ideologies and systems, they argued, could at least live together peacefully under the DCRK scheme, even if this was not a perfect solution.

What made the DCRK proposal different from the earlier confederation proposals was the presumption that the confederation would be a "unified national government" rather than a provisional and temporary arrangement leading eventually to a unified government for Korea. The confederation of two separate systems was proposed in the DCRK plan as a permanent condition. The success of this scheme, however, would presuppose absolute guarantees and safeguards for the independence of each region, free from interference by the other side. This condition appears difficult to fulfill under the present state of North-South Korean relations.[30]

Another new element in the 1980 plan was the new emphasis on the representation of overseas nationals in the confederal assembly. This feature represented an attempt by Pyongyang to establish a close link with overseas Korean nationals who are either unhappy over political repression in the south or neutral toward the controversy between the north and the south on Korean unification. So long as the Pyongyang government refuses to discuss the unification question with the current regime in the south, however, the DCRK proposal will be seen by many thoughtful overseas Korean nationals as a strategic plan by North Korea to bypass South Korea in inter-Korean relations. It will be interpreted as a revolutionary plan to subvert and undermine political stability in the south. For the time being, the DCRK proposal remains a blueprint with a low probability of implementation.

North-South Collaboration. As for more specific measures on North-South relations, the Pyongyang government seemed to agree that—barring a military solution to Korean unification—the elimination of mutual distrust and tensions between the north and the south was an indispensable first step toward Korean unification. This goal incorporates the merits of the "multifaceted collaboration and exchange" that the Pyongyang side proposed during the meeting of the North-South Coordinating Committee in 1972.[31]

The North's demand for simultaneous problem solving in all areas—military, political, economic, cultural, and humanitarian—made this plan unfeasible in the view of the Seoul government. A comprehensive approach is contrary to the more selective, gradual, step-by-step approach that Seoul prefers. From the standpoint of conflict resolution and management, the different approaches taken by the respective Korean authorities on implementing the three principles (of national, peaceful, and democratic reunification) merely reflect the variance in their understanding of the other's intentions and capabilities. The differences also reflect the stalemate in inter-Korean relations and underscore the importance of acquiring a modicum of initial trust and empathy, essential for any meaningful dialogue and for arriving at a compromise solution of the unification issue.[32]

The UDRK Plan: South Korea

South Korea's unification policy in the 1980s was formulated as part of an overall package of President Chun Doo Hwan's government, designed to overcome the negative domestic legacy of the Yushin system and to provide a new direction for the Fifth Republic of Korea. During the 1980 interim period and the first year of the new order in 1981, the

Chun government was preoccupied with restoring political order and reforming domestic political institutions. As political stability was gradually restored at home, however, the Chun government took a number of activist postures on internal and external issues; this included revitalizing its unification posture. A new appointive body called the Advisory Council on Peaceful Unification was created in 1981, giving President Chun an organizational instrument for manipulating public opinion at home and abroad on matters of Korean unification and South Korea's unification policy. Chun's 1982 proposal to establish the United Democratic Republic of Korea (UDRK) was preceded by a summit proposal in 1981.

The Summit Proposal. On January 12, 1981, President Chun proposed an exchange of visits between the top leaders of Seoul and Pyongyang. "I invite President Kim Il Sung of North Korea to visit Seoul without any condition attached and free of any obligation," Chun declared, adding that he was also "prepared, at any time, to visit North Korea if he invites me on the same terms as I offer." Not only would Kim's personal safety be guaranteed while he was in Seoul; Chun also said that his government would "extend all possible cooperation to him if he wishes to travel to any place of his choice in order to take a firsthand look at the actual situation in Seoul, other cities, or rural areas."[33]

This extraordinary proposal was made not "to argue over things past," Chun declared, but "to provide decisive momentum to creating mutual trust" between the two Korean authorities and "to pave the way to peaceful unification through unconditional resumption of the suspended dialogue." After reiterating his conviction that "any problems between the South and the North can be resolved if we work strenuously to narrow our differences following the historical exchange of visits between the highest authorities," Chun concluded his proposal with a statement that seemed to retain the gradualist and incrementalist assumptions of South Korea's unification policy in the 1970s: "The day of reunification, our nation's long-cherished goal, will not be far away, if only both sides begin reaching agreement on the most amenable matters in the least sensitive areas and progress toward the more difficult ones."[34]

The proposal for a summit meeting between the top leaders of South and North Korea was reiterated on June 5, 1981, when President Chun was about to take off on a tour of the five ASEAN countries. Declaring that he had not the "slightest doubt that this proposal will provide a breakthrough toward unification," Chun stated that his earlier proposal had received "broad domestic and international support and encouragement" and therefore that the North Korean authorities should "make an affirmative response." After renewing his call to President Kim to accept his earlier proposal, Chun added that "it does not matter whether President Kim visits Seoul first or I visit Pyongyang first" and that "the North Koreans can choose." He furthermore extended the scope of his invitation by stating that it might be possible that "we meet each other at some other place," if necessary, such as "Panmunjom, or a third country or any other place convenient" to him, thereby leaving "the choice of venue to the North Korean authorities."[35]

Once a summit meeting was realized, President Chun added that he hoped "to discuss frankly all questions raised by both sides, including . . . both South and North Korean unification formulae." As far as his own government was concerned, Chun declared, "all the necessary preparations for a dialogue" had been completed. After reiterating that North Koreans could "choose the date for the meeting . . . the sooner the better," Chun suggested that the North Koreans could "consult constructively with any person representing the Republic of Korea at any place in the world" or could work, if they prefer, "through an authoritative international organization or institution, including the Secretary-General of the United Nations."[36]

Particularly noteworthy in the June 5, 1981, proposal was the opening statement of President Chun, which reflected the philosophy of realism and pragmatism. President Chun admonished once again that "those advocating unification through communization by force of arms incorrectly understand the people's demand for peaceful unification and their delusions about war." But, he added, "For each of us to grasp accurately the true intentions and real situation of the other is essential to dispelling prejudice, self-righteousness, distrust, and miscalculation." This conviction, Chun continued, was what had motivated him to make the earlier summit proposal of January 12.

The January 22, 1982, Proposal. The 1982 proposal of the Seoul government, put forth in the New Year policy statement by President Chun Doo Hwan before the National Assembly, was more comprehensive and specific than earlier proposals for achieving national reunification. It was also positive and forward-looking in its approach to overcoming the impasse and stalemate in inter-Korean relations.

The 1982 proposal recognized and reaffirmed the basic principles of unification, advocating a national, peaceful, and democratic approach. Korean unification should be accomplished, as President Chun put it, "on the principle of national self-determination and through democratic and peaceful procedures that reflect the free will of the entire people." The new unification formula, according to Chun, "was originally prepared in anticipation of a South-North Summit meeting," an indication of preplanning and careful preparation.

The most reasonable way to peaceful unification, in the words of President Chun, was "to adopt a constitution of a unified Korea," and to organize a "Consultative Conference for National Reunification" (CCNR) to draft it. The adoption of a draft constitution would reflect "the promotion of national reconciliation" and also affirm the commitment of the Korean people "to the ideas of nationalism, democracy, liberty, and individual well-being," according to Chun. Once the draft constitution was approved and adopted by the people through a national referendum, further constitutional procedures for establishing a national unified government of Korea would be put into effect. This basic act of making a constitution would resolve all the procedural and subsidiary matters of forming a government, Chun claimed. "It is my understanding that such issues as the political ideology, the name of the country, the basic domestic and foreign policy directions, the form of government and the methods and dates of the general elections for a unified legislature will have to be discussed and agreed on in the CCNR in the course of drafting the constitution," he explained.[37] Chun stated that the Seoul government would present its "draft of a constitution for a unified country to the CCNR" and urged the Pyongyang side to do likewise so that "the two versions can be studied and forged into a single draft."

To make the adoption of a draft constitution for a unified country possible, President Chun proposed a number of specific measures. First, the south and the north should normalize relations and "take concrete steps to bring about national reconciliation." This could be done, according to Chun, by "the conclusion of a provisional Agreement on Basic Relations between South and North Korea" that would feature the following seven provisions:

> First, relations between South and North Korea shall be based on the principle of equality and reciprocity pending unification.
> Second, the South and the North shall abandon all forms of military force and violence, as well as the threat thereof, as a means of settling issues between them and seek peaceful solutions to all problems through dialogue and negotiation.
> Third, South and North Korea shall recognize each other's existing political order and social institutions and shall not interfere in each other's internal affairs in any way.
> Fourth, the South and the North shall maintain the existing regime of armistice in force while working out measures to end the arms race and military confrontation in order to ease tension and prevent war on the Korean peninsula.
> Fifth, in order to eliminate national suffering and the inconvenience resulting from the partition of the land and to promote an atmosphere of national trust and reconciliation, the South and the North shall progressively open their societies to each other through various forms of exchange and cooperation. To substantially advance the interests of the people, the South and the North shall facilitate free travel between the two halves of the peninsula, including the reunion of separated families, and shall promote exchanges and cooperation in the fields of trade, transportation, postal service, communications, sports, academic pursuits, education, culture, news gathering and reporting, health, technology, environmental protection, and so forth.
> Sixth, until unification is achieved, both parties shall respect each other's bilateral and multilateral treaties and agreements concluded with third countries, irrespective of differences in ideologies, ideals and institutions, and consult with each other on issues affecting the interests of the Korean people as a whole.

Seventh, the South and the North shall each appoint a plenipotentiary envoy with the rank of cabinet minister to head a resident liaison mission to be established in Seoul and Pyongyang. The specific functions of the liaison missions shall be determined by mutual consultation and agreement, with each party providing the liaison mission from the other party with all necessary facilities and cooperation to ensure its smooth functioning.[38]

President Chun appealed once again to North Korea to "expeditiously accept the proposal for a meeting between the top leaders of the South and the North in order to conduct frank and open-minded discussion on all issues noted above." Finally, he concluded his statement on the new unification formula by urging that "high-level delegations from the South and the North, headed by cabinet-rank chief delegates, meet together at the earliest possible date in a preparatory conference to work out the necessary procedures for a South-North summit meeting" and to assure that "if North Korea is agreeable to the proposal for a preparatory conference, the Government of the Republic of Korea has already made the necessary preparations to send a delegation."[39] The seven provisions of the Agreeement on Basic Relations Between South and North Korea in many ways resembled the provisions of an agreement entered into between West and East Germany. The acceptance of the German formula as the basis for Korean unification, in Pyongyang's view, would be tantamount to the institutionalization of the status quo of divided nationhood. Pyongyang is therefore opposed to the South Korean proposal for a basic relations agreement.

The February 1, 1982, Proposal. On February 1, 1982, ten days after President Chun's pronouncement of his "new unification formula," the minister of national unification of the Seoul government made public twenty "pilot projects," the more specific implementation plans of the new South Korean unification policy. These measures, although they still remain largely on the drawing board, were interesting and boldly designed. If accepted by the Pyongyang authorities in the future, any one of these twenty "pilot projects" would work to advance the cause of Korean reunification by increasing the level of North-South Korean interaction and integration. For political reasons, however, the February 1 proposal of the Seoul government was dismissed by the Pyongyang government as had been the January 22 unification policy proposal.[40]

The February 1, 1982, proposal included specific implementation plans for a wide range of military, economic, cultural, athletic, and humanitarian measures for inter-Korean cooperation. Included in the pilot projects were such daring ideas as opening a Seoul-Pyongyang highway (item 1), joint management of homeland visits by overseas Koreans and their free travel between the two sides via Panmunjom (item 4), and free access to the two sides through Panmunjom for all foreign visitors (item 8). These were interspersed with the more familiar measures of postal exchanges and reunion of separated families (item 2), the creation of joint fisheries zones for fishermen of the two sides (item 9), and mutual goodwill visits by representatives from various interest groups (item 10). The more imaginative proposals included the opening of Mt. Sorak and Mt. Kumgang (the Diamond Mountains) as a joint tourist zone (item 3), the opening of Inchon and Chinnampo harbors for free trade between the south and the north (item 5), and access to each other's regular radio programs (item 6).

The proposed measures in the more salient issue area of military collaboration included the creation of sports facilities inside the DmZ for goodwill matches (item 17), the complete removal of military facilities from within the DmZ (item 19), discussion of measures to control arms, and the installation of a direct telephone line between officials responsible for military affairs (item 20). Measures in the cultural area of inter-Korean collaboration included free press coverage by the journalists of the two sides, who would be allowed to travel freely to each other's area to cover a story (item 11), joint research on national history (item 12), and a joint academic survey to study the ecological systems of fauna and flora inside the Demilitarized Zone (item 18). In the area of economic cooperation and trade between the two sides, proposals covered the trading of daily necessities (item 14), joint development and utilization of natural resources (item 15), and the exchange of technicians and exhibitions of manufactured products (item 16). Finally, athletic and sports collaboration projects included participation of North Korean delegations in the 1986 Asian Games and the 1988 Summer Olympics to be held in Seoul, and their entry into the south via Panmunjom (item 7), and the exchange of goodwill matches in various fields of sports, with participation in international games under the auspices of a single delegation (item 13).[41]

These comprehensive projects, however unrealistic their implementation might be under the existing stalemate in North-South dialogue, were received abroad as a set of positive and welcome ideas. Although they may reflect "a bit of pacificatory commonsense," these ideas were to be welcomed as "a touch of morning calm in a stormy world," editorialized the *Economist* of London. Moreover, noted the author, "if one of Chun's motives in issuing his appeal to the North was to propitiate doubting allies, no matter. It is the sensible act, not the questioned reason, that counts."[42]

North Korea's Reaction to the South Korean Proposals. North Korea has depicted the South Korean leaders as "insincere" and "intransigent" on the unification issue. North Korean officials draw a sharp contrast between their own position and that of South Korea, claiming that Pyongyang stands for the cause of "national" reunification of the Korean people while Seoul "criminally" harbors "the conspiracy of perpetuating the national division and split." Although this simplified and exaggerated claim is misleading and self-serving, it requires further discussion because the outside world needs a cognitive map of the North Korean leadership's proposed solutions to Korean reunification.

North Korea has dismissed the Seoul government's proposals for "peaceful unification" as a ploy for the consolidation of the status quo on the Korean Peninsula. It also condemns these proposals as a plot by the "national splitists" to advance a "two Koreas conspiracy." From Pyongyang's perspective, Seoul is hypocritical in its alleged quest for the reunion of separated families, the standard expression of South Korea's supposed humanitarian concerns. Ho Jong-suk, chairman of the Committee to Aid Overseas Koreans, has condemned the South Korean authorities for allegedly pressuring and intimidating Korean residents overseas (especially in the United States and Europe) to prevent them from visiting North Korea. In November 1981, upon returning from her trip to Vienna to attend an international conference on Korean unification, Ho said, "Facts prove that its talks about 'humanitarianism,' 'finding separated families,' 'dialogue,' 'peaceful unification,' and so forth are all lies and deception and a camouflage for covering up its ugly colour in seeking division, fascism and treachery."[43]

The Seoul government's January and June 1981 proposals for an exchange of state visits by President Kim Il Sung and President Chun Doo Hwan were not worthy of serious discussion, officials and academicians in North Korea claimed, describing them as "an insult to the reunification cause." When pressed to explain how the principle of "great national unity," one of the three principles of unification, could be effectively sustained if certain individuals and groups were excluded from the unification talks, North Korean officials maintained that their Great Leader Kim Il Sung could not be equated with the "ringleader of butchers" and a "national traitor."[44]

When reminded that North Korea had taken a similar position in regard to Park Chung Hee and yet had eventually been compelled to deal with him, one official insisted that Chun Doo Hwan was worse than any previous dictator because of his crimes against the Korean people—notably the massacre of the patriotic people of Kwangju in May 1980. North Korea would wait to negotiate on the unification question, he stated, until the present South Korean regime was replaced by "patriotic groups" and "democratic personages who possess a nationalist conscience."[45] As it requires two parties to tango diplomatically, this uncompromising, self-righteous position by North Korea bars any possibility for an effective dialogue between Pyongyang and Seoul on the unification question for the time being.

In response to South Korea's January 22 and February 1, 1982, proposals for the UDRK plan, North Korea issued a statement on February 10, in the name of the Committee for Peaceful Unification of the Fatherland, proposing a joint meeting of the "one hundred politicians of the south and the north." In so doing Pyongyang not only named 50 representatives for its side but also the other 50 to represent South Korea, excluding from this list the leaders of President Chun's government. Kim Il Sung did not highlight the unification issue in his 1983 New

Year's message, contrary to long-standing practice. However, Kim used other occasions to reiterate North Korea's basic position that "democratization and independence of South Korea is the key to reunification." In his written answer to the questions submitted by the Japanese *Asahi Shimbun* on January 1, 1983, Kim stated that North Korea had no intention to invade the south and that he would strive to realize "the peaceful reunification" of Korea.[46] Despite these verbal assurances North Korea could not convince South Korea that its strategy of fostering revolution in the south and overthrowing the Chun government had been abandoned. North Korea's demand that the U.S. troops withdraw from the south has not been dropped either, the Seoul government pointed out.

Comparative Assessment: Continuity and Change

The unification policies and proposals of North and South Korea in the 1980s appeared to be a drastic departure from the plans and proposals of the 1970s. A closer look at the underlying postulates and assumptions of the new policies, however, reveals elements of both change and continuity between the earlier and later plans of the respective regimes and also, of course, between the latest North Korean and the South Korean plans. The differences between new and old unification policies are more pronounced for South Korea than for North Korea, yet the policies of both north and south show more continuity than change.

Similarities

South Korea. Institutionalizing the relaxation of tension in the Korean Peninsula was one of the basic postulates of South Korea's unification policy in the 1970s. The principle of "peaceful" unification agreed to by Park's government in the 1972 joint communiqué was in harmony with the Seoul government's strategic goal of consolidating the peace process in the Korean Peninsula. The proposal for the conclusion of a South-North nonaggression agreement, announced on January 18, 1974, and repeated on August 15, 1974, was an attempt on the part of South Korea to attain this goal.

Although the 1982 proposal on the new unification formula used different expressions, the commitment of South Korea to institutionalizing the relaxation of tensions and maintaining peace in the Korean Peninsula had not been abandoned nor modified by Park's successor Chun Doo Hwan. Instead of proposing a nonaggression agreement, the Seoul government now spoke of a "Provisional Agreement on Basic Relations," but the underlying assumption and strategic consideration—promoting peace as a precursor to unification—remained. Not surprisingly, therefore, Chun's January 22, 1982, unification policy statement (not to be confused with the February proposal) contains such provisions on basic relations as: desistance from using force of arms and other violence (item 2), recognition of existing political orders and social institutions and non-interference in internal affairs (item 3), and maintenance of the existing regime of armistice (item 4).

The 1982 unification policy of Chun's government also incorporated some of the provisions already stated in the June 23, 1973, Special Foreign Policy Statement Regarding Peaceful Unification. As previously noted, the 1973 statement was issued at the time of the South-North negotiations to provide the basis for the simultaneous entry into the United Nations by both South and North Korean governments, thereby institutionalizing the de facto coexistence and peace between the two regimes in the Korean Peninsula. Because of opposition by North Korea, which made a counterproposal for joining the United Nations under the single name of the Confederal Republic of Koryo, South Korea's strategic plan for admission into the United Nations as separate entities failed to materialize.

The January 1982 policy statement also continued to advocate the institutionalization of peace in the Korean Peninsula by maintaining already-established diplomatic institutions and procedures. It recommended honoring international treaties and agreements, both bilateral and multilateral, concluded by the respective Korean authorities with third countries (item 6). Although it made the qualifications that this agreement would last until unification and that South and North Korea would consult with each other on issues affecting the interests of the Korean people as a whole, the basic strategic goal behind South Korea's proposal remained the same. South Korea had to think in terms of preserving its security pact with the United States and legalizing the arrangement for the U.S. troop presence in the south. In this sense, as North Korea would no doubt maintain, there was no basic change in South Korea's policy for maintaining the status quo in the Korean Peninsula. The substance of the unification formula of the 1970s and the 1982 version of South Korea's unification policy are the same.

North Korea. Pyongyang's unification policy and proposals in the 1980s likewise did not greatly deviate from the unification policies of the 1970s. In fact, continuity and consistency are the hallmarks of the north's unification policy and strategies. Between the Fifth KWP Congress in 1970 and the Sixth KWP Congress in 1980 no significant changes were noticeable in North Korea's policy stand and perception of Korean unification. In 1970 Kim Il Sung pointed out the necessity to carry out "South Korea's revolution" so as to force "U.S. Imperialist Forces" out of Korea and to liquidate the "fascist regime of Park Chung Hee." In 1980 Kim Il Sung used different expressions for identical themes. He mentioned democratization of South Korea and U.S. troop withdrawal as prerequisites for Korean reunification. He appealed to South Koreans to overthrow the "fascist military dictatorship of Chun Doo Hwan" and also to demand U.S. troop withdrawal from South Korea. This revolutionary line that is the underpinning of the unification policy of North Korea did not change at all.

The differences between the DCRK proposal and the old notion of the confederation of Koryo that Kim had proposed in 1973 were cosmetic. In presenting his five-point formula for "peaceful unification" on June 23, 1973, at a mass Pyongyang rally welcoming visiting Secretary-General Gustav Husak of the Czechoslovakian Communist Party Central Committee, Kim Il Sung mentioned "a north-south federation system under the name of the Confederal Republic of Koryo." He proposed that the north and south should join the United Nations as a single member under this name instead of under separate names. Although the 1980 proposal went into more detail as to the organization and procedures for the proposed federation, Kim's basic scheme for unification was not new.

The status and character of "a unified state" envisioned by each Korean regime differed sharply. While South Korea advocated a "centralized" unified state, North Korea proposed a "confederal" or "federated" unified state. In spite of these different legalistic expressions, however, the real preference may be quite the opposite of what each Korean regime has publicly represented as its official view.

New Elements

Despite basic similarities, new elements were noticeable in the respective regimes' unification policies and strategies in the 1980s, especially in those laid out by the Seoul government. Incrementalism was one of the important basic premises of South Korean unification policy in the 1970s. Without necessarily abandoning this commitment to a step-by-step approach to inter-Korean relations, the 1982 unification formula of Seoul did incorporate more daring, concrete, and specific ideas regarding the implementation of the necessary steps for bringing about peaceful unification.

The 1982 unification formula of President Chun, for instance, advocated the adoption of "a constitution of a unified Korea" through the convocation of a "Consultative Conference for National Reunification." The adoption of the constitution would be preceded by a series of necessary intermediate steps. As Figure 8.1 shows, the first step would be a conference to arrange for a summit meeting between the highest authorities of North and South Korea. The summit meeting itself would be the second step. Next, according to the South Korean formula, would be the conclusion of a provisional agreement on basic relations between the south and the north, incorporating seven specific principles and procedures for unification. Steps to follow would include: (1) the formation of the CCNR, (2) the drafting of a constitution for a unified Korea, (3) a national referendum to approve the draft constitution, and (4) general elections under the constitution to form a unified legislature and a unified government.

The specification of detailed procedures and concrete steps was something entirely new to South Korea's unification politics. Apart from the

FIGURE 8.1
South Korea's Unification Formula Based on a Step-by-Step Approach

---

Step 1. Preparatory Conference to Arrange a South-North Summit Meeting

Step 2. Summit Meeting Between the Highest Authorities of South and North Korea

Step 3. Conclusion of a Provisional Agreement on Basic Relations Between North and South Korea

    Seven Point Principles:
        1. equality and reciprocity
        2. no use of force to settle issues
        3. no interference
        4. maintain armistice in force
        5. promote cooperative measures
        6. respect each other's treaties concluded with third parties
        7. exchange a resident liaison mission

Step 4. Unification Formula Put into Effect Through:

    1. the formation of the Consultative Conference on National Reunification (CCNR)
    2. the drafting of a constitution for a unified Korea
    3. a national referendum to approve the draft constitution
    4. general elections for a unified legislature and a unified government

Step 5. Eastablishment of a Unified Democratic Republic Through the Principles of National Self-Determination and National Reconciliation

---

Source: Young Whan Kihl, "South Korea's Unification Policy in the 1980's: An Assessment," Korea and World Affairs: A Quarterly Review 6, 1 (Spring 1982): p. 87.

question of whether these proposed procedures were feasible, the very fact that the Seoul government was presenting its thinking and staking its honor on a public pledge was a positive and encouraging development for the cause of Korean unification.

Also noteworthy in the 1982 pronouncements were expressions evoking a new spirit of nationalist zeal. The 1982 policy claimed that unification could neither be "pursued exclusively or arbitrarily by any specific class or group" nor used to advance specific ideologies, ideals, or institutions. Unification must grow, instead, out of "the commitment of the entire people" and should be "attained through the promotion of national reconciliation." Whether these expressions signified a new direction or simply new rhetoric has yet to be proved by concrete action.

Differences Between the Plans of the North and the South

The 1982 unification formula of South Korea was a logical response and alternative to North Korea's October 1980 proposal on the creation of a confederal state. Along with the similarities already noted between the DCRK plan of North Korea and the UDRK plan of South Korea, there are four noteworthy differences.

First is the difference in the character and composition of the unified state envisioned by the two proposals. Whereas the South Korean formula seeks to establish a "centralized" unified democratic republic, the North Korean confederation scheme proposes a "federal" unification under which two regional governments would coexist. Ironically, North Korea has claimed that this "incomplete" unification is "the most realistic and reasonable way to reunify the country" because it would leave "the ideas and social systems existing in North and South Korea as they are." South Korea has proposed a unified state that is more complete and that would incorporate "the ideals of nationalism, democracy, liberty and individual well-being." This approach is defended by the spokesman of the Seoul government as the most realistic, equitable, and therefore most justifiable way to reunify the country.[47]

Second is the difference in approach to unification. Whereas the South Korean unification formula calls for the normalization of inter-Korean relations as a necessary step toward eventual unification, the North Korean proposal advocates the formation of a confederal republic as the initial act, to be followed by measures promoting mutual exchange and transaction between the north and south. South Korea's formula thus envisions inter-Korean cooperation and exchanges *before* the act of unification; North Korea's proposal does not stipulate these developments until *after* a federal republic is securely established. These different visions reflect South Korea's gradualist approach to unification and North Korea's insistence upon a "once-and-for-all" political act of unification. In this sense the latest versions of South and North Korea's unification formulae do not deviate greatly from the propositions of the 1970s.

The third difference lies in the method of attaining unification and the scope of popular participation. The South Korean unification formula details specific procedures such as drafting a constitution and holding a national referendum and a general election to create a unified legislature and government. The CCNR would be created to represent the views of the "entire people" of the two halves. North Korea's confederal scheme is much less detailed, although specific individuals and groups are excluded from participation in the unification process and in such bodies as "the Supreme National Confederal Conference or the Confederal Standing Committee." Likewise, the Grand National Conference, recently renamed the Meeting to Expedite Unification, would not be open to incumbent South Korean government leaders and others whom the North Koreans consider to be unacceptable.

The final difference is between the kinds of policies to be formulated and pursued by a unified state. Whereas the South Korean formula leaves the question open pending unification, the North Korean confederal scheme superimposes what it calls the "ten major policies." These policies would, for instance, commit the unified state of Korea to becoming a "neutral nation," not participating in an alliance or bloc and instead following an independent foreign policy. The unification formula of South Korea would let the democratic procedure of representation dictate the character of policies to be followed by the government of a united Korea.

Concluding Remarks: Power and Motivation

In analyzing the unification policies and proposals it is important to differentiate between the stated official view and the cognitive perceptions of those in power. It is also useful to ascertain whether the leadership suffers from cognitive dissonance or misperception of the actual political situation. In diplomatic affairs, there is usually a huge gap between official policy pronouncements and the strategic considerations underlying these pronouncements.

North Korea officially advocates a plan of confederation between the north and the south, but its true intention may be to "communize" South Korea by inciting a revolution. South Koreans point to three North Korean strategies that they feel are directed toward this goal: (1) consolidation of the "democratic" base in the north for the achievement of an all-Korea revolution, (2) the struggle against "U.S. Imperialism," and (3) the organization of the South Korean masses under the strategy of a united front against South Korea's current regime. Likewise, South Korea advocates "a unified state" of North and South Korea, but its true intention may be to buy time to surpass North Korea economically. South Korea's real aim, notwithstanding the rhetoric of unification, is most likely the achievement of peaceful coexistence. Rapid economic development in the south has been made possible, the ruling elite would claim, because of the continued domestic stability and the absence of armed clashes between the north and the south in the post–Korean War years. In assessing the cognitive dissonance that prevails among the respective Korean leaders, one may recall that "any unification can be brought about only on a basis of equality." As the gap between the two Korean states and societies increases in terms of the capability and strength of both regimes, the possibility for system integration decreases proportionally.

Some basic concepts and theories of politics may be employed in analyzing the unification prospects of divided Korea. First of all, although divided territorially, Korea is still a nation in the sense that a nation is a group of people that have a set of characteristics in common, such as language, culture, past history, future destiny, ethnicity, and so on. However, since 1945 Korea has seen the emergence and consolidation of two separate states and regimes. A state is a political and juridical concept; a regime is a governing arrangement that has become institutionalized and regularized in a society. The state and regime also have a territorial base with a government capable of exercising at least three ruling functions: security-military, foreign relations, and taxation. If any of these governing functions are delegated to parts of the state such as provinces or districts, the state is then considered "federal." Otherwise the state is "unitary." A federal state embodies a single political organization that is decentralized with respect to some internal functions. A confederation is more than a single state, because the control of internal power is not centralized and monopolized but is delegated to the constituent units.

North Korea rejects the reunification formula of one nation/two states, whereas South Korea rejects the formula of one state/two governments. For North Korea a change in the status quo is considered desirable from a short-term perspective; South Korea prefers measures to freeze the current situation. Also, North Korea basically pursues a strategy of federalism, whereas South Korea follows a strategy of functionalism to bring about the goals of national reunification. The basic questions that arise regarding inter-Korean relations and the reunification of divided Korea are many and difficult to reconcile. How would power and authority be organized and allocated between the suprastructure and infrastructures? Would the suprastructure (all-Korea bodies) delegate decisionmaking authority to the infrastructures (the respective political systems), or vice versa? If so, how and to what extent? Which of the government functions—security-military, foreign relations, taxation, education and culture—would be delegated?

From the standpoint of an international integration theory, one must define the relationship between the two political regimes in order to work out an acceptable formula for organizing power and allocating authority between the two component units of divided Korea. Whereas North Korea, under the confederal scheme, subscribes to the formula of "one state/two regimes," South Korea basically defends a formula of "one nation/two states" that resembles the German solution of coexistence between the two halves.

Whether peace and normalization of relations should precede unification or vice versa is a chicken-and-egg question. Without dwelling upon the question of the true motivation of leaders, however, any discussion of Korean unification is incomplete. Underlying the current deadlock of the inter-Korean dialogue on unification are nagging questions about the political will and the strategic calculations of the incumbent political leadership.

The issue of Korean reunification must be viewed in its proper historical context. It is one thing to recognize the ardent desire of the Korean people for reunifying their divided nation as a "just and legitimate" cause; whether this goal may realistically be accomplished in a given situation is an entirely different matter. There is and always will be a gap between ideal and real, between desire and fulfillment, between possibility and performance. This distinction needs to be recognized and kept in mind in analyzing and evaluating the respective unification plans and proposals. At the same time, a psychological perception shared by many individuals and groups is undeniably "real," and should not be dismissed.

Many Koreans perceive divided Korea as a victim of great-power conflict in East Asia, and consider the territorial partition of their country as the consequence of international rivalry at the end of World War II. Because of this perception, our analysis of the problem of Korean unification began by specifying the origin of Korean partition and the emergence of separate Korean regimes. Without specifying the developmental process of the issue, any discussion of Korean unification would remain incomplete. An analytical distinction between "Korea as a problem" and "Korean unification as a problem" is also necessary. The problem of Korean unification is a manifestation of the larger question of the geopolitical role and the structural problem that the Korean Peninsula poses internationally. To the extent that the root cause of the Korean problem is Korea's territorial division, the solution to the Korean problem must be sought through reunifying the divided country. Korean unification is the first necessary step toward solving the larger Korean problem.

9
Conclusion: Regimes in Contest

The preceding chapters have examined the process of how two contrasting states and societies have emerged in the Land of the Morning Calm. The Korean Peninsula in the 1980s is a divided land, a country bisected politically and physically with a communist north and a noncommunist south. The two mutually antagonistic political regimes pursue incompatible public policies and programs. Whereas an authoritarian, capitalist, and civilianized military regime rules the south, a totalitarian, socialist, and familistic dictatorial regime prevails north of the Demilitarized Zone that marks the border of the two opposing camps. A divided nation is neither natural nor stable; not surprisingly, the relationship that exists between the two regimes of divided Korea is abnormal and tension-ridden, a state of estrangement and hostility to say the least.

How did this tragic division occur in the first place, and why does a situation of estrangement and anomaly persist on the Korean Peninsula? What are the relevant factors that led to the emergence of the system of regimes in contest in the Korean Peninsula? And how can one explain the politics of high risk, one of the dominant features of Korean politics? Before attempting to present some hypotheses regarding Korea's political development, this chapter will summarize the major similarities and differences of the political regimes, societies, and states of North and South Korea, concluding with certain speculations regarding the problems and prospects, both short-term and long-range, that divided Korea will confront in the remainder of the 1980s.

Systems and Regimes in Perspective

Although North and South Korea have traversed separate paths of political development since 1945, by the 1980s both seem to have reached destinations that are remarkably similar in terms of the structure and orientation of their political systems. Both Korean states are highly centralized, bureaucratic, and elitist in their structuring of political authority and their allocation of political power and influence. Moreover, both Korean states have pursued highly successful public policies and programs of modernization. In both the north and the south, these programs have facilitated the transformation of the once tradition-bound society of Korea—the "Hermit Kingdom"—into a more prosperous, dynamic, and self-sustaining modern society. Within this overall resemblance in authority structure and similarity in policy goals and orientation, however, a number of important contrasts between the two Korean regimes are clearly evident.

System Convergence Versus Regime Divergence

Both Korean regimes have experienced what may be called "authority inflation."[1] Political life in Korea, in the context of divided nationhood, has become central to all socioeconomic activities for most Koreans throughout the post–World War II era. "Politics takes command" seems to be the most appropriate description of public life in both sides of divided Korea, whether in the socialist north or in the capitalist south.[2] Characteristic features of this "politicized" environment are enhanced state authority and centralized governmental power.

Whether the political systems and political developments of the two Korean states have ipso facto converged or diverged is of course a matter of theoretical perspective.[3] Also, system convergence is certainly disputable as a testable proposition and hypothesis.[4] What stands out as an empirical fact, however, is that in the post-1972 years the Korean regimes have both adopted various measures to strengthen central authority and especially the position of the supreme leader in their respective political systems. This system convergence is rather striking in view of the radically different ideology and orientation of the two political regimes in divided Korea, and the contrast in their policy goals and in the basis for political participation.

This apparent convergence, however, should not conceal the basically divergent and contrasting ruling structures that have become entrenched in the respective Korean societies in the 1980s. Despite the projected image of a democratic people's republic, North Korea in the 1980s has fashioned a governing structure that resembles Korea's ancient "Hermit Kingdom." South Korea in the 1980s has developed an authoritarian ruling structure dominated by the civilianized military, in spite of its pledge to build a "just and democratic" society. While pleading independence and self-reliance, under the slogan of Juche, North Korea practices the politics of dependence on the Great Leader; the cult of personality requires that the 20 million North Koreans give their "absolute loyalty" to President Kim Il Sung and now to his son Jong Il as heir and successor. While preaching democracy, "purification," and the building of a democratic welfare society, the ruling circle in South Korea has been enmeshed in financial scandals, raising the suspicion of plutocratic and oligarchic rule by the military, the bureaucracy, and big business.

Whereas Marxism's first "monarchy" or "hereditary dynasty" is about to emerge in the north, capitalism's bureaucratic authoritarian system is rising in the south. While teaching the political gospel of "mass-line democracy" to the people, Kim Il Sung could not trust anyone except his own son to succeed him. Despite the rhetoric of constitutional democracy, Chun Doo Hwan does not permit popular presidential elections and relies heavily upon support by the military and technocracy.

External policies pursued by the respective Korean regimes are also in contrast. In spite of its tightly controlled, xenophobic, and self-enclosed regime, North Korea's socialist "Hermit Kingdom" has decided to "go global" in the 1980s, acquiring a universal mission to preach and carry out its revolutionary tasks beyond its border, as a way of legitimizing political succession at home and isolating South Korea from other Third World countries. Enmeshed in the network of complex interdependence, South Korea's dependence on its major allies for security and trade is rationalized in terms of forestalling the aggressive intent of North Korea; to divert attention from the domestic repression of democratic voices, the South Korean government promotes an activist diplomacy. Functional resemblance in authority structure has thus produced different styles and policies in the two Koreas' domestic and foreign politics in the 1980s.

The drafting of new constitutions in 1972 (both Koreas), and 1980 (South Korea), for instance, indicated that the two Korean states had raised the level of political institutionalization, but without giving a corresponding degree of emphasis to increasing the level of political participation by the citizenry. The ruling elites of the respective Korean states relied more heavily upon political mobilization from the top than upon voluntary and active political participation of the citizenry from below. For this reason the power of the ruling elite, especially the position of the supreme leader, has been drastically expanded at the expense of representative institutions and the procedures for political participation of the masses.[5] Why did this transformation in authority structure, this "authority inflation," take place in the respective Korean states?

Security State Versus Welfare Society

One explanation for authority inflation in divided Korea lies in the character of political elites that came to exercise authority and to implement public policies. Both Korean regimes are led by strong-willed personalities who have consciously cultivated the image of tough executive leadership in politics and have also deliberately recruited a following of dedicated and loyal cadres. Because of the reliance on patron-client ties between leader and follower, the dynamics of Korean domestic politics is best explained not by the model of policy disputes based on functional groupings in society but by the model of factionalism, in which the personal network of relationship is regarded as more important.[6]

The overall policy goals adopted by the two Korean regimes are heavily security- and defense-oriented, although the development of an economically viable welfare society has not been overlooked in the process. Due to the geopolitical situation and Korea's divided nationhood, each Korean regime has built a strong security state, transforming the once civilian, nonmilitaristic society of traditional Korea into what might be called "garrison" or "national security" states.[7]

The political leaders of the respective Korean states have also successfully put into effect a program of modernization to build a welfare society. Because of the natural tension and conflict between the goals of national security and socioeconomic welfare, the political process and the policy agenda in the respective Korean states largely revolve around the central question of how to allocate finite resources and to control limited budgets. Both Korean regimes are beginning to experience considerable difficulties in attaining both a security state and a welfare society.

Unitarianism Versus Pluralism

In drawing a comparison between the two states of North and South Korea, we need to guard against an overly simplistic and deterministic interpretation of Korean politics. Although the two Korean regimes in the 1980s both have a strong central authority structure, they are strikingly different in the style and operation of politics. The two states and societies are incompatible in basic ideology and values, and the two regimes are mutually antagonistic in political policies and preferences.

North Korea is a more thoroughly monolithic state. In the north, the masses are led by the supreme leader and mobilized to render absolute loyalty and dedication to him, whereas the masses in the south are generally dissatisfied with self-righteous and repressive regimes and policies. North Korea unashamedly pursues a program of building a "unitary" system, but South Korea is more pluralistic. Even if the virtues of consensus and unity are extolled in the south, dissension and diversity are a fact of political life, although not often tolerated. How can we account for this variation between the two halves of divided Korea? A number of hypotheses may be suggested.

Explaining System Transformation

Korea as a divided nation system contains two regimes in contest. Each Korean state and society has attained different degrees of system transformation. Whereas North Korea has become more monolithic and unitary, maintaining a high degree of cohesion among the ruling elites and between elites and masses, South Korea has remained somewhat pluralistic in social basis, with competition among ruling elites. There has been no system integration, however, between the two halves of divided Korea, not between the ruling elites of the respective Korean states and not between the ruling elites and the masses in the respective Korean societies. The national reunification of divided Korea, as the ultimate system integration of a divided land, thus far remains largely a symbolic issue with much rhetoric and little substance. What factors and causes explain the success of system transformation within and the failure of intersystem integration between the two halves of divided Korea?

FIGURE 9.1
Explaining System Transformation in Divided Korea

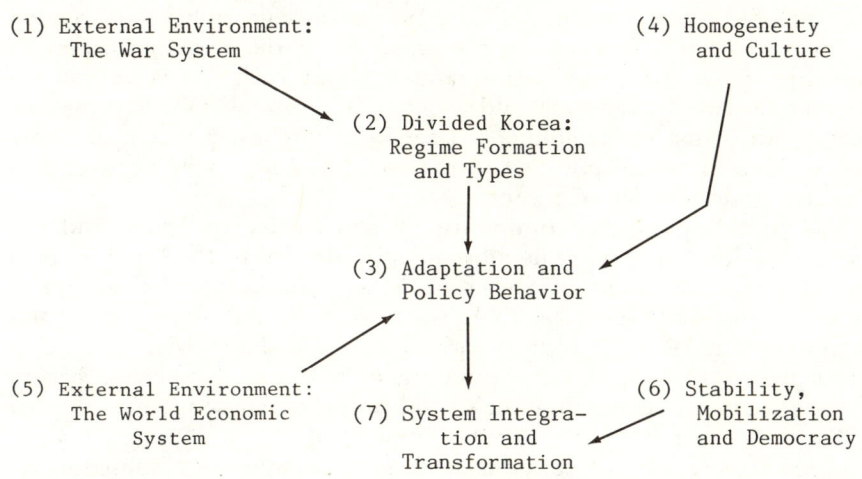

──────► signifies the direction of influence. Numbers 2, 3, and 7 are dependent variables; 1 and 5 are externally generated independent variables; and 4 and 6 are internally generated independent variables.

An explanation of system transformation and integration in divided Korea may proceed along several lines of discussion: historical-cultural, psychological, sociological, economic, or political. Four topics will be examined in turn to account for the consequences of political developments in the 1980s in divided Korea. These are (1) external influences upon domestic politics, (2) homogeneity, culture, and integration, (3) the state and society in the periphery, and (4) stability, mobilization, and democracy. As Figure 9.1 indicates, some of these serve as determining factors in the regime formation and policy behavior of the respective Korean states and societies, affecting in turn the process of system integration and transformation in divided Korea. No one of these individual factors provides sufficient explanation, but when all of these hypotheses are taken together, we may be able to identify the underlying reasons for the phenomenon of systemic change and transformation in Korea as a divided nation system.

External Influences Upon Domestic Politics

Both regime formation and regime types in divided Korea owe much to the pressure generated in the external international environment. The two mutually hostile regimes of divided Korea are the consequence of international politics in World War II, the Korean War, and the system of security alliances entered into by each Korea with the outside powers. The policy behavior of the respective Korean regimes also reflects the imprint of external pressures. Domestic and foreign policies in divided Korea have been a function of the response of the Korean regimes to pressures generated from within and without each Korea as well as between the two Korean states and societies. The capitalist world economic system, for instance, has influenced foreign economic policies, not only in the capitalist south but also in the socialist north, with their expansionistic trade policies of recent years.

The founding of the communist system of North Korea and the socialist policies and programs subsequently adopted by the North Korean regime were clear signs of Soviet influence. Unlike socialist countries such as China and Cuba, North Korea belongs to the more general and common category of communist regimes established by Soviet occupation forces in World War II. The founding of a liberal democratic system and the capitalist economic policies and programs subsequently adopted by South Korea reflected in turn the imprint of U.S. occupation policies in 1945–1948. The close political and economic ties subsequently cultivated by South Korea with the United States, and also with Japan since the 1965 ROK-Japan diplomatic normalization treaty, have maintained this influence.

The competitive spirit of inter-Korean rivalry also led to the adoption of programs of progressive legislation and social reform, such as the land reform acts. The land reform legislation of 1947–1949 in the south, for instance, followed the land reform acts of 1946 in the north. The series of five-year economic plans, first introduced in the south in 1962, was no doubt influenced by the successful economic development plans already in effect in the north. The Saemaul movement of rural modernization adopted in 1971 in the south was a functional equivalent of the successful agricultural development measures already implemented in the north.[8]

The signing of the South Korean–U.S. mutual security treaty in 1954 was followed by defense treaties in 1961 between North Korea and the Soviet Union and between North Korea and China. The May 16, 1961, military coup in the south gave Kim Il Sung an impetus for concluding defense treaties with his communist allies. The policies of strengthening diplomatic ties with the noncommunist nations and of expanding trade, adopted by North Korea since 1971, were also no doubt stimulated by South Korea's successful policy implementation of external linkages in the 1960s.

Militarization and authoritarian political control in the respective Korean regimes in the 1970s naturally resulted from the mirror image of mutual suspicion and threat perception shared by the two Korean regimes toward one another. The national security states that have emerged in the respective halves of divided Korea are a logical consequence of the traumatic and disruptive life experiences the Korean people have gone through in recent times. Many Koreans view the external environment as hostile and threatening, and believe that self-reliance and independence are the only assured means of coping with this threatening environment. It is no wonder, then, that the search for national security and political stability has become a powerful motive force for the Korean people in the post–World War II era.

In the light of these historical experiences, we may hypothesize that in a divided nation system that was externally imposed, *the regime type and policy output are influenced more by the external forces of the international system* and less by the internal forces of domestic politics.[9] With the passage of time, as the divided nation system takes firm root, however, the policy behavior of the respective regimes will be influenced increasingly by (1) internal indigenous factors such as political culture and (2) the international political economy and the world economic system. The degree of system integration and transformation will likewise be subject to (1) the cumulative impact of the capacity for system adaptation and the policy behavior of the respective regimes and (2) the degree of stability, mobilization, and democracy that prevails in the respective halves of the divided nation.

Homogeneity, Culture, and Integration

The rival political systems in divided Korea, once firmly entrenched, owe their political development to the internal factors of Korea's indigenous culture. The cultural imprint of Korea has been manifest in the ways in which the Korean political regimes were able to adjust to the changing situation both within and outside the Korean Peninsula. In surveying their adaptive behavior, what stands out as noteworthy is that the two Korean states and societies, once independent, became increasingly more assertive; they were no longer dependent variables in East Asian regional politics, as they had been at the time of territorial partition in 1945. Instead, they continued to strive toward political independence and autonomy. Evidence of the indigenous cultural impact on specific policy behavior of the respective Korean regimes is overwhelming.

The Korean people are well known for a high degree of cultural, ethnic, and linguistic homogeneity as well as for their long historical continuity as a unified nation. This central aspect of Korea's culture and history has had a definite bearing upon the pattern of subsequent socioeconomic development and upon the prospects for political integration. The Confucian cultural mores, with their emphasis upon hierarchy, loyalty, and group orientation, seem to have played a role not only in the political adaptation of the respective Korean states and societies but also in the implementation of domestic and foreign legislation, including that on national reunification. The fact of ethnic and cultural homogeneity is the reason that national reunification is generally regarded as a salient issue by the present generation of Korean nationals both within and outside the country.

As part of a homogeneous nation in the Confucian cultural tradition, both Korean states and societies are exposed to positive values for attaining modernization. Koreans are achievement-oriented and hardworking, and they value educational attainment and self-discipline. Several East Asian countries of the Confucian cultural tradition, irrespective of their different political systems and ideologies, have been mentioned as the most successful countries in attaining rapid economic development in recent decades.[10] These include Japan, North and South Korea, China and Taiwan, Hong Kong, and Singapore. Confucian cultural mores have been singled out as the most important factor in enabling rapid economic development in these East Asian countries.[11]

Ethnic and cultural homogeneity is a double-edged sword, however. It may be positive or negative in promoting or deterring political integration and social harmony between the two regimes. The experience of divided Korea seems to indicate that if the positive and integrative forces of homogeneity were applied to each Korean state and society the achievement would be astounding, as shown by the attainment of an economic miracle of rapid development by both the capitalist south and the communist north. However, when these forces are directed against one another, the result is quite different. Hostility and the struggle for competing legitimacy, rather than harmony and complementary cooperation, have been the rule in relations between the two halves of the divided Korean nation. The effects of zero-sum, cutthroat competition and the politics of high risk are readily apparent.

Under normal conditions a high degree of cultural homogeneity would facilitate the process of intersystem integration and national reunification. However, the condition of divided nationhood presents a unique and extraordinary situation, a kind of acute crisis. Under this abnormal and exceptional circumstance, cultural and ethnic homogeneity may act to accentuate political conflict rather than to heal wounds, driving an edge between the two halves of the divided nation. The rationale for this proposition, as suggested by Gregory Henderson, is that the act of partitioning a nation resembles that of splitting an atom.[12] Just as it is easier to split an atom than to fuse one, it is easier to divide a nation than to reunite it. Without relying on extraordinary means and outside force, it is difficult for either an atom or a nation to merge. The power generated in the process of either fission or fusion is enormous, and may be proportionate to the degree of homogeneity or purity of the entity. Fusion generally takes more effort and energy than fission, so if the atom-nation analogy is valid, it should be more difficult to reintegrate a homogeneous nation than it is to partition or split a nation-state in the first place.[13]

Once split, a divided nation is like Humpty-Dumpty: once broken, its parts cannot be put back together again. The possibility of reunifying a divided nation also decreases with the passage of time. Not only does the degree of homogeneity erode with time; new patterns and different configurations of vested interests also emerge. Under such circumstances the reintegration of divided Korea through normal diplomatic channels and through the political process of negotiation is difficult to attain. This is the story of North-South Korean dialogue on unification in the 1970s.

A judicious balance and harmony between the internal and external forces seems to be in order if the reunification or reintegration of divided Korea is to come about. The extent of cultural influence and imprint will vary between the two component parts of a divided nation system. It may be hypothesized that *the higher the degree of cultural homogeneity, the stronger the intensity of mutual suspicion and animosity between the component parts of the divided nation and so the more difficult the prospects for reintegration.*

The State and Society in the Periphery

The political status of the respective Korean regimes in world politics and their policy behavior also reflect the process of internalizing the norms of the world's political and economic relations. As divided Korea is "a microcosm of the world divided," so Korea united would be the barometer of a new world unity.[14] Although a united Korea's possible contribution to the welfare of the world remains an unexplored potential, divided Korea is the reality today that dictates the parameters of policymaking and behavior for the respective Korean regimes. The status of divided Korea in the world arena of politics and economics has changed over time, rising and falling with the ebb and flow of the world's political trends and developments.

During the heyday of the Cold War in the 1950s and 1960s, divided Korea was a focal point in the East-West political struggle for ideological predominance between the two superpowers, the United States and the Soviet Union. With the rise of the Third World bloc of nations and the emergence of North-South economic issues in world politics in the 1960s and 1970s, however, divided Korea receded into the background, becoming a peripheral issue, a regional and local concern in international relations. The continuous military preparedness and tension in the Korean Peninsula as well as the emerging economic status of Korea, however, may renew and reactivate concern over Korea in the future. This potential hinges upon the fact that divided Korea could generate a renewal of inter-Korean armed conflict, which might spill over into a regional conflict. These factors would also contribute to possible political fallout and disruption if economic failure or collapse of the respective Korean regimes ever occurs.

Why a common challenge in the external environment elicits different responses by the two regimes of divided Korea remains an unanswered question.[15] In the post–Korean War era, both Korean regimes took measures to consolidate political authority from within rather than to participate actively in external relations. Whereas North Korea has pursued a basic strategy of autonomy and independent development of its economy since the mid-1950s, South Korea adopted a strategy of interdependent development of the economy through establishing links with the outside, and since the early 1960s, through expanding its manufactured exports. North Korea has also expanded its links with the outside world since the early 1970s in both diplomatic and trade relations, modifying its earlier stand of self-reliance and isolation in external relations. An explanation for the policy behavior of the respective Korean regimes may be found through analyzing the political economy of divided Korea and its linkage with the international system.

Both Korean regimes have been victims of circumstances beyond their control. As cases of delayed industrialization within the world capitalist economic system, the requirements for North and South Korea's entry into the world economy were different and the costs have been generally higher for them than for countries that industrialized early.[16] State institutions have been strengthened to direct and coordinate the process of catching up economically with the rest of the world through rapid industrialization.

To say that North Korea is immune from the capitalist world economy, the DPRK's official view of its "Juche" economy, is misleading and inaccurate. Although North Korea practices socialism, it is not immune to the economic impact of the outside world as long as it participates in the world trade system. The pattern of economic development in capitalist South Korea is of course even more subject to the ebb and flow of the world economy insofar as its development strategy relies heavily upon rapid increases of manufactured exports in the world trade system.

Both North Korea and South Korea are peripheral to the world economic system. In this sense both regimes of divided Korea are equally vulnerable and subject to the danger of domination by the central nations of the world system. The obvious difference between the two is that whereas North Korea operates as a peripheral socialist state, South Korea operates as an integral part of a system of peripheral or semiperipheral capitalist states, more popularly known as NICs (newly industrializing countries).[17]

The political impact of the world's economic system varies between capitalist South Korea and socialist North Korea. Capitalism in the south created a social base of power distinct from the domain of the state, made up of entrepreneurs and business elites, yet socialism in the north eliminated the independent base of political and social groups and strengthened instead the domain of the state. Even though capitalism in South Korea has led to authoritarian politics, not democracy, the emergence of a private power base may at least counteract and counterbalance the state power.[18] Socialism in North Korea, despite the rhetoric of democracy and populism, has led to the rise of totalitarianism. The power of the state is vested in the hands of a power elite that practices hereditary rule and unitarianism.[19]

Stability, Mobilization, and Democracy

Both Korean regimes, as national security states, are motivated in their policy behavior by a concern for national security and military defense. Their policy behavior is also affected by the desire of governmental elites to guide the process of modernization and to cushion the impact of rapid socioeconomic change caused by the implementation of government-led developmental policies and programs. External security threats and internal developmental needs are used by the political leadership in each Korean state to enhance its claim to legitimacy.

Whereas the North Korean regime feels genuinely threatened by the presence of U.S. troops in the south, and fears the possible revival of Japanese militarism and the negative fallout of Sino-Soviet rivalry, the South Korean regime is driven by the fear of a renewed Korean war resulting from invasion and attack by communist North Korea. The perception of external threat and the resulting fear underlie the political thinking and policy behavior of the respective Korean regimes. This externally induced fear reinforces the claims made by the respective regimes to justify imposing ironclad domestic control measures upon the population. The maintenance of internal order and political stability, given highest priority by the respective regimes, is cited as a justification for perpetuating repressive domestic policies.

Excessive concern for national security and political stability provides the psychological underpinning for rigid political control and regimentation in both Korean states. The rationale given by the ruling circle is that any government is better than no government at all or a situation bordering on anarchy. The opposition forces in the south and in the north have been silenced in the name of maintaining greater national unity, harmony, and consensus. Factionalism is abhorred by Kim Il Sung in the north, and intraparty feuding and wrangling was severely criticized by Park Chung Hee in the south. Political stability was regarded as the basis for attaining economic development policy in the south, and this was misused as the pretext for perpetuating a repressive authoritarian rule.[20] Excessive concern for the maintenance of political order and stability was fueled by the perception of real or imagined external threat.

Both Korean states and societies have also been affected by progress in socioeconomic modernization and development. Rapid urbanization and industrialization, with the associated rural exodus and urban migration, lead to an increasing demand for popular participation in the development process. The political consequences of rapid socioeconomic development and change have been far-reaching.[21] Traditional mores and norms no longer fit, although their effect lingers on, and people's attitudes, expectations, and values are changing. Citizens are demanding a more participatory role for the masses in the decisionmaking process. Under the circumstances of rapid socioeconomic change and increasing domestic pressures, the governments of the respective Korean states must not only provide appropriate policy measures to accommodate the new demands but must also respond positively to the changing needs and situations in society. The more responsive measures adopted by both regimes will no doubt bolster claims of a democratic and populous rule in the respective Korean states.[22]

Actual developments in the two Korean states have, unfortunately, not been encouraging from the standpoint of promoting democracy in Korea. Instead of letting the political institutions progress commensurate with the pace of socioeconomic modernization, the progress of political development has been curtailed and manipulated arbitrarily by the ruling elite in the respective Korean states. The governing elites have intervened in the process of political development in order to exploit and profit from the effects of rapid socioeconomic change and the attendant demands for participation by the public. Elite intervention in political life and the political process of change, by Kim Il Sung's followers in the north and by military leaders in the south, has led to political decay and political underdevelopment.

The question of how to make political institutions and processes conform with the pace of socioeconomic modernization remains a challenge and an unresolved issue in Korea. What Korea needs is not only democracy on paper but also democracy in practice: not only the rhetoric of democracy or the "mass-line principle of leadership" extolled in North Korea, but also the substance of genuine self-government and autonomy. If either Korea were to become a democratic state, political development would not lag behind economic development and social modernization. Both political development *and* economic development must be encouraged and sustained.

Problems and Prospects

What problems will the respective Korean societies confront in the days ahead? Of the many critical issues facing divided Korea, three may be listed as among the most important for the immediate future. These are (1) maintaining effective political order and stability, (2) sustaining economic growth and social development, and (3) nurturing new cultural values appropriate for the Korean people. From a longer historical perspective, the evolution of a national consensus on political purpose, including an agreement on measures for Korean reunification, is a pressing issue for the Korean people.

Adequate approaches to these issues must be found if the current political leaders in North and South Korea are to stay in power and to succeed in their claims for political rule and legitimacy. In the immediate future Korea as a divided nation promises to continue to be a land subject to political surprises, turmoil, and excitement. Of all the changes that have swept modern Korea since 1945, political upheavals have probably been the most dramatic, especially in South Korea.[23] These dramatic political events have included national liberation from Japan, military occupation by the United States and the Soviet Union, internal insurrection, communist-inspired insurgency in the south, and guerrilla warfare. Civil war between the north and the south resulted in internationalization of the Korean conflict, foreign intervention, bloody political purges in the north, and in the south the Student Revolution, the coups of 1961 and 1980, Park's assassination in 1979, and regional insurrection and rioting in Kwangju. Under the circumstances, political stability and order will remain an important policy issue and a matter of grave concern for policymakers and public alike in both South Korea and North Korea. Of course, there is no guarantee that the future of Korean politics will be less troublesome and violent than the history of Korean politics in the past.

Political activity in the respective states and societies of divided Korea will continue to be dynamic and volatile. The political culture of the respective Korean societies represents a mixture of Confucian cultural traditions and indigenous Korean characteristics. If the Confucian culture is a theoretical system, borrowed from China but internalized with the passage of time, the indigenous Korean characteristics are in practice a counterweight to Confucian norms. Korean society, on the one hand, is orderly, hierarchical, and disciplined, a reflection of Confucian cultural norms. On the other hand, Korean society is also egotistic, rambunctious, restless, and egalitarian. If the Confucian tradition emphasizes the group, stressing loyalty to the family, harmony, and consensus, indigenous Korean culture is more oriented toward the individual, stressing creativity, initiative, and an enterprising spirit. This conflict in Korean culture, attributed by anthropologist Vincent Brandt to a yin-yang dichotomy, represents a synthesis of the alien Confucian and the indigenous shamanistic traditions.[24]

The short-term political issues for North Korea will involve, as a minimum, assuring political succession, sustaining economic development, and maintaining ideological education. Pressing issues for South Korea will be reactivating the process of economic growth, initiating political development, and promoting measures for social and cultural enrichment. The leadership in the north must tackle the difficult problems of assuring an orderly transition of power beyond current leader Kim Il Sung (the political succession issue), implementing ambitious developmental projects effectively, educating the young, and indoctrinating the masses according to the ruling ideology of Juche. The South Korean leadership must deal with the equally difficult problems of reviving and sustaining the earlier momentum for economic growth (what the Chun government calls the second economic miracle), and ensuring an orderly transition of power by honoring President Chun's pledge to step down in 1988. It must evoke a new spirit of cooperation and reconciliation, and promote South Korea's image abroad by measures such as successfully hosting the 1988 Summer Olympic Games scheduled for Seoul.

Internal cohesion and unity among the ruling elites provide the basis for maintaining political stability. Political stability was seen as the primary contributing factor for South Korea's successful economic development and modernization in the 1960s and 1970s.[25] Since political change and stability remains an important issue, appropriate measures for assuring an orderly transfer of power must be taken in South Korea as in North Korea. The threats to political stability and order in divided Korea are both external and internal. Foreign invasion by the opposing regime across the DmZ poses an external threat; domestic opposition and antisystem activities from within constitute an internal threat.

The serious long-term challenges that confront the leaders of divided Korea include solving the reunification issue and evolving a consensus on national purpose and commitment. A national consensus is needed because of the inability of both regimes of divided Korea to cushion the effects of socioeconomic change that continue to undermine the social fabric and political stability. To avoid social cleavage and possible disruption in the respective Korean societies, the latent conflict between established forces and newly emerging forces must be resolved and reconciled. This conflict is manifested in acute confrontation between different forces and groups in society. In South Korea, the confrontation is between a predominantly military ruling elite, led by former general Chun Doo Hwan, and a group of young radical reformers, consisting primarily of student activists, radical clergy, and discontented intellectuals. In North Korea the confrontation is between a faction of Kim Jong Il's followers in the party, recruited as members of the TRT movement, and the potential anti-Kim forces in and out of the ruling party, such as careerists, bureaucrats, and old cadres.

Included in the list of more specific long-term issues and problems for South Korea are resolving regional conflict, especially harmonizing the aspirations and legitimate grievances of the Cholla provinces with anti-Cholla prejudices, and diminishing the lopsided imbalance in life-styles and opportunity structures between Seoul and the rest of the country.[26] Bridging the gap in life-styles and value systems between the rich and the poor, the urban and the rural residents, the professional-managerial class and the manual workers, the Christians and non-Christians, is an important social issue in the south, as is the ongoing confrontation between the government and student activists. Included in the list of long-term problems for North Korea is the need to reconcile the tension between two groups: the ideologues and loyalists on one hand and the technocrats and pragmatists on the other. This difficult matter is a question of harmonizing the interests of the red versus the expert in the communist system. Also facing North Korea is the growing gap between party cadres and ordinary citizens, in terms of the distribution of benefits by the state, and between the reality and rhetorics of North Korea's claim for "earthly paradise," especially as the socialist "Hermit Kingdom" is increasingly exposed to outside influences.

The two Korean states and societies that have emerged in the 1980s, one generation after the country was partitioned, are secure and firmly entrenched, and are unlikely to disappear in the forseeable future. If the present system of divided Korea continues—and all indicators point in that direction—the prospects for system integration of Korea through reunification will become increasingly difficult. For a change in the status quo of the Korean Peninsula to occur, the impetus must come from both within and without the respective Korean societies and states. The dynamics of the ongoing process of competition between the two Korean states and societies will determine the shape of the future, and the success of the political leadership in determining each state's direction and in managing the process of change will be the key to the success or failure of each Korean regime as a viable political entity.

In their quest to reunify and reintegrate the divided nation of Korea, the Korean people at present appear to be "dreaming the impossible dream."[27] For this dream to come true, there must be a thorough overhaul of the existing order, requiring a wholesale change in political attitudes and belief systems. The challenge that faces both the North and South Korean regimes is to inculcate new values of political problem solving, that is, to change the nature and character of the issues from high-risk to low-risk politics, and to shift from the politics of confrontation to the politics of negotiation. Politics, by definition, is the art of the possible, and it deals with the question of power. Political power is by nature not absolute but relative, even if absolute claims are often advanced. Needless to say, the needed transformation in values and institutions will not take place overnight. The hope is that the two Korean societies will nevertheless struggle to meet this challenge, paving the way toward making the "impossible dream" of reunification a reality.

Appendix

List of Countries Maintaining Diplomatic Relations with South Korea and North Korea as of June 1982(a)

A. Countries maintaining diplomatic relations with both the Republic of Korea and the Democratic People's Republic of Korea (67)

*Australia	Guyana	Niger
Austria	Iceland	Nigeria
Bangladesh	India	Norway
Barbados	Indonesia	Papua New Guinea
Botswana	Iran	Portugal
Burma	Jamaica	**Rwanda
Cameroon	Jordan	St. Lucia
Central African Rep.	Kenya	St. Vincent
Chad	Lebanon	Senegal
Comoros	Lesotho	Sierra Leone
Costa Rica	Liberia	Singapore
Denmark	Libya	Sri Lanka
Dominica	**Madagascar	Sudan
Equatorial Guinea	Malaysia	Sweden
Ethiopia	Maldives	Switzerland
Fiji	Malta	Thailand
Finland	Mauritania	Tunisia
Gabon	Mauritius	Uganda
Gambia	Mexico	Upper Volta
Ghana	Nauru	Vanuatu
**Grenada	Nepal	Venezuela
Guinea	Nicaragua	Western Samoa
		Zaire

B. Countries maintaining diplomatic relations with the ROK but not with the DPRK (50)

Antigua and Barbuda	Guatemala	Peru
Argentina	Haiti	Philippines
Bahrain	Honduras	Qatar
Belgium	Israel	Saudi Arabia
Bolivia	Italy	Solomon Islands
Brazil	Ivory Coast	Spain
Canada	Japan	Suriname
Chile	Kiribati	Swaziland
***China (Taiwan)	Kuwait	Tonga
Colombia	Luxembourg	Turkey
Djibouti	Malawi	Tuvalu
Dominican Republic	Morocco	United Arab Emirates
Ecuador	Netherlands	United Kingdom
El Salvador	New Zealand	United States
France	Oman	Uruguay
Germany (FRG)	Panama	Vatican
Greece	Paraguay	

C. Countries maintaining diplomatic relations with the DPRK but not with the ROK (37)

Afghanistan	Egypt	Sao Tomé and Principe
Albania	Germany (GDR)	Seychelles
Algeria	Guinea-Bissau	Somalia
Angola	Hungary	Syria
Benin	Kampuchea	Tanzania
Bulgaria	Laos	Togo
Burundi	Mali	USSR
Cape Verde	Mongolia	Vietnam
China (PRC)	Mozambique	Yemen Arab Republic
Congo	Pakistan	Yemen (PKRY)
Cuba	Poland	Yugoslavia
Czechoslovakia	Romania	Zambia
		Zimbabwe

D. Countries that have diplomatic relations with the DPRK and consular relations with the ROK (2)

Egypt   Pakistan

E. Countries that have consular relations with the ROK but do not have full diplomatic relations with either country (1)

Iraq

F. Countries that have resident DPRK trade missions but do not have diplomatic relations with the DPRK and do not maintain trade missions in Pyongyang (3)

France   Kuwait   Peru

G. Others (2)

The Palestine Liberation Organization maintains an office in Pyongyang but not in Seoul.
The Vatican maintains diplomatic relations with the ROK but not with the DPRK.

Source: Reprinted from US State Department. "Diplomatic Relations of ROK and DPRK: Assessments and Research." <u>Unclassified</u>. May 26, 1982. Washington, D.C.: US State Department Bureau of Intelligence and Research, 1982.

a. Includes the countries which have established, or have announced their intention to establish, official relations.
* Relations temporarily suspended with North Korea.
** Status of ties with South Korea uncertain, though ROK Government claims formal relations have not been broken.
*** South Korea maintains its diplomatic recognition of the authorities on Taiwan.

Notes

Chapter 1

1. For a similar view on divided Korea as exhibiting the politics of competing legitimacy, see Samuel S. Kim, "Research on Korean Communism: Promise Versus Performance," *World Politics* 32, 2 (January 1980).
2. Gregory Henderson, "North and South Korea," in Steven L. Spiegel and Kenneth N. Waltz, eds., *Conflict in World Politics* (Cambridge, Mass.: Winthrop Publishers, 1971), p. 197.
3. Glenn D. Paige, "Toward a Theory of Korean Political Leadership Behavior," in Dae-Sook Suh and Chae-Jin Lee, eds., *Political Leadership in Korea* (Seattle: University of Washington Press, 1976), p. 226.
4. Han-Kyo Kim, "Korea and Comparative Political Studies" (Prepared for presentation at a panel organized by the Association of Korean Political Scientists in North America in conjunction with the Annual Convention of the American Political Science Association, September 3–5, 1982, Denver, Colorado), pp. 6–7.
5. Glenn D. Paige, "Some Implications for Political Science of the Comparative Politics of Korea," in Fred W. Riggs, ed., *Frontiers of Development Administration* (Durham, N.C.: Duke University Press, 1970), p. 152.
6. Adam Przeworski and Henry Teune, *The Logic of Comparative Social Inquiry* (New York: John Wiley, 1969).
7. For an indispensable reference guide to the study of North Korea's political system, see Dae-Sook Suh, *Korean Communism 1945–1980: A Reference Guide to the Political System* (Honolulu: University Press of Hawaii, 1981). See also Robert A. Scalapino and Chong-Sik Lee, *Communism in Korea*, 2 vols. (Berkeley and Los Angeles: University of California Press, 1972), particularly vol. 2, *The Society*.
8. C. I. Eugene Kim, "Government and Politics," in Han-Kyo Kim, ed., *Studies on Korea: A Scholar's Guide* (Honolulu: University Press of Hawaii, 1980), pp. 301–337. See also the seven-volume series, *Studies in the Modernization of the Republic of Korea, 1945–1975* (undertaken jointly by the Harvard University Institute for International Development and the Korea Development Institute), especially Edward S. Mason et al., *The Economic and Social Modernization of the Republic of Korea* (Cambridge, Mass.: Harvard University Council on East Asian Studies, 1980).
9. On the strengthened role of the state in the modern era, see Barrington Moore, Jr., *Social Origins of Dictatorship and Democracy: Lord and Peasant in the Making of the Modern World* (Boston: Beacon Press, 1966). See also Albert

Hirschman, *The Passions and the Interests: Political Arguments for Capitalism Before Its Triumph* (Princeton, N.J.: Princeton University Press, 1977).

10. Max Weber, *The Theory of Social and Economic Organization,* trans. A. Henderson and Talcott Parsons (New York: Oxford University Press, 1947), pp 145–154, as cited in Robert A. Dahl, *Modern Political Analysis,* 2d ed. (Englewood Cliffs, N.J.: Prentice-Hall, 1970), p. 5. See also Bertrand Badie and Pierre Birnbaum, *The Sociology of the State,* trans. Arthur Goldhammer (Chicago: University of Chicago Press, 1983).

11. For a plea to reassess the changing nature of state and societal relationships in the modern era, see Theda Skocpol, "Bringing the State Back In," *Items* 36, 1 and 2 (June 1982):1–8.

12. The choice of "conspiratorial" to characterize the 1961 and 1980 coups is deliberate. The military coups in South Korea were not "exclusionary corporatist coups," as were some Latin American coups. In Korea, organized labor was not involved in the political process either by Syngman Rhee in the First Republic or by Chang Myon in the brief reign of the Second Republic. For a theoretical discussion of the military role in politics, see Alfred Stepan, *The State and Society: Peru in Comparative Perspective* (Princeton, N.J.: Princeton University Press, 1978), pp. 73–113.

13. Skocpol, "Bringing the State Back In," p. 4.

14. On the question of political succession as decided by the Sixth KWP Congress in 1980, see Chong-Sik Lee, "Evolution of the Korean Workers' Party and the Rise of Kim Chong-il," *Asian Survey* 22, 5 (May 1982):434–448.

15. Ibid. See also Robert A. Scalapino, "Current Dynamics of the Korean Peninsula," *Problems of Communism* 30, 6 (November-December 1981):16–31.

16. For an annotated bibliography of English-language studies on Korean government and politics, see Chapters 12, 14, and 15 (dealing with South Korea, inter-Korean relations, and North Korea respectively) in Han-Kyo Kim, *Studies on Korea.*

17. An exception is Bae-ho Hahn, "The Parties and Politics in Two Koreas: A Preliminary Analysis," *Proceedings of the International Conference on the Problems of Korean Unification* (Seoul: Asiatic Research Center, Korea University, 1971), as reprinted in C. I. Eugene Kim and Young Whan Kihl, eds., *Party Politics and Elections in Korea* (Silver Spring, Md.: Research Institute on Korean Affairs, 1976), pp. 152–162. See also Bae-ho Hahn, "Nampukhanui chongch'i ch'eje pikyo sosol 1 & 2" [Toward a comparative analysis of the South and North Korean political systems 1 & 2], *Asea Yon'gu* 14, 3 (September 1971):3–48, and 15, 1 (March 1972):1–19; Joungwon Alexander Kim, *Divided Korea: The Politics of Development* (Cambridge, Mass.: Harvard University Press, 1975); and Sung Chul Yang, *Korea and Two Regimes: Kim Il Sung and Park Chung Hee* (Cambridge, Mass.: Schenkman Publishing Co., 1981).

18. For a useful anthology of the various prevailing approaches and paradigms in the discipline of political science, see various issues of *Political Science Annual: An International Review,* Vols. 1–6 (Indianapolis, Ind.: Bobbs-Merrill Co., 1969 through 1975); and the eight-volume series in the *Handbook of Political Science* (Reading, Mass.: Addison-Wesley Publishing Co., 1977) edited by Fred I. Greenstein and Nelson W. Polsby.

19. Examples of recent Korean-language studies that use a monosystemic approach to North and South Korean politics may be found in Un-t'ai Kim et al., *Han'guk chongch'iron* [On Korean politics] (Seoul: Pakyongsa, 1976), and Ch'ang-sun Kim et al., *Pukhan chongch'iron* [On North Korean politics] (Seoul: Kukdong Munje Yon'guso, 1976, and Pukhan Yon'guso, 1979).

20. Chong-Sik Lee, "Stalinism in the East: Communism in North Korea," in Robert A. Scalapino, ed., *The Communist Revolution in Asia* (Englewood Cliffs, N.J.: Prentice-Hall, 1969), pp. 120-150; C. I. Eugene Kim, "Personalism in North Korea," *Problems of Communism,* January-February 1978, pp. 64-67; R. A. Scalapino and Chong-Sik Lee, *Communism in Korea* 2:752-756, 784-785; Ilpyong J. Kim, *Communist Politics in North Korea* (New York: Praeger Publishers, 1975); Yong-P'il Rhee, "Characteristics of North Korean Political System," *Unification Policy Quarterly* (Seoul) 4, 3 (Autumn 1978):16-33; Dongbok Lee, "Hereditary Succession in North Korea and Its Impact on Inter-Korean Relations" (Prepared for the Second International Symposium on Korea at La Trobe University, Melbourne, Australia, November 20-22, 1980); James B. Palais, "Democracy in South Korea, 1948-72," in Frank Baldwin, ed., *Without Parallel: The American-Korean Relations Since 1945* (New York: Pantheon Books, 1974); Bruce G. Cumings, ed., special supplement on "Imperialism and Repression: The Case of South Korea," *Bulletin of Concerned Asian Scholars* 9, 2 (April-June 1977):2-41.

21. This practice of dichotomizing political systems is by no means unique to the study of North and South Korea. A study that uses a similar scheme of dichotomization in comparative political studies is Zbigniew Brzezinski and Samuel P. Huntington, *Political Power: USA and USSR* (New York: Viking Press, 1967).

22. This theme wil be elaborated further in subsequent discussions. For instance, see notes 55 and 56 below.

23. On North Korea's economic system in general, see Joseph Sang-hoon Chung, *The North Korean Economy: Structure and Development* (Stanford, Calif.: Hoover Institution Press, 1974). Among many existing studies, a useful overview of South Korea's economy is Paul W. Kuznets, *Economic Growth and Structure in the Republic of Korea* (New Haven, Conn.: Yale University Press, 1977).

24. On North Korea's economic development strategy, see DPRK, *The Building of an Independent National Economy in Korea* (Pyongyang: Foreign Languages Publishing House, 1977); Ellen Brun and Jacques Hersh, *Socialist Korea: A Case Study in the Strategy of Economic Development* (New York: Monthly Review Press, 1976). On South Korea's economic development strategy, see the Harvard University series, "Studies in the Modernization of the Republic of Korea," op. cit.

25. On North Korea's self-reliance as a strategy for development, see Gordon White, "North Korean Chuch'e: The Political Economy of Independence," *Bulletin of Concerned Asian Scholars* 7, 2 (April-June 1975):44-54; Adrian Foster-Carter, "North Korea: Development and Self-Reliance, A Critical Appraisal," *Bulletin of Concerned Asian Scholars* 9, 1 (January-March 1977):45-57.

26. On the concept of a world capitalist system, and Korea as a semiperipheral country, see Immanuel Wallerstein, "Semiperipheral Countries and the Contemporary World Crisis," *Theory and Society* 3 (Winter 1976):461-483. According to this view, North and South Korea are "socialist peripheral" and "capitalist peripheral" states respectively. See also Immanuel Wallerstein, *The Capitalist World-Economy: Essays* (New York: Cambridge University Press, 1979).

27. For a Marxist perspective on the economic contrast between North and South Korea, see Gerhard Breidenstein and W. Rosenberg, "Economic Comparison of North and South Korea," *Journal of Contemporary Asia* 5, 2 (1975):165-203. See also Gavan McCormack and Mark Selden, eds., *Korea North and South: The Deepening Crisis* (New York: Monthly Review Press, 1978).

28. On political culture generally, see Gabriel Almond and Sidney Verba, *The Civic Culture* (Boston: Little, Brown & Co., 1963); Lucian W. Pye and Sidney Verba, eds., *Political Culture and Political Development* (Princeton, N.J.: Princeton University Press, 1965). See also Gabriel Almond and Sidney Verba, *The Civic Culture Revisited* (Boston: Little, Brown & Co., 1980).

29. Pye and Verba, *Political Culture,* p. 513. See especially Sidney Verba, "Conclusion: Comparative Political Culture," pp. 512–560.

30. Actually, political economy is an old discipline, predating the recent academic specialization that culminated in the separate disciplines of economics and political science. To differentiate the current mode of political economy study from classical political economy, some students advocate a new designation, "new political economy." For instance, see Warren F. Ilchman and Norman T. Uphoff, *The Political Economy of Change* (Berkeley: University of California Press, 1969), Chapter 2.

31. Webster's Third New International Dictionary defines "political economy" as a "branch of the art of government concerned with directing government policies toward promotion of the wealth of the government and of the community as a whole."

32. Joe A. Oppenheimer, "Small Steps Forward for Political Economy," *World Politics* 33, 1 (October 1980):121.

33. Bruce R. Scott, John W. Rosenblum, and Audrey T. Sproat, *Case Studies in Political Economy: Japan 1854–1977* (Cambridge, Mass.: Harvard Business School, 1980), p. 1.

34. Ibid.

35. On a recent effort to apply the "linkage politics" concept to the study of political parties, see Kay Lawson, ed., *Political Parties and Linkage: A Comparative Perspective* (New Haven, Conn.: Yale University Press, 1980). See also James N. Rosenau, ed., *Linkage Politics* (New York: Free Press, 1969); James N. Rosenau, "Theorizing Across Systems: Linkage Politics Revisited," in Jonathan Wilkenfeld, ed., *Conflict Behavior and Linkage Politics* (New York: David McKay, 1973).

36. In the words of Edward Wright, who spent many years in Seoul as a trained observer, "The political process in Korea is highly centralized and personalized, and the people are quite authority conscious. The nitty-gritty of political life and accomplishment is largely in terms of one's place and status in the social and political hierarchy and, related, in terms of the direct personal influence one can exert on superiors and subordinates." Edward Wright, ed., *Korean Politics in Transition* (Seattle: University of Washington Press, 1975), p. 3.

37. Choe Jae-suk, *Han'gukinui sahoejok songkyok* [Social character of the Koreans] (Seoul: Kaemunsa, 1976), especially pp. 79–128.

38. Elsewhere, I have analyzed the technique of rural mobilization in South Korea in the 1970s. See Young Whan Kihl, "Politics and Agrarian Change in South Korea: Rural Modernization by 'Induced' Mobilization," in Raymond Hopkins, Donald Puchala, and Ross Talbot, eds., *Food, Politics, and Agricultural Development: Case Studies in the Public Policy of Rural Modernization* (Boulder, Co.: Westview Press, 1979), pp. 133–169.

39. Young Whan Kihl, Chong Lim Kim, and Seong-tong Pai, "Masses-Elite Linkage and Political Development in South Korea," in Graciela de la Lama, ed., *Japan and Korea 2* (Mexico City: El Colegio de Mexico, 1982), pp. 122–140.

40. W. Howard Wriggins, *The Ruler's Imperatives: Strategies for Political Survival in Asia and Africa* (New York: Columbia University Press, 1969).

41. On Korea's political participation studies, see various articles in Chong Lim Kim, ed., *The Political Participation in Korea: Democracy, Mobilization, and Stability* (Santa Barbara, Calif.: Clio Press, 1980), and also in the special issue, "Symposium: Political Participation in Korea," *Journal of Korean Studies* 1 (1979):73–223.

42. On South Korea's voting and election behavior, see C. I. Eugene Kim and Young Whan Kihl, *Party Politics and Elections*.

43. Chong Lim Kim, *Political Participation in Korea*, p. 127.

44. Ibid., p. 125.

45. Ibid., pp. 133, 137.

46. Young Whan Kihl, "Politics and Agrarian Change."

47. Chong Lim Kim, *Political Participation in Korea*, p. 212.

48. For a discussion of political participation and development, see Samuel P. Huntington and Joan M. Nelson, *No Easy Choice: Political Participation in Developing Countries* (Cambridge, Mass.: Harvard University Press, 1976).

49. Chong Lim Kim, *Political Participation in Korea*, p. 138.

50. Young Whan Kihl, Chong Lim Kim, and Seong-tong Pai, "Masses–Elite Linkage." By the same authors, see also "Sahoe pulsin p'ungjowa chongch'i munhwa" [Social distrust and political culture], *Sintong'a* 134 (October 1975):86–99.

51. Some of the results of this survey have been reported in various publications, including, for instance, Chong Lim Kim, *Political Participation in Korea*.

52. For an interesting account of North Korea based on a visit by a group of political scientists from the United States, see C. I. Eugene Kim and B. C. Koh, eds., *Journey to North Korea: Personal Perceptions* (Berkeley: University of California Institute of East Asian Studies, 1983).

53. Benjamin B. Weems, *Reform, Rebellion, and the Heavenly Way* (Tucson: University of Arizona Press for the Association for Asian Studies, 1964).

54. Frank Baldwin, "Participatory Anti-Imperialism: The 1919 Independence Movement," *Journal of Korean Studies* 1 (1979):123–162.

55. On the theme of Korean politics as a high-risk system and as a zero-sum game, see Young Whan Kihl, "Linkage and Democratic Orientation of Party Elites in South Korea," in Kay Lawson, ed., *Political Parties and Linkage: A Comparative Perspective* (New Haven, Conn.: Yale University Press, 1980), pp. 75–99.

56. On the concept of Korea's "truncated" political culture and history, I owe thanks to Chong Lim Kim for his initial suggestion. For a discussion of this theme as applied to Korean politics, see Chong Lim Kim, Young Whan Kihl, and Seong-tong Pai, "Han'guk chongch'i munhwae danch'eung" [Segmentation of Korea's political culture], *Wolgan Chungang*, March 1977, pp. 124–135.

Chapter 2

1. For a historical overview of Korean nationalism, see Chong-Sik Lee, *The Politics of Korean Nationalism* (Berkeley and Los Angeles: University of California Press, 1965). Also, on the early phase of Korea's nationalist efforts prior to 1910, see C. I. Eugene Kim and Han-Kyo Kim, *Korea and the Politics of*

Notes to Chapter 2

Imperialism: 1876–1911 (Berkeley and Los Angeles: University of California Press, 1967).

2. My formulation of the concept of political development in terms of attaining threefold tasks is indebted to Gabriel A. Almond and G. Bingham Powell, Jr., *Comparative Politics: System, Processes and Policy,* 2d ed. (Boston: Little, Brown & Co., 1978). In place of a threefold task, Almond and Powell identify five problem areas of political development, namely, state building, nation building, participation, economy building, and distribution (p. 22).

On the concept of political development in general, see Almond and Powell, ibid., especially pp. 19–23, 359–390. See also the seven-volume study on political development sponsored by the Committee on Comparative Politics of the Social Science Research Council in the 1960s and published subsequently by the Princeton University Press in the 1970s. This series includes: (1) *Communications and Political Development* (1963), ed. Lucian W. Pye, (2) *Bureaucracy and Political Development* (1963), ed. Joseph LaPalombara, (3) *Political Modernization in Japan and Turkey* (1964), ed. Robert E. Ward and Dankwart A. Rustow, (4) *Education and Political Development* (1965), ed. James S. Coleman, (5) *Political Culture and Political Development* (1965), ed. Lucian W. Pye and Sidney Verba, (6) *Political Parties and Political Development* (1966), ed. Joseph LaPalombara and Myron Weiner, and (7) *Crises in Political Development* (1971), ed. Leonard Binder, James S. Coleman, Joseph LaPalombara, Lucian W. Pye, Sidney Verba, and Myron Weiner. Two additional books found to be helpful are Samuel P. Huntington, *Political Order in Changing Societies* (New Haven, Conn.: Yale University Press, 1969); and Helio Jagribe, *Political Development: A General Theory and a Latin American Case Study* (New York: Harper & Row, 1973). Huntington argues, for instance, that political development "involves the creation of political institutions sufficiently adaptable, complex, autonomous, and coherent to absorb and to order the participation of these new groups and to promote social and economic change in the society" (p. 266).

3. For a discussion of the circumstances surrounding Korean partition, see Bruce G. Cumings, *The Origins of the Korean War: Liberation and the Emergence of Separate Regimes, 1945–1947* (Princeton, N.J.: Princeton University Press, 1981), pp. 101–131.

4. As quoted in In K. Hwang, *The Neutralized Unification of Korea* (Cambridge, Mass.: Schenkman Publishing Co., 1980), p. 1.

5. On the establishment of the demarcation line along the 38th parallel, see Shannon McCune, "The Thirty-Eighth Parallel in Korea," *World Politics* 1, 2 (January 1949):223–232; Arthur L. Grey, Jr., "The Thirty Eighth Parallel," *Foreign Affairs* 29, 3 (April 1951):482–487; Soon Sung Cho, *Korea in World Politics, 1945–1950: An Evaluation of American Responsibility* (Berkeley and Los Angeles: University of California Press, 1967), pp. 47–57; Leland M. Goodrich, *Korea, A Study of U.S. Policy in the United Nations* (New York: Council on Foreign Relations, 1956), pp. 11–12. See also U.S. Congress, House Committee on Foreign Affairs, *Hearing on H. Rept. 5330, Korea Aid,* 81st Cong., 1st Sess. (Washington, D.C.: Government Printing Office, 1959), pp. 118–119; Hak-Joon Kim, *The Unification Policy of South and North Korea: A Comparative Study* (Seoul: Seoul National University Press, 1977), pp. 27–36.

6. U.S. Department of State, Foreign Relations of the United States, Diplomatic Papers, *The Conferences at Cairo and Teheran, 1943* (Washington, D.C.: Government Printing Office, 1961), pp. 399–404; U.S. Department of State, *In Quest of Peace and Security: Selected Documents on American Foreign Policy, 1941–1951* (Washington, D.C.: Government Printing Office, 1951), p. 6.

7. U.S. Department of State, Foreign Relations of the United States, Diplomatic Papers, *The Conference of Berlin, 1945,* 2 vols. (Washington, D.C.: Government Printing Office, 1960), Vol. 1, pp. 925–926; Vol. 2, p. 351.
8. Harry S Truman, *Memoirs by Harry S Truman,* Vol. 2, *Years of Trial and Hope* (New York: Doubleday and Co., 1956), p. 317.
9. U.S. Department of the Army, *United States Army in the Korean War: South to Naktong, North to the Yalu,* Prepared by Roy E. Appleman, Office of the Chief of Military History (Washington, D.C.: Government Printing Office, 1961), pp. 2–4. Appleman's account is based on his interview with General Hull in 1952.
10. U.S. Department of the Army, *Korea 1950,* Prepared by Walter G. Hermes, Office of the Chief of Military History (Washington, D.C.: Government Printing Office, 1952), p. 4.
11. U.S. Department of State, *Foreign Relations of the United States,* Vol. 4, "The British Commonwealth and the Far East" (Washington, D.C.: Government Printing Office, 1969), p. 1039.
12. Ibid., pp. 1037–1040.
13. Truman, *Memoirs* 1:440.
14. Truman, *Memoirs* 2:317.
15. U.S. Department of the Army, *U.S. Army in the Korean War, Truce Tent and Fighting Front,* Prepared by Walter G. Hermes, Office of the Chief of Military History (Washington, D.C.: Government Printing Office, 1965), pp. 6–7. See also the statement of Secretary of State James F. Byrnes, U.S. Department of State, *Bulletin,* December 30, 1945, 1035.
16. This hypothesis is discussed by Hak-Joon Kim, *Unification Policy,* pp. 34–35.
17. Goodrich, *Korea,* pp. 13–14.
18. The Soviet occupation policy of North Korea has not been fully reported to the outside world. However, see Henry Chung, *The Russians Came to Korea* (Seoul and Washington, D.C.: Korean Pacific, 1947), and Nikita Khrushchev, *Khrushchev Remembers,* Introduction, commentary, and notes by Edward Crankshaw, trans. and ed. Strobe Talbott (Boston: Little, Brown & Co., 1970), for some interesting remarks on the Soviet role in the Korean War.
19. Although the United States consulted the Chungking KPG leaders, it decided that they were totally unrepresentative of Koreans, a position later changed in October 1945 by the U.S. occupation forces in South Korea.
20. The Korean reaction to these and other situations will be examined in the next section of this chapter.
21. On Korea under Japanese colonial rule, see Andrew J. Grajdanzev, *Modern Korea: Her Economic and Social Development Under the Japanese* (New York: Institute of Pacific Relations, 1944).
22. On Korea on the eve of the U.S. arrival in Inchon, September 1945, see Gregory Henderson, *Korea: The Politics of the Vortex* (Cambridge, Mass.: Harvard University Press, 1968), pp. 113–148; Cumings, *Origins of the Korean War,* pp. 137–151. See also George M. McCune, *Korea Today* (Cambridge, Mass.: Harvard University Press, 1950), pp. 38–60.
23. Professor Cumings estimates the total of repatriated Koreans to South Korea between October 1945 and December 1947, from places like Japan, China, Manchuria, and North Korea, to be 2,380,821 (approximately 15 percent of South Korea's total population at that time). Cumings, *Origins of the Korean War,* p. 60.

24. On the activities of the People's Committee at the national level and in the provinces throughout South Korea in 1945–1946, see ibid., pp. 68–100, 167–381.

25. Chong-Sik Lee, *Politics of Korean Nationalism*, pp. 237–273; Dae-Sook Suh, *The Korean Communist Movement: 1918–1948* (Princeton, N.J.: Princeton University Press, 1970) especially pp. 294–329.

26. On the volatility of political party movement in South Korea at this time, see Ki-ha Yi, *Han'guk chongdang paltalsa* [History of the development of political parties in Korea] (Seoul: Uihoe Chongch'isa, 1961).

27. For political maneuvers and movements in North Korea in 1946, see Robert A. Scalapino and Chong-Sik Lee, *Communism in Korea*, Vol. 1 (Berkeley and Los Angeles: University of California Press, 1972), pp. 376–380.

28. R. A. Scalapino and Chong-Sik Lee, *Communism in Korea* 1:313–382. See also Ch'ang-sun Kim, *Pukhan sip-o-nyonsa* [Fifteen-year history of North Korea] (Seoul: Chimungak, 1961).

29. On a fascinating story of this era of Kim Il Sung in the Soviet Union, 1940–1945, see Un Yim [pseudo.], *Kita Chosen oocho seiritisu hishi: Kinnichisei seiten* [Secret history of the founding of North Korean dynasty: Kim Il Sung's true accounts] (Tokyo: Jiyusha, 1982). This is an eyewitness account by a former close associate of Kim Il Sung who subsequently took political refuge in the Soviet Union. Although the authenticity of this book remains to be established, the content is rich and new in many instances. Since the book was written by a Korean communist who now resides in the Soviet Union, many hitherto-untold inside accounts are revealed to the outside world. For an English translation, see Un Lim, *The Founding of a Dynasty in North Korea: An Authentic Biography of Kim Il Sung* (Tokyo: Jiyusha, 1982).

30. Ibid., p. 111.

31. On the activities of Korean communists in China, from whom the Yenan faction was recruited, see R. A. Scalapino and Chong-Sik Lee, *Communism in Korea* 1:170–180.

32. Ibid., pp. 350–363.

33. Henderson, *Korea*, pp. 123–125. For criticism of U.S. Korea policy in 1945–1946 by U.S. advisors serving in Korea at the time, see John C. Aldwell and L. Frost, *The Korea Story* (Chicago: Henry Regnery Co., 1952); and Richard D. Robinson, "Korea: The Betrayal of a Nation" (Typescript, 1947).

34. Cumings, *Origins of the Korean War*, p. xxiv.

35. Ibid., p. 154.

36. Ibid., p. 169.

37. Ibid., p. 173.

38. Ibid., pp. 174–175.

39. For an account of the activities of the U.S.-Soviet Joint Commission on Korea, see Soon Sung Cho, *Korea in World Politics*, pp. 114–136.

40. Ibid., pp. 161–183.

41. Joseph Sang-hoon Chung, *The North Korean Economy: Structure and Development* (Stanford, Calif.: Hoover Institution Press, 1974), pp. 5–6.

42. Ibid., p. 59.

43. For an interesting study of the Oriental Development Company, see Karl Moskowitz, "The Creation of the Oriental Development Company: Japanese Illusions Meet Korean Reality," *Occasional Papers on Korea: Number Two*, ed. James B. Palais for the Joint Committee on Korean Studies of the American

Council of Learned Societies and the Social Science Research Council, March 1974, pp. 73–121.

44. Nena Vreeland et al., *Area Handbook for South Korea* (Washington, D.C.: Government Printing Office, 1975), p. 255.

45. Ibid., p. 256.

46. On the controversy over the character of the Korean War as it started in 1950, see I. F. Stone, *The Hidden History of the Korean War* (New York: Monthly Review Press, 1952); Harold Joyce Noble, *Embassy at War* (Seattle: University of Washington Press, 1975); John Goulden, *Korea: The Untold Story of the War* (New York: Times Books, 1982); Glenn D. Paige, *The Korean Decision: June 24–30, 1950* (New York: Free Press, 1968).

47. On the question of who fired the first shot, see Noble, *Embassy at War*, pp. 219–237. For a more sympathetic view on North Korea's attack, see Jon Halliday, "The Korean War: Some Notes on Evidence and Solidarity," *Bulletin of Concerned Asian Scholars* 11, 3 (July-September 1979):2–18.

48. Press Release by the DPRK Permanent Observer Mission to the United Nations, June 22, 1981, p. 1.

49. Pyongyang Radio, June 25, 1950, at 11:00 A.M., as cited in Noble, *Embassy at War*, p. 313.

50. Frank Baldwin in Noble, *Embassy at War*, p. 315.

51. This and other materials are to be found in U.S. General Headquarters, Far East Command, *Research Supplement: Documentary Evidence of North Korean Aggression* (October 30, 1950, folder, MacArthur Memorial), as cited in Noble, *Embassy at War*, p. 315.

52. The prevailing view is that North Korea made a Sunday predawn attack on South Korea. North Korea, however, claims that South Korea attacked first and it merely responded in self-defense. DPRK, *Facts Tell* (Pyongyang: Foreign Languages Publishing House, 1960). Also, for a more sympathetic view on North Korea's claim, see Jon Halliday, "The Korean War: Some Notes on Evidence and Solidarity," *Bulletin of Concerned Asian Scholars* 11, 3 (July-September 1979):2–18.

53. On the internationalization of the civil war, see Harry Eckstein, ed., *Internal War: Problems and Approaches* (Glencoe, Ill.: Free Press, 1964).

54. On North Korea's factional politics, see Koon Woo Nam, *The North Korean Communist Leadership, 1945–1965: A Study of Factionalism and Political Consolidation* (University, Ala.: University of Alabama Press, 1974), pp. 101–120. See also Dae-Sook Suh, "Communist Party Leadership," in Dae-Sook Suh and Chae-Jin Lee, eds., *Political Leadership in Korea* (Seattle: University of Washington Press, 1976), pp. 159–191.

55. On December 18, 1955, the party newspaper, *Nodong Sinmun*, carried an item titled: "Special Trial of the Supreme Court of the Republic Concerning the Ringleader of American Imperialist Spies and Traitor of the Fatherland Pak Hon-yong." Earlier, on February 15, 1953, the *Nodong Sinmun* carried an attack on Pak Hon-yong entitled "There Is No Room in Our Party Ranks for Those Who Are Not Candid."

56. Kim Il Sung, "On Eliminating Dogmatism and Formalism and Establishing Juche in Ideological Work" (Speech to party propagandists and agitators, December 28, 1955), as reported in Kim Il Sung, *On the Building of the Workers' Party of Korea*, 2 (Pyongyang: Foreign Languages Publishing House, 1978), pp. 71–98.

57. Ibid., p. 80.

58. Ibid.
59. Ibid., p. 81.
60. For further discussion of factionalism and purges within the KWP, see R. A. Scalapino and Chong-Sik Lee, *Communism in Korea* 2:688–690, passim.
61. See R. A. Scalapino and Chong-Sik Lee, *Communism in Korea* 1:514–515.
62. On North Korea's communist politics in the post–Korean War era, see R. A. Scalapino and Chong-Sik Lee, *Communism in Korea* 1:463–558. Also, on policy disputes regarding the developmental strategy, see Ilpyong J. Kim, *Communist Politics in North Korea* (New York: Praeger Publishers, 1975).
63. Byong-sik Kim, *Modern Korea: The Socialist North, Revolutionary Perspectives in the South* (New York: International Publishers, 1970), p. 41.
64. R. A. Scalapino and Chong-Sik Lee, *Communism in Korea* 2:528.
65. See Joseph Sang-hoon Chung, *North Korean Economy*, pp. 12–13.
66. Byong-sik Kim, *Modern Korea*, p. 51.
67. Ibid., p. 56.
68. Ibid., pp. 60–65.
69. For the text of the 1970 KWP bylaws, see Dae-Sook Suh, *Korean Communism 1945–1980: A Reference Guide to the Political System* (Honolulu: University Press of Hawaii, 1981), pp. 525–544.
70. R. A. Scalapino and Chong-Sik Lee, *Communism in Korea* 2:1273.
71. North Korea's defense treaties with the Soviet Union and China are discussed in R. A. Scalapino and Chong-Sik Lee, *Communism in Korea* 1:584–585.
72. For further analysis of South Korea's political development in the 1954–1971 period, see the following: John Kie-Chiang Oh, *Democracy on Trial* (Ithaca, N.Y.: Cornell University Press, 1968); David C. Cole and Princeton N. Lyman, *Korean Development: The Interplay of Politics and Economics* (Cambridge, Mass.: Harvard University Press, 1971); Sung-Joo Han, *The Failure of Democracy in South Korea* (Berkeley and Los Angeles: University of California Press, 1974); Kwan-Bong Kim, *The Korea-Japan Treaty Crisis and the Instability of the Korean Political System* (New York: Praeger Publishers, 1964); C. I. Eugene Kim, ed., *A Pattern of Political Development: Korea* (Kalamazoo, Mich.: Korea Research Publications, 1964); Se-Jin Kim and Chang-Hyun Cho, eds., *Government and Politics of Korea* (Silver Spring, Md.: Research Institute on Korean Affairs, 1972); Hahn-been Lee, *Korea: Time, Change and Administration* (Honolulu: East-West Center Press, 1968); W. D. Reeve, *The Republic of Korea: A Political and Economic Study* (London: Oxford University Press, 1963). For a discussion of the Chang Myon government's interest in developing a five-year plan, see Hahn-been Lee, *Korea*, p. 130.
73. For a more sympathetic account of President Rhee, see Robert Oliver, *Syngman Rhee and American Involvement in Korea, 1942–1960: A Personal Narrative* (Seoul: Panmun Book Co., 1978).
74. On South Korea's inept politics in the 1950s, see John Kie-Chiang Oh, *Democracy on Trial;* Hahn-been Lee, *Korea;* and Reeve, *Republic of Korea*.
75. On the era of the 1960 Student Revolution in South Korea, see John Kie-Chiang Oh, *Democracy on Trial;* Sung-Joo Han, *The Failure of Democracy*.
76. Sung-Joo Han, *The Failure of Democracy*. See also Cole and Lyman, *Korean Development*.
77. See Se-Jin Kim, *The Politics of the Military Revolution in Korea* (Chapel Hill: University of North Carolina Press, 1971). A fascinating story about the

conspiracy for the 1961 coup is told by former KCIA chief Kim Hyong-wuk, who took part in the planning and execution of the coup. His memoirs, initially published in Japan, are available in Korean, although the question of their authenticity has not been settled. Kim Hyong-wuk, who testified before the U.S. House Subcommittee on the Investigation of Korean-American Relations in 1977–1978, subsequently disappeared from a Paris hotel in September 1979, and is now believed to have been kidnapped to South Korea and ordered to be executed by Park Chung Hee before the latter's assassination in 1979 by then–KCIA chief Kim Jae-kyu. For the Korean version of Kim's testimony, see Hyong-wuk Kim, *Kwonryokkwa ummo: Chon-KCIAbujang Kim Hyong-wukui suki* [Power and conspiracy: Ex–KCIA chief Kim Hyong-wuk's account] (Toronto: New Korea Times Co., 1982). On Kim's supposed kidnapping, see especially pp. 311–319.

78. See Kwan-Bong Kim, *Korea-Japan Treaty Crisis*, pp. 180–216.

79. On South Korea's 1963 and 1967 presidential elections, see C. I. Eugene Kim, "Significance of the 1963 Korean Elections," *Asian Survey* 4, 3 (March 1964): 765–773; C. I. Eugene Kim, "Patterns in the 1967 Korean Elections," *Pacific Affairs* 41, 1 (Spring 1968):60–70.

80. Kwan-Bong Kim, *Korea-Japan Treaty Crisis*.

81. On South Korea's involvement in the Vietnam War, see Frank Baldwin, ed., *Without Parallel: The American-Korean Relations Since 1945* (New York: Pantheon Books, 1974):27–30.

82. Which side actually initiated the proposal for conducting the inter-Korean dialogue in 1970 is disputed, however, as both sides claim to have been the first to come forward with the proposal for the talks on Korean unification in 1971.

83. Huntington, *Political Order*, p. 266.

Chapter 3

1. On Korea's response to détente, see Young Whan Kihl, "Korean Response to Major Power Rapprochement," in Young C. Kim, ed., *Major Powers and Korea* (Silver Spring, Md.: Research Institute on Korean Affairs, 1973), pp. 139–164. Also, on North Korea's response in particular, see B. C. Koh, "The Korean Workers' Party and Detente," *Journal of International Affairs* 28, 2 (1974):175–187.

2. In fact, Henry Kissinger states in his memoirs that Kim Il Sung was in Beijing when he was there on July 10, 1971, indicating that North Korea/China consultation was very direct. Henry Kissinger, *White House Years* (Boston: Little, Brown & Co., 1979), pp. 728, 751. Kissinger's account of Kim's China trip has not been confirmed by either Beijing or Pyongyang.

3. *Pyongyang Times*, August 24, 1971, p. 2.

4. The text of the North-South joint communiqué of July 4, 1972, appears in ROK, *A White Paper on South-North Dialogue in Korea* (Seoul: South-North Coordinating Committee, Seoul Side, 1979), pp. 90–92. See also Young Whan Kihl, "Korean Response," pp. 150–157.

5. For an anlysis of the first and second five-year plans (1962–1966 and 1967–1971), see Paul W. Kuznets, *Economic Growth and Structure in the Republic of Korea* (New Haven, Conn.: Yale University Press, 1977), pp. 196–209.

6. On economic change in South Korea, see Parvez Hasan, *Korea: Problems and Issues in a Rapidly Growing Economy* (Baltimore: Johns Hopkins University Press for the World Bank, 1976); Parvez Hasan and D. C. Rao, *Korea: Policy*

Issues for Long-Term Development (Baltimore: Johns Hopkins University Press for the World Bank, 1979).

7. This and other issues are discussed in Young Whan Kihl and Dong-Suh Bark, "Food Policies in a Rapidly Developing Country: The Case of South Korea," *Journal of Developing Areas* 16, 1 (October 1981):47–80; and Dong-Suh Bark and Young Whan Kihl, "Shiknyang chongch'ek suripkwa lheng: Hangukui kyongu" [Food policy making and implementation: The Korean case], *Korean Journal of Public Administration* 17, 2 (1979):214–234. Also, on the Saemaul movement in South Korea, see Young Whan Kihl, "Politics and Agrarian Change in South Korea: Rural Modernization by 'Induced' Mobilization," in Raymond Hopkins, Donald Puchala, and Ross Talbot, eds., *Food, Politics, and Agricultural Development: Case Studies in the Public Policy of Rural Modernization* (Boulder, Co.: Westview Press, 1979), pp. 133–169.

8. On the 1971 election results, see C. I. Eugene Kim, "The Meanings of 1971 Korean Elections: A Pattern of Political Development," *Asian Survey* 12, 3 (March 1972):213–224.

9. B. C. Koh, "Convergence and Conflict in the Two Koreas," *Current History*, November 1973, pp. 205–208.

10. *New York Times*, October 20, 1972.

11. On the Nixon Doctrine, as regards the Korean Peninsula, see Young Whan Kihl, "The Nixon Doctrine and South-North Korea Relations," *Korean Journal of International Studies* 4, 3 and 4 (October 1973):105–123.

12. On Park's defense of the Yushin reforms, see Park Chung Hee, *Korea Reborn: A Model for Development* (Englewood Cliffs, N.J.: Prentice-Hall, 1979), pp. 37–66. See also Michael Keon, *Korean Phoenix: A Nation from the Ashes* (Englewood Cliffs, N.J.: Prentice-Hall, 1977).

13. For the text of the 1972 constitution, see Se-Jin Kim and Chang-Hyun Cho, eds., *Korea: A Divided Nation* (Silver Spring, Md.: Research Institute on Korean Affairs, 1976), pp. 287–307.

14. Ibid., Article 53 of the Yushin Constitution.

15. *Korea Annual 1975* (Seoul: Hapdong News Agency, 1975), pp. 329–331.

16. Ibid.

17. On Kim Chi-ha, see Sugwon Kang, "The Politics and Poetry of Kim Chi-ha," *Bulletin of Concerned Asian Scholars* 9, 2 (April-June 1977):3–7.

18. Kim Chi-ha, *Cry of the People and Other Poems* (Kanagawa-ken, Japan: Autumn Press, 1974), p. 90.

19. For the text, see *Korea Annual 1976* (Seoul: Hapdong News Agency, 1976), pp. 328–330.

20. Dae-Sook Suh, "Communist Party Leadership," in Dae-Sook Suh and Chae-Jin Lee, eds., *Political Leadership in Korea* (Seattle: University of Washington Press, 1976), p. 164.

21. Dae-Sook Suh, *Korean Communism 1945–1980: A Reference Guide to the Political System* (Honolulu: University Press of Hawaii, 1981), pp. 174–175.

22. Robert S. Simmons, *The Strained Alliance: Peking, P'yongyang, Moscow and the Politics of the Korean Civil War* (New York: Free Press, 1975), p. 108.

23. Pyongyang Radio, November 3, 1970.

24. See ROK, *White Paper on South-North Dialogue*.

25. B. C. Koh, "Korean Workers' Party," p. 186.

26. Ibid., p. 178. See note 3 for the source for the August 16 speech.

27. The text of Kim's speech of April 18, 1975, appears in Kim Il Sung, *For the Independent Peaceful Reunification of Korea*, rev. ed. (New York: Weekly Guardian Associates, 1976), pp. 175–183.
28. See Young Whan Kihl, "Korea's Future: Seoul's Perspective," *Asian Survey* 17, 11 (November 1977):1064–1076.
29. For North Korea's stand on South Korea's 1953 truce agreement, see DPRK, *Facts Tell* (Pyongyang: Foreign Languages Publishing House, 1960).
30. An excerpt of the text of Kim's report to the Fifth KWP Congress appears in Kim Il Sung, *Independent Peaceful Reunification*, pp. 69–82.
31. On the question of North Korea's payment difficulty and debts, see Adrian Foster-Carter, "North Korea: Development and Self-Reliance: A Critical Appraisal," *Bulletin of Concerned Asian Scholars* 9, 1 (January-March 1977):55–57.
32. On Kim's indirect reply to Park's proposal on the simultaneous entry into the United Nations, June 23, 1973, see Kim Il Sung, *Independent Peaceful Reunification*, pp. 145–152.
33. DPRK, *On the Socialist Constitution of the Democratic Peoples' Republic of Korea* (Pyongyang: Foreign Languages Publishing House, 1975).
34. See Bong Baik, *Kim Il Sung: Biography*, 3 vols. (Tokyo: Miraisha, 1969–1970). See also Sung Chul Yang, *Korea and Two Regimes: Kim Il Sung and Park Chung Hee* (Cambridge, Mass.: Schenkman Publishing Co., 1981).
35. Chong-Sik Lee, *Korean Workers' Party: A Short History* (Stanford, Calif.: Hoover Institution Press, 1978), p. 133.
36. Ibid.
37. Ibid.
38. On the cult of personality of Kim Il Sung, see B. C. Koh, "The Cult of Personality and the Succession Issue," in C. I. Eugene Kim and B. C. Koh, eds., *Journey to North Korea: Personal Perceptions* (Berkeley: University of California Institute of East Asian Studies, 1983), pp. 25–41.
39. On democratic requirements as applied to South Korea, see Young Whan Kihl, "Linkage and Democratic Orientation of Party Elites in South Korea," in Kay Lawson, ed., *Political Parties and Linkage: A Comparative Perspective* (New Haven, Conn.: Yale University Press, 1980).

Chapter 4

1. This claim is made by both international agencies and the South Korean authorities. See for instance, Organization for Economic Cooperation and Development, *The Impact of the Newly Industrializing Countries on Production and Trade in Manufactures*, Report by the Secretary-General (Paris: OECD, 1979); John A. Mathieson, *The ADCs: Emerging Actors in the World Economy* (Washington, D.C.: Overseas Development Council, 1979).
2. For the latest estimate of South Korea's GNP, see: *Asia Yearbook 1982* (Hong Kong: Far Eastern Economic Review, 1982). See also World Bank, *World Bank Atlas* (Washington, D.C.: World Bank, 1981). This claim, however, must be tempered by the fact that in 1980 South Korea registered a negative growth of -5.6 percent of the economy.
3. For numerous studies on the Korean economy, see Paul W. Kuznets, *Economic Growth and Structure in the Republic of Korea* (New Haven, Conn.: Yale University Press, 1977); Parvez Hasan, *Korea: Problems and Issues in a Rapidly Growing Economy* (Baltimore: Johns Hopkins University Press for the

World Bank, 1976); Parvez Hasan and D. C. Rao, *Korea: Policy Issues for Long-Term Development* (Baltimore: Johns Hopkins University Press for the World Bank, 1979).

4. Chong-Sik Lee, "South Korea in 1980: The Emergence of a New Authoritarian Order," *Asian Survey* 31, 1 (January 1981):125–143.

5. This has also been the case with some Latin American countries, including Brazil, Chile, and Argentina. For Latin American cases, see Guillermo A. O'Donnell, *Modernization and Bureaucratic-Authoritarianism: Studies in South American Politics* (Berkeley: University of California Institute of International Studies, 1973 and 1979); and David Collier, ed., *The New Authoritarianism in Latin America* (Princeton, N.J.: Princeton University Press, 1979).

For typical examples of the liberal assumption of modernization-democracy links, see Seymour Martin Lipset, "Some Social Requisites of Democracy: Economic Development and Political Legitimacy," *American Political Science Review* 53 (March 1959):69–105; James S. Coleman, "Conclusion: The Political Systems of the Developing Areas," in Gabriel A. Almond and James S. Coleman, eds., *The Politics of the Developing Areas* (Princeton, N.J.: Princeton University Press, 1960), pp. 532–576; and Phillips Cutright, "National Political Development: Measurement and Analysis," *American Sociological Review* 27 (April 1963):253–264.

6. On the man Kim Jae-kyu and his motive as Park's assassin, see a fascinating study written in Korean: Chong-Sik Lee, *Ingan Kim Jae-kyu* [The life of Kim Jae-kyu] (Paoli, Pa., 1980). See also Chong-Sik Lee, "South Korea 1979: Confrontation, Assassination, and Transition," *Asian Survey* 20, 1 (January 1980):63–76.

7. The Yushin reforms, as already noted in the preceding chapter, were proclaimed by President Park Chung Hee in October 1972 in the form of a constitutional amendment giving him unlimited powers, including the right to declare a state of national emergency. For further background information on Park's Yushin system, see U.S. Congress, House Subcommittee on International Organizations of the Committee on International Relations, *Report on Investigation of Korean-American Relations,* 95th Cong., 2d Sess. (Washington, D.C.: Government Printing Office, 1978).

8. For a discussion of this and subsequent political developments in South Korea following Park's assassination, see Chong-Sik Lee, "South Korea 1980."

9. On the long-standing enmity between Kim Jong-pil and Lee Hu-rak, which dated back to 1962–1963, see Kwan-Bong Kim, *The Korea-Japan Treaty Crisis and the Instability of the Korean Political System* (New York: Praeger Publishers, 1964).

10. On Korean politics at the time of the Student Revolution and the military coup in 1960 and 1961, see Sung-Joo Han, *The Failure of Democracy in South Korea* (Berkeley and Los Angeles: University of California Press, 1974); John Kie-Chiang Oh, *Korea: Democracy on Trial* (Ithaca, N.Y.: Cornell University Press, 1968); and Se-Jin Kim, *The Politics of Military Revolution in Korea* (Chapel Hill: University of North Carolina Press, 1971).

11. Lee Hu-rak served as President Park Chung Hee's secretary-general in the Blue House and later became director of the Korean Central Intelligence Agency. Park Chong-kyu was chief of the Presidential Security Force.

12. Kim Dae-jung, a dissident politician, was the New Democratic Party presidential candidate in the 1969 election. Subsequently, Kim went into self-imposed exile, but was kidnapped from a Tokyo hotel on August 8, 1973, by

a KCIA agent and brought back to South Korea a few days later to stand trial for the alleged crime of violating the presidential election law. In December 1982, Kim Dae-jung was released from prison and allowed to travel to the United States with his family for medical reasons.

13. General Chung Ho-yung's Special Forces were flown into Kwangju in May 1980 to recover the city from the rioters. In 1982 General Chung was promoted and reassigned as commander of the Third Field Army. In 1984 Chung was made Army Chief of Staff.

14. *Korea Herald,* September 2, 1980.

15. O'Donnell, *Modernization.* See also Collier, *The New Authoritarianism,* especially pp. 23–25, 364–365.

16. The constitution of the Fifth Republic is generally considered to be more democratic than, for instance, the Yushin constitution, which it replaced. The bylaws and the circumstances of adopting the constitution, however, left much to be desired from the standpoint of democratic procedure.

17. This definition of state, similar to Marxian or neo-Marxian positions, is widely adopted by students of Latin American politics of authoritarianism. See, for instance, Collier, *The New Authoritarianism,* p. 403.

18. The inclusion or exclusion of previously active popular sectors, such as the working class, is an important criterion differentiating the types of political regime, according to O'Donnell. See, for instance, Guillermo O'Donnell, "Tensions in the Bureaucratic-Authoritarian State and the Question of Democracy," in ibid., pp. 285–318.

19. For the distinction between autocracy and authoritarianism, see Amos Perlmutter, *Modern Authoritarianism: A Comparative Institutional Analysis* (New Haven, Conn.: Yale University Press, 1981), pp. 1–7.

20. On this analysis of military factionalism, see *Dokrip Sinmun* [Korean Independent Monitor] (Philadelphia), February 5, 1982. General Ro Tae-wu and General Kim Bok-dong were classmates and also became brothers-in-law.

21. Ibid.

22. *Dokrip Sinmun,* December 24, 1982.

23. *Korea Herald,* January 15, 1982, Supplement, p. 2.

24. Ibid.

25. *Hanguk Ilbo,* January 19, 1982, p. 4.

26. *Korea Herald,* January 15, 1982.

27. On bureaucratic authoritarianism in Latin America, see O'Donnell, *Modernization;* Collier, *The New Authoritarianism;* and Guillermo O'Donnell, "Reflections on the Patterns of Change in the Bureaucratic Authoritarian State," *Latin American Research Review* 8, 1 (1978):3–27.

28. On the political parties and party system of Korea, see various chapters in C. I. Eugene Kim and Young Whan Kihl, *Party Politics and Elections in Korea* (Silver Spring, Md.: Research Institute on Korean Affairs, 1976). See also Young Whan Kihl, "Linkage and Democratic Orientation of Party Elites in South Korea," in Kay Lawson, ed., *Political Parties and Linkage: A Comparative Perspective* (New Haven, Conn.: Yale University Press, 1980), pp. 75–99.

29. *Dong-A Ilbo,* October 17, 1981, p. 2, "Tidbits" column, as reported in Joint Publications Research Service (JPRS) 79351, November 3, 1981 (Korean Affairs Report No. 170), p. 4. Pyongyang's uncompromising stance was dropped on January 10, 1984, however, as it proposed to conduct a tripartite talk on Korean unification that includes North Korea, the U.S., and South Korea.

30. The five minor parties in the National Assembly include: Min-Kwon Dang [Democratic Right Party], Shin-Jung Dang [New Politics Party], and Min-Sa Dang [Democratic Socialist Party], which control two seats respectively; and Kunro-Nongmin Dang [Working Farmers Party] and Chayu-Minjok Dang [Free Nationalist Party], which each control a single seat. For the details of these statistics, see *Hanguk Ilbo,* January 19, 1982.

31. On the reporting of campus disturbances, see *Chungang Ilbo,* November 3, 1981, and *Hanguk Ilbo,* November 3, 1981, as reported in JPRS 79520, November 24, 1981 (Korean Affairs Report No. 175), pp. 19–21.

32. On labor legislation, see Nakagawa Nobuo, "Problems Confronting the Struggle for Democratization in Korea," *Gekkan Shakaito* (Tokyo), August 1981, pp. 173–181, as reported in JPRS 79290, October 23, 1981 (Korean Affairs Report No. 167), pp. 22–31.

33. Ibid.

34. In accordance with this new law, the famous Ch'onggye Clothing Workers Labor Union, which represented some 2,000 clothing workers, was ordered by the mayor of Seoul to disband as of January 22, 1981. This union, in existence since November 1970, represented workers employed by small business enterprises in the P'yonghwa market in Seoul and was famous for the incident of Chon T'ae-il, who burned himself to death in an appeal for the guarantee of the workers' legitimate rights. Ibid.

35. *Far Eastern Economic Review,* November 27, 1981, p. 30.

36. Ibid.

37. On mass line as a technique of Kim's leadership, see Ilpyong J. Kim, *Communist Politics in North Korea* (New York: Praeger Publishers, 1975), pp. 49–55.

38. Dong-bok Lee, "Hereditary Succession in North Korea and Its Impact on Inter-Korean Relations" (Prepared for presentation at the Second International Symposium on Korea at La Trobe University, Melbourne, Australia, November 20–22, 1980).

39. Chong-Sik Lee, *Korean Workers' Party: A Short History* (Stanford, Calif.: Hoover Institution Press, 1978), pp. 133–134.

40. Ibid., p. 133.

41. Chong-Sik Lee, "Evolution of the Korean Workers' Party and the Rise of Kim Chong-il," *Asian Survey* 22, 5 (May 1982):434–448.

42. Morgan Clippinger, "Kim Chong-il in the North Korean Mass Media: A Study of Semi-Esoteric Communication," *Asian Survey* 21, 3 (March 1981):289–309.

43. Foreign Broadcast Information Service (FBIS), *Daily Report,* Asia and the Pacific, October 14, 1980, as cited in Young C. Kim, "North Korea in 1980: The Son Also Rises," *Asian Survey* 21, 1 (January 1981):112–113.

44. Ibid. Also, a philosophy professor at Kim Il Sung University gave an explanation identical to the party line to a visiting team of academicians from the United States in July 1981 at a seminar session in Pyongyang. On the latter, see C. I. Eugene Kim and B. C. Koh, eds., *Journey to North Korea: Personal Perceptions* (Berkeley: University of California Institute of East Asian Studies, 1983), p. 36.

45. C. I. Eugene Kim and B. C. Koh, eds., *Journey to North Korea: Personal Perceptions* (Berkeley: University of California Institute of East Asian Studies, 1983), p. 37.

46. Clippinger, "Kim Chong-il in the North Korean Mass Media," pp. 290–291.
47. Ibid., p. 291. For illustrative examples, see B. C. Koh, "The Cult of Personality and the Succession Issue," in C. I. Eugene Kim and B. C. Koh, eds., *Journey to North Korea,* pp. 25–41.
48. Clippinger, "Kim Chong-il in the North Korean Mass Media," p. 290.
49. Ibid., p. 291.
50. B. C. Koh, "The Cult of Personality and the Succession Issue," in C. I. Eugene Kim and B. C. Koh, eds., *Journey to North Korea,* p. 37.
51. Young C. Kim, "North Korea in 1980," p. 113.
52. Chong-Sik Lee, "Evolution of the Korean Workers' Party," p. 434.
53. Koon Woo Nam, *The North Korean Communist Leadership, 1945-1965: A Study of Factionalism and Political Consolidation* (University, Ala.: University of Alabama Press, 1974).
54. September 18 and 19, 1980, issues of the *People's Daily,* as reprinted in *Koria Hyoron* 238 (January 1982):52–55.
55. For a description of this musical play at Mansudae Art Theatre, see C. I. Eugene Kim and B. C. Koh, *Journey to North Korea,* p. 14.
56. For some of the visitors' impressions of North Korea, see ibid.
57. For instance, see Fred J. Carrier, *North Korean Journey: The Revolution Against Colonialism* (New York: International Publishers, 1975); Henry Scott Stokes, "Competition Between the Two Koreas Pays Off in Great Prosperity for Both," *New York Times,* August 11, 1980, p. A10.
58. See also Harrison Salisbury, *To Peking and Beyond: A Report on the New Asia* (New York: Quadrangle, 1973), pp. 16 and 17.
59. Chae-Jin Lee, "Economic Aspects of Life in North Korea," in C. I. Eugene Kim and B. C. Koh, *Journey to North Korea,* p. 48.
60. Ibid., p. 44.
61. Ibid.
62. Ibid.
63. Ibid., pp. 45–46.
64. Ibid., p. 46.
65. The myth of paradise is shattered by the North Koreans who defected to South Korea in 1983. For accounts of North Korea by two defectors—an air force captain and an army captain, see *Korea Herald,* March 5, and May 18, 1983. A third North Korean—a lumberjack—defected to the south in 1983 by crossing the DmZ.
66. Carl J. Friedrich and Z. K. Brzezinski, *Totalitarian Dictatorship and Autocracy* (Cambridge, Mass.: Harvard University Press, 1965).
67. Robert A. Scalapino and Chong-Sik Lee, *Communism in Korea,* Vol. 2 (Berkeley and Los Angeles: University of California Press, 1972), pp. 752–756.
68. Guillermo O'Donnell, "Reflections on Patterns of Change," p. 6.
69. Warren F. Ilchman and Norman T. Uphoff, *The Political Economy of Change* (Berkeley: University of California Press, 1969). On the theme of Korea's "vortex" politics, see Gregory Henderson, *Korea: The Politics of the Vortex* (Cambridge, Mass.: Harvard University Press, 1968).

Chapter 5

1. On the concept of high-risk politics, see Lester G. Seligman, "Political Parties and the Recruitment of Political Leadership," in Lewis J. Edinger, ed.,

Political Leadership in Industrialized Societies (New York: John Wiley, 1967), pp. 302–304. See also Chong Lim Kim and Seong-tong Pai, *Legislative Process in Korea* (Seoul: Seoul National University Press, 1981), pp. 127–128.

2. For instance, see Edward W. Wagner, *The Literati Purges: Political Conflict in Early Yi Korea* (Cambridge, Mass.: East Asian Research Center, distributed by Harvard University Press, 1974).

3. On Kim Il Sung's independent foreign policy line between Russia and China, see Chin O. Chung, *P'yongyang Between Peking and Moscow: North Korea's Involvement in the Sino-Soviet Dispute, 1958–1975* (University, Ala.: University of Alabama Press, 1978). On Chuch'e (Juche) or Chuch'esong in Korean politics, see B. C. Koh, "Chuch'esong in Korean Politics," *Studies in Comparative Communism* 7, 1 and 2 (Spring and Summer 1974):83–97.

4. Herman Kahn is a typical U.S. scholar who takes such a view. See, for instance, Herman Kahn, *World Economic Development: 1979 and Beyond* (Boulder, Co.: Westview Press, 1979), pp. 121, 329. See also Roy Hofheinz, Jr., and Kent E. Calden, *Eastasia Edge* (New York: Basic Books, 1982).

5. For a critical perspective on Kimilsungism, see Gavan McCormack, "North Korea: Kimilsungism: Path to Socialism?" *Bulletin of Concerned Asian Scholars* 13, 4 (October-December 1981):50–61.

6. Wagner, *The Literati Purges*. See also James B. Palais, *Politics and Policy in Traditional Korea* (Cambridge, Mass.: Harvard University Press, 1975), pp. 15–16, 46–50.

7. Gregory Henderson, *Korea: The Politics of the Vortex* (Cambridge, Mass.: Harvard University Press, 1968), especially Chapter 4, "Colonial Totalitarianism," pp. 72–112.

8. Ibid., p. 193.

9. On the political theory of mass society, see William Kornhauser, *The Politics of Mass Society* (Glencoe, Ill.: Free Press, 1959).

10. For a criticism of Henderson's mass society politics thesis, see Bruce G. Cumings, "Is Korea a Mass Society?" *Occasional Papers on Korea: Number One*, ed. James B. Palais for the Joint Committee on Korean Studies of the American Council of Learned Societies and the Social Science Research Council, April 1974, pp. 65–81.

11. Ibid., pp. 65–66.

12. Ibid., p. 77.

13. On the study of *yuji* in South Korea, see Young Whan Kihl, "Political Roles and Participation of Community Notables: A Study of Yuji in Korea," in Chong Lim Kim, ed., *The Political Participation in Korea: Democracy, Mobilization, and Stability* (Santa Barbara, Calif.: Clio Press, 1980), pp. 85–117; Young Whan Kihl, "Local Elites, Power Structure and Legislative Process in Korea," *Journal of Korean Studies* 3 (1981):147–180.

14. Chong Lim Kim, "Elite Political Culture: Cognitive Dimension" (Typescript, n.d.), pp. 12–13.

15. On my experience of talking with members of North Korean elites in 1981, see C. I. Eugene Kim and B. C. Koh, eds., *Journey to North Korea: Personal Perceptions* (Berkeley: University of California Institute of East Asian Studies, 1983), pp. 99–117.

16. On political leadership in Korea, North and South, see Dae-Sook Suh and Chae-Jin Lee, eds., *Political Leadership in Korea* (Seattle: University of Washington Press, 1976).

17. There are few studies of political elites in Korea based on social origin and career background. However, see Bae-ho Hahn and Kyu-taik Kim, "Korean Political Leaders (1952–62): Their Social Origins and Skills," *Asian Survey* 3, 7 (July 1963):305–323; Chong Lim Kim and Byung-kyu Woo, "Social and Political Background of Korean National Assemblymen: The Seventh National Assembly," *Asian Forum* 3 (July-September 1971):123–137.

18. Dae-Sook Suh, "Communist Party Leadership," in Dae-Sook Suh and Chae-Jin Lee, *Political Leadership*, pp. 159–191, especially pp. 186–189.

19. Ibid., p. 218.

20. Ibid., p. 217.

21. Hahn-been Lee, *Korea: Time, Change and Administration* (Honolulu: East-West Center Press, 1968), pp. 177–186.

22. See, for instance, Chong Lim Kim and Seong-tong Pai, *Legislative Process in Korea;* Chong Lim Kim and Byung-kyu Woo, "Intra-Elite Cleavages in the Korean National Assembly," *Asian Survey* 11, 6 (June 1971):544–561; Bae-ho Hahn and Ha-Ryong Kim, "Party Bureaucrats and Party Development," in Dae-Sook Suh and Chae-Jin Lee, *Political Leadership*, pp. 67–90; Dong-Suh Bark and Chae-Jin Lee, "Bureaucratic Elite and Development Orientations," in Dae-Sook Suh and Chae-Jin Lee, *Political Leadership*, pp. 91–133; Young Whan Kihl, "Leadership and Opposition Role Perception Among Party Elites in Korea," *Asian Forum* 5, 3 (July-September 1973), pp. 17–42 (also in *Korea Journal*, 13, 9 (September 1973), pp. 3–22).

23. See Chapter 1 under the subheading "Dominant Features of Korean Politics."

24. On Chuch'esong in Korean politics, see B. C. Koh, "Chuch'esong," pp. 83–97.

25. For a rave review of North Korea's accomplishments, see Byong-sik Kim, *Modern Korea: The Socialist North, Revolutionary Perspectives in the South* (New York: International Publishers, 1970).

26. Kim Il Sung, *On the Juche Idea* (Pyongyang: Foreign Languages Publishing House, 1979), p. 1.

27. Ibid.

28. Ibid., p. 4.

29. Kim Il Sung, *Selected Works*, Vol. 4 (Pyongyang: Foreign Languages Publishing House, 1971), pp. 229–230.

30. The text of the 1972 constitution of North Korea appears in: Dae-Sook Suh, *Korean Communism 1945–1980: A Reference Guide to the Political System* (Honolulu: University Press of Hawaii, 1981), pp. 499–522.

31. Kim Il Sung, *On the Juche Idea*, p. 5.

32. Bruce G. Cumings, "Kim's Korean Communism," *Problems of Communism*, 23 (March-April 1974):33.

33. Sung Chul Yang, *Korea and Two Regimes: Kim Il Sung and Park Chung Hee* (Cambridge, Mass.: Schenkman Publishing Co., 1981), p. 202.

34. The Chongsanri method and the Chollima movement are inscribed in the 1972 Socialist constitution of North Korea.

35. As cited in Sung Chul Yang, *Korea and Two Regimes*, p. 202.

36. Ibid.

37. Article 12 of the 1972 constitution, in Dae-Sook Suh, *Korean Communism*, p. 503.

38. On South Korea's Saemaul movement, see Parvez Hasan, *Korea: Problems and Issues in a Rapidly Growing Economy* (Baltimore: Johns Hopkins University

Press for the World Bank, 1976), pp. 159–164; Young Whan Kihl, "Politics and Agrarian Change in South Korea: Rural Modernization by 'Induced' Mobilization," in Raymond Hopkins, Donald Puchala, and Ross Talbot, eds., *Food, Politics, and Agricultural Development: Case Studies in the Public Policy of Rural Modernization* (Boulder, Co.: Westview Press, 1979), pp. 133–169.

39. Park Chung Hee, *Pak Chong-hi taet'ongryong ui chido inyom kwa hengdong ch'olhak* [The leadership principles and the action philosophy of president Park Chung Hee] (Seoul: Maeil Kyongje Sinmunsa, 1977), p. 198, as cited in Sung Chul Yang, *Korea and Two Regimes*, pp. 267, 286. See also Park Chung Hee, *Korea Reborn: A Model for Development* (Englewood Cliffs, N.J.: Prentice-Hall, 1979), pp. 21–24.

40. Young Whan Kihl, "Linkage and Democratic Orientation of Party Elites in South Korea," in Kay Lawson, ed., *Political Parties and Linkage: A Comparative Perspective* (New Haven, Conn.: Yale University Press, 1980), pp. 75–99.

41. On Yushin Korea, see the discussion in Chapter 3 under the subheading "Park Chung Hee's Yushin Korea."

42. On "Korean democracy," see Seung-jo Han, *Hankuk minjuchuuiwa chongch'i palchon* [Korean democracy and political development] (Seoul: Popmunsa, 1976).

43. Sung Chul Yang, *Korea and Two Regimes*, p. 354. Economic development, according to Cole and Lyman, was Park's "source of final legitimization." David C. Cole and Princeton N. Lyman, *Korean Development: The Interplay of Politics and Economics* (Cambridge, Mass.: Harvard University Press, 1971), p. 80.

44. Sung Chul Yang, *Korea and Two Regimes*, p. 354.
45. Ibid.
46. Ibid., p. 355.
47. Ibid., p. 356.
48. Ibid.
49. Ibid., pp. 356–357.
50. Ibid., p. 357.
51. Ibid., pp. 357–358.
52. Ibid., p. 358.
53. Ibid.
54. A comparative study of Chun Doo Hwan and Kim Jong Il, similar to Yang's study of Kim Il Sung and Park Chung Hee, needs to be undertaken, however, in the years ahead.

55. The following information on Chun Doo Hwan is extracted from Gumsong Ch'on, *Hwanggang eso puk'ak kiseul kkaji: Ingan Chon Du-hwan* [From the Hwang River to Puk'ak Mountain: The man Chun Doo Hwan] (Seoul: Tongso Munhwasa, 1981).

56. Ibid., pp. 236–237.
57. Ibid.
58. Ibid., pp. 264, 270.

59. Kim Jong Il's biographical data are not readily available. The information on him in this study is derived from a Japanese source, Kokusai Kankei Kyodo Genkyusho, ed., *Kita Chosen: Seshu teki shakaishugi no kuni* [North Korea: Hereditary socialist country] (Tokyo: Seikatsu Shobo, 1978).

Chapter 6

1. On my conception of what "political economy" stands for, see the discussion in Chapter 1 and also notes 1:30 through 1:34.

2. A similar approach to political economy analysis and policymaking is presented by a group of economists at Harvard Business School. See Bruce R. Scott et al., *Case Studies in Political Economy: Japan 1854-1977* (Cambridge, Mass.: Harvard Business School, 1980).

3. There is no systematic comparative analysis of the economic systems of North and South Korea. On the economic system of North Korea, see Joseph Sang-hoon Chung, *The North Korean Economy: Structure and Development* (Stanford, Calif.: Hoover Institution Press, 1974); Ellen Brun and Jacques Hersh, *Socialist Korea: A Case Study in the Strategy of Economic Development* (New York: Monthly Review Press, 1976). Of the numerous accounts of the South Korean economy, see Parvez Hasan, *Korea: Problems and Issues in a Rapidly Growing Economy* (Baltimore: Johns Hopkins University Press for the World Bank, 1976); Parvez Hasan and D. C. Rao, *Korea: Policy Issues for Long-Term Development* (Baltimore: Johns Hopkins University Press for the World Bank, 1979); and Paul W. Kuznets, *Economic Growth and Structure in the Republic of Korea* (New Haven, Conn.: Yale University Press, 1977).

4. Joseph Sang-hoon Chung, *North Korean Economy*, pp. 152-155.

5. On the economic development in South Korea prior to 1976, see the seven-volume series, *Studies in the Modernization of the Republic of Korea: 1945-1975*, undertaken jointly by the Harvard University Institute for International Development and the Korea Development Institute, and published by the Harvard University Council on East Asian Studies. See, especially, Edward S. Mason et al., *The Economic and Social Modernization of the Republic of Korea* (Cambridge, Mass.: Harvard University Council on East Asian Studies, 1980), pp. 484-494.

6. *Korea's Economy* (Washington, D.C.: Korea Economic Institute) 2, 4 (May 1983):1.

7. This characterization of states as "soft" or "hard," based on their capability for implementing development policy measures, was initially advanced by Gunnar Myrdal. For an example that characterizes South Korea as a "hard state," see Mason et al., *Economic and Social Modernization*, p. 486.

8. Joseph Sang-hoon Chung, *North Korean Economy;* and U.S. CIA, *Handbook of Economic Statistics, 1979* (Washington, D.C.: CIA, August 1979), as cited in Gordon White, "North Korean Juche: The Political Economy of Self-Reliance," in Manfred Bienefeld and Martin Godfrey, eds., *The Struggle for Development: National Strategies in an International Context* (New York: John Wiley & Sons, 1982), pp. 337-338.

9. Ibid.

10. Mason et al., *Economic and Social Modernization*, p. 97.

11. Ibid.

12. Economic Planning Board, as cited in *Korea: Executive Guide* (New York: Citibank, 1982), pp. 13-14.

13. Ibid.

14. White, "North Korean Juche," in Bienefeld and Godfrey, *Struggle for Development*, pp. 332-336.

15. Scott et al., *Case Studies*. See also Warren F. Ilchman and Norman T. Uphoff, *The Political Economy of Change* (Berkeley: University of California Press, 1969).

16. Ilchman and Uphoff, *Political Economy*.

17. World Bank, *World Development Report 1982* (Washington, D.C.: World Bank, 1982), pp. 143-155.

18. Statistical data for this table come from various sources, including the *World Bank Atlas* for 1978, 1979, and 1980, published by the World Bank, Washington, D.C. Other information, unattainable elsewhere, is taken from: ROK, *Economic Comparison Between South and North Korea 1977* (Seoul: Research Center for Peace and Unification, 1977); and ROK, *A Statistical Comparison Between South and North Korea* (Seoul: Korean Overseas Information Service, 1978).

19. *Asia Yearbook 1982* (Hong Kong), pp. 10-11.

20. Nena Vreeland et al., *Area Handbook for North Korea* (Washington, D.C.: Government Printing Office, 1976), p. 40. See also Nena Vreeland et al., *Area Handbook for South Korea* (Washington, D.C.: Government Printing Office, 1975).

21. Vreeland et al., *Area Handbook, North;* Vreeland et al., *Area Handbook, South,* p. 38.

22. This is the conclusion also arrived at in a U.S. CIA study, *Korea: The Economic Race Between the North and the South: A Research Paper* (Washington, D.C.: National Foreign Assessment Center and the Library of Congress, 1978). See also the sources listed in note 8 above. For a more sympathetic view of North Korea, however, see Gerhard Breidenstein and W. Rosenberg, "Economic Comparison of North and South Korea," *Journal of Contemporary Asia* 5, 2 (1975):165-203.

23. See the various issues of the *World Bank Atlas,* and *Asia Yearbook 1982,* p. 8.

24. U.S. CIA, *Korea: The Economic Race,* p. 2.

25. Ibid., p. 6.

26. Ibid.

27. Ibid.

28. Ibid.

29. On the strategic role of Korea in the East Asian balance of power, see William Barnds, ed., *The Two Koreas in East Asian Affairs* (New York: New York University Press, 1976); Young C. Kim and Abraham M. Halpern, eds., *The Future of the Korean Peninsula* (New York: Praeger Publishers, 1977); Franklin B. Weinstein and Fuji Kamiya, eds., *The Security of Korea: U.S. and Japanese Perspectives on the 1980s* (Boulder, Co.: Westview Press, 1980); Richard Solomon, ed., *Asian Security in the 1980s: Problems and Policies for a Time of Transition* (Santa Monica, Calif.: Rand Corporation, 1979); and Stuart E. Johnson, *The Military Equation in Northeast Asia* (Washington, D.C.: Brookings Institution, 1979).

30. C. I. Eugene Kim and Han-Kyo Kim, *Korea and the Politics of Imperialism: 1876-1911* (Berkeley and Los Angeles: University of California Press, 1967), pp. 203-205.

31. On traditional Korea, see James B. Palais, *Politics and Policy in Traditional Korea* (Cambridge, Mass.: Harvard University Press, 1975).

32. "New Study Raises U.S. Estimate of North Korean Army Strength," *New York Times,* January 4, 1979; and U.S. Arms Control and Disarmament Agency, *World Military Expenditures and Arms Transfers: 1971-1980* (Washington, D.C., 1983).

33. As reported in Kokusai Kankei Kyodo Genkyusho, ed., *Kita Chosen: Seshu teki shakaishugi no kuni* [North Korea: Hereditary socialist country] (Tokyo: Seikatsu Shobo, 1978), pp. 21-22, 151-153.

34. Ibid.

35. U.S. Congress, Senate Committee on Foreign Relations, *U.S. Troop Withdrawal From the Republic of Korea, A Report to the Committee by Senators Hubert H. Humphrey and John Glenn, January 9, 1978*, 95th Cong., 2d Sess. (hereafter cited as Humphrey-Glenn Report) (Washington, D.C.: Government Printing Office, 1978), p. 33. See also Ralph N. Clough, *Deterrence and Defense in Korea: The Role of U.S. Forces* (Washington, D.C.: Brookings Institution, 1976).

36. U.S. Congress, Humphrey-Glenn Report, pp. 43–44; Clough, *Deterrence*, p. 15.

37. The estimates of the military capabilities of North and South Korea are based on published works outside the respective Korean states. See, for instance, International Institute for Strategic Studies, *The Military Balance 1981–82* (London: IISS, 1982); Japan Self-Defense Force, *Boei hakusho* [Defense white paper] (Tokyo: Japan Government Publications Center, 1980); *Asia Yearbook 1982*.

38. Ibid. For recent attempts to assess the military balance in the Korean Peninsula, see Richard L. Sneider, "Prospects for Korean Security," in Solomon, *Asian Security*, pp. 104–147.

39. Ibid.

40. U.S. Congress, Humphrey-Glenn Report.

41. Young-Ho Lee, "Military Balance and Peace in the Korean Peninsula," *Asian Survey* 21, 8 (August 1981):852–864.

42. U.S. Congress, Humphrey-Glenn Report, pp. 35, 39.

43. Ibid., p. 40.

44. For instance see U.S. CIA, *Korea: The Economic Race*.

45. U.S. Department of State, "Diplomatic Relations of Republic of Korea and Democratic People's Republic of Korea (Washington, D.C.: Department of State, 1982). Unclassified.

46. For further elaboration of North Korea's foreign policy behavior early in the 1970s, see Byung Chul Koh et al., *Pukhan oekyo-ron* [On North Korea's foreign policy] (Seoul: Kyong Nam University Press, 1977). Also, for a plea to do a systematic comparative analysis of North and South Korea's foreign policy behavior, see Samuel S. Kim, "Research on Korean Communism: Promise Versus Performance," *World Politics* 32, 2 (January 1980):281–310.

47. Frederica M. Bunge, ed., *North Korea: A Country Study*, Area Handbook Series of the U.S. Department of the Army (Washington, D.C.: Government Printing Office, 1981), pp. 152, 255.

48. Ibid.

49. Ibid., 255.

50. David I. Steinberg, *The Economic Development of Korea: Sui Generis or Generic?* USAID Evaluation Special Study No. 6 (Washington, D.C.: USAID, 1981), p. 26. See also David I. Steinberg, "Development Lessons from the Korean Experience—A Review Article," *Journal of Asian Studies* 42, 1 (November 1982):91–104.

51. Ibid.

52. *Far Eastern Economic Review*, March 3, 1983.

53. Bunge, *North Korea*, p. 155.

54. *Korea's Economy* (Korean Economic Institute, Washington, D.C.) 2, 2 (March 1983):4–6.

55. Ibid.

56. Sung-Hwan Jo, "Direct Foreign Private Investment," in Chong-Kee Park, ed., *Macroeconomic and Industrial Development in Korea* (Seoul: Korea Development Institute, 1980), pp. 131, 178.
57. Ibid.
58. Ibid.
59. Ibid., 178-179.
60. For instance, see Herman Kahn, *World Economic Development: 1979 and Beyond* (Boulder, Co.: Westview Press, 1979); Roy Hofheinz, Jr., and Kent E. Calden, *Eastasia Edge* (New York: Basic Books, 1982).
61. Hofheinz and Calden, *Eastasia Edge*.
62. Lewis A. Coser, *The Functions of Social Conflict* (Glencoe, Ill.: Free Press, 1956).

Chapter 7

1. *Korea Times,* December 16, 1981, p. 2.
2. Prime Minister Yu Chang-soon and Deputy Prime Minister Kim Joon-sung were recruited from the business community, where they had been chairman of the Korea Trader's Association and governor of the Bank of Korea respectively. In the cabinet shift announced on January 4, 1982, the portfolios of economic planning, finance, energy, construction, and unification were newly appointed, changing six members in a cabinet of twenty-five.
3. The text of Chun's 1982 New Year's address appeared in the *Korea Herald,* January 23, 1982.
4. Ibid.
5. In making this and similar statements on political parties and party politics in general, Chun is obviously simplifying the complex issue of political parties and party activities. For a study of political parties and party movement in Korea, see the collection of essays in C. I. Eugene Kim and Young Whan Kihl, eds., *Party Politics and Elections in Korea* (Silver Spring, Md.: Research Institute on Korean Affairs, 1976). See also Young Whan Kihl, "Linkage and Democratic Orientation of Party Elites in South Korea," in Kay Lawson, ed., *Political Parties and Linkage: A Comparative Perspective* (New Haven, Conn.: Yale University Press, 1980), pp. 75-99.
6. President Chun was mistaken in making this generalized observation: the Second Republic (1960-1961) was an obvious exception.
7. *Korea Herald,* January 23, 1982.
8. Ibid.
9. On Park Chung Hee's rather skeptical views on party politics, see Kwan-Bong Kim, *The Korea-Japan Treaty Crisis and the Instability of the Korean Political System* (New York: Praeger Publishers, 1964); and C. I. Eugene Kim and Young Whan Kihl, *Party Politics and Elections.*
10. See Chong-Sik Lee, "South Korea in 1980: The Emergence of a New Authoritarian Order," *Asian Survey* 31, 1 (January 1981):125-143.
11. The advantage of the DJP as the governing party was made evident from the fact that it had raised a party fund of 5.76 billion won (U.S. $8 million), 92 percent of the total funds raised by all the political parties in 1981. The two major opposition parties, Democratic Korea Party and Korea National Party, succeeded in raising only 5 percent and 2 percent of the total party funds respectively. *Hanguk Ilbo,* January 19, 1982, p. 4.
12. *New York Times,* May 21, 1982.

13. *New York Times,* July 11, 1982.
14. Ibid.
15. *Far Eastern Economic Review,* September 8, 1983, pp. 56–58.
16. *Korea Herald,* March 2, 1982.
17. FBIS, Asia and the Pacific, June 9, 1983, E-1.
18. *Far Eastern Economic Review,* August 25, 1983.
19. *Korea Times,* June 15, 1983, p. 8, as reported in FBIS, Asia and the Pacific, June 16, E-1.
20. *Korea Herald,* July 8, 1983. Hahm, Kim Jae-ik, and Suh were all killed in the October 1983 bombing in Rangoon.
21. FBIS, Asia and the Pacific, June 3, 1983, E-2.
22. *Korea Herald,* August 26, 1983.
23. For a discussion of South Korea's strategy for economic development, see the series entitled *Studies in the Modernization of the Republic of Korea, 1945–1975,* published by the Council on East Asian Studies of Harvard University.
24. The case in point was the proposal to make the banking industry—largely state owned and operated—into a predominantly privately owned and operated industry.
25. *Far Eastern Economic Review,* September 18, 1981, pp. 112–114.
26. Korean overseas construction contracts from 1966 through the end of 1982 totaled U.S. $57.3 billion, of which Middle Eastern contracts accounted for more than 90 percent. In 1981 alone, Korea's overseas construction contracts amounted to U.S. $13.6 billion. See *Korea's Economy* 2, 8 (August 1983):1–2.
27. *Dong-A Ilbo,* November 28, 1981.
28. *Far Eastern Economic Review,* August 4, 1983, pp. 40–41.
29. Ibid.
30. Ibid.
31. *Korea Herald,* November 21, 1981, p. 5.
32. *News Review* (Seoul), January 23, 1982, p. 20.
33. *Korea Herald,* February 7, 1982.
34. *New York Times,* November 12, 1983.
35. FBIS, Asia and the Pacific, June 6, 1983, E-1.
36. *Korea Herald,* June 8, 1983.
37. *Korea Herald,* October 5, 1983.
38. *New York Times,* October 10, 1983.
39. *Korea Herald,* October 11, 1983.
40. *Pyongyang Times,* October 15, 1983.
41. Former diplomat Lee Bum-suk was also chief negotiator at the North-South Red Cross talks in Panmunjom in 1972–1973. He became foreign minister in 1982.
42. See Chapter 8 for further analysis of the unification issue. See also Young Whan Kihl, "South Korea's Unification Policy: An Assessment," *Korea and World Affairs* 6, 1 (March 1982):73–95.
43. The careful planning of Chun's unification strategy was evident from the fact that ten days after his speech the Seoul government came forward with a follow-up proposal to put Chun's plan into effect. See ibid., and also Chapter 8.
44. *Des Moines Register,* October 21, 1983, p. 7-C; *Korea Herald,* October 23, 1983.
45. Kim Il Sung, "Let Us Vivaciously Develop the Three Great Revolutions and Further Accelerate the Socialist Construction," *Kulloja* [The Workers], March 1975.

46. Ibid.
47. Kim Il Sung, *Report to the Sixth Congress of the Workers' Party of Korea on the Work of the Central Committee*, October 10, 1980 (Pyongyang: Foreign Languages Publishing House, 1980), pp. 35–37.
48. Chong-Sik Lee, *Korean Workers' Party: A Short History* (Stanford: Hoover Institution Press, 1978):131–132.
49. Chong-Sik Lee, "Evolution of the Korean Workers' Party and the Rise of Kim Chong-il," *Asian Survey* 22, 5 (May 1982):435.
50. A typical example of this view may be found in Dong-bok Lee, "Hereditary Succession in North Korea and Its Impact on Inter-Korean Relations" (Prepared for presentation at the Second International Symposium on Korea at La Trobe University, Melbourne, Australia, November 20–22, 1980.) See also Ilpyong J. Kim and Dong-bok Lee, "After Kim: Who and What in North Korea," *World Affairs* 142, 4 (Spring 1980):258.
51. Kim Il Sung, *Tasks of the People's Government in Modelling the Whole of Society on Juche Idea*, Speech at the joint meeting of the KWP Central Committee and the DPRK Supreme People's Assembly on April 14, 1982. Text issued by the DPRK Permanent Observer Mission to the UN, Press Release No. 32 (April 15, 1982).
52. Ibid.
53. Ibid.
54. Ibid.
55. Morgan Clippinger, "Kim Chong-il in the North Korean Mass Media: A Study of Semi-Esoteric Communication," *Asian Survey* 21, 3 (March 1981):297.
56. Ibid.
57. Ibid., p. 294.
58. Ibid., p. 295.
59. Ibid.
60. *Vantage Point*, 6, 2 (February 1983):13.
61. Kim Jong Il, "The Workers' Party of Korea Is a Juche-type Revolutionary Party Which Inherited the Glorious Tradition of the DIU" (Pyongyang: Foreign Languages Publishing House, 1972), p. 2.
62. Ibid., Open letter mailed via German Democratic Republic, dated November 1982.
63. FBIS, Asia and the Pacific, July 7, p. D-7.
64. *Naewoe Tongsin*, 337 (June 24, 1983).
65. *New York Times*, May 20, 1982; and FBIS, Asia and the Pacific, December 9, 1982, pp. E-1, E-2.
66. *New York Times*, November 29, 1983.
67. Kim Il Sung, *Report to the Sixth Congress*, p. 41.
68. *Korea Today* 1 (1978):18–28, as cited by Dae-Sook Suh, "North Korea 1978: The Beginning of the Final Push," *Asian Survey* 19, 1 (January 1979):52.
69. Foreign trade deficits in these years reached, for instance, U.S. $597 million in 1974, $317 million in 1975, and $422 million in 1976. For details, see Table 6.9.
70. *Vantage Point* 6, 1 (January 1983):12–15.
71. *Vantage Point* 6, 2 (February 1983):12.
72. FBIS, Asia and the Pacific, July 21, 1983, p. D-9.
73. Young-Ho Lee, "Military Balance and Peace in the Korean Peninsula," *Asian Survey* 21, 8 (August 1981):852–864. Also, see the discussion in Chapter 6.

74. FBIS, Asia and the Pacific, June 30, 1983, p. D-9.
75. As reported in *Chungang Ilbo,* May 13, 1983.
76. FBIS, Asia and the Pacific, May 19, 1983, p. D-6.
77. *Vantage Point* 6, 9 (September 1983):19.
78. Ibid.
79. *Korea Today,* December 1982, p. 4.
80. Ibid.
81. As reported in the *Korea Herald,* September 9, 1983.
82. *Asahi Shimbun,* October 30, 1983, as reported in the *Korea Herald,* November 3, 1983.
83. *Des Moines Register,* November 8, 1983; *New York Times,* November 9, 1983.
84. On the evolution of President Carter's plan for U.S. troop withdrawal from Korea, see Larry Niksch, "U.S. Troop Withdrawal from South Korea: Past Shortcomings and Future Prospects," *Asian Survey* 21, 3 (March 1981):325–341.
85. On Congressman Stephen J. Solarez's report on his trip to North Korea, see U.S. Congress, House Committee on Foreign Affairs, *The Korean Conundrum: A Conversation with Kim Il Sung, Report of a Study Mission to South Korea, Japan, the People's Republic of China and North Korea, July 12–21, 1980,* 97th Cong., 1st Sess. (Washington, D.C.: Government Printing Office, 1981).
86. Young C. Kim, "North Korea in 1980: The Son Also Rises," *Asian Survey* 21, 1 (January 1981):118.
87. Press Release, DPRK Permanent Observer Mission to the UN, March 22, 1983.
88. *Nodong Sinmun,* November 11, 1983. Also, FBIS, Asia and Pacific, November 14, 1983, p. D-7.
89. *Far Eastern Economic Review,* May 12, 1983, pp. 16–17; and the *Washington Post,* November 11, 1983.
90. FBIS, Asia and the Pacific, April 28, 1983, p. E-2.
91. *Korea Herald,* July 28, 1983.
92. Press Release, DPRK Permanent Observer Mission to the UN, January 13, 1983.
93. FBIS, Asia and the Pacific, January 25, 1983, p. D-1.
94. FBIS, Asia and the Pacific, July 1, 1983, p. E-4.
95. FBIS, Asia and the Pacific, July 11, 1983, p. C-2.
96. *Shincho,* June 30, 1983, as reported in FBIS Asia and the Pacific, June 24, 1983, p. E-1.
97. Ibid. The Korea-Japan Trade Co. is a business firm affiliated with Chochongryon, the Association of Korean Residents in Japan.
98. See Chin O. Chung, *P'yongyang Between Peking and Moscow: North Korea's Involvement in the Sino-Soviet Dispute, 1958–1975* (University, Ala.: University of Alabama Press, 1978).
99. For a recent analysis of this issue, see: Helen-Louise Hunter, "North Korea and the Myth of Equidistance," *Korea and World Affairs* 4, 2 (Summer 1980):268–269.
100. As cited in Dae-Sook Suh, "North Korea 1978: The Beginning of the Final Push," *Asian Survey* 19, 1 (January 1979):53.
101. For reports on the treaty with Libya, see *Korea Today* (Pyongyang), January 1983; on the treaty with Ethiopia, see the *Pyongyang Times,* October

26, 1983; and on the secret agreement with Grenada, see the *New York Times,* November 5, 1983.

102. Press Release, DPRK Permanent Observer Mission to the UN, April 5, 1983. The theme of south-south cooperation was also emphasized by *Nodong Sinmun,* November 16, 1983. See FBIS, Asia and the Pacific, November 18, 1983, p. D-13.

103. Ibid., March 12, 1983.

104. *Des Moines Register,* September 7, 1983, p. 8 A; *New York Times,* November 19, 1983. This figure of U.S. $640 million military credit sale to Zimbabwe in 1983 as reported in the wire service, if correct, represents a substantial amount of bilateral transaction between North Korea and the newly independent African country.

105. FBIS, Asia and the Pacific, July 5, 1983, p. D-16.

106. *Pyongyang Times,* October 1, 1983.

107. *Asahi Shimbun,* January 1, 1983, as cited in *Vantage Point,* 6, 1 (January 1983):16.

108. Press Release, DPRK Permanent Observer Mission to the UN, September 26, 1983.

109. *Pyongyang Times,* October 15, 1983.

110. *New York Times,* November 5, 1983.

111. FBIS, Asia and the Pacific, November 7, 1983, p. D-1.

112. Michael G. Fry and Arthur N. Gilbert, "A Historian and Linkage Politics," *International Studies Quarterly* 26, 3 (September 1982):425–444.

113. James N. Rosenau, *The Adaptation of National Societies: A Theory of Political System Behavior and Transformation* (New York: McCaleb-Seisler Publishing Co., 1970).

Chapter 8

1. For some examples of Korea's nationalist sentiment regarding divided nationhood, see the discussion in Chapter 2.

2. Johan Galtung, "Divided Nations as Process: One State, Two States, and In-Between: The Case of Korea," *Journal of Peace Research* 9 (1972):345–360.

3. For an analysis of the July 4, 1972, joint communiqué, see Young Whan Kihl, "Korean Response to Major Power Rapprochement," in Young C. Kim, ed., *Major Powers and Korea* (Silver Spring, Md.: Research Institute on Korean Affairs, 1973), pp. 139–164. Also, see the discussion in Chapter 3.

4. On South Korea's unification policy and position on the South-North dialogue, see Park Chung Hee, *Toward Peaceful Unification* (Seoul: Kwangmyong Publishing Co., 1976); ROK, *A White Paper on South-North Dialogue in Korea* (Seoul: South-North Coordinating Committee, Seoul Side, 1979); "Unification Policy," in ROK, *A Handbook of Korea* (Seoul: Korean Overseas Information Service, 1979), pp. 409–442; Se-Jin Kim, ed., *Korean Unification: Source Materials with an Introduction,* (Seoul: Research Center for Peace and Unification, 1976).

5. Park Chung Hee, *Toward Peaceful Unification,* pp. 88–92.

6. Ibid., pp. 103–109.

7. Ibid., pp. 76–79.

8. Ibid., pp. 72–75.

9. Young-Ho Lee, "South Korea's Unification Policy" (Paper prepared for presentation at the International Workshop on Korean Unification: Analysis, Evaluation, Prescription, held at Hotel Sorak Park, Sokcho, Korea, November

21–23, 1981, and sponsored by the Advisory Council on Peaceful Unification Policy), pp. 14–15.

10. As cited in ROK, *A Handbook of Korea*, p. 420.

11. Park Chung Hee, *Toward Peaceful Unification*, pp. 18–23.

12. Young Whan Kihl, "Korean Response," pp. 139–150.

13. B. C. Koh, "Convergence and Conflict in the Two Koreas," *Current History*, November 1973, pp. 205–208.

14. On North Korea's unification policy and position on the North-South dialogue, see Kim Il Sung, *For the Independent Peaceful Reunification of Korea*, rev. ed. (New York: Weekly Guardian Associates, 1976); Young Whan Kihl, "The Issue of Korean Unification: North Korea's Policy and Perceptions," in C. I. Eugene Kim and B. C. Koh, eds., *Journey to North Korea: Personal Perceptions* (Berkeley: University of California Institute of East Asian Studies, 1983), pp. 99–117. See also Hak-Joon Kim, *The Unification Policy of South and North Korea: A Comparative Study* (Seoul: Seoul National University Press, 1977).

15. This and the following analysis are based on interviews with North Korean officials and scholars in Pyongyang, July 1981. On the report of my trip to North Korea, see Young Whan Kihl, "North Korea: A Reevaluation," *Current History* 81, 474 (April 1982). See also Young Whan Kihl, "The Issue of Korean Unification."

16. It is no accident that the underground movement in South Korea, which is actively supported and controlled by North Korea, is called the Revolutionary Party for Reunification.

17. Young Whan Kihl, "The Issue of Korean Unification," p. 102.

18. Ibid.

19. Ibid., p. 103.

20. Ibid.

21. Ibid., p. 106.

22. Ibid.

23. Pyongyang's official response is contained in the talk by Kim Il, DPRK vice-president and chairman of the Committee for the Peaceful Reunification of the Fatherland, January 26, 1982. Press Release No. 5, DPRK Permanent Observer Mission to the UN, January 26, 1982.

24. For the text of Kim's proposal on the DCRK Plan, see Kim Il Sung, *Report to the Sixth Congress of the Workers' Party of Korea on the Work of the Central Committee*, October 10, 1980 (Pyongyang: Foreign Languages Publishing House, 1980), especially "Let Us Reunify the Country Independently and Peacefully," pp. 59–81.

25. Ibid., p. 65.

26. Ibid.

27. Ibid., pp. 64–65.

28. Ibid., pp. 71–81.

29. Young Whan Kihl, "The Issue of Korean Unification," p. 109.

30. Interestingly, while South Korea advocates the "centralized" unified state, North Korea proposes a "confederal or federated" unified state.

31. On North Korea's five-point proposal on "peaceful unification," as presented on June 23, 1973, see Kim Il Sung, *Independent Peaceful Reunification*, pp. 145–151.

32. This position is discussed further in Young Whan Kihl, "Korean Response."

33. On President Chun's proposal of January 12, 1981, see the *Korea Herald*, January 13, 1981.
34. Ibid.
35. On President Chun's proposal of June 5, 1981, see the *Korea Herald*, June 6, 1981.
36. Ibid.
37. On President Chun's proposal of January 22, 1982, see the *Korea Herald*, January 23, 1982.
38. Ibid.
39. Ibid.
40. On South Korea's "pilot projects" proposal of February 1, 1982, see the *Korea Herald*, February 2, 1982.
41. Ibid.
42. *Economist* (London), February 6, 1982, pp. 16, 19.
43. Press Release No. 109, November 26, 1981, DPRK Permanent Observer Mission to the United Nations, p. 13. This international conference was attended by North Koreans and overseas Koreans in Europe and North America who were critical of the Chun Doo Hwan government in the South.
44. Young Whan Kihl, "The Issue of Korean Unification," p. 607.
45. Ibid.
46. *Vantage Point* 6, 1 (January 1983):16.
47. On the interpretation of this difference, see Dong-bok Lee's comment in the *Korea Herald*, January 23, 1982.

Chapter 9

1. The term "authority inflation" as used here refers to the situation in which the regime's status and resources have been inflated or exaggerated beyond their proper place in society. For a discussion of the concept of "political inflation and deflation," see Warren F. Ilchman and Norman T. Uphoff, *The Political Economy of Change* (Berkeley: University of California Press, 1969), pp. 136–159.
2. This is a Maoist developmental model. For the relevance of the "politics takes command" approach to the study of Korean politics, see Glenn D. Paige, "Some Implications for Political Science of the Comparative Politics of Korea," in Fred W. Riggs, ed., *Frontiers of Development Administration* (Durham, N.C.: Duke University Press, 1970).
3. Adam Przeworski and Henry Teune, *The Logic of Comparative Social Inquiry* (New York: John Wiley, 1969).
4. On "convergence hypotheses" as applied to the study of U.S.-Soviet politics, see Zbigniew Brzezinski and Samuel P. Huntington, *Political Power: USA and USSR* (New York: Viking Press, 1967).
5. See Young Whan Kihl, "Political Institutions and Participation in the Two Koreas: Comparison" (Prepared for presentation at a workshop sponsored by the Joint Committee on Korean Studies, Social Science Research Council, and American Council of Learned Societies, San Juan, Puerto Rico, January 16–18, 1976). A modified version of this paper was also presented at the Thirtieth International Congress on Human Sciences in Asia and North Africa, August 1976, Mexico City. See Young Whan Kihl, "Some Aspects of Political Participation and Culture of the Two Koreas," in Graciela de la Lama, ed., *Japan and Korea* 2 (Mexico City: El Colegio de Mexico, 1982), pp. 54–73.

6. For a similar point of view as applied to the study of Chinese politics, see Lucian Pye, *The Dynamics of Chinese Politics* (Cambridge, Mass.: Oelgeschlager, Gunn and Hain, 1981), especially pp. 159–161. Also, on the theory of patron-client ties in politics, see Steffen Schmidt et al., *Friends, Followers and Factions* (Berkeley: University of California Press, 1978).

7. The concept of a "garrison state" was suggested initially by Harold Lasswell. For an interesting application of this concept to South Korea's politics, see Jai-hyup Kim, "The Political Involvement of Military Elites: A Comparative Study of a 'Garrison State' in Japan during the 1930s and 1940s and Korea during the 1960s and 1970s" (Ph.D. diss., Indiana University, 1976).

8. Man-Gap Lee, ed., *Toward a New Community: Reports of International Research-Seminar on the Saemaul Movement* (Seoul: Institute of Saemaul Undong Studies for Seoul National University, 1981). For my analysis of the Saemaul undong, see Young Whan Kihl, "Politics and Agrarian Change in South Korea: Rural Modernization by 'Induced' Mobilization," in Raymond Hopkins, Donald Puchala, and Ross Talbot, eds., *Food, Politics, and Agricultural Development: Case Studies in the Public Policy of Rural Modernization* (Boulder, Co.: Westview Press, 1979). Also, as an example of the increasing attention given to South Korea's Saemaul undong, see Arthur Goldsmith, "Popular Participation in South Korea's New Community Movement," *Rural Development Participation Review* (Cornell University Rural Development Committee, Ithaca, N.Y.) 3, 3 (Spring 1982):1–7.

9. For a stimulating discussion of the impact of the international system upon domestic politics, see Peter Gourevitch, "The Second Image Reversed: The International Sources of Domestic Politics," *International Organization* 32, 4 (Autumn 1978):881–912.

10. Ray Hofheinz, Jr., and Kent E. Calden, *Eastasia Edge* (New York: Basic Books, 1982).

11. Ibid.

12. Gregory Henderson, "North and South Korea," in Steven L. Spiegel and Kenneth N. Waltz, eds., *Conflict in World Politics* (Cambridge, Mass.: Winthrop Publishers, 1971), pp. 197–198.

13. See Ray Johnston, ed., *The Politics of Division, Partition and Unification* (New York: Praeger Publishers, 1976).

14. Sung Chul Yang, *Korea and Two Regimes: Kim Il Sung and Park Chung Hee* (Cambridge, Mass.: Schenkman Publishing Co., 1981), p. x.

15. In this regard, see James N. Rosenau, *The Adaptation of National Societies: A Theory of Political System Behavior and Transformation* (New York: McCaleb-Seisler Publishing Co., 1970).

16. See Alexander Gershenkron, *Economic Backwardness in Historical Perspective* (Cambridge, Mass.: Harvard University Press, 1963).

17. Immanuel Wallerstein, *The Capitalist World-Economy: Essays* (New York: Cambridge University Press, 1979).

18. Leroy P. Jones and Il Sakong, *Government, Business and Entrepreneurship in Economic Development: The Korean Case* (Cambridge, Mass.: Harvard University Council on East Asian Studies, 1980).

19. For a symposium discussion on the question of capitalism, socialism, and democracy in the modern era that has implications for the study of North and South Korean politics, see "Capitalism, Socialism, and Democracy: A Symposium," *Commentary* 65, 4 (April 1978):29–70.

20. This theme of political stability enabling economic development in South Korea underlies the Harvard University Institute for International Development and Korea Development Institute seven-volume joint series, *Studies in the Modernization of the Republic of Korea, 1945–1975*. For comprehensive reviews of this study, see Karl Moskowitz, "Korean Development and Korean Studies—A Review Article," and David I. Steinberg, "Development Lessons from the Korean Experience—A Review Article," *Journal of Asian Studies* 42, 1 (November 1982):63–90 and 91–104 respectively.

21. For an interesting recent discussion of South Korea's social trends, see Vincent S. R. Brandt, "Social Trends, Environmental Factors, Political Culture and National Integration in South Korea" (Prepared for the Hudson Institute Workshop on "Future Prospects for the Korean Peninsula in a World Context," June 12–15, 1982, and for the Columbia University Seminar on Korea, December 1982).

22. On the political participation of the South Korean citizenry, see Chong Lim Kim, ed., *The Political Participation in Korea: Democracy, Mobilization, and Stability* (Santa Barbara, Calif.: Clio Press, 1980); and a special issue on the Symposium on Political Participation in Korea, *Journal of Korean Studies* 1 (1979).

23. Brandt, "Social Trends."
24. Ibid., p. 25.
25. Moskowitz, "Korean Development," pp. 71, 86.
26. Brandt, "Social Trends," p. 25.
27. Gari Ledyard, "To Dream the Impossible Dream: Korean Unification" (Prepared for the Conference on a Century of United States–Korean Relations, Woodrow Wilson Center, Washington, D.C., June 1982).

Abbreviations

ADC	advanced developing country
ASEAN	Association of Southeast Asian Nations
CCNR	Consultative Conference for National Reunification
CCP	Chinese Communist Party
COMECON	Council of Mutual Economic Assistance
CPSU	Communist Party of the Soviet Union
DCRK	Democratic Confederal Republic of Koryo
DIU	Down-with-Imperialism Union
DJP	Democratic Justice Party
DKP	Democratic Korea Party
DmZ	Demilitarized Zone
DPRK	Democratic People's Republic of Korea
DRP	Democratic Republican Party
EPB	Economic Planning Board
FBIS	Foreign Broadcast Information Service
IISS	International Institute for Strategic Studies
IPU	Inter-Parliamentary Union
JPRS	Joint Publications Research Service
JSP	Japan Socialist Party
KCIA	Korean Central Intelligence Agency
KDP	Korean Democratic Party
KIP	Korean Independence Party
KNP	Korea National Party

KPA	Korean People's Army
KPG	Korean Provisional Government
KWP	Korean Workers' Party (or Workers' Party of Korea)
LDC	less-developed country
LDP	Liberal Democratic Party (Japan)
NDP	New Democratic Party
NIC	newly industrializing country
OECD	Organization for Economic Cooperation and Development
OPEC	Organization of Petroleum Exporting Countries
PLO	Palestine Liberation Organization
PRC	People's Republic of China
ROK	Republic of Korea
SKWP	South Korean Workers' Party
SPA	Supreme People's Assembly
TRT	Three Revolutions Teams
UDRK	United Democratic Republic of Korea
UNDP	United Nations Development Program
UNESCO	United Nations Educational, Scientific and Cultural Organization
USAFIK	United States Armed Forces in Korea
USAMGIK	United States Army Military Government in Korea
WHO	World Health Organization (UN)

Bibliography

PRIMARY SOURCES

Official Publications and Documents

Democratic People's Republic of Korea (DPRK). *The Building of an Independent National Economy in Korea*. Pyongyang: Foreign Languages Publishing House, 1977.

_____. *The Bylaws of the Workers' Party of Korea*. Pyongyang: Korean Workers' Party, 1970. In Dae-Sook Suh, *Korean Communism: 1945-1980: A Reference Guide to the Political System*, pp. 525-544. Honolulu: University Press of Hawaii, 1981.

_____. *Facts Tell*. Pyongyang: Foreign Languages Publishing House, 1960.

_____. *On the Socialist Constitution of the Democratic People's Republic of Korea*. Pyongyang: Foreign Languages Publishing House, 1975.

International Institute for Strategic Studies (IISS). *The Military Balance 1981-1982*. London: IISS, 1982.

Japan Self-Defense Force. *Boei hakusho* [Defense white paper]. Tokyo: Japan Government Publications Center, 1980.

Organization for Economic Cooperation and Development (OECD). *The Impact of the Newly Industrializing Countries on Production and Trade in Manufactures*. Report by the Secretary-General. Paris: OECD, 1979.

Republic of Korea (ROK). *Economic Comparison Between South and North Korea 1977*. Seoul: Research Center for Peace and Unification, 1977.

_____. *A Handbook of Korea*. Seoul: Korean Overseas Information Service, 1979.

_____. *A Statistical Comparison Between South and North Korea*. Seoul: Korean Overseas Information Service, 1978.

_____. *A White Paper on South-North Dialogue in Korea*. Seoul: South-North Coordinating Committee, Seoul Side, 1979.

U.S. Central Intelligence Agency (CIA). *Korea: The Economic Race Between the North and the South: A Research Paper*. Washington, D.C.: National Foreign Assessment Center and the Library of Congress, 1978.

U.S. Congress. House. Committee on Foreign Affairs. *Hearing on H. Rept. 5330, Korea Aid*. 81st Cong., 1st Sess. Washington, D.C.: Government Printing Office, 1959.

_____. *The Korean Conundrum: A Conversation with Kim Il Sung, Report of a Study Mission to South Korea, Japan, the People's Republic of China and North Korea, July 12-21, 1980*. 97th Cong., 1st Sess. Washington, D.C.: Government Printing Office, 1981.

U.S. Congress. House. Subcommittee on International Organizations of the Committee on International Relations. *Report on Investigation of Korean-American Relations.* 95th Cong., 2d Sess. Washington, D.C.: Government Printing Office, 1978.

U.S. Congress. Senate. Committee on Foreign Relations. *U.S. Troop Withdrawal from the Republic of Korea, A Report to the Committee by Senators Hubert H. Humphrey and John Glenn, January 9, 1978.* 95th Cong., 2d Sess. Washington, D.C.: Government Printing Office, 1978.

U.S. Department of the Army. *Korea 1950.* Prepared by Walter G. Hermes, Office of the Chief of Military History. Washington, D.C.: Government Printing Office, 1952.

———. *U.S. Army in the Korean War, Truce Tent and Fighting Front.* Prepared by Walter G. Hermes, Office of the Chief of Military History. Washington, D.C.: Government Printing Office, 1965.

———. *United States Army in the Korean War: South to Naktong, North to the Yalu.* Prepared by Roy E. Appleman, Office of the Chief of Military History. Washington, D.C.: Government Printing Office, 1961.

U.S. Department of State. *Foreign Relations of the United States.* 8 vols. Vol. 4, "The British Commonwealth and the Far East." Washington, D.C.: Government Printing Office, 1969.

———. Foreign Relations of the United States, Diplomatic Papers, *The Conference of Berlin, 1945,* 2 vols. Washington, D.C.: Government Printing Office, 1960.

———. Foreign Relations of the United States, Diplomatic Papers, *The Conferences at Cairo and Teheran, 1943.* Washington, D.C.: Government Printing Office, 1961.

———. *In Quest of Peace and Security: Selected Documents on American Foreign Policy, 1941–1951.* Washington, D.C.: Government Printing Office, 1951.

———. *Korea, 1945–1948.* Washington, D.C.: Government Printing Office, 1948.

———. *North Korea: A Case Study in the Techniques of Takeover.* Washington, D.C.: Government Printing Office, 1961.

———. *The Record of Korean Unification 1943–1960.* Washington, D.C.: Government Printing Office, 1960.

U.S. General Headquarters, Far East Command. *Research Supplement: Documentary Evidence of North Korean Aggression.* October 30, 1950, folder, MacArthur Memorial. Cited in Harold Joyce Noble, *Embassy at War,* p. 315. Seattle: University of Washington Press, 1975.

World Bank. *World Bank Atlas.* Washington, D.C.: World Bank, 1981.

———. *World Development Report 1982.* Washington, D.C.: World Bank, 1982.

Memoirs and Reports

Khrushchev, Nikita. *Khrushchev Remembers.* Introduction, commentary, and notes by Edward Crankshaw; translated and edited by Strobe Talbott. Boston: Little, Brown & Co., 1970.

Kim, Hyong-wuk. *Kwonryokkwa ummo: Chon-KCIAbujang Kim Hyong-wukui suki* [Power and conspiracy: Ex-KCIA chief Kim Hyong-wuk's account]. Toronto: New Korea Times Co., 1982.

Kim, Il Sung. *For the Independent Peaceful Reunification of Korea.* Rev. ed. New York: Weekly Guardian Associates, 1976.

———. "Let Us Vivaciously Develop the Three Great Revolutions and Further Accelerate the Socialist Construction." *Kulloja* [The Workers], March 1975.
———. "On Eliminating Dogmatism and Formalism and Establishing Juche in Ideological Work." Speech to party propagandists and agitators, December 28, 1955. Reported in Kim Il Sung, *On the Building of the Workers' Party of Korea* 2:71–98. Pyongyang: Foreign Languages Publishing House, 1978.
———. *On the Juche Idea*. Pyongyang: Foreign Languages Publishing House, 1979.
———. *Report to the Sixth Congress of the Workers' Party of Korea on the Work of the Central Committee,* October 10, 1980. Pyongyang: Foreign Languages Publishing House, 1980.
———. *Selected Works*. Vol. 4. Pyongyang: Foreign Languages Publishing House, 1971.
———. *Tasks of the People's Government in Modelling the Whole of Society on Juche Idea*. Speech at the joint meeting of the KWP Central Committee and the DPRK Supreme People's Assembly on April 14, 1982. Text issued by the DPRK Permanent Observer Mission to the UN, Press Release No. 32 (April 15, 1982).
Kissinger, Henry. *White House Years*. Boston: Little, Brown & Co., 1979.
Park, Chung Hee. *Korea Reborn: A Model for Development*. Englewood Cliffs, N.J.: Prentice-Hall, 1979.
———. *Pak Chong-hi taet'ongryong ui chido inyom kwa hengdong ch'olhak* [The leadership principles and the action philosophy of president Park Chung Hee]. Seoul: Maeil Kyongje Sinmunsa, 1977.
———. *Toward Peaceful Unification*. Seoul: Kwangmyong Publishing Co., 1976.
Truman, Harry S. *Memoirs by Harry S. Truman*. Vol. 2, *Years of Trial and Hope*. New York: Doubleday and Co., 1956.

Newspapers and Periodicals

Korean and Japanese Language

Asahi Shimbun (Tokyo).
Chungang Ilbo (Seoul).
Dokrip Sinmun [Korea Independent Monitor] (Philadelphia).
Dong-A Ilbo (Seoul).
Hanguk Ilbo (Seoul).
Korea Hyoron (Tokyo).
Minju Chosun (Pyongyang).
Naewoe Tongsin (Seoul).
Nodong Sinmun (Pyongyang). *Nodong Sinmun* is the organ of the Central Committee of the Korean Workers' Party.
Sankei Shimbun (Tokyo).
Shincho (Tokyo).

English Language

Asia Yearbook 1982 (Hong Kong).
Des Moines Register (Des Moines).
Far Eastern Economic Review (Hong Kong).
Korea's Economy (Korea Economic Institute, Washington, D.C.).

Korea Herald (Seoul).
Korea Times (Seoul).
Korea Today (Pyongyang).
New York Times (New York).
People's Daily (Beijing).
Press Releases, DPRK Permanent Observer Mission to the United Nations (New York).
Pyongyang Times (Pyongyang).
Vantage Points: Development in North Korea (Seoul).

SECONDARY SOURCES

Books and Monographs

Korean and Japanese Language

Choe, Jae-suk. *Han'gukinui sahoejok songkyok* [Social character of the Koreans]. Seoul: Kaemunsa, 1976.
Ch'on, Gum-song. *Hwanggang eso Puk'ak kiseul kkaji: Ingan Chon Du-hwan* [From the Hwang River to Puk'ak Mountain: The man Chun Doo Hwan]. Seoul: Tongso Munhwasa, 1981.
Han, Seung-jo. *Hanguk minjuchuuiwa chongch'i palchon* [Korean democracy and political development]. Seoul: Popmunsa, 1976.
Hayashi, Takehiko. *Kita Chosen to Minami Chosen* [North Korea and South Korea]. Tokyo: Saimaru Press, 1971.
Kim, Ch'ang-sun. *Pukhan sip-o-nyonsa* [Fifteen-year history of North Korea]. Seoul: Chimungak, 1961.
Kim, Ch'ang-sun et al. *Pukhan chongch'iron* [On North Korean politics]. Seoul: Kukdong Munje Yon'guso, 1976; and Pukhan Yon'guso, 1979.
Kim, Un-t'ai et al. *Han'guk chongch'iron* [On Korean politics]. Seoul: Pakyongsa, 1976.
Koh, Byung Chul, Se-Jin Kim, Jae Kyu Park, Young-Ho Lee, and Chang-Yoon Choi. *Pukhan oekyo-ron* [On North Korea's foreign policy]. Seoul: Kyong Nam University Press, 1977.
Kokusai Kankei Kyodo Genkyusho, ed. *Kita Chosen: Seshu teki shakaishugi no kuni* [North Korea: Hereditary socialist country]. Tokyo: Seikatusu Shobo, 1978.
Lee, Chong-Sik. *Ingan Kim Jae-kyu* [The life of Kim Jae-kyu]. Paoli, Pa., 1980.
Tamaki, Motoi. *Chosen minshushugi jinminkyowakoku no jinwato genjitsu* [DPRK's myth and reality]. Tokyo: Koria Hyoronsha, 1978.
Yi, Ki-ha. *Han'guk chongdang paltalsa* [History of the development of political parties in Korea]. Seoul: Uihoe Chongch'isa, 1961.
Yim, Un [pseud.]. *Kita Chosen oocho seiritsu hishi: Kinnichisei seiten* [Secret history of the founding of North Korean dynasty: Kim Il Sung's true accounts]. Tokyo: Jiyusha, 1982.

English Language

Adwell, John C., and L. Frost. *The Korea Story*. Chicago: Henry Regnery Co., 1952.
Almond, Gabriel A., and G. Bingham Powell, Jr. *Comparative Politics: System, Processes and Policy*. 2d ed. Boston: Little, Brown & Co., 1978.

Almond, Gabriel, and Sidney Verba. *The Civic Culture*. Boston: Little, Brown & Co., 1963.
——— . *The Civic Culture Revisited*. Boston: Little, Brown & Co., 1980.
Badie, Bertrand, and Pierre Birnbaum. *The Sociology of the State*. Translated by Arthur Goldhammer. Chicago: University of Chicago Press, 1983.
Baik, Bong. *Kim Il Sung: Biography*. 3 vols. Tokyo: Miraisha, 1969–1970.
Baldwin, Frank, ed. *Without Parallel: The American-Korean Relations Since 1945*. New York: Pantheon Books, 1974.
Barnds, William, ed. *The Two Koreas in East Asian Affairs*. New York: New York University Press, 1976.
Brun, Ellen, and Jacques Hersh. *Socialist Korea: A Case Study in the Strategy of Economic Development*. New York: Monthly Review Press, 1976.
Brzezinski, Zbigniew, and Samuel P. Huntington. *Political Power: USA and USSR*. New York: Viking Press, 1967.
Bunge, Frederica M., ed. *North Korea; A Country Study*. Area Handbook Series of the U.S. Department of the Army. Washington, D.C.: Government Printing Office, 1981.
Carrier, Fred J. *North Korean Journey: The Revolution Against Colonialism*. New York: International Publishers, 1975.
Cho, Soon Sung. *Korea in World Politics, 1945–1950: An Evaluation of American Responsibility*. Berkeley and Los Angeles: University of California Press, 1967.
Chung, Chin O. *P'yongyang Between Peking and Moscow: North Korea's Involvement in the Sino-Soviet Dispute, 1958–1975*. University, Ala.: University of Alabama Press, 1978.
Chung, Henry. *The Russians Came to Korea*. Seoul and Washington, D.C.: Korean Pacific, 1947.
Chung, Joseph Sang-hoon. *The North Korean Economy: Structure and Development*. Stanford, Calif.: Hoover Institution Press, 1974.
Clough, Ralph N. *Deterrence and Defense in Korea: The Role of U.S. Forces*. Washington, D.C.: Brookings Institution, 1976.
Cole, David C., and Princeton N. Lyman. *Korean Development: The Interplay of Politics and Economics*. Cambridge, Mass.: Harvard University Press, 1971.
Coleman, James S. "Conclusion: The Political Systems of the Developing Areas." In Gabriel A. Almond and James S. Coleman, eds., *The Politics of the Developing Areas*, pp. 532–576. Princeton, N.J.: Princeton University Press, 1960.
Collier, David, ed. *The New Authoritarianism in Latin America*. Princeton, N.J.: Princeton University Press, 1979.
Coser, Lewis A. *The Functions of Social Conflict*. Glencoe, Ill.: Free Press, 1956.
Cumings, Bruce A. *The Origins of the Korean War: Liberation and the Emergence of Separate Regimes, 1945–1947*. Princeton, N.J.: Princeton University Press, 1981.
Dahl, Robert A. *Modern Political Analysis*. 2d ed. Englewood Cliffs, N.J.: Prentice-Hall, 1970.
Eckstein, Harry, ed. *Internal War: Problems and Approaches*. Glencoe, Ill.: Free Press, 1964.
Friedrich, Carl J., and Z. K. Brzezinski. *Totalitarian Dictatorship and Autocracy*. Cambridge, Mass.: Harvard University Press, 1965.
Gershenkron, Alexander. *Economic Backwardness in Historical Perspective*. Cambridge, Mass.: Harvard University Press, 1963.
Goodrich, Leland M. *Korea, A Study of U.S. Policy in the United Nations*. New York: Council on Foreign Relations, 1956.

Goulden, John. *Korea: The Untold Story of the War.* New York: Times Books, 1982.
Grajdanzev, Andrew J. *Modern Korea: Her Economic and Social Development Under the Japanese.* New York: Institute of Pacific Relations, 1944.
Han, Sung-Joo. *The Failure of Democracy in South Korea.* Berkeley and Los Angeles: University of California Press, 1974.
Harrison, Selig S. *The Widening Gulf: Asian Nationalism and American Policy.* New York: Free Press, 1978.
Hasan, Parvez. *Korea: Problems and Issues in a Rapidly Growing Economy.* Baltimore: Johns Hopkins University Press for the World Bank, 1976.
Hasan, Parvez, and D. C. Rao. *Korea: Policy Issues for Long-Term Development.* Baltimore: Johns Hopkins University Press for the World Bank, 1979.
Henderson, Gregory. *Korea: The Politics of the Vortex.* Cambridge, Mass.: Harvard University Press, 1968.
―――. "North and South Korea." In Steven L. Spiegel and Kenneth N. Waltz, eds., *Conflict in World Politics*, pp. 197–220. Cambridge, Mass.: Winthrop Publishers, 1971.
Hirschman, Albert. *The Passions and the Interests: Political Arguments for Capitalism Before Its Triumph.* Princeton, N.J.: Princeton University Press, 1977.
Hofheinz, Roy, Jr., and Kent E. Calden. *Eastasia Edge.* New York: Basic Books, 1982.
Huntington, Samuel P. *Political Order in Changing Societies.* New Haven, Conn.: Yale University Press, 1969.
Huntington, Samuel P., and Joan M. Nelson. *No Easy Choice: Political Participation in Developing Countries.* Cambridge, Mass.: Harvard University Press, 1976.
Hwang, In K. *The Neutralized Unification of Korea.* Cambridge, Mass.: Schenkman Publishing Co., 1980.
Ilchman, Warren F., and Norman T. Uphoff. *The Political Economy of Change.* Berkeley: University of California Press, 1969.
Jagribe, Helio. *Political Development: A General Theory and a Latin American Case Study.* New York: Harper & Row, 1973.
Jo, Sung-Hwan. "Direct Foreign Private Investment." In Chong-Kee Park, ed., *Macroeconomic and Industrial Development in Korea*, pp. 129–184. Seoul: Korea Development Institute, 1980.
Johnson, Stuart E. *The Military Equation in Northeast Asia.* Washington, D.C.: Brookings Institution, 1979.
Johnston, Ray, ed. *The Politics of Division, Partition and Unification.* New York: Praeger Publishers, 1976.
Jones, Leroy P., and Il Sakong. *Government, Business and Entrepreneurship in Economic Development: The Korean Case.* Cambridge, Mass.: Harvard University Council on East Asian Studies, 1980.
Kahn, Herman. *World Economic Development: 1979 and Beyond.* Boulder, Co.: Westview Press, 1979.
Keon, Michael. *Korean Phoenix: A Nation from the Ashes.* Englewood Cliffs, N.J.: Prentice-Hall, 1977.
Kihl, Young Whan. "Korean Response to Major Power Rapprochement." In Young C. Kim, ed., *Major Powers and Korea*, pp. 139–164. Silver Spring, Md.: Research Institute on Korean Affairs, 1973.
―――. "Linkage and Democratic Orientation of Party Elites in South Korea." In Kay Lawson, ed., *Political Parties and Linkage: A Comparative Perspective*, pp. 75–99. New Haven, Conn.: Yale University Press, 1980.

———. "Politics and Agrarian Change in South Korea: Rural Modernization by 'Induced' Mobilization." In Raymond Hopkins, Donald Puchala, and Ross Talbot, eds., *Food, Politics, and Agricultural Development: Case Studies in the Public Policy of Rural Modernization*, pp. 133-169. Boulder, Co.: Westview Press, 1979.
———. "Some Aspects of Political Participation and Culture of the Two Koreas." In Graciela de la Lama, ed., *Japan and Korea 2*, pp. 54-73. Mexico City: El Colegio de Mexico, 1982.
Kihl, Young Whan, Chong Lim Kim, and Seong-tong Pai. "Masses-Elite Linkage and Political Development in South Korea." In Graciela de la Lama, ed., *Japan and Korea 2*, pp. 122-140. Mexico City: El Colegio de Mexico, 1982.
Kim, Alexander Joungwon. *Divided Korea: The Politics of Development*. Cambridge, Mass.: Harvard University Press, 1975.
Kim, Byong-sik. *Modern Korea: The Socialist North, Revolutionary Perspectives in the South*. New York: International Publishers, 1970.
Kim, C. I. Eugene, ed. *A Pattern of Political Development: Korea*. Kalamazoo, Mich.: Korea Research Publications, 1964.
Kim, C. I. Eugene, and Young Whan Kihl, eds. *Party Politics and Elections in Korea*. Silver Spring, Md.: Research Institute on Korean Affairs, 1976.
Kim, C. I. Eugene, and Han-Kyo Kim. *Korea and the Politics of Imperialism: 1876-1911*. Berkeley and Los Angeles: University of California Press, 1967.
Kim, C. I. Eugene, and B. C. Koh, eds. *Journey to North Korea: Personal Perceptions*. Berkeley: University of California Institute of East Asian Studies, 1983.
Kim, Chi-ha. *Cry of the People and Other Poems*. Kanagawa-ken, Japan: Autumn Press, 1974.
Kim, Chong Lim, ed. *The Political Participation in Korea: Democracy, Mobilization, and Stability*. Santa Barbara, Calif.: Clio Press, 1980.
Kim, Chong Lim, and Seong-tong Pai. *Legislative Process in Korea*. Seoul: Seoul National University Press, 1981.
Kim, Hak-Joon. *The Unification Policy of South and North Korea: A Comparative Study*. Seoul: Seoul National University Press, 1977.
Kim, Han-Kyo, ed. *Studies on Korea: A Scholar's Guide*. Honolulu: University Press of Hawaii, 1980.
Kim, Ilpyong J. *Communist Politics in North Korea*. New York: Praeger Publishers, 1975.
Kim, Kwan-Bong. *The Korea-Japan Treaty Crisis and the Instability of the Korean Political System*. New York: Praeger Publishers, 1964.
Kim, Se-Jin. *The Politics of the Military Revolution in Korea*. Chapel Hill: University of North Carolina Press, 1971.
Kim, Se-Jin, ed. *Korean Unification: Source Materials with an Introduction*. Seoul: Research Center for Peace and Unification, 1976.
Kim, Se-Jin, and Chang-Hyun Cho, eds. *Government and Politics of Korea*. Silver Spring, Md.: Research Institute on Korean Affairs, 1972.
———. *Korea: A Divided Nation*. Silver Spring, Md.: Research Institute on Korean Affairs, 1976.
Kim, Young C., and Abraham M. Halpern, eds. *The Future of the Korean Peninsula*. New York: Praeger Publishers, 1977.
Korea Annual 1975. Seoul: Hapdong News Agency, 1975.
Korea Annual 1976. Seoul: Hapdong News Agency, 1976.
Korea: Executive Guide. New York: Citibank, 1982.

Kornhauser, William. *The Politics of Mass Society.* Glencoe, Ill.: Free Press, 1959.
Kuznets, Paul W. *Economic Growth and Structure in the Republic of Korea.* New Haven, Conn.: Yale University Press, 1977.
Lawson, Kay, ed. *Political Parties and Linkage: A Comparative Perspective.* New Haven, Conn.: Yale University Press, 1980.
Lee, Chong-Sik. *Korean Workers' Party: A Short History.* Stanford, Calif.: Hoover Institution Press, 1978.
―――. *The Politics of Korean Nationalism.* Berkeley and Los Angeles: University of California Press, 1965.
―――. "Stalinism in the East: Communism in North Korea." In Robert A. Scalapino, ed., *The Communist Revolution in Asia*, pp. 120–150. Englewood Cliffs, N.J.: Prentice-Hall, 1969.
Lee, Hahn-been. *Korea: Time, Change and Administration.* Honolulu: East-West Center Press, 1968.
Lee, Man-Gap, ed. *Toward a New Community: Reports of International Research-Seminar on the Saemaul Movement.* Seoul: Institute of Saemaul Undong Studies, for Seoul National University, 1981.
Lim, Un. *The Founding of a Dynasty in North Korea: An Authentic Biography of Kim Il-Sung.* Tokyo: Jiyusha, 1982.
McCormack, Gavan, and Mark Selden, eds. *Korea North and South: The Deepening Crisis.* New York: Monthly Review Press, 1978.
McCune, George M. *Korea Today.* Cambridge, Mass.: Harvard University Press, 1950.
Mason, Edward S. et al. *The Economic and Social Modernization of the Republic of Korea.* Cambridge, Mass.: Harvard University Council on East Asian Studies, 1980.
Mathieson, John A. *The ADCs: Emerging Actors in the World Economy.* Washington, D.C.: Overseas Development Council, 1979.
Mitchell, A. "South Korea: Vision of the Future for Labor Surplus Economies?" In Manfred Bienefeld and Martin Godfrey, eds., *The Struggle for Development: National Strategies in an International Context*, pp. 189–216. New York: John Wiley & Sons, 1982.
Moore, Barrington, Jr. *Social Origins of Dictatorship and Democracy: Lord and Peasant in the Making of the Modern World.* Boston: Beacon Press, 1966.
Nam, Koon Woo. *The North Korean Communist Leadership, 1945–1965: A Study of Factionalism and Political Consolidation.* University, Ala.: University of Alabama Press, 1974.
Noble, Harold Joyce. *Embassy at War.* Seattle: University of Washington Press, 1975.
O'Donnell, Guillermo A. *Modernization and Bureaucratic-Authoritarianism: Studies in South American Politics.* Berkeley: University of California Institute of International Studies, 1973 and 1979.
Oh, John Kie-Chiang. *Democracy on Trial.* Ithaca, N.Y.: Cornell University Press, 1968.
Oliver, Robert. *Syngman Rhee and American Involvement in Korea, 1942–1960: A Personal Narrative.* Seoul: Panmun Book Co., 1978.
Paige, Glenn D. *The Korean Decision: June 24–30, 1950.* New York: Free Press, 1968.
―――. *The Korean People's Democratic Republic.* Hoover Institution Series No. 11. Stanford, Calif.: Hoover Institution Press, 1966.

———. "North Korea and the Emulation of Russian and Chinese Behavior." In A. Doak Barnett, ed., *Communist Strategies in Asia: A Comparative Analysis of Governments and Parties*, pp. 228–261. New York: Praeger Publishers, 1963.

———. "Some Implications for Political Science of the Comparative Politics of Korea." In Fred W. Riggs, ed., *Frontiers of Development Administration*. Durham, N.C.: Duke University Press, 1970.

———. "Toward a Theory of Korean Political Leadership Behavior." In Dae-Sook Suh and Chae-Jin Lee, eds., *Political Leadership in Korea*, pp. 223–236. Seattle: University of Washington Press, 1976.

Palais, James B. "Democracy in South Korea, 1948–72." In Frank Baldwin, ed., *Without Parallel: The American-Korean Relations Since 1945*, pp. 318–357. New York: Pantheon Books, 1974.

———. *Politics and Policy in Traditional Korea*. Cambridge, Mass.: Harvard University Press, 1975.

Perlmutter, Amos. *Modern Authoritarianism: A Comparative Institutional Analysis*. New Haven, Conn.: Yale University Press, 1981.

Przeworski, Adam, and Henry Teune. *The Logic of Comparative Social Inquiry*. New York: John Wiley, 1969.

Pye, Lucian W., and Sidney Verba, eds. *Political Culture and Political Development*. Princeton, N.J.: Princeton University Press, 1965.

Reeve, W. D. *The Republic of Korea: A Political and Economic Study*. London: Oxford University Press, 1963.

Rosenau, James N. *The Adaptation of National Societies: A Theory of Political System Behavior and Transformation*. New York: McCaleb-Seisler Publishing Co., 1970.

———. "Theorizing Across Systems: Linkage Politics Revisited." In Jonathan Wilkenfeld, ed. *Conflict Behavior and Linkage Politics*. New York: David Mckay, 1973.

Rosenau, James N., ed. *Linkage Politics*. New York: Free Press, 1969.

Rudolph, Philip. *North Korea's Political and Economic Structure*. New York: Institute of Pacific Relations, 1959.

Sakamoto, Yoshikazu. *Korea as a World Order Issue*. World Order Models Project Occasional Paper No. 3. New York: Institute for World Order, 1978.

Salisbury, Harrison. *To Peking and Beyond: A Report on the New Asia*. New York: Quadrangle, 1973.

Scalapino, Robert A., and Chong-Sik Lee. *Communism in Korea*. 2 vols. Berkeley and Los Angeles: University of California Press, 1972.

Scalapino, Robert A. and Jun-Yop Kim, eds. *North Korea Today: Strategic and Domestic Issues*. Berkeley, Calif.: University of California Institute of East Asian Studies, 1983.

Scott, Bruce R., John W. Rosenblum, and Audrey T. Sproat. *Case Studies in Political Economy: Japan 1854–1977*. Cambridge, Mass.: Harvard Business School, 1980.

Seligman, Lester G. "Political Parties and the Recruitment of Political Leadership." In Lewis J. Edinger, ed., *Political Leadership in Industrialized Societies*, pp. 294–315. New York: John Wiley, 1967.

Simmons, Robert S. *The Strained Alliance: Peking, P'yongyang, Moscow and the Politics of the Korean Civil War*. New York: Free Press, 1975.

Solomon, Richard, ed. *Asian Security in the 1980s: Problems and Policies for a Time of Transition*. Santa Monica, Calif.: Rand Corporation, 1979.

Steinberg, David I. *The Economic Development of Korea: Sui Generis or Generic?* USAID Evaluation Special Study No. 6. Washington, D.C.: USAID, 1981.
Stepan, Alfred. *The State and Society: Peru in Comparative Perspective.* Princeton, N.J.: Princeton University Press, 1978.
Stone, I. F. *The Hidden History of the Korean War.* New York: Monthly Review Press, 1952.
Suh, Dae-Sook. "Communist Party Leadership." In Dae-Sook Suh and Chae-Jin Lee, eds., *Political Leadership in Korea,* pp. 159–191. Seattle: University of Washington Press, 1976.
―――. *Korean Communism: 1945–1980: A Reference Guide to the Political System.* Honolulu: University Press of Hawaii, 1981.
―――. *The Korean Communist Movement: 1918–1948.* Princeton, N.J.: Princeton University Press, 1970.
Suh, Dae-Sook, and Chae-Jin Lee, eds. *Political Leadership in Korea.* Seattle: University of Washington Press, 1976.
Vreeland, Nena, Rinn-Sup Shinn, Peter Just, and Philip W. Moeller. *Area Handbook for North Korea.* Washington, D.C.: Government Printing Office, 1976.
Vreeland, Nena, Peter Just, Kenneth W. Martindale, Philip W. Moeller, and Rinn-Sup Shinn. *Area Handbook for South Korea.* Washington, D.C.: Government Printing Office, 1975.
Wagner, Edward W. *The Literati Purges: Political Conflict in Early Yi Korea.* Cambridge, Mass.: East Asian Research Center, distributed by Harvard University Press, 1974.
Wallerstein, Immanuel. *The Capitalist World-Economy: Essays.* New York: Cambridge University Press, 1979.
Weber, Max. *The Theory of Social and Economic Organization.* Translated by A. Henderson and Talcott Parsons. New York: Oxford University Press, 1947.
Weems, Benjamin B. *Reform, Rebellion, and the Heavenly Way.* Tucson: University of Arizona Press, for the Association for Asian Studies, 1964.
Weinstein, Franklin B., and Fuji Kamiya, eds. *The Security of Korea: U.S. and Japanese Perspectives on the 1980s.* Boulder, Co.: Westview Press, 1980.
White, Gordon. "North Korean Juche: The Political Economy of Self-Reliance." In Manfred Bienefeld and Martin Godfrey, eds., *The Struggle for Development: National Strategies in an International Context,* pp. 323–354. New York: John Wiley & Sons, 1982.
Wriggins, W. Howard. *The Ruler's Imperatives: Strategies for Political Survival in Asia and Africa.* New York: Columbia University Press, 1969.
Wright, Edward, ed. *Korean Politics in Transition.* Seattle: University of Washington Press, 1975.
Yang, Sung Chul. *Korea and Two Regimes: Kim Il Sung and Park Chung Hee.* Cambridge, Mass.: Schenkman Publishing Co., 1981.

Periodicals

Korean and Japanese Language

Bark, Dong-Suh, and Young Whan Kihl, "Shiknyang chongch'ek suripkwa iheng: Hangukui kyongu" [Food policy making and implementation: The Korean case]. *Korean Journal of Public Administration* (Seoul) 17, 2 (1979):214–234.
Han, Bae-ho. "Nampukhanui chongch'i ch'eje pikyo sosol 1 & 2" [Toward a comparative analysis of the South and North Korean political systems, 1 &

2]. *Asea Yŏn'gu* (Seoul) 14, 3 (September 1971):3-48; and 15, 1 (March 1972):1-19.

Kim, Chong Lim, Young Whan Kihl, and Seong-tong Pai, "Han'guk chongch'i munhwae danch'eung" [Segmentation of Korea's political culture]. *Wolgan Chungang* (Seoul), March 1977, pp. 124-135.

_____. "Sahoe pulsin p'ungjowa chongch'i munhwa" [Social distrust and political culture]. *Sintong'a* 134 (October 1975):86-99.

Tamaki, Motoi. "Chosen Rodoto dairokkaidaikai no mondaiten" [KWP sixth party congress: Problem areas]. *Koria Hyoron*, December 1980, January 1981, February 1981, and March 1981 issues.

English Language

Baldwin, Frank. "Participatory Anti-Imperialism: The 1919 Independence Movement." *Journal of Korean Studies* 1 (1979):123-162.

Breidenstein, Gerhard, and W. Rosenberg, "Economic Comparison of North and South Korea." *Journal of Contemporary Asia* 5, 2 (1975):165-203.

"Capitalism, Socialism, and Democracy: A Symposium." *Commentary* 65, 4 (April 1978):29-70.

Clemens, Walter C. "GRIT at Panmunjom: Conflict and Cooperation in a Divided Korea." *Asian Survey* 13, 6 (June 1973):531-559.

Clippinger, Morgan. "Kim Chong-il in the North Korean Mass Media: A Study of Semi-Esoteric Communication." *Asian Survey* 21, 3 (March 1981):289-309.

Cumings, Bruce G. "Is Korea a Mass Society?" *Occasional Papers on Korea: Number One*. Edited by James B. Palais for the Joint Committee on Korean Studies of the American Council of Learned Societies and the Social Science Research Council, April 1974, pp. 65-81.

_____. "Kim's Korean Communism." *Problems of Communism* 23 (March-April 1974):27-41.

Cumings, Bruce G., ed. "Imperialism and Repression: The Case of South Korea." Special supplement, *Bulletin of Concerned Asian Scholars* 9, 2 (April-June 1977):2-41.

Cutright, Phillips. "National Political Development: Measurement and Analysis." *American Sociological Review* 27 (April 1963):253-264.

Foster-Carter, Adrian. "North Korea: Development and Self-Reliance, A Critical Appraisal." *Bulletin of Concerned Asian Scholars* 9, 1 (January-March 1977):45-57.

Fry, Michael G., and Arthur N. Gilbert. "A Historian and Linkage Politics." *International Studies Quarterly* 26, 3 (September 1982):425-444.

Galtung, Johan. "Divided Nations as Process: One State, Two States, and In-Between: The Case of Korea." *Journal of Peace Research* 9 (1972):345-360.

Goldsmith, Arthur. "Popular Participation in South Korea's New Community Movement." *Rural Development Participation Review* (Cornell University Rural Development Committee, Ithaca, N.Y.) 3, 3 (Spring 1982):1-7.

Gourevitch, Peter. "The Second Image Reversed: The International Sources of Domestic Politics." *International Organization* 32, 4 (Autumn 1978):881-912.

Grey, Arthur L., Jr. "The Thirty Eighth Parallel." *Foreign Affairs* 29, 3 (April 1951):482-487.

Hahn, Bae-ho. "The Parties and Politics in Two Koreas: A Preliminary Analysis." *Proceedings of the International Conference on the Problems of Korean Unification.* Seoul: Asiatic Research Center, Korea University, 1971.

Hahn, Bae-ho, and Kyu-taik Kim. "Korean Political Leaders (1952–62): Their Social Origins and Skills." *Asian Survey* 3, 7 (July 1963):305–323.

Halliday, Jon. "The Korean War: Some Notes on Evidence and Solidarity." *Bulletin of Concerned Asian Scholars* 11, 3 (July-September 1979):2–18.

Harrison, Selig S. "One Korea?" *Foreign Policy* 17 (Winter 1974-1975):35–62.

Hunter, Helen-Louise. "North Korea and the Myth of Equidistance." *Korea and World Affairs* 4, 2 (Summer 1980):268–269.

Kang, Sugwon. "The Politics and Poetry of Kim Chi-ha." *Bulletin of Concerned Asian Scholars* 9, 2 (April-June 1977):3–7.

Kihl, Young Whan. "Leadership and Opposition Role Perception Among Party Elites in Korea." *Asian Forum* 5, 3 (July-September 1973):17–42. Also in *Korea Journal* 13, 9 (September 1973):3–22.

_____. "Local Elites, Power Structure and Legislative Process in Korea." *Journal of Korean Studies* 3 (1981):147–180.

_____. "Korea's Future: Seoul's Perspective." *Asian Survey* 17, 11 (November 1977):1064–1076.

_____. "The Nixon Doctrine and South-North Korea Relations." *Korean Journal of International Studies* 4, 3/4 (October 1973):105–123.

_____. "North Korea: A Reevaluation." *Current History* 81, 474 (April 1982):155–159, 180–182.

Kihl, Young Whan, and Dong-Suh Bark. "Food Policies in a Rapidly Developing Country: The Case of South Korea." *Journal of Developing Areas* 16, 1 (October 1981):47–80.

Kim, C. I. Eugene. "The Meanings of 1971 Korean Elections: A Pattern of Political Development." *Asian Survey* 12, 3 (March 1972):213–224.

_____. "Patterns in the 1967 Korean Elections." *Pacific Affairs* 41, 1 (Spring 1968):60–70.

_____. "Personalism in North Korea." *Problems of Communism*, January-February 1978, pp. 64–67.

_____. "Significance of the 1963 Korean Elections." *Asian Survey* 4, 3 (March 1964):765–773.

Kim, Chong Lim, and Byung-kyu Woo. "Intra-Elite Cleavages in the Korean National Assembly." *Asian Survey* 11, 6 (June 1971):544–561.

_____. "Social and Political Background of Korean National Assemblymen: The Seventh National Assembly." *Asian Forum* 3 (July-September 1971):123–137.

Kim Ilpyong J., and Dong-bok Lee. "After Kim: Who and What in North Korea." *World Affairs* 142, 4 (Spring 1980):246–267.

Kim, Samuel S. "Research on Korean Communism: Promise Versus Performance." *World Politics* 32, 2 (January 1980):281–310.

Kim, Young C. "North Korea in 1980: The Son Also Rises." *Asian Survey* 21, 1 (January 1981):112–124.

Koh, B. C. "Chuch'esong in Korean Politics." *Studies in Comparative Communism* 7, 1 and 2 (Spring and Summer 1974):83–97.

_____. "Convergence and Conflict in the Two Koreas." *Current History*, November 1973, pp. 205–208.

_____. "The Korean Workers' Party and Detente." *Journal of International Affairs* 28, 2 (1974):175–187.

Ledyard, Gari K. "The Historical Necessity of Korean Unification: Past History, Present Imperatives, Future Prospects." *Journal of International Studies* (Seoul) 4, 2 (1975):39–51.
Lee, Chong-Sik. "Evolution of the Korean Workers' Party and the Rise of Kim Chong-il." *Asian Survey* 22, 5 (May 1982):434–448.
―――. "South Korea in 1980: The Emergence of a New Authoritarian Order." *Asian Survey* 31, 1 (January 1981):125–143.
―――. "South Korea 1979: Confrontation, Assassination, and Transition." *Asian Survey* 20, 1 (January 1980):63–76.
Lee, Young-Ho. "Military Balance and Peace in the Korean Peninsula." *Asian Survey* 21, 8 (August 1981):852–864.
Lipset, Seymour Martin. "Some Social Requisites of Democracy: Economic Development and Political Legitimacy." *American Political Science Review* 53 (March 1959):69–105.
McCormack, Gavan. "North Korea: Kimilsungism: Path to Socialism?" *Bulletin of Concerned Asian Scholars* 13, 4 (October-December 1981):50–61.
McCune, Shannon. "The Thirty-Eighth Parallel in Korea." *World Politics* 1, 2 (January 1949):223–232.
Moskowitz, Karl. "The Creation of the Oriental Development Company: Japanese Illusions Meet Korean Reality." *Occasional Papers on Korea: Number Two*. Edited by James B. Palais for the Joint Committee on Korean Studies of the American Council of Learned Societies and the Social Science Research Council, March 1974, pp. 73–121.
―――. "Korean Development and Korean Studies—A Review Article." *Journal of Asian Studies* 42, 1 (November 1982):63–90.
Nakagawa, Nobuo. "Problems Confronting the Struggle for Democratization in Korea." *Gekkan Shakaito* [Socialist Party Monthly] (Tokyo), August 1981, as reported in JPRS 79290, October 23, 1981. Korean Affairs Report No. 167, pp. 22–31.
Niksch, Larry. "U.S. Troop Withdrawal from South Korea: Past Shortcomings and Future Prospects." *Asian Survey* 21, 3 (March 1981):325–341.
O'Donnell, Guillermo. "Reflections on the Patterns of Change in the Bureaucratic Authoritarian State." *Latin American Research Review* 8, 1 (1978):3–38.
Oppenheimer, Joe A. "Small Steps Forward for Political Economy." *World Politics* 33, 1 (October 1980):121–151.
Porter, Gareth. "Time to Talk with North Korea." *Foreign Policy* 34 (Spring 1979):52–73.
Rhee, Yong-P'il. "Characteristics of North Korean Political System." *Unification Policy Quarterly* (Seoul) 4, 3 (Autumn 1978):16–33.
Scalapino, Robert A. "Current Dynamics of the Korean Peninsula." *Problems of Communism* 30, 6 (November-December 1981):16–31.
Skocpol, Theda. "Bringing the State Back In." *Items* 36, 1/2 (June 1982):1–8.
Steinberg, David I. "Development Lessons from the Korean Experience—A Review Article." *Journal of Asian Studies* 42, 1 (November 1982):91–104.
Suh, Dae-Sook. "North Korea 1978: The Beginning of the Final Push." *Asian Survey* 19, 1 (January 1979):51–57.
"Symposium: Political Participation in Korea." Speical issue, *Journal of Korean Studies* 1 (1979):73–223.
Wallerstein, Immanuel. "Semiperipheral Countries and the Contemporary World Crisis." *Theory and Society* 3 (Winter 1976):461–483.

White, Gordon. "North Korean Chuch'e: The Political Economy of Independence." *Bulletin of Concerned Asian Scholars* 7, 2 (April-June 1975):44–54.

Unpublished Sources

Choi, Sung-il. "A Typological Model of Political Development: Korea as a Preliminary Test." Ph.D. diss. Lawrence: University of Kansas, 1971.
Ha, Young-sun. "Nuclearization of Small States and World Order: The Case of Korea." Ph.D. diss. Seattle: University of Washington, 1979.
Kihl, Young Whan. "Political Institutions and Participation in the Two Koreas: Comparisons." Prepared for presentation at a workshop sponsored by the Joint Committee on Korean Studies, Social Science Research Council, and American Council of Learned Societies, San Juan, Puerto Rico, January 16–17, 1976.
Kim, Chong Lim. "Elite Political Culture: Cognitive Dimension." Typescript, n.d.
Kim, Han-Kyo. "Korea and Comparative Political Studies." Mimeo. Prepared for presentation at a panel organized by the Association of Korean Political Scientists in North America in conjunction with the Annual Convention of the American Political Science Association, September 3–5, 1982, Denver, Colorado.
Kim, Jai-hyup. "The Political Involvement of Military Elites: A Comparative Study of a 'Garrison State' in Japan during the 1930s and 1940s and Korea during the 1960s and 1970s." Ph.D. diss. Indiana University, 1976.
Ledyard, Gari. "To Dream the Impossible Dream: Korean Unification." Prepared for the Conference on a Century of United States–Korean Relations, Woodrow Wilson Center, Washington, D.C., June 1982.
Lee, Dong-bok. "Hereditary Succession in North Korea and Its Impact on Inter-Korean Relations." Mimeo. Prepared for presentation at the Second International Symposium on Korea at La Trobe University, Melbourne, Australia, November 20–22, 1980.
Lee, Young-Ho. "The Political Culture of Modernizing Society: Political Attitudes and Democracy in Korea." Ph.D. diss. New Haven, Conn.: Yale University, 1969.
―――. "South Korea's Unification Policy." Mimeo. Prepared for presentation at the International Workshop on Korean Unification: Analysis, Evaluation, and Prescription, at Hotel Sorak Park, Sokcho, Korea, November 21–23, 1981.
Loo, Robert Kalei Wah Kit. "A Comparative Study of Governmental Treatment of Interest Groups in South Korea and North Korea, 1954–1964." Ph.D. diss. New York: New York University, 1970.
Renick, Roderick Dhu, Jr., "Political Communication: A Case Study of U.S. Propaganda in North Korea and South Korea." Ph.D. diss. New Orleans: Tulane University, 1971.
Robinson, Richard D. "Korea: The Betrayal of a Nation." Typescript, 1947.
Winn, Gregory F. T. "Arms, Attitudes and Decisions: The Probability of Conflict in North East Asia with Particular Emphasis on the Korean Peninsula." Ph.D. diss. Los Angeles: University of Southern California, 1979.
Yim, Dong-jae. "Factional Ties in Seventeenth-Century Korea: A Reevaluation of Traditional Concepts." Ph.D. diss. Cambridge, Mass.: Harvard University, 1976.
Yoo, Han-jong. "The Two Koreas: A Comparative Political Analysis of a Divided Nation." Ph.D. diss. New York: New York University, 1977.

Index

Ade, Shintaro, 194
Afghanistan, 190, 196
Agreement on Basic Relations between South and North Korea, 219–220
Agriculture
 collectivization in, 46
Almond, Gabriel, 12
An, Seug-tak, 186
Angola, 197
Antigua, 152
Arms race, 145–150
Arms sales
 by DPRK, 197–198, 276(n104)
Artists
 in DPRK, 100
ASEAN. *See* Association of Southeast Asian Nations
Asian Games, 177, 221
Association of Southeast Asian Nations (ASEAN), 176
Authoritarianism
 in DPRK, 65–72, 101–104, 231–234
 in ROK, 59–65, 72, 101, 103–104, 231–234
"Authority inflation," 232, 233, 278(n1), 278(n2)

Baldwin, Frank, 40
Banking industry
 in ROK, 273(n24)
Benin, 197
Blue House attack, 51
Bonesteel, C. H., III, 30
Brandt, Vincent, 243
Brezhnev, Leonid, 91

Brunei, 198
Brzezinski, Z. K., 102
Bureaucratic authoritarianism, 6, 102–103, 121
Burma, 176–177, 198–199
Bush, George, 173

Cairo conference, 29
"Campaign to Capture the Red Flag of the Three Revolutions," 184
Canada, 176
Capitalism, xii, 7, 11, 131, 232, 240–241
Carter, Jimmy, 68, 173, 192, 211
CCNR. *See* Consultative Conference for National Reunification
CCP. *See* Chinese Communist Party
Central African Republic, 197
Cha, Ji-chol, 76
Ch'a, Kyu-ho, 80
Ch'ae, Hi-chong, 186
Chae, Mun-shik, 166
Chang, Myon, 19, 48, 49, 250(n12)
Chang, Taek-sang, 35
Chang, To-yong, 36
Chang, Yong-ja, 164
Chayu-Minjok Dang (Free Nationalist Party), 264(n30)
Chiang, Jing-kuo, 128
Chiang Kai-shek, 29, 40, 128
Chin, Iee-chong, 166, 179, 211
China. *See* People's Republic of China
Chinese Communist Party (CCP), 56, 91
Cho, Man-sik, 33, 34, 43

297

Cho, Pyong-ok, 35
Choe, Ch'ang-ik, 45
Ch'oe, Yong-gwon, 34, 97
Ch'ollima movement, 117, 184, 267(n34)
Chon, T'ae-il, 264(n34)
Chong, Il-gwon, 36
Ch'onggye Clothing Workers Labor Union, 264(n34)
Chongsanri method, 118, 267(n34)
Choson inmin konghwaguk, 32
Choson Munhak, 95
Choson Yesul, 95
Choy, Kyu Ha, 77, 79, 80
Chuch'e. *See Juche*
Chuji, Kuno, 194, 195
Chun Doo Hwan, 16, 74, 75, 80, 83, 84, 118, 120, 233, 243, 268(n54), 272(n6)
  assassination attempt against, 177, 178–179, 195, 198–199, 211
  assumption of power by, 78–79
  DJP and, 85–86
  economic devleopment and, 168, 170–171
  economic policy of, 131–132, 165
  foreign policy of, 172–179
  international opposition to, 278(n43)
  "new unification formula" of, 161
  opposition to, 85, 87–90, 163, 166–167, 172, 278(n43)
  on party activities, 272(n5)
  personal history of, 122–126
  political development and, 161–163
  power base of, 84
  power consolidation by, 81, 82, 84, 160–161, 163–164, 165, 166
  reunification and, 41, 211, 212, 213, 216–220, 222–224, 225, 273(n43)
  U.S. and, 193
Chung, Ho-yung, 80, 84, 263(n13)
Chung, Seung-hwa, 77, 78
Chun-kuk, Hyon, 194
Churchill, Winston, 29
Civil unrest, 20–22, 128–129
  in ROK, 51, 64–65, 76, 77, 79, 88–89, 244–245
Civil War. *See* Korean War
Cold War, xi, 28, 31–32, 52, 157, 159, 196, 239

Collectivization
  in DPRK, 46
COMECON. *See* Council of Mutual Economic Assistance
Committee for Peaceful Unification of the Fatherland, 222
Commodity prices
  in DPRK, 100–101
Communism, xii–xiii, 6, 108, 127–128
  in ROK, 212
Communist Party of the Soviet Union (CPSU), 91
Confederal Republic of Koryo, 224–225
Confucianism, 16, 108, 127, 141, 158, 237–238, 243
Constabulary Forces, 35–36
Consultative Conference for National Reunification (CCNR), 161, 218–219, 225, 228
Corporatism, 8
Council of Mutual Economic Assistance (COMECON), 136
CPSU. *See* Communist Party of the Soviet Union
Cross-recognition, 174–175. *See also* North-South dialogue
Cuba, 236
Cultural tradition, 237–238. *See also* Political culture
Cumings, Bruce, 109, 117, 255(n23)

Daewoo business group, 201
DCRK. *See* Democratic Confederal Republic of Koryo
Defense, 145–150
  spending, 146–147
  See also National security
Defense treaties
  DPRK, 47, 48, 56
Democracy. *See* Political participation
Democratic Confederal Republic of Koryo (DCRK), 23, 214–216, 227. *See also* Reunification
Democratic Front for the Reunification of the Fatherland, 213
Democratic Justice Party (DJP), 85–86, 87, 161, 165, 272(n11)
Democratic Korea Party (DKP), 87, 272(n11)

Democratic People's Republic of Korea
(DPRK)
  Administrative Council, 70
  Central People's Committee, 70
  Confederal Standing Committee, 228
  Grand National Conference, 228
  Labor Law, 38
  Land Reform Act, 37
  Nationalization Law, 37
  Permanent Observer Mission, 69
  Provisional People's Committee, 38
  ROK unrest and, 51
  State Planning Commission, 133
  Supreme National Confederal
    Conference, 228
  Supreme People's Assembly (SPA),
    34
Democratic Republican Party (DRP),
  50, 62, 77, 78
Democratization
  of ROK, 212
Deng Xiaoping, 91, 97, 191
Diplomatic competition, 150–152,
  172–178
DIU. See Down-with-Imperialism
  Union
DJP. See Democratic Justice Party
DKP. See Democratic Korea Party
Domestic politics
  world environment and, 236–237
Down-with-Imperialism Union (DIU),
  185
DPRK. See Democratic People's
  Republic of Korea
DRP. See Democratic Republican Party
Dulles, John Foster, 40, 193

Economic development, 11, 133,
  134(table), 135(table), 136,
  140–145, 201
  in DPRK, 45–46, 47–48, 66, 69,
    117–118, 187–189, 201, 243
  international influences on, 240
  plans for, 45–46, 47–48, 66,
    132–133, 187, 188, 236
  policy choices and, 138, 139(table),
    140
  in ROK, 75, 168, 170–171
Economic miracle, xii, 65, 119, 168
Economic performance, 158

  in DPRK, 133, 134(table)
  in ROK, 133, 135(table), 136,
    168–171
Economic policy, 131, 136–140
Economic system, 7, 8, 10–11
Education, 139(table), 141, 143,
  144–145
  ideological, 180, 243
  in ROK, 171
Egypt, 152, 197
Elections, 17–18
  in ROK, 49, 50–51, 60–62
Elite structure, 115–116
EPB. See Republic of Korea, Economic
  Planning Board
Equity, 136, 138
Ethiopia, 197
Evren, Kenan, 176

Federation of Korean Labor Unions,
  89
Fifth Republic, 74
  Command of the Special Forces, 83
  constitution of, 263(n16)
  corruption in, 164
  Defense Security Command, 83–84
  labor law in, 89
  Legislative Council on National
    Security, 81, 82, 89
  Martial Law Decree No. 10, 79
  Metropolitan Defense Command,
    83–84
  Military Civilian Standing Committee,
    80–81, 82
  National Conference for Unification,
    81
  opposition forces in, 87–90
  Public Servants' Ethics law, 86
  ruling coalition of, 83–86
  Special Committee for National
    Security Measures, 82
  state building in, 161–163
  structure of, 81–86
  See also Chun Doo Hwan; Republic
    of Korea
Finland, 198
First Republic, 49, 53, 116, 250(n12).
  See also Rhee, Syngman
Flying Horse movement. See Ch'ollima
  movement

Foreign aid, 154–157
Foreign policy
  of DPRK, 68, 69, 189, 191, 192, 197, 198, 199–200, 201, 224
  of ROK, 51, 172–179, 200, 201
Foreign relations, 150–152, 233, 247–248
  DPRK and, 189–199
"Four Great Military Policylines," 147
Fourth Republic. See Park Chung Hee; Yushin system
France, 152
Friedrich, Carl J., 102

Gabon, 176
Galtung, Johan, 205
Geng Biao, 191, 192
Great Britain, 29
Grenada, 197, 198
Growth. See Economic development
Guinea, 197
Guyana, 197

Hahm, Pyong-choon, 167
Harvard Business School, 14
Henderson, Gregory, 5, 109, 238
"Hermit Kingdom," xii, xv, 232–233
Hidden History of the Korean War, The, 40
Hierarchy, political, 16
Hirohito (emperor), 30
Ho Chi Minh, 91
Ho, Chong, 49
Ho, Dam, 187
Ho, Gai-i, 44
Ho, Hwa-pyong, 84n, 85
Ho, Jong-suk, 186, 221
Ho, Sam-su, 84n, 85
Hodge, John R., 36
Hong Kong, 238
Hoxha, Enver, 90
Hu Yaobang, 186, 191
Hua Guofeng, 97, 195
Hull, John E., 29
Huntington, Samuel P., 19, 53
Husak, Gustav, 225
Hwang, Chang-yop, 186
Hyon, Jun-kuk, 194
Hyon, Ho-pom, 95
Hyon, Jun-hyok, 43

Hyon, Mu-kwang, 186
Hyundai business group, 201

Ideology, 6, 108–109, 116, 117, 119, 130–131, 234
Ilshin Steel, 164
Immigration
  postwar, 32, 33, 34, 255(n23)
Incrementalism, 207–208, 225
Industrialization, 109, 110, 130, 140, 144, 181, 240
  in DPRK, 118, 138
  in ROK, 59, 119
Industrial Labor Unions, 89
Inter-Parliamentary meetings (IPU), 176
Intraelite conflict
  in DPRK, 45
Iran, 197
Iraq, 152

Jaju, 119, 122
Japan, 21, 22, 122, 146, 157, 160, 198, 200, 201, 236, 238, 241, 243, 255(n23)
  colonial policy of, 32, 35
  DPRK and, 194–195
  ideology and, 108–109
  PRC and, 196
  ROK and, 11, 51
  Self-Defense Forces of, 173
  support from, 172–174
  Third Republic and, 51
  trade with, xiii, 153, 154, 169, 189
  U.S. and, 55, 56, 61, 67
  World War II surrender of, 29, 30, 31
Japan–Republic of Korea Treaty, 194
Jarip, 119
Johnson, Lyndon B., 30
Joint Communiqué on North South Dialogue, 57, 206, 207, 209, 210, 213
Juche, xii, 6–7, 11, 44, 45, 90, 94, 102, 108, 116–117, 122, 136, 152, 179–183, 187, 200, 201, 232, 240, 243
July 4 Joint Communiqué. See Joint Communiqué on North South Dialogue
Jung, Nae-hyok, 167

KAL007, 175, 176, 198
Kang, Kon, 34
Kang, Song-san, 187, 211
Kang, Yang-uk, 186
Katsushi, Fujii, 193
KDP. *See* Korean Democratic Party
Kennedy, John F., 30
Kenya, 176
"Kerb" scandal, 164–165
Khrushchev, Nikita, 45
Kim, Bok-dong, 84, 124
Kim, Ch'ek, 34
Kim, Chi-ha, 63
Kim, Chong Lim, 18–19
Kim, Ch'un Ch'u, 122
Kim, Dae-jung, 60, 78, 79–80, 88, 166, 262–263(n12)
Kim, Han-kyo, 5
Kim, Hwan, 186
Kim, Hyong-wuk, 259(n77)
Kim, Il, 34, 187
Kim Il Sung, xii, 6, 9, 13, 16, 20, 33, 35, 58, 98, 99, 102, 103, 115, 123, 126, 127, 144, 179, 209, 232, 236, 241, 242, 243, 259, 268(n54)
  economic development and, 69, 117–118, 187–189, 201
  foreign policies of, 68, 69, 189, 191, 192, 197, 198, 201, 224
  ideology and, 108, 116
  Korean War and, 39, 40
  leadership abilities of, 120–122
  opposition to, 45
  political perceptions of, 182–183
  power consolidation by, 43–45, 47, 65–66, 69–70, 71
  PRC and, 68, 191, 192
  regime stability and, 90–97
  reunification and, 52, 67, 68, 214, 217, 222, 224–225
  society building and, 46, 47–48
  Soviet Union and, 195
  Third World and, 197
  U.S. and, 192, 193
  U.S.-China relations and, 55, 56
  in World War II, 34
  See also Juche
Kim, Jae-ik, 167
Kim, Jae-kyu, 36, 75–76, 78, 163, 259(n77)
Kim, Jae-uk, 44
Kim, Jin-man, 77, 171
Kim Jong Il, 98, 99, 120, 179, 180, 191, 244, 268(n54)
  personal history of, 122–123, 126–127
  power consolidation by, 184–185
  rise to power of, 181–182, 184–187
  "speed battle" and, 183–184
  See also Political succession, in DPRK
Kim, Jong-pil, 50, 76, 78, 79, 83, 171
Kim, Jong-suk, 126
Kim, Joon-sung, 272(n2)
Kim, Jung-rin, 186
Kim, Kiu-sik, 33
Kim, Ku, 33
Kim, Kyung-won, 167
Kim, Sang-hyop, 165, 179
Kim, Song-ju. *See* Kim Il Sung
Kim, Tu-bong, 34, 35, 45
Kim, Yong-ju, 58, 96–97, 126
Kim, Yong-nam, 186, 187
Kim, Young-sam, 64, 78, 79, 83, 163, 166
Kimilsungism. *See* Juche
KIP. *See* Korean Independence Party
Kissinger, Henry, 174, 259(n2)
Kita Chosen oocho seiritisu hishi, 256(n29)
KNP. *See* Korea National Party
Koguryo Dynasty, 122
Konguk chumbi-wiwonhoe, 32
Kong Yung Construction, 164
Konjon, 32
Korean Airlines incident, 175, 176, 198
Korea National Party (KNP), 87–88, 272(n11)
Korean Communist Party, 35
Korean Democratic Party (KDP), 33
Korean Independence Party (KIP), 33
Korean Military Academy, 36, 84n, 124
Korean National Police, 35, 36
Korean People's Army (KPA), 147, 149
Korean People's Republic, 32
Korean Scholarship Foundation, 171
Korean War, xi, 39–42, 52, 90, 98, 122, 158, 209, 213, 241, 243
  casualties in, 42(table)
  causes of, 40–41, 257(n52)

Korean Workers' Party (KWP), 7, 8, 18, 35, 74, 91, 102, 116, 181
  Central Committee, 66, 115
  ideology and, 117
  Kim Il Sung and, 71
  political succession and, 92–94, 96
  power consolidation by, 47
  purge of, 43–45, 47
  Socialist Constitution and, 70, 72, 118
Kornhauser, William, 109
Koryo Dynasty, 108
KPA. *See* Korean People's Army
Kulloja, 95
Kunayev, D. A., 195
Kunro-Nongmin Dang (Working Farmers Party), 264(n30)
Kuomintang, 91
Kuwait, 152
Kwangju uprising, 13, 21, 74, 80, 88, 213, 243, 263(n13)
Kwon, Ik-hyon, 165, 167
Kwon, Jong-dal, 164
KWP. *See* Korean Workers' Party

Labor Committee Law, 89
Labor Dispute Settlement Law, 89
Labor-Employer Council Law, 89
Labor Standard Law, 89
Labor Union Law, 89
Labor unions
  in ROK, 89–90, 264(n34)
Land reform, 37–39, 54, 236
  in DPRK, 37
Leadership
  political elites and, 115–116
  principles of, 116–120
Lebanon, 152
Lee, Bum-suk, 178, 273(n41)
Lee, Chol-hi, 164
Lee, Chong-Sik, 96, 181
Lee, Hahn-been, 116
Lee, Hu-rak, 58, 76, 78, 79, 83, 88, 96, 171, 262(n11)
Lee, Kyu-dong, 124
Lee, Kyu-kwang, 124–125, 164
Lee, Kyu-seung, 124–125
Lee, Soon Ja, 124
Lesotho, 152, 197

"Let Us Advance Under the Banner of Marxism-Leninism and the Juche Idea," 185
Li Xiannian, 56
Liberation, 13, 32–39
  foreign occupation and, 32–36
  establishment of regimes and, 36–39
Libya, 152, 197, 198
Linkage politics, 15, 199–201, 239

MacArthur, Douglas, 30, 40
Madagascar, 197
Manchuria, 255(n23)
Mao Zedong, 74, 91, 92, 97, 117, 184, 191
March First Independence Movement, 22
Marshall, George C., 29
Marxism, 232
Media
  in DPRK, 95
Meeting to Expedite Unification, 228
Mexico, 152
Mikoyan, Nikolai, 45
Military expenditures, 146(table), 146–147
  in DPRK, 189
Military postures, 145–150
Min-Kwon Dang (Democratic Right Party), 264(n30)
Min-Sa Dang (Democratic Socialist Party), 264(n30)
Mitterrand, François, 152
Mobilization, 17–18
  in DPRK, 183–184
  See also Political participation
Modernization, 19, 241
Mohamad, Datuk Seri Mahathir, 176
Mubarak, Mohamed Hosni, 193, 197
Myongsong group, 165
Myrdal, Gunnar, 269(n7)

Nakasone, Yasuhiro, 173, 174, 194
National Assembly, 7, 264(n30)
  in Fifth Republic, 81, 87–88
  in Yushin system, 61, 62
Nationalism, 27, 28–29, 227
Nationalization, 38
National security, 178, 233–234, 237, 241, 279(n7)

National Security Law, 90
Natural resources, 143
Nauru, 152
NDP. *See* New Democratic Party
Nelson, Joan M., 19
Nepal, 197
New Democratic Party (NDP), 60, 77
New Korea Company, 38
New People's Party, 34–35
Newly industrializing countries (NIC), 11, 75
Nicaragua, 197
Nigeria, 176
Nixon, Richard, 51, 55
Nixon Doctrine, 51, 56, 60, 61, 67–68, 147
Nodong Ch'ongnyon, 95
Nodong Sinmun, 95
Non-aligned nations movement
 DPRK and, 197–198
North Korea. *See* Democratic People's Republic of Korea
North Korean Workers' Party, 35. *See also* Korean Workers' Party
North-South Coordinating Committee, 213, 216
North-South dialogue, 57–59, 67, 69, 72, 151, 174–175, 178–179, 198–199, 213–214, 230, 239, 259(n82). *See also* Reunification

O, Jin-u, 92
O'Donnell, Guillermo, 82, 103
Oh, Se-ung, 166
Oil, 143
Olympics, 177–178, 221
"On the Juche Idea," 185
Oppenheimer, Joe, 14
Ordinance No. 173, 38
Oriental Development Company, 38

Paige, Glenn, 5–6
Paik, Ung-taik, 85
Pak, Ch'ung-hoon, 81
Pak, Gum-ch'ol, 47
Pak, Hon-yong, 44
Pak, Il-u, 44
Pak, Song-chol, 34, 58, 97, 186, 197
Pakistan, 152, 197
Palestine Liberation Organization, 152

Park, Chong-kyu, 77, 79, 262(n11)
Park Chung Hee, 10, 36, 48, 50, 53, 67, 79, 81, 83, 88, 108, 118, 123, 124, 125, 126, 161, 163, 224, 241, 259(n77), 262(n7), 262(n11), 268(n54)
 assassination of, 65, 74, 75–76, 77, 78, 213, 243
 "coup in office." *See* Yushin system
 economic development and, 59, 131
 foreign policy of, 201
 ideology and, 119
 leadership abilities of, 120–122
 martial law decrees of, 61
 power base of, 59–60
 power consolidation by, 60–65
 reunification policy of, 207, 208, 209, 222, 223
Park, Se-jik, 84–85
Partition, 22, 28–32, 52, 128, 199, 230, 238–239
Party politics
 in ROK, 162–163
Peng Dehuai, 45
People's Committee, 32
People's Daily, 97
People's Republic of China (PRC), 149, 153, 158, 160, 174–175, 180, 197, 199–200, 236, 238, 255(n23), 259(n2)
 aid from, 154, 155, 196
 Cultural Revolution of, 67, 184, 201
 DPRK and, 47, 48, 56, 67–68, 190–192
 Japan and, 196
 Kim Il Sung and, 68, 191, 192
 Kim Jong Il and, 186
 Korean War and, 41
 military assistance from, 191, 192
 partition and, 29
 political succession in, 97
 society building and, 46
 Soviet Union and, 195–196, 241
 trade with, 153, 189
 U.S. and, 55–59, 61, 196
Peru, 152
Policy analysis, 15–16
Political cleavage
 in ROK, 110, 113, 113(table), 114(table)

304   Index

Political culture, 11–13, 16–22,
    102–129, 231–232, 243, 252(n36)
  definition of, 11
  dominant features, 16–22
  opinion surveys, 110–114
  traditional beliefs, 107–110
Political economy, 13–15, 130–159,
    252(n30), 252(n31)
  definition of, 14
  ideology and, 130–131
  performance, 132–136, 140–146
  world economy and, 136, 152–157
Political participation, 17–19, 110,
    111–112(table), 233, 242, 263(n18)
  in DPRK, 90–97, 181–182, 185–187,
    243
  in PRC, 97
  in ROK, 244
Political succession
  in DPRK, 90–97, 181–182, 185–187,
    243
  in PRC, 97
  in ROK, 244
Political system
  in DPRK, 6–8, 9–11, 65–72, 102,
    103–104
  in ROK, 6–8, 9–11, 59–65, 72, 103
  typology, 9–11
Politics of defiance. *See* Civil unrest
Population, 141, 142(table)
Potsdam Declaration, 29
PRC. *See* People's Republic of China
"Provisional Agreement on Basic
    Relations," 224
Provisional People's Committee, 34
Przeworski, Adam, 6
Pye, Lucian, 12

Rapprochement. *See* United States,
    PRC and
Rangoon bombing, 173, 177, 178–179,
    198–199. *See also* Burma
Reagan, Ronald, 173, 174, 193, 196
Reaganomics, 168
Real Name Deposit Law, 165
Realpolitik, 163
Recession, 64
Red Cross talks, 57, 67, 209, 213,
    273(n41). *See also* North-South
    dialogue

Red Guards. *See* People's Republic of
    China, Cultural Revolution of
Reformism
  in DPRK, 37–38
  in ROK, 38–39, 51
Regime stability, 101–104, 241–243,
    244
  in DPRK, 90–97, 101–102
  in ROK, 103–104
Repatriation, 32, 33, 34, 255(n23)
Republic of Korea
  Advisory Council on Peaceful
    Unification, 217
  Economic Planning Board (EPB),
    133, 170
  Farmland Reform Law, 38
  Interim Legislative Assembly, 36
  National Assembly. *See* National
    Assembly
  National Conference for Unification,
    77, 209
  National Democratic Youth and
    Student Federation, 63
  National Land Administration, 38
  Supreme Council for National
    Reconstruction, 50
  See also Fifth Republic; Second
    Republic; Third Republic; Yushin
    system
Research strategies, 9–16
Reunification, 52, 174, 178, 199,
    205–230, 245, 263(n29)
  cultural traditions and, 238–239
  DPRK policy on, 52, 67, 68,
    209–212, 214, 217, 222, 223, 224–
    225, 227–228, 277(n30)
  ROK policy on, 206–209, 211, 212,
    213, 216–220, 222–224, 225,
    226(fig), 227–228, 229–230,
    273(n43), 277(n30)
Revolutionary Party for Reunification,
    277(n16)
Rhee, Syngman, 10, 33, 36, 39, 41,
    48–49, 53, 83, 91, 118, 125, 179,
    250(n12)
Ro, Tae-wu, 80, 84, 124
ROK. *See* Republic of Korea
Roosevelt, Franklin D., 29
Rosenau, James N., 201
Rusk, Dean, 30

Russo-Japanese War, xi, 199
Rwanda, 197

Saemaul movement, 17, 59, 118–119, 138, 162, 236
Samsung business group, 201
Sato, Eisaku, 68
Second republic, 49, 53, 116, 250(n12), 272(n6)
Sejong (king), 122
Senegal, 176
Service sector, 140
Seven-Point Declaration for Peace and Unification, 207
Seychelles, 152, 197, 198
Shanghai Joint Communiqué, 58
Shin-Jung Dang (New Politics Party), 264(n30)
Shultz, George, 173, 193
Sihanouk, Nordom (prince), 56
Silla Dynasty, 122
Singapore, 238
Sino-Japanese War, xi, 21, 199
SKWP. *See* South Korean Workers' Party
Socialism, 131, 240–241
Socialist Constitution, 70, 72, 118
Society building
  in DPRK, 45–48, 72, 73
  in ROK, 73
Solarez, Stephen J., 192
Somalia, 198
Son, Kwan-hi, 186
Son, Song-pil, 186
"Song of Paradise, The," 98
South Korea. *See* Republic of Korea
South Korean–U.S. mutual security treaty, 236
South Korean Workers' Party (SKWP), 35, 44. *See also* Korean Workers' Party
Soviet Union, 149, 153, 174–175, 176, 179, 190, 195, 199–200
  Afghanistan invasion, 190, 196
  aid from, 154, 155
  defense treaties with, 48
  military presence, 236, 243, 255(n18)
  partition and, 28–32
  postwar occupation by, 22, 39
  PRC and, 195–196, 241

society building and, 46
trade with, 153, 190
See also Cold War
SPA. *See* Democratic People's Republic of Korea, Supreme People's Assembly
Special Foreign Policy Statement Regarding Peaceful Unification, 224
"Speed Battle Youth Shock Brigade," 184
Stalin, Joseph, 29, 71, 91, 92
Standards of living, 139(table)
  in DPRK, 99–100
State building, 53–54
  in DPRK, 33–35, 36–38, 39
  in ROK, 33, 35–37, 38–39, 48–52, 161–163
States, 7–8, 263(n17), 269(n7)
Stone, I. F., 40
Student movement, 172, 244
  in ROK, 13, 21, 48, 49, 53, 62, 79, 88–89, 125, 243
Student Revolution, 13, 21, 48, 49, 53, 79, 125, 243
Suh, Suk-joon, 167, 170
Suharto, 176
System transformation, 234–242

Taean work system, 118
Taiwan, 238
"Team Spirit" exercise, 173, 193
Technology transfer, 189, 195
"Ten Principles for Firmly Establishing the Party's Unitary Ideology System," 183
Teune, Henry, 6
Third Republic, 53, 83
  economic policies of, 51
  establishment of, 50
  Japan and, 51
  leadership in, 116
  reform measures of, 51
  See also Park Chung Hee
Third World, 176–178, 180, 197–198, 239
Three revolutions, 179, 182–185
Three Revolutions Teams (TRT), 92–93, 123, 126, 180, 184
Togo, Yoneda, 194

Tonghak Rebellion, 21
Trade, 153–154, 155–156(table)
  by DPRK, xiii, 153, 189, 190
  and DPRK deficit, 274(n69)
  by ROK, 154, 169
Travel
  in DPRK, 100
Treaty of Friendship, Cooperation and Mutual Assistance with China, 56, 192
Treaty of Friendship, Cooperation and Mutual Assistance with the Soviet Union, 190
TRT. See Three Revolutions Teams
Truman, Harry S, 29, 30

UDRK. See United Democratic Republic of Korea
Uganda, 198
UNDP. See United Nations, Development Program
  UNESCO. See United Nations, Educational, Scientific and Cultural Organization
Unification. See Reunification
United Arab Emirates, 152
United Democratic Republic of Korea (UDRK), 23, 217–223, 227
  DPRK reaction to, 221–223
  See also Reunification
United Nations, 150, 152, 207, 218, 224, 225
  Development Program (UNDP), 156
  Educational, Scientific and Cultural Organization (UNESCO), 69
  Korean War and, 41
  state building and, 36–37, 49
United States, 11, 122, 160, 200
  aid from, 154, 155
  DPRK and, 68, 192–194
  Fifth Republic and, 88–89
  investments from, 157
  Japan and, 55, 56, 61, 67
  Korean War role of, 40, 41
  military presence of, 145, 147, 149–150, 192, 198, 211, 224, 236, 243, 255(n19)
  partition and, 28–32
  postwar occupation by, 22, 39
  PRC and, 55–59, 61, 196

  state building and, 35–36, 38, 49
  State-War-Navy Coordinating Committee, 30
  support from, 172–173
  Third Republic and, 51
  trade with, 153, 154, 169
  See also Cold War
United States Army Military Government in Korea (USAMGIK), 35–36, 38
Upper Volta, 197
Urban Industrial Mission, 64, 89
Urbanization, 138, 140
U San Yu, 177
USAMGIK. See United States Army Military Government in Korea
U.S.-Japan Security Pact, 174
U.S.-Soviet Joint Commission on Korea, 36
U.S.S. Pueblo incident, 51

Vanuatu, 152
Verba, Sidney, 12
Vietnam, 51, 61, 196
Vietnam War, 51

Wage scale
  in DPRK, 99–100
Walker, Richard, 194
Weber, Max, 7
Weinberger, Caspar, 173
WHO. See World Health Organization
"Who Prepared and Provoked a War of Aggression in Korea," 40
Worker-Peasant Red Guard, 147, 149
"Workers' Party of Korea Is a Juche-type Revolutionary Party Which Inherited the Glorious Tradition of the DIU, The," 185
World Health Organization (WHO), 69
Wright, Edward, 252(n36)
Wu Xueqian, 191

Yalta conference, 29
Yang, Hyong-sop, 186
Yang, Sung Chul, 121
Yenan Koreans, 34–35
Yi Dynasty, 108–109, 122, 146, 199
Yi, Hyo-sun, 47
Yi, Jong-ok, 187, 190

Yi, Kang-kuk, 44
Yi, Pom-sok, 36
Yi, Seung-yop, 44
Yi, Song-gye, 108
Yi, Sun-sin, 122
Yi, Yong-ik, 186
Yim, Chun-chu, 186
Yim, Hwa, 44
Yim, Un, 256(n29)
Yo, Un-hyong, 32
Yo, Yon-ku, 186
Yon, Hyong-mok, 186
Yon'gesomun, 122
Yu, Chang-soon, 165, 272(n2)

Yujonghoe, 62, 76, 209
Yun, Ki-bok, 186
Yun, Po-son, 35, 50
Yushin system, 8, 59–65, 82–83, 118, 209, 262(n7)
   constitution of, 62–64
   judiciary in, 62
   leadership principles in, 118–119
   repressiveness of, 62–65
   See also Park Chung Hee

Zambia, 197
Zhao Ziyang, 191, 193
Zhou Enlai, 67
Zimbabwe, 197, 198, 276(n104)